BURMA 1942

Burma 1942

The Road from Rangoon to Mandalay

Alan Warren

continuum

Continuum International Publishing Group

The Tower Building
11 York Road
London
SE1 7NX

80 Maiden Lane
Suite 704
New York
NY 10038

www.continuumbooks.com

First published 2011

British Library Cataloguing-in-Publication Data
A catalogue record for this book is available from the British Library.

ISBN 978-1441-15250-3

Designed and typeset by Fakenham Prepress Solutions, Fakenham, Norfolk NR21 8NN
Printed and bound in India

Table of Contents

Preface

The city of Rangoon, the capital of the colony of Burma, lay on the north bank of the broad, muddy Irrawaddy river, twenty-five miles inland from the sea. Glittering in the sunlight, an immense volume of water flowed past the city towards the Bay of Bengal. The waterfront of Rangoon was crowded with acres of docks, warehouses and rows of steel cranes.

On the eve of the Second World War Burma was the world's largest rice exporter. Millions of people – a population greater than Burma's own – were dependent on the supplies of rice loaded into the holds of freighters by the port's Indian labour force, under the watchful eyes of shipping agents and the representatives of merchant houses. On the banks of the river above the docks were timber mills; teak log rafts were floated down river from the forests of northern Burma to be sawed in the mills.

Beyond the docks lay a thriving commercial district, the city's main railway station and the government's office buildings. Rangoon was a bustling metropolis and had acquired something of the atmosphere of colonial Shanghai. A rectilinear grid of wide, straight streets had been laid out shortly after Britain's permanent annexation of the city in 1852. Solid bank architecture was in abundance on the main thoroughfares; American motorcars, buses, bullock carts and rickshaws jostled with pedestrians for right of way; the market stalls of the bazaars presented a colourful scene. Women with coiled black hair and high cheekbones carried baskets on their heads, and wore dresses made of brightly coloured materials. The city's mostly Indian and Burmese populace lived in crowded residential districts beyond the city centre. Down river at Syriam, the tall chimneys of the Burmah Oil Company's refinery made the air grey and misty with smoke.

Near the Governor's House, the golden shrine of the Shwedagon Pagoda shimmered magnificently over Rangoon and dominated the skyline. The great pagoda was one of the most revered places of pilgrimage in the Buddhist world, and the principal historical reason for the city's existence at such a location. The golden, gilt-covered spire of the pagoda rose 300 feet into the air above a terraced platform on a hill surrounded by the slender, gold-tipped spires of smaller pagodas and shrines. On the stairways to the raised terrace, and banked around foreground shrines, masses of flowers

– marigolds, lotus and jasmine – scented the air with strong perfume. Carved stonework featured guardian ogres, winged gorgons and other fabulous beasts. The pagodas were tended by shaven-headed priests in robes. By night the towering Shwedagon Pagoda loomed mysteriously through the darkness.

On 23 December 1941 Burma seemed far from the dramas of the war underway in Europe. After the fall of France to Nazi Germany, the British Isles had been blockaded and was only separated from occupied Europe by the width of the English Channel. Japan's recent raid on Pearl Harbor and invasion of British Malaya had been a major jolt to Burma's colonial rulers. Anxiety was growing beneath the surface of local society, though an exterior effort to remain calm prevailed; a manner that was often misinterpreted as complacency by journalists on fleeting visits to the colony.

Rangoon was dangerously close to Japanese airfields in Thailand and Indochina. The city was protected by a single radar unit and a thin chain of observer posts in the jungle-clad mountains of the Thai-Burma frontier. The observer corps was dependent on the civilian telephone system to send messages to the Royal Air Force's headquarters. Rangoon was without anti-aircraft guns; few shelters were prepared for the civilian population.

At Mingaladon airfield, fifteen miles to the north of Rangoon, a small force of Allied fighter aircraft stood ready to oppose any Japanese incursions into the skies of southern Burma. The RAF's No. 67 Squadron was equipped with Buffalo fighters; most of the squadron's pilots were New Zealanders. The second of the two fighter squadrons at Mingaladon belonged to the American Volunteer Group and flew P-40B Tomahawks. This squadron was one of the 'Flying Tiger' units raised to aid Nationalist China in its war against Japan. Mechanics had awoken before daylight to arm, fuel and warm-up the engines of aircraft. A dawn patrol was flown, after which pilots breakfasted and lounged in the shade of tents not far from the gravel runways.

The Japanese Air Force had paid little attention to southern Burma in the early days of the Pacific war, but Japanese commanders had decided to disturb Rangoon from its slumbers. Just before 10 a.m. on 23 December, a fine tropical day, the operations room at Mingaladon airfield received a report of approaching hostile aircraft. The sirens rang out in downtown Rangoon, though many people dismissed them as another practice alert. There were a few clouds in the air and a light breeze blew from seaward.

A large force of Japanese bombers and fighters had taken to the skies from airfields in Thailand and Indochina. The raiders sped westwards through the air towards Rangoon over the glittering waters of the Gulf of Martaban in tight V-formations. Many of the bombers were twin-engine Ki-21 Mitsubishis. The wings of the twin-engine bombers were set back at the midpoint of the fuselage to give a hawk-like silhouette. The 2200-pound bomb load carried by the aircraft was sufficient to do a great deal of damage to a crowded city of the orient. The Mitsubishis were painted pale grey underneath and light brown and green on the upper side; red discs on the wings and fuselage proclaimed the nationality of the bomber. The city and Mingaladon airfield were the intended targets. The warehouses along the docks were crammed with American military supplies destined for transport to Nationalist China along the fabled Burma Road.

At Mingaladon Allied pilots ran for their aircraft; climbed into cramped cockpits; put on radio headphones; adjusted their parachute harnesses; switched on their radios. The engines coughed and roared into action. The pilots eased forward on the throttle to taxi to the end of the runway for a hasty take-off. A dozen Tomahawks and fifteen Buffaloes took to the air through clouds of dust. The pilots retracted the landing gear of their aircraft, and climbed in circles towards 20,000 feet under a blinding sun. The propellers of the fighters hungrily clawed at the tropical air. From high above, the runways of Mingaladon formed a light coloured triangular shape, surrounded by patches of vegetation and green-brown rice fields.

Two RAF Buffalo fighters piloted by Sergeants C. V. Bargh and G. Williams were already aloft on patrol over Rangoon. These young men were amongst the first to see the approaching Japanese aircraft. As the Buffaloes circled high overhead, ground controllers heard over the radio the excited voice of a New Zealander: 'Hell! Showers of them. Look, Willie, showers of them!'[1] At Mingaladon an American aircraft mechanic recalled:

> After the scramble we gathered around our barracks and stood looking up into the sky, just like a bunch of tourists … We heard engines, and high in the sky we saw small silver specks flying in a V-formation. Someone started counting, and when he reached twenty-seven, he yelled, 'They're not ours. We don't have that many.' I jumped into the nearest slit trench about the same time I heard the whoosh, whoosh of the bombs coming down.[2]

In Rangoon Indians, Burmans, Chinese, Anglo-Indians, Anglo-Burmans, Karens and Europeans poured onto the streets, instead of finding shelter, curious to watch the aerial display.

From the ground the aircraft were clearly and impressively visible in the sky, right overhead. Crowds of dock labourers gathered in Strand Road, unaware of their vulnerable state; women and children at market stalls paused to study the sky. The whistle of falling bombs and the sounds of explosions soon caused mass panic amongst those gazing skywards. Little had been done to warn the populace of the dangers of air attack. The streets became strewn with the mutilated corpses of the dead and dying; the injured hauled themselves to overflowing hospitals as best they could. Anti-personnel bombs and sticks of high explosive started many fires amongst wooden houses of the crowded residential districts.

Burma was about to be engulfed by the Second World War. Since the outbreak of war in Europe, there had been a gradual raising of the military tempo in the colony; but Burma was towards the bottom of beleaguered London's priorities. Burma was in theory India's eastern outer bastion, but for almost a hundred years the military focus of British India had been the North-west Frontier, which was the gateway to Afghanistan and central Asia.

There was nothing accidental about war coming to Burma in the days and weeks after Imperial Japan raided the United States Pacific Fleet at Pearl Harbor, Hawaii to set in motion the Pacific war. In the wake of the Pearl Harbor raid, Japan set out to seize South-east Asia and the western Pacific to complete the building of a self-sufficient empire. It was planned to capture Britain's fortress of Singapore as a high priority. The Imperial Japanese Army was already occupying large swathes of China, where war had been raging for several years.

The Japanese planned to take Burma as an integral part of the Greater East Asia Co-prosperity Sphere. The rice industry and other raw materials of Burma were of great value. Japanese possession of Burma was necessary to cover the flank of Japan's intended conquests elsewhere in South-east Asia. Japanese possession of Burma would also cut the route from the outside world to the Chinese armies resisting Japanese forces in the Chinese interior. The Burma Road leading into south-west China had become the last remaining route along which American supplies could be sent to Chiang Kai-shek's Nationalist regime.

The consequences of the loss of Burma would be profound. This book seeks to present a fresh study of the series of events that make up the Burma campaign of 1942. The combatants helped to determine the course and shape of the war in South-east Asia through the battles they won and lost on land, at sea and in the air. Victory or defeat in particular battles had the power to alter the trajectory of the conflict to the benefit or doom of many people. The examination of warfare helps to restore the significance of dramatic human action to history. The Second World War remains a fascinating area of study; its enduring influence on the nations involved is strangely undiminished by the passage of time.

For permission to reproduce illustrations I am grateful to the Australian War Memorial. I would like to express my thanks to all those who have helped me during the preparation of this book. I am grateful for the confidence and support of my publishers and editors, in particular Claire Lipscomb, Nicola Rusk, Kim Storry and Barbara Archer.

List of Maps

List of Illustrations

Between pages 84 and 85

1. The spire of the Shwedagon Pagoda, Rangoon.
2. General Sir Archibald Wavell and General T.J. Hutton, March 1942.
3. Generalissimo Chiang Kai-shek, Madame Chiang and Lt-General Joseph W. Stilwell, Maymyo, Burma, April 1942.
4. Brewster Buffalo fighter aircraft lined-up on an airfield.
5. Rangoon, 6 March 1942: smoke from demolitions rises over the city.
6. The battleship HMS *Warspite*, Indian Ocean 1942.
7. The aircraft carrier HMS *Hermes* sinking off the coast of Ceylon, 9 April 1942.
8. A view of the demolished Ava bridge in the Irrawaddy river near Mandalay.

British Burma and Imperial Japan

Burma is a land of vivid jungle ranges and coastal mangrove swamps; the landscape teems with wildlife; animal and insect noises fill the night hours. Burma is the size of France and Britain combined. The territory is a vast region, though it can seem small on the map sandwiched between India and China. Great rivers running north to south traverse a central plain that is surrounded by mountains on three sides. The Himalayan mountains – the roof of the world – separate Burma from China to the north. To the east and west, mountain ranges stretching southwards from the Himalayas separate Burma from Thailand and India respectively. The western coast of Burma is a swampy strip of plain and bamboo forest. In south-east Burma the Tenasserim peninsula stretches away from the rest of the country like an elephant's trunk; the peninsula forms the eastern flank of the Bay of Bengal.

Burma's principal river, and one of the great rivers of the world, is the Irrawaddy. The name Irrawaddy is derived from Sanskrit and means 'land of refreshment'. The river is over 1200 miles in length. At its southern extremity it empties into the Bay of Bengal in a mass of tributaries. There are three other major rivers in Burma that flow from north to south. The Chindwin is an inland tributary of the Irrawaddy in the north-west of the country. The confluence of the Irrawaddy and Chindwin is a vast sheet of water in the monsoon season. To the east of the Irrawaddy, the Sittang and Salween rivers also run south to empty into the sea. The northern stretch of the Salween river, which flows out of China, divides Burma from Thailand. But Burma has many other smaller rivers as well. The countryside is riven with *chaungs* – watercourses – that are dry in the hot season and torrents when the rains come.

The weather of Burma is dominated by two monsoon seasons. From mid-October to mid-May the north-east monsoon prevails. Rain is rare in the dry season and the climate is pleasantly cool late in the calendar year. The heat, however, begins to rise uncomfortably in March as the north-east winds abate and die out. April and May is a period of sweltering heat and humidity. The blue, clear skies and glaring white sunlight of the hot weather comes to an end when dark clouds begin to roll across the horizon to herald the arrival of the south-west monsoon. The rainy season lasts from mid-May to mid-October; the rains are very heavy in most parts of the territory, and exceptionally heavy in particular coastal regions and the northern mountain ranges. The drenching of the monsoon causes malaria to be endemic in many parts of Burma.

Burma is an ancient land and has been inhabited for many centuries. Successive waves of migratory tribes entered the valley of the Irrawaddy after crossing the mountains to the north. Merchants from India and other parts of South-east Asia reached Burma from the sea, and brought other influences with them. Early tribal societies gradually united to form local kingdoms and dynasties based on stockaded towns and villages.

In Europe the land of Burma was first mentioned around 1300 in Marco Polo's writings about his travels in Asia; Marco Polo was a Venetian in the service of Kublai Khan. It was the Portuguese who discovered the sea route from Europe around the Cape of Good Hope to India in 1497. The Portuguese were the earliest European merchant presence in Burma, and were followed by the Dutch, French and British. In the eighteenth century the Portuguese settlement at Syriam, in the Irrawaddy delta, was one of the main trading posts for Europeans on the south coast. Burma was defenceless from the sea; the Irrawaddy river gave access to a fertile hinterland.

In Bengal the British-controlled East India Company had established a common frontier with the kingdom of Burma by 1784. Burmese raiding across the border into British territory was a constant irritation. Finally, in 1824 Governor-General Amherst dispatched an army to overawe the Court of Ava. The stockaded village of Rangoon in the Irrawaddy delta was captured by a British force landed by the navy.

The conflict proved a stalemate and towards the close of 1826 a treaty was arranged to end the war. British forces evacuated Rangoon under the terms of the treaty. Forty thousand British and East India Company soldiers had been involved in the conflict; 15,000 of these men died, mostly from fevers, dysentery and cholera. The five British Army regiments of the initial landing force lost over 3100 dead.[1] After the war the coastal strips of Arakan and Tenasserim were annexed by the East India Company; Assam was also ceded to Britain. Moulmein became the main British-Indian port and garrison town in southern Burma.

In 1852 another war led to the complete British occupation of the Irrawaddy delta of lower Burma. The trigger for conflict was a series of disputes between British merchants and Burmese officials; Governor-General Dalhousie was unwilling to tolerate this consistent challenge to British prestige. The war, however, was more efficiently managed on this occasion. The naval component of the amphibious expedition that sailed from India was commanded by Rear-Admiral Sir Charles Austin, who was the younger brother of the novelist Jane Austin. In April 1852 an invasion force landed from the Irrawaddy river to capture Rangoon; the town was badly damaged by bombardment and looting as it was seized. The province of Pegu was annexed to the crown.

The British cleared the old town of Rangoon at the foot of the Shwedagon Pagoda. By the end of 1853 a new city was under construction. The colonial city was given a chess-board design of wide streets. European-style public buildings and church spires were erected in a land of Buddhist pagodas and monasteries. New forms of civil administration were imposed on southern Burma by the Indian Civil Service. Courts of law and government departments were established along Indian lines. The opening of the Suez Canal in 1869 led to a dramatic increase in the number of steamships trading at Rangoon; Burma's first stretch of railway was completed in 1877.

But Britain was not the only European power working to acquire territory in South-east Asia. A new challenger emerged when the French began to occupy parts of Indochina in the 1860s. French contacts with King Thibaw in Upper Burma aroused the suspicion of the authorities at Rangoon. A Burmese mission travelled to Europe in the mid-1880s and had discussions with the French that included arrangements for the supply of modern arms. This helped spur London into action. British officialdom set out to manufacture a pretext for invading Upper Burma.

The Secretary of State for India, Lord Randolph Churchill, later explained: 'It is French intrigue which has forced us to go to Burmah; but for that element we might have treated [King] Theebaw with severe neglect.' Lord Curzon would proclaim:

> India is like a fortress ... with mountains for her walls ... beyond these walls ... extends a glacis of varying breadth and dimension. We do not want to occupy it, but we cannot afford to see it occupied by our foes. We are quite content to let it remain in the hands of our allies and friends, but if rivals and unfriendly influences creep up to it ... we are compelled to intervene.[2]

The proverbial road to Mandalay was the mighty Irrawaddy river. An army of 10,000 men in a flotilla of river steamers and launches commanded by Major-General Sir Harry Prendergast VC was assembled in British-controlled territory. On 22 October 1885 an ultimatum was dispatched that included the demand that King Thibaw conduct his external relations solely through the British authorities in India. This was rejected and Prendergast's flotilla crossed the frontier on 14 November. After a brief engagement at Minhla the force steamed onwards; Mandalay had been entered by the end of the month.

King Thibaw's Kingdom of Ava was annexed to make the whole of Burma a British colony; Thibaw and Queen Supayalat were sent into exile in India.

The palace in Mandalay was renamed Fort Dufferin, in honour of the Viceroy of India, the Earl of Dufferin. The palace compound was an impressive set of buildings. Salmon-pink walls one and a quarter miles long surrounded the compound; a lotus-filled moat was crossed by four bridges; within the walls were the palace, other housing and tree-lined roads. Beyond Fort Dufferin lay a crowded city. The 800-foot high Mandalay Hill was covered by pagodas and temples. The Irrawaddy lay to the west of Mandalay; the skyline beyond the river was dotted with white pagodas on the summits of hills.

Several years of conflict followed the initial annexation of Upper Burma. During the late 1880s 32,000 troops were committed to the final pacification of the territory. Rudyard Kipling described the conflict as a subalterns' war. There were many deaths from jungle fever during the five-year campaign to subdue bands of rebels and dacoits.

Unified Burma became a province of the Indian empire, a decision that would be consistently unpopular with Burmans, who were the majority ethnic population in Burma. The Burman majority lived in most parts of central and southern Burma. Minority ethnic groups, however, had not benefited from authoritarian Burman kingship. For minority communities like the Karens of the south, and the hill peoples of the north, the British were preferable to other conquerors. The Shan States in the north-east of the colony were divided into a series of semi-autonomous principalities and ruled by hereditary rajahs.

Religious toleration made foreign rule palatable, as did law and order in place of despotism. Buddhist priests dressed in saffron-coloured robes and with shaven heads continued to be a common sight on the streets of towns and villages. British officials, soldiers and businessmen enjoyed their service in Burma. Amid the tropical greenery, a fertile, healthy and peaceful colony gradually prospered. Tourists were enchanted by the moonlight reflections on the waterways.

Colonial Rangoon steadily grew in size and complexity. In Pagoda Road, Jubilee Hall was built to celebrate Queen Victoria's sixty years on the throne. The Secretariat complex was completed early in the twentieth century and featured a large dome. Ornate pavilions and band-stands decorated Dalhousie Park; Buddhist monasteries clustered at the foot of Pagoda Hill. New residential suburbs of spacious houses set in colourful gardens for civil servants and prosperous merchants were established to the north of the pagoda district near Victoria Lake.

On the river front, trained elephants worked in the timber yards; rice-mills prepared the crop for export. At the docks hydraulic cranes and electric flood-lighting kept the port abreast with modernity. The city's population in the 1881 census was 134,176. This figure had increased to more than

400,000 by 1931, over half of whom were Indian; 30,000 Chinese and sizeable European, Anglo-Indian and Anglo-Burmese communities added to the ethnic variety of Rangoon. The immigrants from India were both Muslim and Hindu. Regular passenger services connected the capital of the colony with other major ports of the British empire.

Burma's railway system was steadily extended to link the main towns with the cities of Rangoon and Mandalay. The steamers of the Irrawaddy Flotilla Company plied the great rivers of the colony. At Mandalay the railway bifurcated, one line heading north-east to Lashio, 120 miles from the Chinese frontier; the second line continued northwards for 250 miles to Myitkyina in the Kachin hills. The mountain ranges of the Indian-Burmese frontier were traversed by only a few tracks and these were vulnerable to floods and landslides.

Burma had great potential in the field of agriculture. Over many generations the rivers had carried thick silt deposits downstream to accumulate in the flat delta region in the south of the country. The colonial administration consistently encouraged the expansion of the rice industry. Western commercial law permitted business companies to operate with financial certainty. Economic development encouraged Indian immigration and internal immigration to lower Burma; this provided the labour force for the rice industry.

In the mid-nineteenth century rice exports from Burma were negligible, but by the 1930s Burma had become the largest rice-exporting territory in the world.[3] Burma, Thailand and Indochina accounted for 70 per cent of the world's rice exports. Burma's share was 37 per cent, which was more than Thailand and Indochina combined. The later two territories exported large quantities of rice to Japan and China; the majority of Burma's rice exports went to India and Ceylon.[4] Burma was a granary for India to draw upon in years of famine and scarcity. In 1941 it was estimated that 63 per cent of Burma's rice production was available for export.[5]

Rice dominated village life in lower Burma. After the ceaseless downpour of the monsoon, buffaloes and men dragged a plough across paddy fields knee-deep in water; women and children then planted green seedlings. The fields dried out and the crop ripened during the brief cool period, when wild flowers bloomed in the jungle alongside the paddy; white mist hung in the mornings after cold nights. A ripened paddy field yielded a breast-high crop like a field of wheat. After harvest, once the hot weather had set in, the rice fields became a dust-coloured plain divided into plots of an acre or two by mud banks baked rock-hard in the sun. The village routine of ploughing, planting and reaping lasted from June to December; then followed celebrations, festivals and preparations for the hot weather and monsoon ahead. Rice stocks were at a peak level in December of each year.[6]

The rice industry was not the only sector of the economy to prosper under colonial rule. The Burmah Oil Company began to develop a field in the arid central plain at Yenangyaung. By the interwar period this oilfield could produce 250 million gallons a year; the oil was piped directly to a refinery near Syriam, which was on the Irrawaddy river to the south-east of Rangoon. Burma was able to supply most of India's demand for oil. Burma also became the world's main source of teak wood. Timber was logged in the forests of the northern region of the colony. Wolfram was mined at Mawchi; tin was mined in Tenasserim.

The First World War largely passed by Burma; it was joked that the colony was the safest place in the empire. Burma, however, was greatly affected by developments taking place elsewhere in the colonial world. The rise of nationalism in India saw a parallel trend in Burma. At first Burma was excluded from the 1919 Government of India Act, but officialdom relented in the face of public pressure. In consequence a new scheme of limited self-government was introduced by the colonial regime in the 1920s. This was the first step towards representative government. In Rangoon the university that had been established after the First World War became a centre of nationalist agitation. The Burman and Indian communities came into conflict as Burmese national consciousness attained new heights; Indian moneylenders were very unpopular with the peasantry. The crisis of the Great Depression caused rice prices to tumble and the peasantry fell deeper into debt.

The Saya San rebellion of 1930–32 broke the spell and reputation of Burma as a colonial Arcadian backwater. Saya San was a former monk; he had the goals of restoring the monarchy and the status of the Buddhist hierarchy. The revolt drew heavily upon religious loyalties; magic spells and amulets were distributed to bands of followers. The rebellion was directed against all foreigners and the collection of taxes, though the brunt fell against the Indians as they were an easy target and more numerous than Europeans. The army and police killed 1300 rebels in the course of restoring the government's authority.[7]

In 1938 another round of disturbances were directed against Indians. A growing level of rural distress was behind the unrest of the Burmese peasantry. Land holdings were getting smaller as the population grew; the class of landless labourers was steadily expanding as mortgaged land was lost to moneylenders. The census of 1931 had estimated the population to be seventeen million, of whom ten million were Burmans. The balance of the population comprised four million Karens, one and half million Shans, one million Indians and numerous smaller ethnic communities.

Social relations between the British and Burmans were outwardly cordial. Just before the outbreak of war in Europe in 1939, the abbot of a small

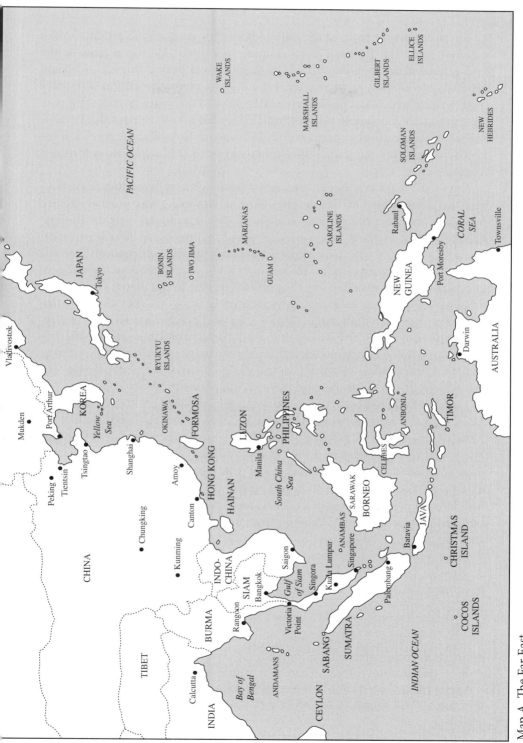

Map A   The Far East

monastery outside Mandalay explained to Lieutenant James Lunt of the Burma Rifles, 'Yes, I like you well enough, better than say the French or the Dutch. But the Burmese are perfectly able to rule themselves and we do not require the British to do this for us. The sooner you go, the better it will be for both the British and the Burmese.'[8] Anti-colonial sentiment was not far below the surface of everyday life.

As part of the constitutional reform process overtaking India, in April 1937 Burma was made a separate colony and given a legislature elected on a narrow franchise. The separation of Burma from India was a source of great satisfaction to the Burmese. A Burma Office ministry came into existence in London; Burma was given a council of ministers and two houses of parliament. The lower house comprised members elected for five year terms; the upper house, the Senate, was half-elected by the lower house and half-appointed by the colonial regime. A Burmese Prime Minister and Cabinet were established in Rangoon. Only the Dominions had a greater degree of self-government.

As part of the reformed regime, the British governor in Rangoon retained control of defence and foreign affairs, and had substantial reserve powers in respect to finance. The elected ministers had only limited power over personnel appointments in Burma's civil service; the hill territories that comprised 40 per cent of Burma also remained under British control. But the local political scene in Rangoon became very different from before – Burma's new constitution was a significant and probably irreversible step down the road to political independence. A number of new political parties and groupings were established to contest the new elections. The most extreme nationalist party was the Thakins, a party that drew heavy support from students in the capital. At this point in time, however, the bulk of the population remained relatively unaffected by modern politics.

Whilst Burma was an Indian province, the Indian Army had been responsible for local defence, but from 1937 Burma had to take control of its own military, and there was not a lot for the new defence department in Rangoon to build upon. For many years Delhi's military planning had been primarily focused on the North-west Frontier, Afghanistan and the Soviet Union. The General Staff noted on 13 August 1927:

> At the present time our policy is to adopt a strict defensive attitude on the north-east frontier since we have no aggressive intentions ourselves, and because we are of the opinion that the Chinese will not for a considerable time be in a position to undertake any important offensive against us, even if they wished to do so.[9]

Efficient sea communications to Rangoon meant there had been little strategic or commercial incentive to build roads or railways across the forbidding terrain of Assam and Manipur lying between Bengal and Burma. The tracks across the Thai-Burmese frontier were also poor. Burma was a land of rivers and there were few bridges across the largest waterways. The ferocity of the monsoon floods made the building of bridges impractical in many places. This was a further discouragement to military preparation.

By the 1930s the Royal Air Force had a role to play in imperial defence alongside the army and navy. The island of Akyab, off the coast of Arakan, was the site of an airstrip that became an important link in the air route from Calcutta to Singapore. The RAF built its main base for Burma at Mingaladon, to the north of Rangoon. But the Royal Navy continued to be Burma's principal defensive shield by virtue of its dominating presence in the Indian Ocean and the waters of South-east Asia. Burma had a 1200-mile coastline running from the frontier with Bengal all the way to Victoria Point, at the southern end of the Tenasserim peninsula.

During the early decades of the twentieth century a new external threat rose up to challenge the position of the European colonial powers in Asia, quite apart from the pressures of local nationalist movements and the immense, though indirect, impact of the First World War in Europe and the Middle East. The rise of Japan as a major power with imperial ambitions badly disrupted the status quo in east Asia. In the fullness of time the long shadow of Japanese militarism would fall upon Burma.

In the last quarter of the nineteenth century a new Japanese regime had set out to modernise the country by importing many branches of Western technology. This was grafted onto Japan's traditional rural society and its austere moral values. Government missions were sent to Europe on ambitious study tours. A modern navy was established in imitation of Britain's Royal Navy; army and constitutional reform borrowed from the customs of France and Germany. An industrial economy was created and this introduced a need for imported raw materials that had not previously existed.

To secure its position in north-east Asia, the Japanese government went to war with China at a favourable opportunity. After an eight-month war China sued for peace in 1895; Japan annexed Formosa (Taiwan) and became the most influential power in Korea. In 1902 Britain formed a defensive alliance with Japan jointly to face down Russian ambitions in Asia and the western Pacific. In 1904 Japan, emboldened by the new alliance with Britain, went to war against Russia.

The conflict was a triumph for Japan; Port Arthur was captured after a costly siege and the Tsarist army pushed northwards into the Manchurian interior. On 27 May 1905 the Russian fleet was destroyed at the battle of Tsushima, near the southern tip of Korea. Almost 5000 Russian sailors were killed in the battle; all the principal Russian warships were sunk or captured. Admiral Togo's fleet had been mostly built in British shipyards. Peace was signed in September 1905; in consequence Japan took control of Port Arthur and the southern section of the Manchurian railway. This was the first defeat of a European power by an Asian state for centuries.

During the First World War Japan entered the conflict against Germany in support of what had proved to be a rewarding alliance with Britain. The Japanese seized German territory in China and the Pacific; Japanese cruisers and destroyers assisted the Royal Navy's campaign against German surface raiders and submarines in the Mediterranean, Indian Ocean and near the Cape of Good Hope.

The Royal Navy emerged victorious from the First World War. The surrendered German High Seas Fleet was scuttled at Scapa Flow in 1919. Britain's position in the Far East, however, was undermined as the United States and Japan had built powerful fleets during the war years. Washington and Tokyo had an obvious interest in the Pacific Ocean. The British government worked to maintain good relations with the United States as an effective long-term policy to restrain Japanese ambitions. The Anglo-Japanese alliance was permitted to lapse in 1923 as there was no question of Britain supporting Japan in a crisis that involved the United States and Canada.

After the First World War the British military was subjected to dramatic reductions, even though London's imperial responsibilities were greater than ever. The financial costs of the war had been immense and the British government willingly embraced the agreements reached at the 1921–22 Washington Naval Conference. A treaty was signed that reduced the size of the world's principal navies. The treaty permitted Britain and the United States a tonnage equivalent to fifteen capital ships, the Japanese nine capital ships, and France and Italy five capital ships apiece.[10] This was a major departure from the policies of successive British governments prior to 1914, which had not accepted naval parity with any other nation. At the end of the 1880s the First Lord of the Admiralty, Lord George Hamilton, had told parliament that the government's aim was to have a naval establishment equal to the next two largest naval powers; this had become known as the 'two-power standard'. The Washington Naval Treaty compelled Britain to accept a much reduced 'one-power standard'.[11] The 1930 London Naval Treaty put further restrictions on naval construction.

Meantime, the Chinese imperial state had finally collapsed. In 1911 the last Manchu emperor was deposed. A Chinese republic was proclaimed the following year, and the country soon fell under the control of regional warlords. Chinese national affairs took another dramatic turn after the founding of the National Party of China – the Kuomintang – in south China in the early years of the 1920s. The Kuomintang, led by Chiang Kai-shek, steadily expanded its control beyond an initial power base in south China. In 1927 Nationalist forces captured Peking; a central government was established at Nanking. The regime at Nanking directly controlled the lower Yangtze valley, and formed alliances and accommodations with many regional leaders. Nanking was a national capital more in name than reality, but the Kuomintang had managed to turn around China's drift towards disintegration that had been underway since the republican revolution. The founding of the Communist Party of China in 1922 would have profound consequences for the future of east Asia, but China appeared to be the Nationalists for the taking in the late 1920s.

In Japan civilian politicians held sway over the military during the 1920s, but the crisis of the Great Depression changed the situation dramatically. The collapse of world trade brought Japan's exported-oriented economy to its knees. Japan's population had more than doubled since the Meiji Restoration. The military became convinced that to survive, Japan needed guaranteed access to the raw materials and markets of the nearby Asian mainland. Under Japan's constitution, the Cabinet was appointed by the emperor and not by Parliament; by imperial edict the army and navy ministers were serving officers. Emperor Hirohito had come to the throne in 1926. Despite his gentle exterior, the emperor consistently supported the policies of the military at home and abroad. Ultra-nationalist military secret societies exercised great power in Japanese politics; civilian politicians were intimidated to fall into line with the will of the Japanese military.

At the height of the Great Depression the Japanese army seized an opportunity to occupy all of Manchuria. The local warlord had unwisely obstructed the Japanese presence in southern Manchuria; hostilities got underway in September 1931. After overrunning Manchuria, Japanese forces entered northern China. A general truce was signed between the Japanese and the Chinese Nationalists in May 1933 to temporarily halt the slide towards general war in east Asia.

The Chinese Nationalists were deeply opposed to Japan's incursions into Manchuria and northern China, but Generalissimo Chiang was willing to bide his time whilst his regime was consolidated. The Nationalists devoted much of their energies during the early 1930s to waging a series of campaigns against the Communists. Chiang was his own military commander; he had succeeded Sun Yat-sen as the Nationalists' leader largely because of his military experience.

An austere man, Chiang was born in 1887 near the old treaty port of Ningpo, the son of a merchant and landlord. As a young man, Chiang had trained at Chinese and Japanese military schools; he had headed a

Kuomintang military mission to the Soviet Union in 1923. Upon return from Russia, Chiang became commandant of the new Whampoa military academy. After he ascended to the leadership of the Kuomintang, Chiang proved to be ruthless and decisive, though he was also a contemplative man with a semi-feudal outlook. Chiang's wife, the vivacious, beautiful, Christian and English-speaking Madame Chiang – Mayling Soong – proved a great asset to her husband when it came to dealing with the Western press.

Against the backdrop of these tumultuous events, the Nationalists worked hard to modernise their army, which was large in numbers but poorly officered, trained and armed. Chiang had turned from Soviet to German military advisers after relations with the Communist Party of China descended into open warfare. In 1933 Colonel-General Hans von Seeckt, the German Army's commander from 1919–26, headed an advisory mission. He was succeeded two years later by General Alexander von Falkenhausen, a shrewd Prussian officer. The Nationalist regime built an army of thirty-one divisions; problems procuring weaponry and ammunition delayed further expansion. These forces were but a small part of the estimated 176 divisions supported by China's various rulers and warlords. Of China's two million men under arms, the Nationalist regime directly commanded about 300,000.[12]

In Europe the Great Depression also disrupted national politics and played a part in catapulting Hitler to power in 1933. Nazi Germany soon left the League of Nations and commenced a major re-armament programme in defiance of the Treaty of Versailles. The system of naval disarmament collapsed when the international naval treaties expired in 1936. Japan swiftly launched an ambitious warship-building programme. Britain was slow to respond and the under-sized Royal Navy was already burdened with many obsolete ships. From 1936 an accelerated naval programme was authorized, though, ironically, the parlous state of the British shipbuilding industry restricted production after it was decided to spend lavishly on the navy.[13]

The crisis in Europe rolled onwards with the outbreak of civil war in Spain in July 1936 and the formation of the Rome-Berlin axis. British planners now had to deal with the risks imposed by three potential first-class enemies: Germany in Europe, Italy in the Mediterranean and Japan in the Far East. The German air threat loomed large in the popular imagination of the British public at this time. Not without good reason, the focus of defence spending shifted to the modernisation of the Royal Air Force. Preparation for warfare in the third dimension took money away from the budgets of both the navy and army. Nonetheless, officials at the Admiralty did their best to make plans with the resources at their disposal. In January 1938 Captain T.S.V. Phillips, Director of Plans at the Admiralty, told a United States envoy that if the Japanese threatened the British Far East a fleet comprising nine battleships, three aircraft carriers and nineteen cruisers could be sent to Singapore.[14] That force would only be available, however, if Europe remained at peace.

Whilst the eyes of the world were transfixed by the ascent to power of Hitler in Germany, in east Asia relations between China and Japan had spiralled towards renewed conflict. Hostilities broke out in northern China on the night of 7 July 1936. Japanese troops on night manoeuvres near the Marco Polo Bridge at Peking were fired on by Chinese soldiers. The opening battle of the Sino-Japanese war took place around the ancient city. On 17 July Chiang Kai-shek publicly called on the Chinese people to resist Japan and ordered reinforcements to north China. Chiang proclaimed:

> [China must] throw the last ounce of our national energy into a struggle for the independent existence of our nation. To seek peace once war has begun would be to invite the subjugation of our nation and the annihilation of our race ... Should we hesitate and vainly hope for temporary safety, we shall perish forever. If we allow one more inch of our territory to be lost, then we would be committing an unpardonable offence against our race.[15]

The Japanese government of Prince Konoye Fumimaro responded by sending reinforcements to northern China. Chiang remained confident. He told the writer Edgar Snow: 'Look at the map and note the smallness of Japan compared to China. Can anyone doubt that we shall triumph?'[16] Japanese troops were soon in control of the Peking-Tientsin region. Before long, the conflict had spread to central China and the Yangtze valley.

The city of Shanghai and the lower Yangtze region was China's economic and political heartland. China's population during this period was estimated to be 4–500,000,000; over a third of these people lived in the Yangtze valley. Britain, United States, France and Japan maintained contingents of troops, police and civil officials in their territorial concessions at Shanghai. European and Japanese warships patrolled the lower Yangtze, which teemed with steamers, tugs, junks and sampans heading for inland towns up to 1000 miles from the sea. By 1937 the population of Shanghai was probably in excess of 4,000,000, to make the city one of the half dozen largest metropolises in the world.

Tensions steadily mounted at Shanghai and fighting broke out on 13 August when Chinese forces attacked the Japanese enclave of the International Settlement. In the weeks ahead, Japanese reinforcements were poured into the Shanghai region by sea. The battle raged across September and October; General Iwane Matsui's army grew to comprise six divisions and several independent brigades. The Japanese did not secure Shanghai until mid-November. The three-month campaign was expensive and caused the Imperial Japanese Army's heaviest losses since the war of 1904–05.

The city of Shanghai had received terrible damage; uncontrolled fires burnt out entire city blocks; a Japanese civilian visitor was reminded of Tokyo after the 1923 earthquake. The foreign settlements became islands surrounded by occupied territory, 'like a postage stamp with the edges torn off' remarked a French journalist. Tokyo authorized an advance on Nanking and Japanese forces entered the city on 13 December. The previous day Japanese aircraft had mistakenly sunk the American gunboat *Panay* on the Yangtze; the British gunboat *Ladybird* was shelled by artillery.

What followed shocked the civilized world. For a month the population of Nanking was subjected to a frenzied, drunken orgy of murder and rape. Japanese soldiers would later bring camera films taken at Nanking to be developed at Japanese-owned photographic shops in Shanghai. Chinese photographic assistants made extra prints of the murderous scenes that helped to spread the story of what had happened.[17] Relatively objective foreign observers put the death toll at several tens of thousands. A vast horde of refugees from the lower Yangtze region fled their homes; many of these people would perish from famine and disease. Imperial Japan's international reputation was ruined by the news of the Nanking campaign, though in Berlin there was a growing appreciation of Tokyo's methods.

The Japanese were unable to convert their victories at Shanghai and Nanking into a victory in the war as a whole. This put paid to a swift Japanese triumph in east Asia. Imperial Japan became caught up in an open-ended war of attrition, which was disconcerting for Japanese leaders who had been raised on stories of the battles at Mukden and Tsushima in the 1904–05 war with Russia. After those great victories the Tsarist regime and international mediators had hastened to give Tokyo a favourable settlement. Nothing like that happened in 1937; the Rape of Nanking did not create the conditions for an outbreak of peace. On 26 December 1937 Chiang declared China's intention to fight a protracted war and not negotiate with Japan. In January 1938 the Konoye cabinet announced they would not accept Chiang Kai-shek's regime as a party to any diplomatic settlement.

During 1938 the Japanese military extended the war and pushed inland across northern and central China. Japanese troops advanced south-wards from the Yellow river along the railway that ran from Peking to Nanking. Japanese forces at Nanking pressed northwards to join hands. Around this time the German military mission with the Nationalists was recalled by the Nazi government. Across the summer months of 1938 the Japanese Central China Expeditionary Force advanced westwards along the Yangtze valley. By late October Wuhan, 400 miles from Nanking, was under Japanese control; Nationalist forces retreated further inland along the Yangtze valley.

To support the offensive in central China, on 12 October an amphibious landing was made near Canton in south China by a three division Japanese force. The city, which was inland from Hong Kong, was swiftly captured to cut the Nationalists' main external supply route. In February 1939 Hainan Island, to the south-west of Hong Kong, was seized. Japanese forces occupied Chinese territory adjacent to the frontier of French Indochina to sever the rail link leading to Hanoi and other French colonial ports.

The Japanese held nine-tenths of China's railway system, and had reached the fringe of South-east Asia, but the stalemate continued. Chiang's hopes that the Western powers would intervene in the conflict had come to very little. According to the British ambassador: 'I had always made it quite plain to General Chiang Kai-shek that it would be impossible for Great Britain to afford any material assistance.'[18] In the absence of international intervention, the Chinese Nationalists had no strategic alternative other than to trade space for time, and trust that China's vast terrain and populace would soak up and overstretch the occupying forces of Japan.

At Chungking, deep inland in the upper Yangtze valley, Chiang's government was re-established in relative security. The Nationalist regime, however, became badly isolated from the mainstream of Chinese life, which would have dire consequences for its future survival. In south-west China a long harsh winter shielded Chungking from Japanese air raids; but, after the seasonal fogs lifted, Japanese bombers returned in the spring of 1939 to carpet bomb the crowded city.

The Japanese military settled down as an army of occupation in eastern China. In many sectors a buffer zone 100 miles wide existed between the Japanese and Chinese armies. Guerrilla forces harried the Japanese in north-west China, where the well-organized communists were pursuing a novel but effective political and military strategy. By late 1939 over one million Japanese troops were in China, organised into twenty-five divisions and numerous independent brigades; these troops were supported by over 500 aircraft.[19]

The Sino-Japanese war had acquired a scale and complexity beyond the previous experience of the Imperial Japanese Army, the commanders of which had no tenable plan for a military victory. Japan's leadership in Tokyo was compelled to draw up and clarify a policy for the long-term occupation of Chinese territory. Occupied China was to be part of a Japanese-controlled 'Greater East Asia Co-prosperity Sphere'. This sphere was to embrace Manchuria, Korea, China and any other territory conquered by Japanese forces. Obviously this Japanese programme ran counter to the political and economic interests of the Western powers. Britain, France and the Netherlands all had colonies in South-east Asia; the United States' principal colonial possession in the region was the Philippines.

Yet the position of the United States in Asia was contradictory. From 1937 onwards America exported vast quantities of iron and oil to Japan, most of which was known to be earmarked for military consumption. United States trade and investment with Japan was five to six times greater than with China. President F.D. Roosevelt had declined to invoke the Neutrality Acts to halt this trade as it would antagonise Japan and was bad for business during a prolonged economic slump.[20] Washington's aid to China during the late 1930s was mostly diplomatic, though money was also loaned to Chungking. Any support Chiang Kai-shek could garner from America was useful given his range of expensive commitments.[21]

America's tolerance of Japanese belligerence was wearing thin, but the half-heartedness of British and American responses to Japan's war in China encouraged Japanese leaders to believe that the Western democracies lacked resolve. Tokyo had no such doubts about the Soviet Union. There were regular clashes between Soviet and Japanese troops along the Manchurian-Siberian frontier. In the summer of 1939 heavy fighting took place at Nomonhan, near the frontier of Manchuria and Outer Mongolia. An armistice was concluded in September of that year. At Nomonhan the Japanese army learnt that the capacity of Soviet forces was not to be underestimated.

Unexpectedly, the Sino-Japanese war raised to international prominence the overland route from Lashio, in north-east Burma, to Kunming, the capital of the Chinese province of Yunnan. As the Japanese had seized control of the Chinese seaboard, the Nationalists had to find a new way to import war material from the outside world. Some goods could be shipped across the land frontier with the Soviet Union, but the deserts of inland China made the route too difficult for the quantities to be of significance. Provided the British authorities in Burma were amenable, the route from Rangoon into south-west China was ideal for transporting equipment and munitions originating in the Western world, especially the United States.

The narrow, twisting road from Lashio to Kunming followed an ancient caravan route that may have been used by Marco Polo in the twelfth century. From Kunming a better road ran onwards to Chungking. At 6000 feet above sea level, Kunming was surrounded by mountains and adjacent to a large lake. At first glance Kunming presented a picturesque scene, though the crowded walled city was rather more squalid when looked at closely; opium smoking was widespread and a large overflow of population lived in sampans and junks on the lake.[22] The French had built a railway over the mountains from Hanoi to Kunming. The Chinese provincial capital and its surrounds had come to serve as an unofficial hill station for colonial Indochina.

The governor of Yunnan province was instructed by the leadership at Chungking to build a new road on the route from Lashio to Kunming. Work on the so-called 'Burma Road' began in earnest at the end of the 1938 monsoon season. Lashio and Kunming were 320 miles apart as the crow flies, but the winding road would need to be over 700 miles in length. The construction of the new road by Chinese engineers and labourers incorporated existing sections of road where possible. Workers were employed or conscripted from amongst the hill tribes of the province or brought in from outside. The road wound around mountain peaks over 9000 feet high, and dropped down into the deep gorges of the Mekong and Salween rivers. The Salween gorge was so deep that the sun only reached the bottom when it was high overhead around midday.[23] Long suspension bridges were built to cross the fast-flowing rivers; many lesser rivers and streams also needed new bridges able to carry heavily loaded motor vehicles. The road looped sharply and dramatically as it rose in and out of valleys and across a succession of steep ridges. There was little modern equipment available; men used picks and shovels to move earth and break down the cliffs and hillsides. Blasting of limestone rock was done with black powder in bamboo tubes as dynamite was seldom available.

The Burma Road was officially opened early in 1939. At Lashio, in north-east Burma, the road met the railway that ran through Mandalay from Rangoon. Between Lashio and Mandalay the line crossed the Gokteik gorge, a half-mile wide chasm. Convoys of lorries began to make the laborious journey along the winding and narrow road to Kunming in China. At best, the Burma Road took five days to traverse and was virtually impassable for much of the rainy season. But with Japanese forces occupying coastal China, the route became a lifeline from Nationalist China to the outside world; it was also a way for Chungking to indirectly involve Britain and the United States in the Sino-Japanese war. The interests of the Anglo-Americans had been damaged by Japan's war in east Asia. In consequence, London and Washington willingly played their part to ensure that war material flowed freely to China along the Burma Road.

2

Preparations for War

War broke out in Europe in September 1939 when Germany invaded Poland. Britain and France declared war on Germany in protest. The crisis over Czechoslovakia the previous year had already made it clear that Europe was fast moving towards a resumption of the conflict suspended by armistice in November 1918. At the outset, the Second World War's direct impact was confined to Europe; but the fall of France and the entry of Italy into the war in June 1940 changed all that. Britain's position in the Mediterranean was badly undermined by the loss of the French fleet as an ally and the acquisition of the Italian navy as an enemy. There was now little chance of the Royal Navy's main fleet heading to the Far East to fight the Japanese. An appreciation by the British Chiefs of Staff in August 1940 acknowledged that state of affairs.

In the middle of 1940 Britain's position in the Far East suffered a further blow. In July Tokyo demanded that Britain close the road from Burma to China. Churchill's government complied given the depth of the crisis in Europe, but felt able to reopen it on 18 October; the period of closure had been during the monsoon season when the road was largely unusable.

Meanwhile, on 25 September Japanese troops entered northern Indochina after the Vichy French government caved in to Japanese demands. This effectively cut all supply routes to China through the Hanoi delta, and further raised the practical and symbolic value of the Burma Road. The Japanese were making it clear they had come to mainland Asia to build a permanent empire. Thailand, Indochina's neighbour, found itself trapped between the traditional colonial powers of the region and the rising tide of Japanese imperialism.

Given Germany's recent conquest of most of continental Europe, Japan leapt at the opportunity to forge an alliance with the European Axis. Prince Konoye's government joined the Axis pact on 27 September. According to Konoye: 'Germany and Italy intend to establish a New Order in Europe and Japan will do likewise in Greater East Asia.' In the event of war with the United States, Japan had the prospect of support from Germany.

The fall of France had compelled the Roosevelt administration to more openly support Britain; Washington was opposed to Germany's militarised foreign policy. Once Japan had joined the Axis it made sense for the United

States to start cutting economic ties with that country. The Americans soon halted the export of aviation-grade gasoline and scrap iron to Japan.

In Europe, the threat of the German army across the English Channel in northern France occupied the attention of British leaders during the later months of 1940. The Middle East and Mediterranean had emerged as the highest military priority after the defence of the United Kingdom. The belief that Japan could be contained by the threat of United States' intervention became the basic assumption behind the British empire's defence policy in the Far East. The bulk of reinforcements destined to reach the Far East were bound for Malaya, which was to be expected given the significance of the Singapore Naval Base. The defence of Burma would have to be organised in the shadow of Britain's commitment to Malaya.

In November 1940 a General Headquarters Far East was opened at Singapore. Air Chief Marshal Sir Robert Brooke-Popham was made Commander-in-Chief Far East. His responsibilities included Burma, Borneo and Hong Kong, in addition to Malaya. Burma was placed under Far East Command operationally but remained attached to India Command for supply and reinforcement purposes.

The peacetime garrison of Burma was not large. This was because as long as the Royal Navy controlled the Bay of Bengal, the colony could not be attacked from the sea. Only two British Army infantry battalions were stationed in Burma: the 2nd King's Own Yorkshire Light Infantry (KOYLI) was at Maymyo and Mandalay; the 1st Gloucestershire (or Glosters) was at Mingaladon and Rangoon. Most British regiments had two battalions: one battalion was usually located somewhere in the empire and maintained at full strength; the other battalion remained in Britain and trained drafts for its companion overseas. The army's peacetime training routine and field manoeuvres were not overly strenuous. A lot of team sport was played at a colonial station to pass the time and build team spirit. The KOYLI had an annual parade and celebration for Minden day, a battle from distant 1759 at which the regiment was present.

The core of Burma Army – as the military in Burma was called after the colony's separation from India – was the Burma Rifles, a regiment transferred from the Indian Army. The Burma Rifles had four battalions in 1939. The battalions of the regiment each comprised four rifle companies, two of Karens and one each of Chins and Kachins. Few ethnic Burmans were recruited as they were suspected of having divided loyalties. The Burma Frontier Force, a large body of military police, was on hand to assist the army if required.

Many officers were seconded from the Indian Army to serve with military units in Burma, but in 1939 a field company of sappers and miners and a

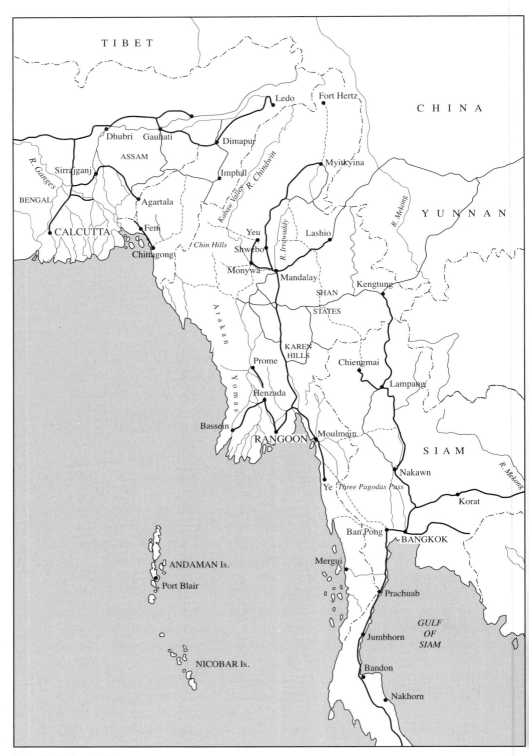

Map B Colonial Burma

mountain battery were the only Indian troops in Burma. The other artillery battery in the colony was a four-gun unit of vintage eighteen pounders belonging to the Burma Auxiliary Force; these guns were mostly used for firing salutes in honour of visiting dignitaries.[1]

Burma Army's headquarters was in Rangoon during the cool season, but for the hot weather civil and military officialdom transferred to the hill station of Maymyo outside Mandalay. The commander of Burma Army was Major-General Donald McLeod, an Indian cavalryman of the Guides. McLeod had written to the Deputy Chief of India's General Staff in 1939: 'I do not regard the land threat very seriously – air attack by Japan from Siamese aerodromes is a big danger.'[2] Born in 1885, McLeod had first seen active service with a punitive expedition on the North-west Frontier in 1908. He had held staff posts in France from 1914–17, and later attended both the Staff College Camberley and Imperial Defence College. In the period before his transfer to Burma, McLeod had commanded a cavalry brigade in India. An American lady described McLeod as 'a sweet old gentleman, tall, a bit heavy, with perfectly white hair and a ruddy complexion.'[3]

After the outbreak of war in 1939, it was decided to raise four more battalions of Burma Rifles by dividing existing units and drawing on recruits from the civil police. The 7th Battalion was half Indian in composition; the 8th Battalion was entirely composed of Sikhs and Punjabi Muslims. A small number of Burmans were recruited for the new units, though this did little to calm Burman resentment at their systematic exclusion from the defence forces of their own country. To provide additional officers, emergency commissions were granted to local Europeans, Anglo-Burmese and Anglo-Indians resident in Burma and working in the administration or commerce. Service in the Burma Auxiliary Force was made compulsory for European British subjects. An Air Observer Corps and Air Raid Precautions (ARP) organization were also set up. At this time the newspapers and cinema newsreels were full of stories of the Luftwaffe's aerial Blitz on Britain. Defence preparations in Burma were hampered by shortages of many types of equipment.

A new governor, Sir Reginald Dorman-Smith, was appointed to Burma on 5 May 1941, to succeed Vice-Admiral Sir Archibald Cochrane. Dorman-Smith was a politician and a former president of the farmers' union. He had been Minister of Agriculture in Prime Minister Chamberlain's government from January 1939 to May 1940, but had lost his post when Churchill's coalition government was formed. Dorman-Smith's posting to Burma had certainly been unexpected; colonial governorships were usually doled out to elderly servants of the state. Dorman-Smith was only forty-one years of age when he arrived in Burma with his wife and two daughters after the long wartime voyage from Britain. Born in Ireland in 1899, as a young man Dorman-Smith had served for a year in the Indian Army; he had retained his citizenship of the Irish Free State after the tumult of Ireland's partition and civil war. Dorman-Smith's exposure to Irish affairs meant that he was well aware that the British empire was moving into a period of profound change.

By the time of Dorman-Smith's arrival in Burma the colony was up to its third ministry since the reformed constitution had come into operation in 1937. Dr Ba Maw had headed a coalition government until March 1939; U Pu was then Prime Minister from that time until September 1940, after which U Saw had become Prime Minister. The two fallen leaders had lost the confidence of the elected members of the legislature.

Prime Minister U Saw was an ambitious and aggressive nationalist; he wanted to trade support of the British war effort in return for a promise of independence straight after the war. The most extreme of the nationalist groupings, the Thakin party, advocated a grant of immediate independence and was openly anti-British. There were, however, only three Thakins in the legislature. The translation of Thakin is 'master'; that was precisely what the Thakins aspired to be in Burma.

U Saw's premiership was full of controversy; he was rumoured to be corruptly selling government posts. U Saw had visited Japan, and he once said of the Japanese: 'We Asiatics have had a poor time since Vasco da Gama rounded the Cape! It was nice to see an Asiatic race able to stand up to you all at last.' (Vasco da Gama was a late fifteenth-century Portuguese navigator.) U Saw conceded, however, that the Japanese were inflicting great suffering on the Chinese people.[4] Dorman-Smith offered to bring his principal ministers into a defence council, though only in an advisory capacity as he was constitutionally responsible for defence. Amongst the Burmese elite nationalism was a powerful influence, though its urgency should not be exaggerated. The pace of politics in the late 1930s had been rapid, and there was strong Burman support for the process of constitutional reform underway and gathering momentum. The non-Burman minorities remained, as always, firmly aligned with the British-led administration.

The colonial regime was always on the lookout for seditious activities, especially after the outbreak of war. Ba Maw, the former prime minister, was jailed for contacts with Japanese agents. The Thakins were in part an underground movement and constantly under the suspicion of authority. The Thakins were particularly influential amongst the students of Rangoon and the organisers of the labour movement. In 1940 many of the party's leaders were arrested under the Defence of Burma Rules. During this crack down the twenty-four-year-old Aung San, the son of a provincial lawyer and prominent political activist, fled the country.

The Japanese had plans to solicit the cooperation of anti-colonial groups in South-east Asia. Colonel Keiji Suzuki was the staff officer responsible for developing links with disaffected local nationalists. In Bangkok he met with Burmese and Indian radicals resident in that city. Suzuki and a companion also travelled to Rangoon to assess the situation.

After Aung San left Burma he contacted Suzuki's group. On 12 November 1940 he was flown to Tokyo for discussions about the raising of a Burmese insurgency in the event of a Japanese invasion of the colony. Aung San returned to Rangoon in secret on 3 March 1941. Over the next three months thirty men were smuggled out of Burma – the so-called 'Thirty Comrades' – to build a leadership for an armed nationalist militia. From Bangkok the men were sent to Japanese bases at Hainan and Formosa for military training.[5]

In theory the colony of Burma was in charge of its own military establishment, but in practice the colony remained heavily dependent on the Indian government in Delhi for defence. The 1919 and 1935 Government of India Acts had introduced a substantial degree of autonomy in provincial government, but Indian defence and foreign policy was retained firmly under the control of the British-dominated central administration and civil service, which was in turn responsible to London and the British Cabinet. When Britain had gone to war with Germany, India went to war as well. The commanders of the Indian Army had consistently advocated that Burma remain under Indian control for defence purposes. Burma was still the outer bastion of north-east India and had shown little sign of being able to manage its own defence in the brief interregnum since 1937.

The Indian Army in 1939 was divided into three major commands, twelve divisional districts and no less than thirty-five brigade area commands. About one-third of the army was deployed in a chain of stations and posts along the North-west Frontier facing Afghanistan. During 1938–39 schemes had been drawn up to modernise the army with financial assistance from the British government, though good intentions were soon overtaken by the speed of events. A pre-war review of the Indian defence establishment had conveniently concluded that the Middle East and Malaya were vital to India's regional security. At the outbreak of war the Indian Army, including British personnel, was 237,500 strong; the army's infantry comprised thirty-seven British, eighty-two Indian and twenty Gurkha battalions.[6]

The Indian Army of the interwar period was not a national or nationalist army in the contemporary sense; but it was a professional army built upon a long and rich military heritage that stretched across the generations since the East India Company had become a significant power in eighteenth century India. Formations from the Indian Army had fought effectively in several overseas theatres during the First World War.

During the 'phoney war' period of 1939–40 India had only a small role to play. The contingents of troops already in Egypt and Malaya were reinforced. After the fall of France, however, the Government of India responded to the crisis by offering to raise five divisions for overseas service. It was planned to raise five more once those first five had departed. The 4th and 5th Indian Divisions were promptly sent to the Middle East; during 1941 the 6th, 8th and 10th Divisions set sail for the Middle East as well; the 9th and 11th Divisions were dispatched to Malaya. A further contingent of Indian troops joined the garrison at Hong Kong.

At the outbreak of war reservists were recalled to the colours; for example, the 10th Baluch Regiment was able to recall 1400 reservists, of whom only two would remain unaccounted.[7] Then in 1940 the recruiting flood-gates were opened to find troops for the new divisions that were to be raised. Regimental depots were swamped by young men eager to secure government employment. During 1941 the Indian Army expanded by means of voluntary recruitment to almost 900,000 officers and men. After a hasty and too-brief basic training period, soldiers were sent to join a unit and undertake more advanced training. In India recruits had to be taught many elementary skills. Young men who had grown up amid bullock carts had to become accustomed to lorries, armoured carriers, mortars, machine guns and radio sets. Newly raised battalions were given a cadre of regulars and then topped up with recruits to make the process of creating an efficient unit doubly difficult. Expanding any army in a hurry presents problems, but there was a major war underway and risks had to be taken.

The Indian Army was organised on a similar basis to the British Army. An infantry battalion had four rifle companies comprising three platoons each, and a headquarters company made up of half a dozen specialist platoons. Indian Army units had a complex social profile. Indian ethnic groups noted for their physique, martial self-image and political reliability – such as Dogras, Garhwalis, Mahrattas, Sikhs, Jats, Rajputs, Pathans and Punjabi Muslims – were heavily recruited. In the army's preferred recruiting grounds boys were encouraged to seek state service in all forms; the army was viewed with respect. The small agricultural holdings of northern India could not support all of a family's sons. Pay, medical care, an impartial system of discipline, and the additional prospect of a pension, provided powerful incentives to enlist.[8]

In practice the peacetime Indian Army had strong ties to the Punjab province. Carefully targeted recruiting in districts closely connected with the government of British-India was vital to the creation of a contented and loyal military. Most infantry battalions comprised a mix of different Indian races and religions, each organised into a separate company as a safeguard against mutiny. A large minority of the regular army was Muslim but there were no all-Muslim regiments.

The Indian Army's ten Gurkha regiments recruited young men from particular tribes and districts of Nepal, the mountain kingdom that lay to the north of India. Nepal was not a formal part of the British empire, but, after the 1814–16 Anglo-Nepalese war, a British Resident was imposed on the court of Nepal; the oldest Gurkha regiments date from that period. Nepal's Maharajah Jang Bahadur Rana paid a state visit to Britain in 1850; he later supported the East India Company in the aftermath of the great mutiny of 1857. The Indian Army was subsequently granted far-ranging recruiting rights in Nepal. In return Nepal's rulers received the diplomatic and monetary backing from Britain they needed to stay in power.[9]

The rich and fertile Kathmandu valley is located in the centre of Nepal; mountains stretch away on either side of the valley. The main tribes in the western mountains are the Magars and Gurungs; to the east live the Rai and Limbu tribes. The majority of Gurkha recruits came from the western mountains, though the 7th Regiment in particular recruited from the eastern tribes. Nepal was still a closed country on the eve of the Second World War. The road-less mountains were high enough to be covered by clouds that might lift abruptly to reveal spectacular views of snow-covered peaks on distant ranges or deep valleys far below. The air was clear and the mountain streams pure. The tribes lived a primitive subsistence life cultivating tiny terraced fields.[10] To be hardy, trustworthy and loyal were essential qualities in the mountains and translated well to army life.

The Gurkha regiments of the Indian Army reproved their value in the 1878–81 Second Anglo-Afghan war, and on numerous campaigns on India's North-west Frontier over the following twenty years. During the first decade of the twentieth century Gurkha recruitment was further expanded to find the manpower for ten regiments of two battalions each; this created a peacetime establishment of 20,000. Extensive overseas service in the First World War added further renown to the reputation of the Gurkha regiments.

The Gurkhas – which is sometimes spelt Gorkha – wore distinct uniforms and headgear; each regiment had its own customs and traditions. Bagpipes had been adopted as a martial instrument as the Gurkhas were also highlanders. The Gurkhas' Hindu religious festivals were encouraged within the military; buffaloes were sacrificed as part of one particular festival. Onlookers were left in no doubt that the kukri, a curved knife, was a useful weapon.[11] The Gurkhas were popular with British officers as they were friendly people by nature, and also because the Gurkhas were outsiders in India, much as the British were.

The senior half of an Indian or Gurkha battalion's officers were holders of a King's Commission, twelve to sixteen at full strength. KCOs came out to India from Britain; they were all British apart from a small number of Indians who had attended Royal Military Academy Sandhurst. The 'Indianisation' of the officer corps was a slow process, but it was speeded up when an officer training academy was opened at Dehra Dun in 1932. Graduates from Dehra Dun were known as 'Indian Commissioned Officers'. By 1939 one in seven officers serving in the Indian Army was an Indian, and these men were concentrated in certain units. The ICOs slowly broke down the monopoly of military leadership hitherto enjoyed by British Sandhurst graduates.[12]

During the Second World War, as in the previous global conflict, the army needed large numbers of Emergency Commissioned Officers. These men were either found within the expatriate community in India or directly transferred from the army in the United Kingdom. ECOs had to hastily learn something of the languages and key religious and cultural beliefs of the men under their command.

Two special types of officers, called jemadars and subedars and holding a Viceroy's Commission, comprised the junior half of an Indian unit's officers. VCOs were Indians promoted from the ranks, usually after at least ten years' service. These men were junior to all officers with a King's or Indian commission, but wore the same rank insignia as lieutenants and captains. Jemadars commanded platoons; a subedar was the senior VCO in a company; the senior VCO in a battalion was the subedar-major. VCOs were the principal link between the army's mostly British officers and the sepoys; the VCOs were the lynch-pin of the colonial army.

A defence review conducted in August 1940 by the Chiefs of Staff in London concluded that war with Japan would lead to air attacks on Burma. The Shan States was considered to be the most likely part of Burma to be invaded from Thailand; the roads leading in that direction from Bangkok were better than those further south leading into Tenasserim.[13] A full-scale land invasion, however, was unlikely as long as Malaya was secure.

Nonetheless, some reinforcement was needed in Burma to augment the slender peacetime garrison. On 7 February 1941 the Chiefs of Staff ordered that a brigade group be dispatched from India. In March and April the 13th Indian Brigade arrived at Rangoon composed of units full of wartime recruits. The brigade group was sent to Mandalay and included two mountain batteries. In the weeks and months ahead units from the Maymyo garrison were sent to the southern Shan States to form the 1st Burma Brigade; steps were also taken to form the 2nd Burma Brigade in Tenasserim.

In July a headquarters for the 1st Burma Division was established at Toungoo. The newly promoted Major-General James Bruce Scott was the division's commander. Scott was nearing fifty years of age and had been commissioned in 1912. He served in the 33rd Punjab Regiment during the First World War, and saw service in Egypt, France and German East Africa. After the war he transferred to the 6th Gurkhas and took part in several frontier campaigns, for which he was twice mentioned in despatches. He took command of the 1/8th Gurkhas late in 1936; the battalion moved from Quetta to Razmak in Waziristan in the spring of 1939. In the autumn of that year Scott was posted to Burma as a brigadier.

Burma would remain a backwater as long as South-east Asia was at peace, but that was not destined to last. On 13 April 1941 a neutrality pact was signed between Japan and the Soviet Union; then on 22 June, to Tokyo's surprise, the Germans invaded the Soviet Union. With the Russians fully engaged resisting the Nazis, Japan was now free to send forces into South-east Asia to complete its domination of the eastern portion of the Asian continent. The next step was to occupy southern Indochina, and the French authorities swiftly capitulated to Japanese demands. Washington was quick to respond and by the end of July the United States had banned the export of oil to Japan. The Western powers combined to place a trade embargo on the Japanese. In 1940–41 Japan imported 80 per cent of oil from the United States; Japan had only enough stockpiled oil to last eighteen months if used at a normal rate.

Washington's rising level of engagement in eastern Asia began more directly to involve the road that ran from Upper Burma into south-west China. This was brought about by the passing of the Lend Lease Act on 11 March 1941. The act permitted the United States government to send war material to Allied powers – such as Britain and the Soviet Union – on the proviso that the bill would be deferred till after the war. China was also declared eligible for Lend Lease supplies. American staff were sent to Rangoon to supervise the onward shipment of an expanded supply of war material for Chungking.

Generalissimo Chiang was eager to receive all possible aid from America. At his headquarters at Chungking, Chiang presided over a National Military Council that had several million soldiers deployed across a dozen designated war zones. Nationalist generals were often regional governors in their own right. Chiang had personal control of a relatively small proportion of all Chinese divisions, but those formations could at least be given preferential access to Western equipment arriving along the Burma Road.[14]

Yet in the autumn of 1941 the Burma Road was only able to carry 6000 tons of supplies per month to Kunming. American officials felt it could carry 30,000 tons per month under optimal conditions and efficient central management. By November a figure of 15,000 tons was achieved, prompted by the vigorous insistence of the Americans that matters needed to improve.[15] Allied shipping carried war material to Rangoon for China regardless of delays further along the pipeline. It was estimated late in the year that 85,000 tons of Lend Lease supplies had been accumulated in warehouses at Rangoon.

Inefficiency, corruption and the genuine difficulty of the route into south-western China combined to retard the transport of war material. Some of the material sent along the Burma Road vanished into China's black market with the assistance of officials who imposed tolls on vehicles passing through their territory. Equipment such as industrial plant could be adapted for illicit civilian purposes; cigarettes and petrol were smuggled as they were very profitable commodities. There was a lack of repair and maintenance facilities, and motor vehicles were stripped for spare parts; the route was littered with the wreckage of road accidents. Efforts by American journalists such as Leland Stowe to expose the Burma Road as a giant racket fell on deaf ears given the general state of crisis in the Allied world.[16]

Chungking came under regular Japanese aerial bombardment. The Chinese air force was no match for the new long-range fighter escorts the Japanese had introduced in the autumn of 1940. The Mitsubishi A6M had an enclosed cockpit and retractable landing gear. It became known as the 'Zero' as the year 1940 was the year 2600 in the calendar of Imperial Japan. At the end of September Japanese bombers raided Kunming from bases near Hanoi; the following month bombers struck the town of Loiwing, close to the China-Burma frontier. The exposed Burma Road might become a regular target for Japanese raiders.[17]

Late in 1940 Chiang asked his chief air force adviser, Claire L. Chennault, to head a mission to recruit pilots and buy modern aircraft in the United States. Chennault, a former United States Army Air Force fighter pilot, had been an adviser to the Chinese air force since 1937 and had attained the rank of colonel. Chennault – 'old leatherface' – was a stocky man from Louisiana, with a strong jaw, a square furrowed face and determined demeanour. When America entered the First World War, Chennault had volunteered for service; he had commenced flight training shortly after the armistice and remained in the military postwar.

The United States' government could see that the Burma Road needed air cover; Chennault's mission was a success. There was no point America shipping supplies to Rangoon, for onwards transport to Kunming and Chungking, if the Japanese air force could interdict the route without opposition.[18] The Nationalists' representative in Washington, T.V. Soong, was Madame Chiang's brother and a keen supporter of the scheme. A front organization was set up – the Central Aircraft Manufacturing Company – through which government finance could be channelled.

During the Spanish Civil War the international precedent had been set of foreign pilots fighting in another country's war. Numerous young Americans had already left for Britain to join the Royal Air Force. On 15 April 1941 President Roosevelt issued a secret executive order allowing American military personnel to resign and fight for China. At the end of a year's service with the 'American Volunteer Group', they would be able to re-join United States forces without loss of seniority. High base pay, bonuses and the prospect of adventure attracted volunteers; 100 pilots and 200 ground crew were recruited; two-thirds of the pilots came from the navy and marines. The pilots of the American Volunteer Group did not hold military rank within the organization, which operated like a civilian airline.[19]

The American Volunteer Group was equipped with 100 P-40B Tomahawk fighters. The aircraft had been a French order at the Curtiss-Wright factory at Buffalo, New York. The contract was taken over by the British after the fall of France, but they were persuaded to waive their right to the aircraft. The P-40s had been modified for the RAF and hence they were called P-40B Tomahawks.[20] The British readily agreed that the Americans could use RAF airfields in Burma for training, prior to their planned departure for service in the skies of the Chinese interior. Mingaladon, Toungoo and Magwe airfields were made available to the Americans. Uncrated Tomahawks were assembled at Mingaladon after shipment to Burma in a Norwegian freighter; the first assembled aircraft arrived at Toungoo on 3 August.

The arrival of the AVG created considerable local excitement, but the air defence of Burma remained in the hands of the RAF. A defence review had estimated that the RAF would need 280 aircraft in Burma, but there was never any prospect of the attainment of that figure.[21] No. 60 Squadron, equipped with Blenheim bombers, arrived in February 1941; No. 221 Group headquarters was formed in April. Later in the year – September – a Buffalo fighter squadron, No. 67 Squadron, arrived from Singapore with a front-line strength of sixteen aircraft. Apart from the squadron and flight commanders, almost all the pilots were New Zealanders, many of whom had come straight from flying school. The young pilots lacked experience but possessed a 'fine aggressive spirit'.[22]

An increased level of support from the United States, and the entry of the Soviets into the war, had improved Britain's strategic position in Europe during 1941. The British government, however, felt obligated to send military aid to Russia given the enormous burden the Red Army was shouldering in the war against Germany. Convoys carrying aircraft, tanks and other equipment began sailing to Russia via the Arctic Circle. This was another strain on a finite pool of Allied merchant shipping. There were few reinforcements available for the Far East; the Middle East was the main destination for army divisions sailing from Britain, India and the Dominions. Nonetheless, three divisions had been sent to Malaya to cover the landward approaches to Singapore fortress, which was a stronger force than the single colonial division in Burma. Towards the end of the year, at Churchill's urging, the modern battleship *Prince of Wales* and old battlecruiser *Repulse* would sail for Singapore to form the nucleus of a fleet for the Far East.

General Sir Archibald Wavell had become the Indian Army's Commander-in-Chief in July 1941. He soon began to cast his one remaining eye over the problems of Burma's defence, though the colony was not his operational responsibility and remained under the control of Far East Command at Singapore. Born in 1883 and the son of a major-general, at Winchester school young Wavell studied the classics; he developed an interest in poetry and history that lasted throughout his life. Commissioned into the Black Watch in 1901, Wavell arrived in southern Africa in time for the closing period of the Boer war. He saw further active service in the North-west Frontier's Bazaar valley in 1908. This was followed by attendance at the Camberley Staff College and a year in Russia as a military observer. In the First World War Wavell lost an eye to a shell splinter at Ypres; after recovery he spent another period in Russia as a liaison officer. By war's end he was a brigadier-general at General Allenby's headquarters in the Middle East.

Wavell was hard-working and his career did not stagnate in the interwar period. By 1937 he was GOC (General Officer Commanding) Palestine and Trans-Jordan. The start of the Second World War found Wavell CIC Middle East. His reputation for intelligence and sound judgement was sorely tested by the many challenges that beset the Middle East Command during the twelve months from June 1940 to June 1941. The Italians were driven out of Egypt and Abyssinia, but, in turn, British forces were pushed out of Greece and Crete. General Rommel and his Afrika Korps besieged the garrison of Tobruk in Libya and a relief force was turned back.

Prime Minister Churchill decided that a change was needed at Cairo; at the close of June 1941 Wavell was informed that he was to trade places with the CIC of the Indian Army. Wavell fair-mindedly commented to his chief of staff: 'I am sure the Prime Minister is right. You will find a new man with new ideas will be a good thing.' At Delhi Wavell quickly realised that Burma needed transfer from Far East Command to his operational control. Wavell visited London in September and lobbied the Chiefs of Staff for this; Governor Dorman-Smith supported the proposed change in policy. Wavell later reported:

The Chiefs of Staff ... refused to alter the existing arrangement, on the ground that the question had been fully considered when the Far Eastern Command was established. The Japanese by this time had invaded Indochina, and thus brought danger to Burma much closer, but this fact was not held to justify the change.[23]

Burma was bound to be a low priority in a command based at Singapore, but might become a higher priority if made a responsibility of the Indian Army. After Air Chief Marshal Brooke-Popham had toured Burma earlier in the year, a dismayed Dorman-Smith had cabled his minister in London that a more energetic personality was needed in the post at Singapore.

Wavell visited Burma in late October 1941; Dorman-Smith wrote of Wavell:

> His mere presence made us all feel much better. He had the wonderful power of inspiring confidence. Small, stocky, not very approachable, yet very kind, he reminded you of the famous physician, the Harley Street specialist, who is called in at the last minute and whom everyone expects will know what to do to save the patient.

An inspection by any senior official was appreciated by the Rangoon authorities given the rarity of the event. Wavell's impression of his tour was unambiguously grim:

> I was very much concerned by the extent of unpreparedness in Burma's defences of which I became aware during my visit. I realised that the number and training of the troops, their equipment, the Intelligence lay out, the size and organization of the staff, the administrative system and the defensive arrangements were quite inadequate.[24]

After his return from Rangoon, Wavell ordered that an additional infantry brigade and mountain battery be sent from India to Burma.

Another official visit to Burma by very important persons had also taken place earlier that month. The famous couple was Sir A. Duff Cooper and Lady Diana. Churchill had sent Duff Cooper, formerly Minister of Information, to the Far East as resident Minister of State. The Coopers stopped in Rangoon before flying to Maymyo to meet with Dorman-Smith. Lady Diana visited the Shwedagon Pagoda, undeterred by the need to enter the temple bare-footed. At Maymyo, in a speech to the Bush Warfare School, Duff Cooper told his listeners that they were unlikely ever to see active service in Burma.[25]

Preparations for the defence of Burma were slowly taking shape, but the ultimate fate of the colony was in the hands of diplomats and governments on opposing sides of the Pacific Ocean. Negotiations were underway between Japan and the United States to end the Western trade embargo. Washington, however, had no intention of resuming the supply of oil unless the Japanese made significant territorial concessions in China. That was not acceptable to the Imperial Japanese Army. The Japanese cabinet was forced to resign; on

17 October General Hideki Tojo became the new Prime Minister. Tojo and his supporters were determined to maintain and expand the army's empire-building ambitions.

Preparations for war against the Western powers gathered renewed momentum; the military pushed aside the doubts of civilian politicians. Orders were sent from Tokyo warning subordinate headquarters that hostilities would commence on 8 December, which would be 7 December to the east of the international date line. The Japanese were gambling that Germany would defeat or contain the Soviets and Britain in Europe; after which an isolated United States might be compelled to accept a peace that recognised Japan's empire in Asia. On the opening day of war the Imperial Japanese Navy was planning a surprise raid on the United States Pacific Fleet at Pearl Harbor, Hawaii.

To preside over the conquest of South-east Asia, a headquarters for the Japanese Southern Army was established at Saigon under the command of Count Terauchi. Southern Army comprised four smaller armies: XIV Army was to invade the Philippines; XV Army was to take Thailand and Burma; XXV Army was to seize Malaya; XVI Army was to overrun the Dutch East Indies. Singapore was the most important Allied base in South-east Asia and the Southern Army's main objective. Across this critical period the bulk of the Imperial Japanese Army remained deployed in China and Manchuria.

Burma had its place in Japanese planning; Burma was to be invaded to protect the flank of Japanese forces advancing on Singapore and the oil fields of the Dutch East Indies. Burma was the last remaining route along which supplies could be sent to Chinese forces resisting Japan's invasion of mainland Asia. The oil, rice and timber of Burma would be useful additional raw materials for the Japanese war effort. A full-scale invasion of Burma, however, would only be possible once it appeared likely that the drive upon Singapore was destined to be crowned with success.

3

The Outbreak of War in South-east Asia

The time had come for Japan to execute its carefully laid plans for war. The Western powers were aware that a crisis was about to break. Daily RAF reconnaissance flights were made from Malaya out over the Gulf of Siam and the South China Sea. On 6 and 7 December aircrew sighted Japanese troop convoys but there were doubts as to whether they were headed for Thailand or Malaya.

As British commanders at Singapore discussed reports of the probable approach of an invasion force, other Japanese fleets were moving out across the western and central Pacific Ocean. In particular a fleet of Japanese aircraft carriers, the most powerful naval strike force in the world, was preparing to make a surprise attack on Pearl Harbor on the morning of 7 December, which would be 8 December in Asia, on the western side of the international date line.

The attack by two waves of carrier aircraft devastated the battleships of the United States Pacific Fleet. The Pearl Harbor raid brought America into the war against Japan in no uncertain fashion. Within a few days Hitler had declared war on the United States in support of Japan. America was thus a part of both the European and Asia-Pacific wings of the Second World War.

The Japanese attack on South-east Asia was planned to follow the outbreak of hostilities. Hong Kong, Thailand, Malaya and the Philippines were all to be invaded. Lieutenant-General Tomoyuki Yamashita's XXV Army was to thrust down the Malayan peninsula towards Singapore. XV Army, commanded by Lieutenant-General Shojiro Iida, was assigned the task of occupying Thailand, after which Burma was also to be invaded. Japanese control of the port of Bangkok and the Thai railways would greatly assist operations in Burma. A full-scale invasion of Burma, however, was conditional on Japanese forces making good progress in Malaya.

At the outbreak of war XV Army comprised 35,440 men.[1] Iida's army, in common with other Japanese army formations, would not be heavily equipped in terms of artillery, tanks or motor transport. But several years of hard campaigning in China had taught the Japanese a great deal about the swift manoeuvre of light infantry across broken terrain. The strength of the Imperial Japanese Army lay in the tremendous spirit of self-sacrifice routinely displayed by virtually every soldier. The samurai ethos and the code of Bushido – the Way of the Warrior – were drawn upon for inspiration. A high level of discipline and obedience was a feature of relations between officers and the men under their command; all ranks would literally fight to the death if given the opportunity to do so for their divine emperor.

General Iida, the commander of XV Army, was an experienced professional soldier and a cultivated man. Prior to his appointment to XV Army, Iida had commanded the Imperial Guards Division in China. His father had commanded a regiment of the Imperial Guards in the war against Russia in 1904–05.[2]

The leading division of XV Army was the 55th Division, which was recruited from rural Shikoku, the smallest of Japan's four main home islands. The division had been raised in 1940 as a cadre and was brought to full strength early in October 1941 as part of the preparations for an expanded war. Reservists were recalled to augment a large body of recently enlisted conscripts. Lieutenant-General Yiroshi Takeuchi and the 112th and 143rd Regiments arrived at Saigon in late November. The division's third regiment was detached for a planned landing on Guam in the western Pacific.

The 33rd Division was XV Army's second principal formation. The division comprised soldiers recruited from a mountainous region north-west of Tokyo and had been deployed to China in 1939. The commander of the 33rd Division was Lieutenant-General Seizo Sakurai; he was fifty-two years of age and a former military attaché at Japan's Paris embassy. Sakurai took command of the 33rd Division in January 1941. The troops of the division were well prepared for a fast-moving campaign that would utilise encircling tactics and improvised landing operations.[3] The 55th Division's order of battle included a reconnaissance regiment, but the 33rd Division did not possess a unit of that type.[4]

XV Army's infantry regiments and battalions had their own light artillery detachments. An infantry regiment had an artillery company armed with seventy-five millimetre mountain guns and an anti-tank company armed with thirty-seven millimetre guns. Each Japanese battalion had two additional seventy-millimetre guns. A lack of ammunition would be the main constraint upon Japanese artillery usage.[5] XV Army was heavily dependent on animal transport and had a limited pool of motor vehicles. The 5th Air Division was to provide General Iida's troops with air support.

In the early hours of 8 December assault landings were made on the coast of Thailand and north-east Malaya. In conjunction with the landings from the sea, the Imperial Guards Division entered Thailand from Indochina. The 55th Division's 143rd Regiment was part of the Malayan invasion fleet, but sheered away northwards from the main convoys to make an opposed landing on the coast of Thailand between Chumphon and Prachuab. By the morning of 8 December the Thai Premier and Japanese ambassador had reached an agreement to permit Japanese forces to pass across Thai territory, but the news took time to spread and fighting at Prachuab lasted into the following day. Seventy-nine XV Army troops were killed in the Thai landing operation.[6] Late in December the Thai and Japanese governments signed a Treaty of Mutual Assistance. The following month Thailand, under pressure from Tokyo, would declare war on Britain and the United States to remove any doubt as to where Thailand stood.

Imperial General Headquarters in Tokyo issued orders for Japanese troops to overrun southern Tenasserim in Burma to establish airfields and isolate Thailand and Malaya. Tenasserim is a long, narrow finger of territory running down the western side of the Kra peninsula; Tenasserim stretches for over 400 miles southwards from Moulmein to Victoria Point. A strip of land thirty to sixty miles wide was Burmese territory, and was divided from Thailand by jungle-covered mountains that could only be traversed in the dry season by a few remote tracks. British commanders had accepted that Victoria Point was indefensible. Japanese aircraft raided RAF airfields in Tenasserim at Victoria Point, Tavoy and Mergui in support of the intended ground invasion. After a heavy raid two-thirds of Mergui's population fled.

After disembarkation on the Thai coast Colonel Uno and the II/143rd Battalion headed cross-country to enter the southern tip of Burma. Upon the approach of Japanese troops a small Burma Frontier Force detachment at Victoria Point was evacuated by motor launch.[7] Japanese troops had entered Victoria Point without opposition by 16 December. The 143rd Regiment was made responsible for protecting the railway running from Bangkok into Malaya, against which a BFF unit would later make an unsuccessful raid. Allied fighters took to the skies to defend Rangoon, though Japanese aircraft, at this stage of the campaign, confined their operations to Tenasserim.

On 11 December 1941 the Chiefs of Staff hastily put Burma back under the operational command of the Indian Army. Prime Minister Churchill signalled General Wavell: 'You must now look east. Burma is placed under your command.' Churchill and his principal military advisers sailed for the United States on 12 December and were not due to return to the United Kingdom for several weeks. The sinking of the capital ships *Prince of Wales* and *Repulse* the previous day, off the eastern coast of Malaya, had been a terrible shock to British commanders at Singapore and London.

There was also the vital question of Nationalist China's involvement in Allied military plans for South-east Asia. Wavell would have a central role to play in drawing up those arrangements. As a whole the Chinese armies were a disunited coalition of warlord forces, but the Kuomintang's regular divisions were a cut above the rest in terms of discipline and organization. Chiang Kai-shek's regime had to both hold down its own territory against the Communists, and maintain a front opposing the Japanese. But, despite these heavy commitments, a large force of Chinese troops was present in Yunnan province as a strategic reserve.

Soon after the outbreak of the Pacific war Chiang Kai-shek met the British military attaché at Chungking, Major-General L.E. Dennys, and offered to send troops to cooperate with Allied forces in Burma. The Burma Road into south-west China was a vital interest for Nationalist China. On 14 December the Chiefs of Staff instructed Wavell to negotiate with Chungking in respect to that matter. On 15–16 December the Chinese leadership offered the 5th and 6th Armies for the defence of Burma, provided they could be given their own zone of operations. Generalissimo Chiang was later to state:

> The way the Chinese Armies acquit themselves in Burma is a matter which touches the honour and pride of China. The eyes of the world will be upon them and they cannot risk defeat. If they are in sufficient numbers they will not be defeated, but if their strength is insufficient I cannot give any guarantee. You must remember that my honour and pride are concerned too and you should listen to my views as to what is best.[8]

The head of the United States military mission at Chungking, Brigadier-General J. Magruder, was present at the interview on 15 December. He reported to Washington that Chiang had made clear his opposition to a piecemeal deployment of Chinese troops in Burma.

At Rangoon, shortly after the outbreak of war, Governor Dorman-Smith met his ministers and reported that 'their attitude was robustly anti-Japanese'. A senior minister told the press: 'Burma is prepared and I am sure that the country will not be found lacking in any effort to resist aggression by the enemy.'[9] Not all people shared that view and Indian citizens began to book their passages by sea to return to their homeland.

Prime Minister U Saw was absent from Burma at this time as he had left for London early in October to press for the granting of immediate independence after the war was ended. On 18 October he had met with Churchill at Chequers, the country residence of British prime ministers. Churchill said that negotiations for further constitutional reform would be unwise at a time of great uncertainty. Provided Britain won the war, the reform process would continue its liberal path in a time of peace. U Saw planned to return to Burma by way of the United States and the Pacific. In America he visited the Japanese Consul-General for the stated purpose of discussing the safety of Burmese students in Japan. U Saw and a colleague, U Tin Tut, the secretary of Burma's Defence Council and a member of the

Indian Civil Service, landed at Pearl Harbor by air on 8 December, the day after the Japanese raid. The wrecked and smoking American battleships were a shocking sight.

U Saw now had to return to Burma via the Middle East; he landed in Portugal on the first stage of the journey. At Lisbon U Saw contacted the Japanese embassy and called upon the ambassador alone. Unbeknown to U Saw and the Japanese ambassador, British intelligence was able to decode cipher messages sent from Japan's Lisbon embassy. The day after the visit of Burma's Prime Minister, the embassy sent a report of the interview to Japan. U Saw had supposedly claimed that if the Japanese invaded Burma, the Burmese would rise against their colonial masters in support of the invasion. U Saw promised to help the Japanese as best he could. The Japanese ambassador may have exaggerated the content of the interview but the Secretary of State for India, Leo Amery, authorized U Saw's incarceration. At Haifa in Palestine U Saw was arrested and detained in east Africa indefinitely.

The new Prime Minister of Burma was Sir Paw Tun. He was Western educated and an experienced minister who believed in the good intentions of the constitutional reform process underway in the colony. Burmese members of the civil service, police and judiciary were of moderate political views in general.

Sir Paw Tun soon authorized the arrest of many Thakin activists; it had long been suspected that Japanese agents were active amongst them. The extreme wing of the Thakins was receptive to overtures from Colonel Suzuki's political officers. Behind Japanese lines preparations were well advanced to form a Japanese-sponsored Burma Independence Army. The BIA would be formally established at Bangkok on 28 December; Aung San was appointed a major-general in the force. The BIA commenced with a small body of Japanese and Burmese personnel, but plans were in place to create a much larger organization.[10]

General McLeod, Burma Army's commander, now had an active war on his hands. His Order of the Day on the outbreak of war in the Far East announced:

> In the air, on the sea, and on the land, Burma is ready to repulse any foe. It is with every confidence that I call on the soldiers to face the enemy with calmness and courage. We shall throw back the invaders and free Burma forever from the threat which has dawned today.

Nonetheless, the 1st Battalion of the Gloucestershire Regiment was retained on garrison duty at Mingaladon and Rangoon to guarantee internal security, despite the immediate threat of Japanese invasion. A detached company was housed at barracks near the Shwedagon Pagoda. The commanding officer of the Glosters, Lieutenant-Colonel Charles Bagot, was a stern disciplinarian who had won the Military Cross as a subaltern on the First World War's western front. The Glosters had left Britain for Egypt as long ago as 1928. After three years in the land of the pyramids, the battalion spent a year at Singapore before arrival in India. Sojourns at three different Indian cantonments had followed; after which the Glosters arrived in Burma in November 1938. Long periods of overseas service, often lasting for the better part of a generation, was typical in the British Army of that era, especially for relatively unfashionable regiments.

Upon mobilisation the Glosters wore an army-type sun helmet as there were no steel helmets available. Armoured Bren carriers, mortars and trucks were also in short supply. The precaution had already been taken of sending the Glosters' colours by air to India to be deposited with Lloyd's Bank in Delhi. The regiment's women and children were dispatched to the hill station of Maymyo outside Mandalay. The Glosters began the campaign with 640 officers and other ranks and eighty-seven attached followers.[11]

At the end of November, just prior to the outbreak of war, the 16th Indian Brigade had arrived in Burma; each battalion of the brigade had been made up to strength with over 300 recruits. The commander of the 1st Burma Division, General Scott, commented of this period: 'Shuffle and reshuffle was the order of the day and commanders did not know from day to day of what their commands were composed.'[12] It had been a shock to Delhi for the north-east frontier facing Burma to spring to life after decades of quietude.

When war broke out in the Far East, General Wavell was instructed by the Chiefs of Staff to retain the 17th Indian Division in India; this formation had been due to sail for Iraq. He was also told that the 18th British Division, currently at sea on the Cape of Good Hope route to the Middle East, would arrive in India in the weeks ahead. London signalled Wavell that he should 'proceed immediately with administrative arrangements for the development of Rangoon as a base for a force which might ultimately reach four divisions and fifteen [RAF] squadrons.'[13] At this time Wavell was optimistic that adequate reinforcements would be sent to India. If all went well, operations in Malaya might be protracted and provide breathing space for Burma to build up its defences. An appreciation prepared by the General Staff in Delhi on 15 December stated: 'Rangoon forms the only effective means of entry into Burma. Its protection is, therefore, of the utmost importance. The road now under construction between Assam and Burma can only be a supplement and can never be a substitute for the port.' It went on to say that 'a force of two divisions should be transported from India to Burma at the earliest possible date'.[14] General McLeod had wasted no time in requesting further reinforcement.

After the capture of Victoria Point, at the southern tip of Burmese Tenasserim, General Iida's XV Army spent the rest of December consolidating Japan's grip on Thailand. Operations in Malaya were the primary Japanese focus in South-east Asia during this period. British commanders at Rangoon had little knowledge of events in Thailand or Japanese intentions, nor was there much likelihood of that situation improving in the absence of an established espionage network. There was the possibility of the Japanese invading Burma at several places along the lengthy Thai-Burmese frontier. The Thai railways could be used by the Japanese to concentrate troops at Chieng Mai in the north of the country; from there the Shan States could be entered with the intention of cutting the main rail and road links from Rangoon to Mandalay.

General McLeod had concluded that a large Japanese army might be based in Thailand, but supply problems would only permit a two-division force to invade Burma by land. As the road network leading into the Shan States was superior to the rough track leading westwards from Raheng to Moulmein, McLeod positioned the 1st Burma and 13th Indian Brigades in the Shan States and the 2nd Burma Brigade in Tenasserim.[15] The 16th Indian Brigade formed a general reserve; Scott's divisional headquarters supervised the troops in the Shan States.

General Wavell next visited Rangoon on 21 December. By this time the Chiefs of Staff had diverted to Malaya the 53rd Brigade of the 18th British Division and the 45th Brigade of the 17th Indian Division. India Command's capacity to reinforce Burma was already on the wane. The following day, 22 December, Wavell signalled the Chief of the Imperial General Staff:

> Burma is essential base for operations against Japan, it is only route for supplies to China, it is integral part of defence of Eastern India, where large proportion of munitions factories are sited. Its security is, therefore, absolutely vital to prosecution of War against Japan. At present time Burma is very far from secure. From lack of aircraft and break down of intelligence system based on Singapore, information of Japanese moves and intentions is completely lacking. At present moment GOC Burma is working blindfold.

Wavell determined that Burma's immediate requirements were another two brigades and a second divisional headquarters.[16]

Before leaving Rangoon, Wavell decided to replace General McLeod as commander of Burma Army. McLeod was nearing retirement age in the normal course of events, and he would be promoted lieutenant-general to ease the pain of his sudden relief. Wavell appointed his chief of staff at Delhi, Lieutenant-General T.J. Hutton, to command Burma Army; Hutton was to fly to Rangoon as soon as could be arranged.

From Rangoon Wavell flew to Chungking on 22 December with the United States Army Air Force's Major-General George H. Brett. Wavell had meetings with Generalissimo Chiang on the two days following his arrival. Brett and Brigadier-General Magruder, the head of the American military mission at Chungking, were present at the talks. Chiang had been hoping for a general discussion of Allied strategy, but Wavell was not commissioned to undertake such a task. The British commander wanted the Chinese to release part of the American Volunteer Group for the air defence of Rangoon, and also to permit British forces to requisition some of the Lend Lease stores building up on the docks. Wavell would write of the Generalissimo that he 'was not a particularly impressive figure at first sight: he speaks no English but makes clucking noises like a friendly hen when greeting one. Madame, of course, speaks perfect English.'[17] Neither Wavell nor Chiang could fathom the other man.

The Chinese had offered to send two armies to Burma earlier in the month; this offer was again discussed. The 6th Army was close to the Burmese frontier and the 5th Army was at Kunming, at the Chinese end of the Burma Road. These armies would need to be supplied by the British, and have a distinct zone of operations. Wavell, however, only accepted a single division of the 6th Army for service in Burma; he asked that a second division be held in reserve close to the Burma-China frontier. Wavell was concerned that Chinese troops might live off the land in Burma and strip the countryside like a swarm of locusts. He still had hopes that British reinforcements would be sent to Rangoon, though it was starting to become apparent that Singapore had an insatiable appetite for any available troops in the region. The civil authorities at Rangoon also pointed out that China had an old claim that Burma was a feudatory of a former Chinese empire, and had never recognised the British annexation of the territory. 'It was desirable', Wavell later wrote, 'that a country of the British Empire should be defended by Imperial troops rather than by foreign.'[18] Brett and Magruder signalled Washington that Wavell had rejected Chiang's offer of troops; Wavell was to be much criticised for his handling of the negotiations.

The situation confronting Allied air forces in Burma was as difficult and fraught as was the case for Burma Army on the ground. The Japanese army's air forces in the region were controlled by Southern Area headquarters. The 5th Air Division was to support XV Army in Burma; the 3rd Air Division was to support the invasion of Malaya. An air division was a balanced force of fighters, bombers and other aircraft types. Mergui airfield had been bombed by the Japanese when the southern tip of Tenasserim was occupied, but there had been no major incursion into the skies of Burma since then.

The American Volunteer Group was at Toungoo when war broke out, still completing its training for service in China. Wavell described the American airmen as 'formidable buccaneers'. The AVG's P-40B Tomahawk was a swift aircraft, whether diving or flying level, and carried heavy armour and a self-sealing fuel tank. The Tomahawks were armed with two point-five calibre nose machine guns and four point-three wing machine guns. The pilots were trained to fight in pairs and to dive to attack hostile aircraft and then climb away to safety. Hit and run was the fighter pilot's principal method in the Second World War; modern fighters were too fast to often indulge in the slow-wheeling dogfights that had been commonplace in the 1914–18 conflict.

On the outbreak of war against Japan the RAF in southern Burma had desperately needed immediate reinforcement. The 3rd Squadron of the AVG – the 'Hell's Angels' – arrived at Mingaladon from Toungoo on 12 December. The RAF and AVG shared an operations room, though different radio transmitters were used on different frequencies for controlling the pilots in the air. The AVG's Tomahawks and the Buffaloes of No. 67 Squadron used separate intersecting runways; when the base was scrambled planes scampered in all directions amid clouds of dust.[19]

The remaining two AVG squadrons flew from Toungoo to Kunming in south-west China on 18 December. Thirty-four Tomahawks made the flight; the fighters carried the markings of the blue and white star of Nationalist China; a row of shark's teeth was painted onto the nose of the aircraft. Ground staff set out in trucks for the long journey by road. Kunming was set on a high plateau astride the ancient trade route from India to China; the winter weather was cold and ice lay on the ground. The weather at Rangoon in December was cooler than during the hot season but was still warm and tropical.

The first major air battle of the campaign took place on 20 December when ten twin-engine Kawasaki Ki-48 bombers set out from Hanoi to bomb Kunming. The bombers flew without an escort and were driven off by American fighters before they could reach the intended target. One Tomahawk made a forced landing when it ran out of fuel, and numerous Japanese aircraft were claimed destroyed by the American pilots. It transpired that three of the bombers had been shot down and all of the remainder received some damage. The AVG's victory was celebrated by the people of Kunming and reported in Chinese newspapers far and wide. The phrase 'Flying Tigers' was coined; the Burma Road seemed to be in the safe hands of the Anglo-American powers.[20]

The air war in southern Burma was also about to enter an entirely new phase. General Michio Sugawara was planning a major bombing raid on Rangoon for 23 December. Mingaladon airfield and the down-town districts of Rangoon were to be the principal targets; the Shwedagon Pagoda would provide an excellent navigation mark from the air. Eighty bombers and thirty fighters were available for the operation. Most of the bombers were twin-engine Ki-21 Mitsubishis. The Ki-21 was a modern type, carried a large crew and could fly at 300 miles per hour. Three squadrons of Ki-21 Mitsubishi bombers would be supported by a squadron of nimble Ki-27 Nakajima fighters – also called a Type 97 fighter – and a squadron of Ki-30 Anns. The Ann was a fighter-bomber and carried a 600-pound bomb; for armament the Ann mounted one forward firing fixed machine gun, and a rear-gunner sat behind the pilot under a greenhouse type canopy.

The morning of 23 December was a fine tropical day; there were few clouds in the air and a light breeze blew from the south. The Japanese aircraft took to the skies from airfields in Thailand and Indochina. Just before 10 a.m. the operations room at Mingaladon reported two waves of approaching raiders. Squadron Leader Robert Milward of No. 67 Squadron was with Mingaladon's commanding officer, Wing Commander N.C.S. Rutter, when the news came through. The base's fighters were hastily ordered to scramble. A dozen Tomahawks and fifteen Buffaloes took off and began climbing for all the height they could manage in the time available. The Japanese aircraft arrived forty minutes after the first warning.[21] A squadron of twin-engine bombers (62nd Sentai) made for Mingaladon with the slower single-engine fighter-bombers (31st Sentai) and fighters (77th Sentai) swarming behind. The other two squadrons of twin-engine bombers (60th and 98th Sentais) headed towards Rangoon city in a separate stream.

A pair of Buffaloes already in the air for a routine patrol were first to attack the bombers heading for Mingaladon. Sergeant Bargh, after an initial dogfight that left his aircraft full of bullet holes, flew out to sea with his windscreen covered in oil. He removed his boot and used a sock to clean the windscreen and then rejoined the fray.[22]

A flight of Tomahawks soon gained sufficient height to attack the incoming Japanese aircraft. From a line astern the fighters peeled off to rake the bombers with machine gun fire. R.T. Smith found a bomber that had fallen out of formation and opened fire from behind at a distance of 200 yards:

> I could see my tracers converging on the fuselage and wing roots as I rapidly undertook him but kept firing until he blew up right in my face. His gas tanks exploded in a huge ball of flame, the concussions tossing my plane upward like a leaf. I fought for control, flying through the detonations, felt a thud as something hit my left wing, let out a shout of triumph into my oxygen mask and thought

By God, I got one of the bastards no matter what happens from now on! I was thinking strictly in terms of 'one' plane, not the six or seven faceless individuals seen only as shadow-figures if at all.[23]

More Tomahawks joined the battle; Chuck Older forced a bomber out of formation trailing smoke. 'I gave it a long burst and the bomber suddenly nose down out of the formation with smoke streaming behind. I saw it roll over into almost a vertical dive and disappear below.'[24] Another bomber crashed on the waterfront; the gun crew on the American freighter *City of Tulsa* made a claim, though the falling aircraft was probably already fatally crippled.[25]

By this time the bombers had completed their bombing run on Mingaladon airfield and closed their bomb-bay doors. On the ground at the airfield seventeen men had been killed in the raid and others wounded. A number of aircraft were wrecked by falling bombs; the operations room was badly damaged by a direct hit; the main hanger and fuel tanks were also hit and the runways cratered.

But the battle in the sky was far from ended. In a further round of aerial combat, Hank Gilbert's Tomahawk was caught in the cross-fire of the bombers' gunners. The stricken P-40B fell earthwards trailing flame and smoke; Gilbert was the AVG's first combat death. Paul Greene's Tomahawk was also shot up by Japanese fighters. He baled out when his aircraft went out of control. Greene's parachute proved to be damaged and he was strafed by fighters as he descended rapidly towards the ground. Greene was knocked out when he hit the earth and awoke to find he was looking along the gun barrel of a British soldier.

The 62nd Sentai – the Ki-21 Mitsubishi squadron that had bombed Mingaladon – lost five bombers out of fifteen in the raid. Lieutenants Sabe, Niioka, Shimada, Shingansho and Ikura perished with their crews. All of the remaining bombers of the squadron had suffered damage.[26]

Meanwhile a further two squadrons of Japanese twin-engine bombers had headed towards the centre of Rangoon. Six Tomahawks of Parker Dupouy's flight were circling over Syriam, down river of Rangoon, on the look-out for incoming raiders. Before long a well-drilled formation of green camouflaged twin-engine bombers were sighted approaching at 17,000 feet. The leading formation of this wave comprised eighteen bombers of the 98th Sentai; the squadron was commanded by Colonel Shigeki Usui.

The Tomahawks attacked in two sections of three aircraft. One Tomahawk was damaged by the air gunners of the bombers and the pilot killed. Two of the bombers were knocked out of formation and shot down in a series of attacks by the American fighters. Three crew baled out of one of the bombers. The body of a Japanese airman was later recovered beneath the folds of a parachute holding a grenade in the frozen claw of his hand.[27] Several other bombers were damaged in the engagement; Colonel Usui was killed by machine gun fire sitting in his co-pilot's seat.

Twenty minutes behind the 98th Sentai's bombing run over downtown Rangoon, the 60th Sentai arrived. From 23,000 feet the twenty-seven Mitsubishis dropped their bomb loads without much opposition and headed for home.

Burmese and Indians had taken to the streets to watch the raid. As the Japanese bombers sailed towards the city an observer on the ground recalled:

> A-gleam in the sunlight, the enemy bombers came on in arrow-head formation. Men climbed out of the trenches to watch them; people stood on the roads with uplifted faces ... Within a few moments they were clapping their hands and cheering. A British [or American] fighter on the tail of a bomber had shot up the Japanese, from which streamed a trail of smoke. The bomber burst into flames, crumpled, fell. Another flared like a spent rocket and dropped. Parachutes opened in the sky. We saw all this and cheered wildly; saw, too, that deadly arrow-head almost above the centre of the city; our fighters had not turned it.

High explosive bombs blasted buildings and people alike; flying glass and collapsing houses caused a stampede that trampled underfoot those who had fallen. According to an Indian shopkeeper: 'It was a pitiable sight to see women with dishevelled hair and babes in arms crying and running where their fear-laden whimsies took them ... More pathetic were children who clung to running men and women, mistaking them for their parents.'[28] Civilian casualties were estimated as 1000 killed and another 1000 badly injured. The docks were paralysed as the labour force fled the city; public transport ground to a halt. A district near to the main docks was burnt out by the bombing; smoke drifted skywards in columns over Rangoon.

The civil defence services broke down when many of the staff fled, though the fire brigade was considered to have performed well in the crisis. An official report said of the civil defence services:

> The handful [of personnel] that were left made superhuman efforts to cope with the carnage but most of the wounded were left unattended until volunteers could be obtained. By then many of them had succumbed to their injuries; others died of shock and haemorrhage after being admitted to hospital.[29]

The raid caused a panic-stricken flight of part of the population. Some people fled into the surrounding jungle; others took to the roads heading northwards towards Prome, the men pushing carts, the women with bundles on their heads and carrying children too young to walk. The people of Rangoon lived in flimsy wooden buildings, without underground shelters; they now knew they were badly exposed to air attack. Governor Dorman-Smith toured the city that afternoon; the dead lay still uncollected in a tropical climate.

The Japanese bombers headed back towards Thailand across the brilliant blue waters of the Gulf of Martaban with their noses down to gather extra speed. The rigid air discipline of the Japanese bomber pilots had impressed their enemies. A Buffalo pilot reported of the bombers that he was 'surprised at [their] speed as I was under the impression that Jap aircraft were not much good'.[30] More than one Buffalo pilot would report that the Japanese were flying German Heinkel 111s of the type used in the Blitz on London. The glass nose of the Ki-21 Mitsubishi gave it a resemblance to a Luftwaffe bomber. On the other hand, some of the Japanese pilots confused the Tomahawks with Spitfires.

According to Japanese records, seven Ki-21 Mitsubishi bombers were shot down and an additional twin-engine bomber crashed on the return journey. Japanese pilots and gunners claimed to have shot down forty-one Allied fighters; Allied combat claims were also excessive. The Buffaloes escaped loss on this occasion, but four Tomahawks were shot down and two pilots killed in the air battles.[31]

Allied ground crew at Mingaladon spent 24 December undertaking repairs on damaged fighters. The pilots rested after the excitement of the previous day or flew standing patrols. The two American pilots killed the previous day were buried in the churchyard of Edward the Martyr, two miles south of Mingaladon. All sense of normality in Rangoon had vanished; preparations for Christmas were thoroughly upset. The air offensive against Rangoon, however, was far from ended.

General Sugawara decided to send another heavy raid to Rangoon on Christmas Day. Three squadrons of Mitsubishi bombers – 12th, 60th and 62nd Sentais – were to take part; the 98th Sentai was given the day off. Major Kato's 64th Sentai flew from Malaya to Bangkok on 24 December to reinforce the planned attack. The squadron flew twenty-five Ki-43 Nakajima Hayabusa fighters. The retractable landing gear on the Ki-43s would cause them to be mistaken by Allied pilots for the already famous Zero fighter. The bombers heading for Mingaladon would each carry a bouquet of flowers to drop on the airfield along with another dose of high explosive.[32] The squadrons of Ki-27 Nakajima fighters and Ki-30 Anns would again take part in the raid. The total strength of the Christmas Day raid would be heavier than two days before; over 150 aircraft were to make the flight to Rangoon.

Christmas Day dawned bright and clear; the Japanese fighters met up with their respective bomber formations over Thailand. Rangoon that morning was visible to keen-eyed Japanese aviators a long way from the target. The radar station at Moulmein gave warning that a large Japanese force was heading for Rangoon. Despite the damage done to the operations room at Mingaladon during the previous raid, the Buffaloes of No. 67 Squadron and the Tomahawks of the AVG were quickly scrambled for action in the blue skies over the capital. Three Tomahawks were already aloft on patrol; the pilots reported the approach of an unidentified formation. Half of the Japanese force headed for Mingaladon and half for the port. The stronger Japanese fighter escort for this raid would make it harder for Allied fighters to attack the twin-engine bombers.

The Buffalo squadron climbed for height in two flights of six aircraft; a further pair of Buffaloes provided top cover. Sergeant E.H. Beable wrote of the engagement that followed:

> Once again because of the inadequate warning system we found ourselves in the unenviable and vulnerable position of having to climb at very low airspeed into the Japanese formation some 5000 feet or more above us. As we gained the level of the bombers we were set upon by a section of fighters which dived from above.[33]

Four Buffalo pilots were killed in the action that followed, Sergeant J. Macpherson in the upper A Flight, and three pilots from the lower B Flight. A fifth Buffalo was damaged and forced to crash-land. According to Flight Lieutenant J. Brandt of B Flight: 'One of my saddest tasks was to bury [Flying Officer John] Lambert and two others without coffins, and not even blankets since they were required by the local hospital.'[34] The Buffalo squadron suffered further material losses when Mingaladon was bombed; three Buffaloes were destroyed on the ground and another five aircraft under assembly were also damaged beyond salvage.

The bombing of the airfield caused more damage to the station's buildings. The runways were again cratered; anti-aircraft emplacements suffered direct hits and their Indian gunners 'were scattered in a bloody broken mess for hundreds of yards around'.[35] General Wavell had just returned from China when the bombers struck; he had left Chungking at dawn that day. His aircraft had briefly landed at Moulmein after the pilot had strayed into the skies of Thailand, before quickly flying on to Rangoon. Wavell was forced to dive for shelter in a slit trench. He recalled: 'When it was all over I counted seventeen bombs which had fallen within fifty yards of the trench, the nearest about a dozen yards away.' Wavell added: 'I cannot say that I was enjoying it, but the abject terror of my companion had the effect of heartening me.'[36]

The American Volunteer Group had a more fortunate Christmas Day than the Buffalo squadron. The Tomahawks had taken off in two flights. George McMillan's flight of seven aircraft headed for a Japanese bomber formation as it turned away from Rangoon after its bombing run. Escorting Ki-43 fighters were in close attendance to the bombers and a fierce dog-fight developed.

Two Tomahawks were damaged and crash-landed in fields; the downed pilots, including McMillan, survived the experience, though they did not turn up at base until the following day.[37]

Christmas Day had been another costly bout of aerial combat over Rangoon. Seven Allied fighters were destroyed in the air and four pilots killed; many Japanese aircraft were claimed shot down by Allied pilots. The AVG squadron's commander reported to Colonel Chennault: 'It was like shooting ducks!'[38] In total ten Japanese aircraft were lost on the raid or crashed on the return journey; one twin-engine bomber reached an airfield at Bangkok carrying three dead crew. Major Kato, commander of the 64th Sentai, wrote in his diary of the raid:

> I felt terribly chagrined while at the same time I felt a strong sense of responsibility for not having trained my men more thoroughly. I offered my apologies to Colonel Kitajima … Spent the whole day in mortification tortured by the sense of responsibility.[39]

Surprisingly, one particular pilot, Sergeant Ri Kontetu, bailed out of his stricken aircraft and was made prisoner. It was exceedingly rare for a Japanese serviceman to be taken alive. Japanese commentators have pointed out dismissively that the pilot concerned was Korean-born.

When there was no further major raid on Rangoon after Christmas Day this was interpreted as a victory for the Allied fighter force. That was good for morale but in reality the Japanese had decided to re-focus upon more urgent operations underway in Malaya and the Dutch East Indies. The pair of raids had been designed to keep the British on the defensive in Burma whilst the push on Singapore rolled forward. Aircraft from both the 3rd and 5th Air Divisions had taken part in the raids.

Civilian casualties from the Christmas Day raid were sixty killed and forty wounded. This was well down on the toll of two days before and is an indication of the extent to which many people had fled the city in the intervening period; either that, or the populace had learned through bitter experience to seek shelter in slit trenches and monsoon ditches at the first sign of trouble. By the afternoon of 26 December the road northwards from Rangoon to Prome was filled with an estimated 100,000 Indian refugees. The refugees were prevented by government officials from crossing the Irrawaddy at Prome in a bid to make them return to the capital.

The Allied air force commander in Burma ruefully estimated that he now had less than thirty aircraft of all types to face the armada of Japanese aircraft obviously stationed well within range of Rangoon. At the end of December a pair of Indian anti-aircraft batteries landed at Rangoon and were deployed around the city and at Moulmein; other anti-aircraft reinforcements were borrowed from Lend Lease stocks on Wavell's authority. On 30 December seventeen Tomahawks of the 2nd AVG Squadron – the 'Panda Bears' – arrived at Mingaladon to relieve the 3rd Squadron.

Whilst the authorities in Rangoon were busy endeavouring to reopen the city for business, General Hutton arrived on 27 December to take up his new post as commander of Burma Army. He had a subdued personality and lacked obvious charisma. A cheeky junior officer wrote that he looked 'more like a head gardener than a general'.[40] Hutton was born in 1890, and had joined the Royal Artillery in 1909. During the First World War he commanded a field battery on the western front, was wounded three times, and awarded the Military Cross and bar. After the armistice he held a succession of staff appointments, which culminated in a posting to India's Western District at Quetta as a major-general in 1938–40. Following that Hutton became deputy and then Chief of the General Staff at Indian Army headquarters. At Delhi he played an important role in the rapid expansion of the army during the early period of the war. To Wavell, the hard-working and reliable Hutton seemed well suited to the role of overhauling Burma's defences.

At Rangoon Hutton would have a wide range of responsibilities; he would be operational commander of Burma Army, as well as head of Burma's War Office and General Staff. Hutton would also be responsible for liaison with Delhi, Dorman-Smith's government, the Royal Navy, RAF and any foreign allied forces in his command area. Hutton reported that

> the Headquarters staff [at Rangoon] was totally inadequate and a few overworked staff officers were struggling to compete with problems quite beyond their powers … There was no intelligence staff worthy of the name … We were usually in complete ignorance of what was happening just over the Thailand border. The same applied regarding internal intelligence.[41]

It was hard to predict the main Japanese line of advance and troop strength in the absence of meaningful information. Rumours had reached Rangoon that Japanese troops had moved into northern Thailand. In consequence a Chinese regiment entered north-east Burma to guard the Mekong river frontier between Burma and Indochina.[42]

The news from elsewhere in South-east Asia was not heartening for Hutton either. In the early hours of 26 December the British garrison at Hong Kong capitulated to Japanese forces attacking from the Chinese mainland. In the Philippines, Japanese columns were pushing the Filipino-American army into the Bataan peninsula near Manila. This Allied force would soon find itself besieged far behind enemy lines. In Malaya General Percival's army had already lost the northern part of the peninsula, and was endeavouring to rebuild a new front in central Malaya covering the city of Kuala Lumpur.

4

The Invasion of Burma

The month of January 1942 began with the Axis powers in a dominant position in the Second World War. The fortunes of the Western Allies and the Soviet Union were at a low ebb. Shortly after Japan's entry to the war, Prime Minister Churchill and a high-level military delegation sailed across the Atlantic to the United States to meet with President Roosevelt and his administration. The main point of agreement reached between American and British leaders at the Arcadia Conference was the decision to make the defeat of Germany their foremost strategic priority. To help secure that grand strategy it was in Britain's interests to defer to the wishes of the Americans whenever possible. For good reason the Americans wanted to create new command arrangements in the Asia-Pacific region to deal with the crisis of Japan's entry to the war. Washington was keen for all Allied forces in South-east Asia to be placed under a single supreme commander and preferably a British officer. Churchill and his Chiefs of Staff reluctantly agreed to put a British general in charge of a new American-British-Dutch-Australian (ABDA) command that would stretch from Burma to the Philippines and include Malaya and the Dutch East Indies. General Wavell was appointed ABDA Supreme Commander.

On 29 December Churchill signalled Wavell at Delhi: 'You are the only man who has the experience of handling so many theatres at once and you know that we shall back you up and see that you have fair play. Everyone knows how dark and difficult the situation is.'[1] When Wavell was given the news of his posting, a military colleague diarised: 'Of all the raw deals he [Wavell] has been given, the miracles he has been asked to produce without even a golden wand to wave, this ABDA Command has been the worst instance.' Wavell remarked, 'I've heard of holding the baby, but this is twins.'[2] Wavell advised against including Burma in the new command; Governor Dorman-Smith did likewise, commenting that 'since India assumed direct responsibility the situation here has been positively dynamic.'[3] But the Americans insisted that Burma be part of ABDA Command as Rangoon and the Burma Road were vital to Chinese interests.

In conjunction with the ABDA arrangements for South-east Asia, a new China war theatre was created under the leadership of Generalissimo Chiang Kai-shek. As a mark of Washington's support, a high-ranking American army general was appointed Chiang's chief of staff. Washington feared the collapse of China given that the bulk of the Japanese army was deployed on the Asian mainland. Still, Roosevelt's administration was not planning to send ground forces to south-west China, and had little to spare anyway at such a dire stage of the war.

Burma Army was now under the command of a headquarters in Java, instead of Singapore or Delhi. General Wavell left for Java by air on 5 January, though ABDA Command did not come into operation until 15 January. In the meantime, at Delhi an interim CIC held the fort until on 16 January General Sir Alan Hartley was appointed the new head of the Indian Army.[4] Senior Allied commanders in the region seemed to be playing an endless game of musical chairs. At Delhi Wavell had been 2000 miles to the north-west of Rangoon; at Lembang, Java he was a similar distance away, only now to the south-east. There were no reliable communications between Burma and Java; cables had to be sent via Delhi and this caused delays. The British Chiefs of Staff sent a signal to Wavell reminding him:

> It is of the highest importance Chiang Kai-shek should be given every possible support and encouragement. We must in conjunction with him ensure that the Burma Road is kept open and that a flow of warlike stores reaches him. Continuation of Chinese resistance is indispensable and will pay good dividend. Americans feel very strongly on this.[5]

Somewhat grudgingly, London and Cairo agreed that several army divisions would need to sail from the Nile delta to join the war against Japan; it would take time, however, to bring that about.

On the ground at Rangoon General Hutton was busy getting to grips with his new responsibilities as commander of Burma Army. He wrote on 10 January that 100,000 tons of American Lend Lease material for Nationalist China was congesting the Rangoon docks; there was another large dump at Lashio in northern Burma. Hutton reported the following:

> To clear Rangoon of its accumulation, assuming no more shipments arrived, would take several months. Included in this lease-lend material there is a great deal of equipment greatly needed for the defence of Burma. Such equipment includes signals equipment of all natures, light automatics, light carriers, explosives, M.T. [motor transport], etc. At present policy is that Burma may not touch this except by express consent of the Chinese Central Government, which is very difficult to obtain.

It was frustrating for Burma Army's commanders and staffs to see a stockpile of valuable Allied military equipment under their noses and yet remain out of reach.

On 10 January Governor Dorman-Smith wired London that Rangoon was calm again after the major air raids of the Christmas period. A local newspaper was able to report: 'Life in the city is returning to normal. Daylight robberies have started again.' Japanese air attacks on Rangoon eased off in January; small hit and run raids by night on Mingaladon airfield and Japanese fighter sweeps over southern Burma by daylight were the most noteworthy events. Large British convoys continued to sail to and from the port of Rangoon without interference. Early in the month Air Vice-Marshal D.F. Stevenson arrived to become the RAF's commander in Burma; sixteen Blenheim IV bombers of No. 113 Squadron landed at Toungoo from Egypt.[6] The Japanese were also expecting air reinforcements in the later half of January to bring the 5th Air Division up to a permanent strength of 150 aircraft.

British senior officers at Rangoon hoped that the Japanese campaign in Malaya would continue to delay a full-scale invasion of Burma. A strong Allied showing in Malaya would at least reduce the scale of any Japanese attack on Burma. The fighting in northern and central Malaya, however, had resulted in swift Japanese victories. As British resistance on the Malayan mainland crumbled it became apparent that a blow against Burma might not be long in coming after all. From mid-January the Indian population of Rangoon again began to stream northwards along the road to Prome, with the intention of seeking sanctuary in India; this time they could not be persuaded to return to the threatened colonial metropolis.

The army in Burma needed another divisional headquarters urgently; the 17th Indian Division's headquarters was dispatched to Rangoon to meet that need. Two of the division's brigades had already been detached to sail for Malaya and Singapore. By mid-January the headquarters of the division had been opened in south-eastern Burma's Tenasserim division. The formation's commander was Major-General J.G. Smyth.

Jackie Smyth was born in 1893 and joined the Indian Army and the 15th Sikhs prior to the First World War, after his education at Repton and Sandhurst. He won the Victoria Cross in France at Festubert in 1915. On the afternoon of 18 May he led a party over several hundred yards of ground swept by the enemy's fire to carry a supply of bombs up to a captured trench that had been under sustained German counter-attack. Smyth and ten Sikh soldiers hauled forward two boxes of bombs by crawling up a small stream and dashing from shell hole to shell hole across ground strewn with corpses. Many of the party became casualties from shrapnel bursts and small arms fire. Lieutenant Smyth, Lance-Naik Mangal Singh and a sepoy only reached the troops in the threatened trench with the bombs after darkness had fallen. Smyth later commented: 'I had indeed been lucky. I had several bullets

through my tunic, one through the top of my service cap and my small cane
had been hit no less than four times.'[7]

Smyth had returned to India in 1916, but his adventures were by no means
over. During the tribal rising on the North-west Frontier that followed the
1919 Anglo-Afghan War Smyth was again at the forefront of the action.
Smyth was brigade-major of the 43rd Brigade when a convoy was ambushed
by Mahsud tribesmen in northern Waziristan's Tochi valley. A relief column
set out successfully to extricate the convoy, though only after a serious
engagement. Captain Henry Andrews of the Indian Medical Service was
awarded a posthumous Victoria Cross for his work treating the wounded;
Smyth and another officer received Military Crosses for their conduct of the
convoy's relief. In his memoirs Smyth mentioned: 'I heard afterwards that
Brigadier-General Gwyn-Thomas had originally recommended me for a
bar to my V.C.'[8] A 'bar', or clasp, is attached to a medal ribbon to denote the
second or subsequent award of the same decoration.

Smyth attended the Camberley Staff College in 1923, and was the Indian
Army's representative instructor at that institution from 1931–34. Further
service on the North-west Frontier followed in the mid-1930s. When war
broke out with Germany in September 1939, Smyth was on leave in Britain
and through the good offices of General Sir John Dill he secured a posting
to the British Expeditionary Force in northern France. In 1940 Smyth was a
brigade commander at Dunkirk; he was the principal Indian Army officer to
hold such a senior appointment in that campaign. Smyth was proud of his
experience fighting Germans in France in two major wars.[9]

Smyth returned to India midway through 1941 and took up a brigade
command near Quetta. Given his recent war experience, he swiftly advanced
to the command of the 19th Indian Division, which was forming at
Secunderabad. On 4 December 1941 he was offered command of the 17th
Indian Division and quickly accepted that post. The division's previous
commander, Major-General H.V. Lewis, had badly injured his knee in an
accident and was no longer fit for active service.[10]

Smyth was intensely ambitious and something of a showman. Captain
Lunt described Smyth in his diary as 'a bright, perky and friendly little man,
with a wonderful ability to put younger officers like me at their ease'.[11] Smyth's
out-going personality was persuasive, but his peers in the army sometimes
saw a different side to him. Lunt, looking back later in life, reflected that Smyth
'was inclined to be cocky, extremely self-confident'.[12] Smyth's self-belief had
been tested when his hitherto excellent health had collapsed after his return
to India. He had developed a painful anal fissure and contracted malaria.
Smyth had been forced into hospital at Quetta where an internal abscess
was discovered and operated upon. To make matters worse, Smyth was still

in hospital when an earthquake caused an evacuation of the buildings and his wound burst open; he left hospital far from recovered and was in pain when walking or sitting.[13] Smyth had accepted his new posts as a divisional commander as he believed that it would be up to six months before his formation was ready to go overseas; by then he might have regained his health.

The military situation in Burma at the time of General Smyth's arrival was in a state of upheaval. At the start of January 1942 Scott's 1st Burma Division was deployed in the Shan States and comprised the 1st Burma and 13th Indian Brigades. The 2nd Burma Brigade was in Tenasserim and principally based at Moulmein. On 14 January the 16th Indian Brigade arrived in Tenasserim from army reserve in accordance with General Hutton's instructions. The 17th Indian Division's headquarters took control of the two brigades in Tenasserim.

One of Smyth's first actions was to send the 16th Brigade to Kawkareik, to the east of Moulmein, to help cover the Thai border. Lieutenant-Colonel Abernethy's 4th Burma Rifles had been in the frontier hills since early December; the unit was badly hit by malaria. The 16th Brigade took them under command and, in exchange, left the 4/12th Frontier Force Regiment at Moulmein. The road from Moulmein heading eastwards towards the Thai-Burma frontier ran through thick jungle and across deep rivers for sixty miles to the Kawkareik pass. One hundred miles south-east of Moulmein there was a second route across the frontier ranges – the Three Pagodas Pass.

On 16 January the 46th Indian Brigade disembarked at Rangoon and was also sent forward to join Smyth's division. This was the last of the 17th Division's original brigades and a much needed reinforcement. The brigade's battalions were all war raised units; for instance, the 3/7th Gurkhas had been raised at Karachi in October 1940 with drafts of 200 men each from the regiment's 1st and 2nd Battalions and an additional 400 recruits.[14] The troops had sailed wearing khaki drill shorts and shirts designed for Middle East service. Many Indian soldiers wore pugarees, which was a cloth strip bound around a helmet. The brigade's commander, Brigadier R.G. Ekin, was an officer of the Frontier Force Rifles; in common with many Indian Army regulars, he was a veteran of the Middle East in 1917–18 and a number of frontier expeditions across the interwar period.

Few artillery reinforcements for Burma Army were available as India had already been stripped of field artillery to reinforce Malaya. Burma Army, at this stage of the campaign, possessed only the 27th Mountain Regiment. The 1st Burma Division had two mountain batteries and the regimental headquarters; the 17th Indian Division was given the regiment's other two mountain batteries. This was a weak force of artillery for a pair of infantry divisions.

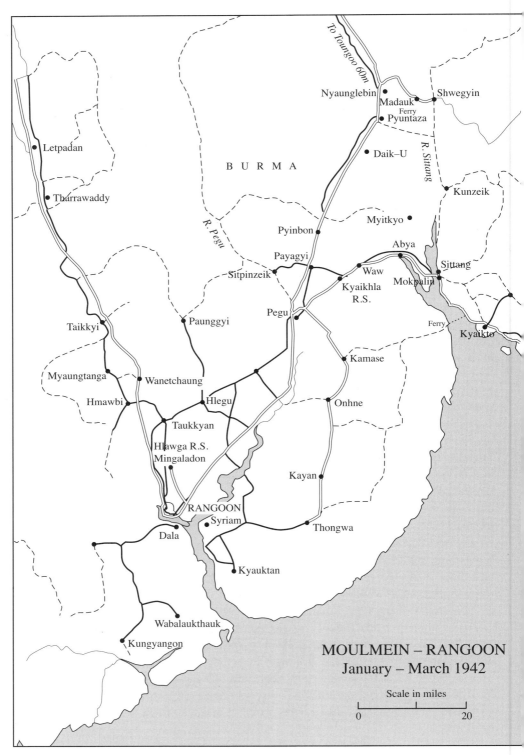

Map C Moulmein-Rangoon

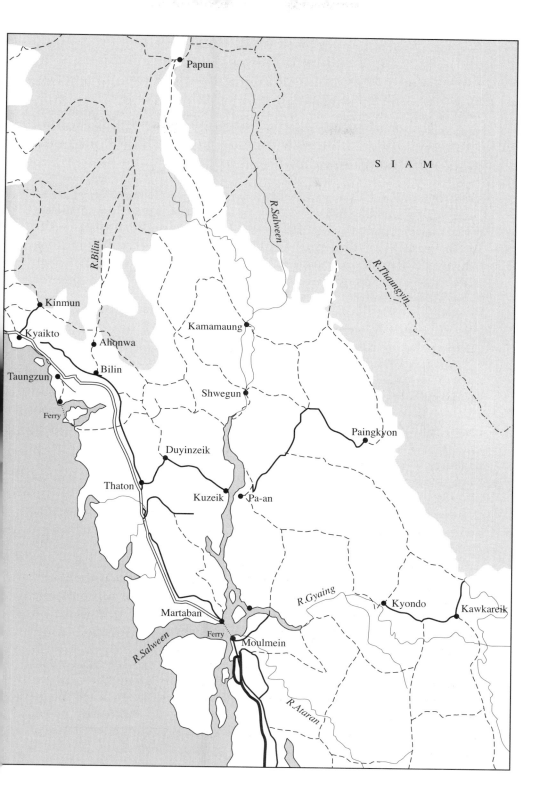

A mountain battery comprised four 3.7-inch howitzers, which could fire shells at high trajectory to a maximum range of 6000 yards. The guns could be broken down into eight mule loads; the barrel was broken into two loads and had to be screwed together to be fired. When a mountain battery travelled by railway or truck the mules had to be loaded aboard, along with the rest of the battery's equipment.[15]

As the 17th Indian Division was taking up positions in Tenasserim, Japanese forces were assembling in Thailand for the invasion of Burma. The campaign in Malaya was progressing well and seemed not to need further reinforcement. The Japanese XV Army's plan was to invade south-eastern Burma from Raheng with Rangoon as the main objective. The shortest route to Rangoon from Raheng ran through Moulmein. It was over forty miles from Raheng to the Thai-Burma frontier near Mae Sot; Japanese engineers set to work to improve the track heading westwards from Raheng. The Japanese did not intend to advance from northern Thailand into the Shan States.

From a newly established headquarters at Raheng, General Iida's staff planned for the 55th Division to lead the offensive across the frontier into the Dawna range and onwards to Moulmein. The 33rd Division was to follow behind and cross the Salween river to the north of Moulmein; both divisions were then to thrust for Rangoon. XV Army would eventually need reinforcement beyond its strength of two infantry divisions, especially if the Chinese intervened in Burma, but that would depend on the course of the campaigns underway elsewhere in South-east Asia. On 22 January Imperial General Headquarters in Tokyo gave authorisation for an invasion of southern Burma.

General Takeuchi's 55th Division had entered Thailand from Indochina and reached Bangkok by rail.[16] Troops of the division headed northwards to Raheng; they then marched to Mae Sot on the Thai side of the frontier. The 55th Division comprised two infantry regiments; a battalion of the division's 143rd Regiment had already occupied Victoria Point. The division was mostly organised on a pack transport basis – mules, oxen, horses and elephants were impressed as transport. Heavy artillery had to be left behind in Thailand; the division's two mountain artillery battalions had only six guns each.

Marching behind the 55th Division was General Sakurai's 33rd Division, which had been serving in central China for the past year. The division had sailed from China to Bangkok. The division's infantry group headquarters, one infantry regiment and two mountain gun battalions had to be left behind in China for lack of shipping space; these units would rejoin their parent division later in the campaign. This left the 33rd Division with just one nine gun battalion of mountain artillery, one engineer company and two horse companies of its transport regiment.[17] Other engineering and transport units were under the direct command of XV Army, but General Iida's force was planning to advance with the minimum of logistical support. The rice crop of southern Burma had been harvested in December and the village granaries were full early in the new year. This was a tremendous benefit for Japanese soldiers accustomed to eating rice at the heart of their diet.

After a long delay the Japanese campaign against Burma was about to enter a new and more dangerous phase for Hutton's defending army. The first step of the new Japanese offensive, however, was directed against Tavoy, far to the south of Moulmein. Tavoy was a large town on the Tenasserim coast with a population of 30,000. Major Oki's III/112th Battalion group of 1500 men, which had been detached from the 55th Division, had left Bangkok on 3 January to make a difficult march over the jungle-covered Tenasserim ranges. Oki's soldiers were heavily laden and relied on horses, oxen and several elephants for transport. Amid very dense terrain the force advanced only two miles per day, until on 14 January the crest of the range was reached. On the following day the troops began to cross a grassy plain leading to the village of Myitta, from which a motorable road ran thirty-four miles to Tavoy.

Tavoy's garrison had an outpost at Myitta. Three companies of the 6th Burma Rifles, a recently raised unit, were deployed on a ridge behind the village. On the night of 17/18 January the Japanese attacked Myitta; the Burma Rifles swiftly collapsed and fled northwards into the jungle. At 9 a.m. on 19 January the Japanese approached the airfield near Tavoy. There was some confused fighting but soon after midday the town was evacuated and Lieutenant-Colonel Cotton and his remaining troops headed northwards for the sanctuary of Moulmein. The hasty withdrawal of RAF personnel had been damaging to the morale of the town's army defenders.

A large supply of high octane fuel was captured by the Japanese as the defence had collapsed too quickly for the implementation of a demolition scheme.[18] Japanese casualties in the operation were twenty-three killed and forty wounded; the ruined 6th Burma Rifles would play little further role in the campaign. From Tavoy the III/112th Battalion turned north and began the long march for Moulmein.[19] To the south of Tavoy, Mergui was cut off; its small battalion-strength garrison – the 2nd Burma Rifles – was evacuated by sea after demolitions were carried out in the local tin and wolfram mines.

Aung San and some of his comrades arrived at Tavoy with the Japanese and set about recruiting for the Burma Independence Army. When news of this filtered through to Rangoon, the authorities proscribed the Thakin party and arrested many more of its activists. The Deputy Commissioner at Mergui, F.H. Yarnold, was evacuated to Rangoon and reported to Dorman-Smith: 'We will never be able to hold up our heads again in Mergui.'[20]

The main Japanese advance from Raheng got underway on 20 January. The 16th Indian Brigade was posted in the hills on the Burmese side of the frontier. The brigade was commanded by Brigadier J.K. Jones and comprised the 1/9th Royal Jats, 1/7th Gurkhas and the 4th Burma Rifles. Jones, a fit man of fifty years of age, was an officer of the 1st Gurkha Rifles; he had spent the First World War in the Warwickshire Regiment. The Jat Regiment had been given the prefix 'Royal' in 1921 as a recognition of distinguished service that included the nineteenth century's First and Second Anglo-Afghan Wars, and France and Mesopotamia during the First World War.

The 16th Brigade's headquarters was by a track near Kawkareik, a town at the western foot of the Dawna range. Troops travelled from Moulmein to Kawkareik partly by river ferry and partly by road; Japanese reconnaissance aircraft kept a careful watch over the route. Eastwards of Kawkareik was thick, jungle-covered hill country, which was penetrated by a sharply bending road. The pass in the range was twenty miles from Kawkareik at Sukli village. To the east of Sukli the road dropped steeply down to plain country near the border. The Thai frontier was close to the village of Myawadi, thirty-eight miles from Kawkareik. From the summit of the Dawna range the Thai airfield at Mae Sot could be seen through field glasses, especially on a clear day. Rumours had reached the ears of Brigadier Jones of the Japanese build-up across the frontier in Thailand. The brigade's Intelligence Officer was Lieutenant Raymond Hall, formerly a local representative of Steele Brothers Trading Company. In the jungle of the Dawna hills tigers roared in the distance at night.

Jones' brigade was equipped with a mixture of animal and motor transport; for example, the 1/7th Gurkhas possessed fifty-two mules, six horses, ten lorries, a water tanker and four motorcycles. The vehicles were painted desert colours and had sun compasses intended for navigation across the featureless wastes of the Middle East.[21] There were not enough lorries to lift all troops and animals at once, but a battalion could at least move its own stores and heavy equipment.

Signalling also posed difficulties for British formations in Burma. Radio sets which worked well in the open terrain of the Middle East proved of limited value in Burma due to the dense landscape, the fungus growth of a humid climate and a shortage of charging batteries. Brigade headquarters laid telephone cable to establish more secure links with battalion headquarters. The civil telephone line from the frontier to Moulmein was another useful form of communication within Tenasserim.

The 16th Brigade was deployed with the 1/7th Gurkhas in the eastern Dawna Hills near the frontier. The 4th Burma Rifles was covering a subsidiary track to the north of the Gurkhas; the 1/9th Jats was in reserve near Kawkareik.

Forty miles south of Kawkareik, Major Burke's B Company of the Gurkhas was in position to watch the bridle track over the Three Pagodas Pass.

The brigade's front line was held by Captain Eric Holdaway's D Company of the Gurkhas. Holdaway's Gurkhas were entrenched in flat country near the frontier village of Myawadi; a single company of Jats was covering the Kwingale pass to the south of Myawadi. Sappers were busy preparing demolitions on the main track through the Dawna Hills. An air raid on Kyondo, to the west of Kawkareik, damaged the landing stage at the Haungtharaw river and sank a steamer.[22]

The Japanese 55th Division's plan was for the II/112th Battalion directly to cross the frontier at Myawadi, whilst the I/112th Battalion crossed the frontier a few miles to the north with the intention of hooking southwards onto the main road. The 55th Division's reconnaissance regiment was to cross the frontier south of Myawadi, and advance along the track leading from Palu to the Kwingale pass. The 143rd Regiment remained in divisional reserve and was poised to reinforce the advance wherever it might be required.

The Japanese crossed the frontier in force at 5 a.m. on 20 January. Captain Holdaway reported to battalion headquarters on the civil telephone line that his company of Gurkhas was under attack; the line went dead at 9.30 a.m. The last report stated that the company was surrounded and short of ammunition. Lieutenant-Colonel White, the battalion's commander, and Lieutenant Hall went forward with a small escort to investigate but were ambushed on the way. Hall was killed in the ambush. To the east the sound of firing from Holdaway's position died away, though most of D Company managed to break out and avoid capture.[23] At dusk White and the rest of the Gurkhas withdrew into the hills to Sukli, which had been subjected to dive-bombing during the day.

On the southern flank of Myawadi there was also fighting that day. 2nd Lieutenant Alan Balls was leading a patrol of Jats in two lorries along the track leading to Palu. The Jats rounded a bend to see a hundred yards away a column of marching Japanese troops led by three mounted officers and four heavily laden elephants. The Japanese troops belonged to the reconnaissance regiment. Indian soldiers hastily opened fire; the frightened elephants crashed into the jungle trumpeting loudly. After nightfall the Japanese had a speedy revenge when they fell upon the Jat company near Kwingale, which collapsed and dispersed into the darkness.[24]

During the night of 20/21 January demolitions were blown on the road in front of Sukli. Brigadier Jones received General Smyth's permission to retreat if he felt his brigade was in danger of encirclement. During the hours of darkness there was a lot of panicky firing. Lieutenant-Colonel Abernethy of the 4th Burma Rifles said of the brigade:

The effect of the jungle on these young soldiers was most marked as they, including British and Indian officers, actually showed me enemy moving in the jungle which was nothing more than the effect of light and shade on trees and undergrowth. There was no enemy in the vicinity.[25]

At first light on 21 January the 16th Brigade's main position at milestone thirty-six was not under threat, though a heavy Japanese air raid hit Kawkareik that morning. Alarm was caused when news was received at brigade headquarters during the day that the Jat company at Kwingale was no longer in position; the route through that place was unprotected. If the Japanese advanced along the track from Palu to Kwingale in strength they could bypass to the south the main route through Sukli and strike directly at Kawkareik. At 6 p.m. Jones ordered a general retreat to commence that night.

The Jats were to provide the brigade's rearguard. It was ordered that surplus vehicles and stores be burnt. Before long, wild rumours and strange noises panicked the brigade's young soldiers. The smell of burning tyres was said to be poison gas; Gurkhas were fired upon by other units that mistook them for Japanese; a rogue elephant stampeded mules carrying the brigade's wireless sets. The Gurkhas' mules also stampeded in terror at a sudden burst of small arms fire and were lost in the jungle.

The brigade's motor transport convoy left Kawkareik at 10 p.m. Eight miles along the road to the south-west a river had to be crossed. The first lorry to use the only heavy-vehicle ferry was overloaded with ammunition; this caused the ferry to sink when the lorry attempted to drive off on the far bank. In consequence, the brigade's transport had to be abandoned on the wrong side of the river.[26]

During the hours of darkness, Gurkhas, Burma Rifles and Jats marched or were driven to Kyondo, the place to the west of Kawkareik from which river boats were usually taken to and from Moulmein. Abernethy ordered his companies of the 4th Burma Rifles on the northern track to make their own way back to Moulmein. According to the war diary of the Jats: 'No clear picture can be painted of this [the situation that night] as it was nothing short of a panic'. There was confusion as to which unit was the rearguard; further panic amongst the brigade headquarters staff added to the tumult. The regimental history of the 7th Gurkhas stated:

> At Kyondo was a scene of utter confusion. Men crowded the bank of the creek which they had no means of crossing: stragglers poured in, and loose animals galloped about too frightened to be approached. The last of the vehicles and such equipment as could not be carried by the men were collected and set on fire.[27]

By the morning of 22 January order had more or less been restored at Kyondo; the last parties and stragglers arrived along the road from

Kawkareik. At Kyondo the remaining motor transport was destroyed and Brigadier Jones sent the wounded and sick onwards in the only two river steamers present.

The 16th Brigade crossed the river at Kyondo in local craft and marched onwards towards Moulmein along the south bank of the Gyaing river. Jones sent a request to Moulmein that river transport be sent to collect the marching troops. Only in the early hours of the morning of 24 January did steamers arrive to pick up the weary soldiers. The steamers sailed down river to Martaban, across the estuary from Moulmein. The Japanese air force was not sighted during this vulnerable period. Abernethy's party of Burma Rifles arrived by steamer a day later. Holdaway's Gurkha company only reached Martaban after an adventurous march of several days. Holdaway was awarded the Military Cross for extricating his men from a tight corner; one Gurkha marched sixty miles to rejoin his unit with a gunshot wound to the stomach and a sword wound to the neck.[28] Major Burke's Gurkha company at the Three Pagodas Pass also eventually rejoined its parent battalion. Radio news bulletins had kept Burke in touch with events.

Jones' brigade arrived at Martaban without its vehicles and mules; the units were badly disorganised. General Hutton in Rangoon was unsure at first if a major Japanese offensive was underway as there had been insufficient fighting to gain a clear picture. Only one company in the whole brigade had fought it out with the invaders in a praise-worthy fashion. Young soldiers had not coped well with the isolation imposed by dense scrub and jungle country. The 16th Brigade's battalions had been deployed in dispersed detachments to invite piecemeal defeat. The Jats' commanding officer was sacked; Hutton considered removing Brigadier Jones as well, but was persuaded by Smyth to give him another chance.

Japanese casualties were not heavy in the Dawna hills, though the II/112th Battalion lost twenty killed and fifty wounded forcing its way along the track from Myawadi.[29] General Takeuchi had expected tougher opposition. Japanese troops entered Kawkareik on 23 January. The following day five RAF Blenheims bombed the town but failed to damage the 55th Division's headquarters, which had quickly taken up residence.

General Wavell at Java was not impressed by news of the engagement around Kawkareik. He commented:

> It is quite clear that the enemy were allowed to gain cheap initial successes through bad handling by the local commanders, lack of training, and in some instances lack of fighting spirit on the part of the troops. It was an unfortunate beginning to the campaign and had serious results in raising the morale of the enemy and depressing that of our own troops.[30]

There had been, however, no particular mystery as to likely Japanese tactical methods. The fighting in Malaya had already revealed that the Japanese army was a very capable fighting force.

5

Battle of Moulmein

After the Japanese had advanced across the Thai-Burmese frontier, and through the Dawna hills, the provincial town of Moulmein came under immediate threat. General Wavell signalled Hutton: 'Cannot understand why with troops at your disposal you should be unable to hold Moulmein and trust you will do so.'[1] Rangoon's intelligence staff estimated that the Japanese had pushed at least one division across the frontier. The General Staff at Delhi was planning to build up the British force in southern Burma to four divisions, but that prospect was still some way off.

On 21 January Hutton had received Wavell's consent to ask Chungking that a second Chinese division be sent to northern Burma. With a serious Japanese invasion underway, British forces needed reinforcement from any available source.[2] Burma Army staff began to transfer stores and petrol from Rangoon to Mandalay as a prudent precaution in the event of the loss of the colony's capital. This was carried out on Hutton's order by his chief administration officer, Major-General E.N. Goddard.

The war in the air continued in tandem with operations on the ground. RAF morale was boosted by news that No. 267 Wing was bound for Burma from the Middle East. The wing comprised three Hurricane squadrons and pilots from all parts of the Allied world, including a number of Canadians and several United States citizens. Some Blenheim bombers had also recently arrived from the Middle East, and were promptly sent to raid the docks at Bangkok. There was only one radar station in Burma, which was located at Moulmein. On 15 January this station was moved to Rangoon for safekeeping as Moulmein was the subject of regular hit and run raids by Japanese aircraft.[3]

For the first three weeks of January the Japanese air force in South-east Asia concentrated on operations in Malaya, but the tempo of aerial activity over southern Burma was stepped up from 23 January. The following day a force of Tomahawks, Buffaloes and two Hurricanes intercepted six Ki-21 Mitsubishi twin-engine bombers near Rangoon. To the joy of Allied fighter pilots, the bombers had left their designated escort of Ki-27 Nakajima fighters trailing behind. The Allied fighters pounced on the unescorted Japanese bombers. According to the American Volunteer Group's Bob Neale:

About the same time 'Tex' Hill and I dove on them, we saw two barrel shaped Buffaloes of the RAF hit them from above. One RAF pilot blew up a bomber in the middle of the Jap formation, and the rest started to run. We just knocked them off like moving targets in a shooting gallery. I ripped up the last plane in the formation. 'Tex' Hill got another that just fell apart under his fire. The second RAF pilot sent the fourth bomber smoking. Then suddenly the leader of the formation blew up. We all ganged up on the last two bombers. It was hard to tell who really got them, with four fighters pouring lead into them.[4]

Japanese records state that five out of six bombers were shot down. When the Japanese fighters belatedly arrived, the Tomahawks shot down three of them without loss. It was a notable authenticated victory for the Allied air forces. Nonetheless, a second Japanese formation managed to slip through undetected that day to strafe and bomb Mingaladon airfield. The Japanese air force had the numbers to swamp the Anglo-American defenders of Rangoon. There were further small night raids on Rangoon towards the end of the month.

A dozen fresh American pilots arrived from China to reinforce the Tomahawk squadron at Mingaladon. Amongst the pilots was C.R. Bond. On 29 January Bond landed at the airfield after a clash with Japanese fighters over Rangoon.

While taxiing past a revetment, I saw quite a crowd around one side of the enclosure. Closer observation revealed a crashed I-96 fighter. The Japanese pilot had apparently been shot out of the air, and he was making a last suicidal attempt to crash into an old RAF Blenheim bomber which was sheltered in the revetment. He had missed it by only a few feet. A RAF airman held up a leather helmet with the pilot's head still in it and with parts of his throat hanging down in a bloody mess. With his other hand the airman pointed two fingers skyward in the usual V-for-victory sign. I returned the V-sign and taxied on. I could not, however, return his broad grin.[5]

According to official records, from 23–29 January the Japanese lost seventeen aircraft on operations; ten RAF and two AVG aircraft were destroyed for the same period.[6] The oil installations at Syriam were never attacked by Japanese bombers. Eventually the anti-aircraft guns sited there had to be relocated for lack of opportunities.

On the ground Japanese troops wasted no time setting out for Moulmein, the 55th Division's next objective on the road to Rangoon. From Kyondo the I/143 Battalion advanced westwards along the north bank of the Gyaing river; the main body of the 143rd Regiment advanced from Kyondo along the south bank of the river. The 112th Regiment (less III Battalion) and the 55th Reconnaissance Regiment pushed into the countryside to the south-west of

Kawkareik. The 112th Regiment then turned westwards towards Moulmein. The reconnaissance troops hooked more deeply to the south-west with the aim of taking the town of Mudon, from where they could approach Moulmein from the south.

Moulmein was a picturesque, tranquil and spacious town; it was one of the largest urban centres in Burma apart from Rangoon and Mandalay. The district had been under British control since 1826 and colonial rule was well accepted. Many Karens lived in Moulmein and were the most loyal of subject peoples. Moulmein was twenty-eight miles inland from the sea on the east bank of the River Salween, just below the Salween's junction with the Gyaing and Ataran rivers. A town with parallel main streets stretched along the bank of the broad estuary. On the western side of the estuary was the smaller town of Martaban.

Moulmein had once been a Portuguese trading post and there was still evidence of Portuguese influences in the town's colonial buildings, which reminded some travellers of Goa or Malacca. Old stone houses with balconies of wrought iron, and windows flanked by heavy columns, sat amid palm trees and recently erected structures with corrugated iron roofs. On a sidewalk near the quayside a stone effigy of Queen Victoria had been erected under a Gothic canopy to commemorate her Diamond Jubilee of 1897. In the timber yards elephants worked to shift the logs.

The main ridge near the town featured a number of pagodas with white, glazed earthenware Buddhas, decorated with gilding and bells that tinkled in the breeze day and night. Kipling had made famous the Moulmein pagoda in his verse. To the east of the town was a landscape of jungle, paddy fields and rubber plantation.

On 17 January the 17th Indian Division's headquarters was established at Moulmein. The 46th Brigade came forward from Rangoon to join Smyth's division, and was held in reserve to the east of the Sittang river. The brigade would not be joined by its transport until the end of the month. The exhausted 16th Brigade had been disembarked at Martaban, after the engagement in the Dawna hills, and needed time to rest and reorganise. The 2nd Burma Brigade was thus solely responsible for the defence of Moulmein on the exposed eastern side of the swollen Salween estuary. Ideally, the lengthy perimeter around the town needed a divisional garrison for a prolonged defence.

Moulmein was subject to regular bombing raids; Major Wilberforce wrote of one particular air raid:

> A squadron of enemy fighter planes appeared overhead. One by one they peeled off and strafed the airfield at low level. There were only two old Buffalo fighter planes on the field and their pilots would have been fully justified in taking cover. Instead these two brave men ran to their planes and took off, determined to give

battle; we could see them bare-headed in their cockpits urging their planes on like jockeys riding to a finish. They never reached more than tree-top height before both were shot into the ground.[7]

The air raids and rumours of the approaching Japanese had caused most of the population of Moulmein to flee to villages in the surrounding countryside.

Brigadier A.J.H. Bourke was the commander of the 2nd Burma Brigade. He had spent the First World War in France and Mesopotamia with the British Army's Connaught Rangers, and had been wounded in each of those theatres. Bourke subsequently transferred to a Punjab regiment of the Indian Army, and took part in a succession of frontier campaigns.

The 2nd Burma Brigade comprised the 7th and 8th Burma Rifles, 3rd Burma Rifles (less two companies), 4/12th Frontier Force Regiment and the 12th Mountain Battery. The 8th Burma Rifles was composed entirely of Sikhs and Punjabi Muslims resident in Burma, many formerly of the military police, and was considered to be the most reliable of the Burma Rifles units. On the other hand, the 3rd Burma Rifles was full of recruits and said to be unsteady.[8] The Frontier Force was an excellent battalion; it was a four-class unit, with Sikhs, Dogras, Punjabi Muslims and Pathans in separate rifle companies. The brigade also included the four Bofors guns of the 3rd Indian Light Anti-Aircraft Battery and some sappers of the 60th Field Company. A detachment of Burma Frontier Force was posted at the airfield to the south-east of Moulmein.

On 23 January General Smyth asked permission for his division to withdraw to the Bilin river, which was to the west of the Salween. Hutton rejected that proposal and directed that Moulmein be stoutly defended. Smyth had previously recommended holding Moulmein with only a single battalion in an outpost role; he described Moulmein as 'a swine of a position to hold'.[9] On 24 January the 17th Division's headquarters was relocated from Moulmein to Kyaikto; Brigadier Bourke remained in local command at Moulmein. The 16th Brigade was ordered to patrol the west bank of the Salween to the north of Moulmein.

On the night of 24/25 January General Wavell made a ten-hour flight from Java to Rangoon in a four-engine heavy bomber for a brief visit. Wavell met with Hutton and ordered him to hold Moulmein for as long as possible without sacrificing the garrison. The two generals agreed that an evacuation would be needed in the event of a strong attack. Wavell correctly suspected that the Japanese advance into Tenasserim had been made by a comparatively small force; thus a defensive battle for Moulmein might be risked.

Hutton, accompanied by Smyth, went to Moulmein on 28 January to inspect the progress of defensive preparations that were intended to make the town a 'second Tobruk'.[10] It was decided that in the event of a serious

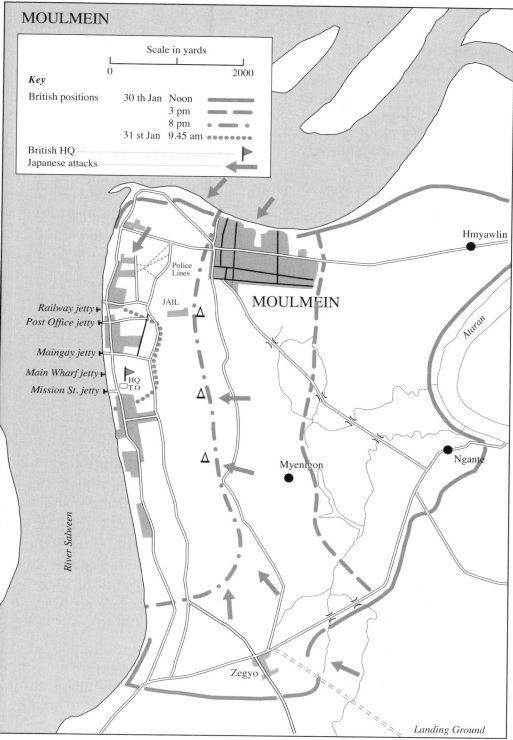

Map D Moulmein

Japanese attack Brigadier Ekin of the 46th Brigade would assume command at Moulmein; this would leave Brigadier Bourke free to handle the garrison's civil and administrative problems.

The four battalions of the 2nd Burma Brigade had to cover a perimeter of twelve miles; the garrison had no mines and was running short of barbed wire and sandbags. Japanese aircraft overhead unsettled elements of the Burma Rifles, and bombing burnt out Moulmein's main bazaar. At night packs of starving pi-dogs howled and roamed the town's deserted streets. In the surrounding countryside law and order broke down as panic spread at the approach of the invaders. Colonel Pelly, the provincial commissioner at Moulmein, conceded that little useful information about the Japanese was arriving from normally loyal village headmen.[11]

At XV Army's headquarters General Iida gave orders on 26 January for the 55th Division to attack Moulmein. The 33rd Division was to follow behind and prepare to cross the Salween river further north at Pa-an. Advancing Japanese forces made contact with Indian troops in vehicles fifteen miles south of Moulmein. A company of the 4/12th Frontier Force Regiment had been detached and posted to Mudon. This company was cut off from Moulmein on the night of 29/30 January, but the troops successfully rejoined their parent unit in the days ahead.

The defenders' perimeter at Moulmein was covered by water on two sides. The course of the Salween, a wide expanse of muddy estuary, covered both the northern flank and the rear of the 2nd Burma Brigade's position. The dominant feature within the perimeter was a long wooded ridge dotted with pagodas that gleamed in the sunshine. The ridge ran from north to south and dominated, in particular, the district of Moulmein that faced westwards onto the estuary. The 7th Burma Rifles held the northern sector of the perimeter; the 8th Burma Rifles covered the southern flank of the perimeter. Lieutenant-Colonel F.D. Taylor's 3rd Burma Rifles (less two companies) held a long stretch of the eastern face of the perimeter from a line of posts behind the Ataran river. The brigade's reserve was Lieutenant-Colonel W.D. Edward's 4/12th Frontier Force (less one company). Major John Hume's 12th Mountain Battery was on hand to support the infantry.

Moulmein airfield, which was outside the main perimeter, was defended by a detachment of the Burma Frontier Force. This detachment of Sikhs was commanded by a Viceroy's Commissioned Officer who had been in General Smyth's regiment in France during the First World War.[12] When this was discovered, the two men exchanged greetings with surprise and delight.

The Japanese force preparing to assault Moulmein on 30 January comprised two infantry regiments and a reconnaissance regiment; ten seventy-five millimetre mountain guns were available to support the advance of the infantry. These guns outranged their British equivalents, but fired a relatively light fourteen-pound shell. Japanese commanders were uncertain as to the strength of Moulmein's garrison, but were determined to attack without delay.

At dawn on 30 January the garrison of Moulmein was on high alert. Observation beyond the perimeter was poor in places given the broken terrain; there were a number of covered lines of approach through patches of paddy field and jungle. A report reached the 8th Burma Rifles in the southern sector of the perimeter that the Japanese were in a village east of the airfield. The Sikhs of D Company marched out to investigate and at 7.30 a.m. they encountered four trucks with troops aboard. The trucks were of Allied make and had been captured by the Japanese at Kawkareik. Lance-Naik Jwala Singh was alert to the ruse and opened fire without order with his light machine gun. The leading truck crashed into a ditch as its driver had been hit and lost control; the second and third vehicles were also shot up and brought to a halt; only the fourth managed to turn around and beat a hasty retreat. An attack developed against the 8th Burma Rifles later in the morning, but, with the support of a section of mountain guns, the Japanese advance was repelled and firing in that quarter died away. The airfield was evacuated and the Burma Frontier Force detachment made its way to safety.

The main Japanese attack got underway mid-morning when troops of the 112th and 143rd Regiments advanced on Moulmein from the east. Japanese troops crossed the Ataran river and occupied the villages of Hmyawlin and Ngante on the west bank; posts of the 3rd Burma Rifles were thrown back in disorder. Meanwhile, at noon Brigadier Ekin of the 46th Brigade arrived at Moulmein after a sixty-mile journey to take command of the garrison. 'The Jap attack had already begun,' wrote Ekin, 'and I had to assume command of troops I had never seen, on ground I did not know.'[13] Brigadier Bourke loyally cooperated despite his untimely supersession in the middle of a battle.

Brigadier Ekin visited the headquarters of the 3rd Burma Rifles at 1 p.m.; he ordered the battalion to pull back to a new line about 2000 yards west of the original front line at the Ataran river. The 4/12th Frontier Force came forward from reserve to occupy the long commanding ridge running north to south within the perimeter. By late afternoon hostile mortar fire had caused the 3rd Burma Rifles to collapse altogether. The advancing Japanese were engaged by the Frontier Force on the ridge; the guns of the 12th Mountain Battery fired in support. Lieutenant-Colonel Edward of the Frontier Force recalled: 'The battle raged all day and as night fell the advantage was still with us, although the Jap forces were increasing and, without reinforcements, holding Moulmein was militarily quite out of the question.'[14]

During the afternoon Smyth had reported to Hutton at Rangoon that the situation at Moulmein had become critical; he advised that the garrison needed either reinforcement or, preferably, withdrawal across the Salween. Hutton agreed and left Smyth to decide the timing of the evacuation. The Japanese advance guard had been forced to deploy and mount an attack, and that was a sufficient delay given the level of risk that had been taken.

Around 6.30 p.m. the headquarters of the 8th Burma Rifles was shelled out of its post in a bungalow. As darkness was falling Ekin ordered this battalion to withdraw to a new line at the southern end of the ridge. The brigadier also received the ominous news that Japanese troops had been sighted in boats on the river to the north of Moulmein. In the evening brigade headquarters, which was on the ridge near the Moulmein pagoda, was pulled back to a bungalow in Salween Park.

About 10 p.m. Japanese troops landed from the river near the timber yard in the northern sector; this was a reserve company of the 143rd Regiment. In the darkness the Japanese surprised and quickly overran a company of the 7th Burma Rifles. The Bofors anti-aircraft guns of the Indian battery were overrun as the Japanese mingled with the retreating infantry and surprised the gunners. The breach blocks of two of the four guns were removed, though not before some of the gunners had perished on Japanese bayonets.

It had become clear to Ekin and Bourke that the garrison needed to evacuate the town swiftly before Japanese artillery could dominate the ferry crossing. The telephone link to divisional headquarters at Kyaikto was working. About midnight Ekin reported that he doubted whether Moulmein could be held during the daylight hours of the coming day. Smyth gave Ekin permission to evacuate; the brigadier gave orders for the flotilla of steamers waiting at Martaban to cross the estuary immediately.

During the hours of darkness there was sporadic firing along the eastern face of the perimeter, but no serious Japanese attack developed from that direction. Brigade headquarters attracted the fire of Japanese infiltraters in the early hours of the morning, and had to be shifted for a second time to the Telephone Exchange near Mission Street Jetty. Fires in nearby river front buildings cast light into the night sky and caused further anxiety for the exhausted brigade staff.

Fifteen paddle steamers of the Irrawaddy Flotilla had been assembled at Martaban in anticipation of an evacuation; Burma was about to have its own miniature Dunkirk-type operation. The steamers arrived at Moulmein about 3 a.m. Brigade orders were issued for the troops to withdraw to a small perimeter covering the quayside and jetties; the evacuation was to commence at 8 a.m. After daylight there was renewed Japanese probing of the contracted perimeter, and the 7th Burma Rifles lost ground in the northern sector. At the southern end of the perimeter, the headquarters company of the 8th Burma Rifles counter-attacked to clear Japanese troops off Salween Park.[15]

During the morning of 31 January the 2nd Burma Brigade managed to successfully embark from Moulmein's river-front, though the Japanese were only held at arm's length with difficulty. Some troops of the Burma Rifles fled to the jetties ahead of schedule and caused a disturbance.[16] The wounded were loaded on stretchers or walked and limped aboard in bandages; the mountain guns fired over open sights and there was skirmishing in the streets near the quayside. Sappers were put aboard the steamers to stiffen the morale of their civilian crews.

The Frontier Force, mountain battery and a detachment of the 8th Burma Rifles were amongst the last troops to leave Moulmein. According to the brigade commander: 'I do not think we should have been able to get out of Moulmein if it had not been for the splendid action of the 4th Sikhs [4/12th Frontier Force] and 12th Mountain Battery as rear-guard to the force.'[17] Major Hume's mountain guns were embarked with difficulty. The anti-aircraft gunners' 2nd Lieutenant Mehar Dass and a party managed to haul one of the Bofors guns to Post Office jetty, but they could not get the piece on a steamer in time. Dass went ashore again to look for stragglers and was taken prisoner.[18]

Shortly after 10 a.m. brigade headquarters left from Mission Street jetty in the last steamer, which was shelled most of the way across the water to Martaban. The crossing of the estuary took an anxious forty to fifty minutes; there were several near misses. Only one of the steamers was sunk by Japanese artillery firing from the ridge, which had been promptly occupied once British forces withdrew from the feature. Captain James Lunt of the brigade's headquarters staff noted that 'it is no credit to the marksmanship of the Japanese gunners' that so little damage was done to the slowly retreating fleet of local shipping.[19]

Japanese aircraft were in the skies overhead during the evacuation, but they bombed Martaban on the western side of the estuary rather than Moulmein. If they had bombed the jetties of Moulmein a disaster might have occurred for British forces. There had been no sign of the RAF and on occasion the civilian crews on the steamers panicked at the sight of aircraft; it was a narrow escape.

According to Brigadier Ekin: 'Moulmein would have been a severe task for the best trained and most experienced staff and units, and we were not in that category! I regard this action as a very considerable achievement by the fighting troops and services.'[20] The evacuation could not have been delayed any longer – if Ekin had waited for nightfall it might have been a failure. The 2nd Burma Brigade evacuated three-quarters of its personnel, but the brigade's transport and anti-aircraft guns were abandoned; the mules were set free to fend for themselves. Some types of weaponry and equipment, however, were lifted to safety. In particular the guns of the mountain battery and the infantry's mortars were saved.

British casualties at Moulmein amounted to 617 officers and men, but most of these personnel were missing and many reappeared over the next few days. Some soldiers of the Burma Rifles deserted and headed for their homes.[21]

One of the officers killed in the Moulmein engagement was Captain A.R. Jardine of the 60th Field Company Queen Victoria's Madras Sappers and Miners. During the last phase of the evacuation the sappers blew up the power station and telephone exchange. Jardine's detachment was then ordered by a staff officer to help defend the quayside as Japanese troops were nearby. A breastwork of rolls of bedding on a jetty was all the shelter on offer. After Jardine was initially wounded, Jemadar Malligarjunan took over command. In the confusion the sappers were left behind and hid under the jetty.

Lieutenant-Colonel Taylor of the 3rd Burma Rifles had also been left behind with two of his officers.[22] This group joined the sappers under the jetty. After dark Taylor

> heard odd sounds coming from an adjacent yard and found that the sappers had disappeared. Peeping round a wall I was staggered to see them industriously building a petrol-barrel raft with their Jemadar giving instructions in whispers. Having completed the raft, they launched it; but the Jemadar, apparently not satisfied, had the raft pulled ashore and taken to pieces to replace a leaking barrel. It was then re-launched, but still the Jemadar was not happy about it, and had it re-built a second time. Then he smiled his satisfaction, came up to me and, saluting, said, 'Raft ready, Sahib.' We climbed aboard, but as we dared not use paddles, the Jemadar and his men stripped and gently slid the raft into the water and guided it to safety.[23]

The sappers and Taylor's party rejoined Burma Army to fight again another day.

Japanese casualties at Moulmein were not heavy. One of the 143rd Regiment's battalions suffered fourteen dead; the 55th Reconnaissance Regiment lost twenty killed and eleven wounded. Overall Japanese losses may not have been more than 200 killed and wounded in the two-day engagement.

The loss of Moulmein left virtually all of Tenasserim in Japanese hands. Tenasserim had been British territory since 1826 and the colonial presence was well accepted in that part of Burma. But Tenasserim had never seemed defensible as the territory lay on the eastern side of the broad Salween river, the first major river barrier in southern Burma. If a larger British garrison had made a more protracted defence of Moulmein, the Japanese could have by-passed the town by crossing the river further north; they had sufficient animal transport and were not dependent on motor roads.

With Moulmein lost to the Japanese, Rangoon was unlikely to receive an early warning of air attack in the future. The Japanese discovered a cache of 5000 drums of aviation spirit near the airfield in a rubber plantation; the fuel helped them to bring the airfield into operation at an early opportunity.[24]

The retirement from Moulmein was by no means the only British retreat underway in South-east Asia at the close of January 1942. The defeated army in Malaya was preparing to fight a final battle in defence of Singapore Island. The future course of events in many parts of the region would be determined in part by the ability of Singapore's heavily reinforced garrison to hold out against General Yamashita's XXV Army. Not far from Singapore, Japanese forces had also commenced landing operations on the Dutch possessions of Borneo, Celebes and Ambon. It was feared that the Japanese might be planning to reach southwards all the way to the north coast of Australia.

6

The Defence of the Salween River

The fighting at Moulmein had revealed to British intelligence the presence of the Japanese 55th Division in south-east Burma. That was a step in the right direction as hitherto little was known about the Japanese order of battle in Thailand. Rumours of Japanese troops in northern Thailand at Chiang Mai and Chiang Rai had reached Rangoon, but Hutton's staff struggled for confirmation from a reliable source. There was the possibility that Japanese forces might thrust into Upper Burma from northern Thailand; Scott's 1st Burma Division remained in the Shan States to meet that contingency. In reality there were no Japanese troops in northern Thailand. Unbeknown to British commanders, General Iida had used both of his divisions to invade southern Burma by the route heading west from Raheng.

By the end of January Hutton had arranged – with Wavell's permission – for a second Chinese division to enter the Shan States; the third division of the Chinese 6th Army was to be brought into reserve close to the Burma-China frontier. Hutton formed a Chinese Liaison Mission to help solve the considerable administrative challenges posed by a foreign army setting up shop in British territory.

The British strategy to defend Burma rested on using the port of Rangoon to build-up strength in the colony faster than Japanese forces could arrive by way of the difficult overland route from Thailand. The next substantial reinforcement to land at Rangoon was the 48th Indian Brigade, which comprised three regular Gurkha battalions. The brigade had been taken from the 19th Indian Division and reached Burma on 31 January. When the Gurkhas were mobilised for overseas service they were unsure of their destination; but the issuance of animal transport and embarkation at Madras indicated they were bound for the war against Japan.

The battalions of the 48th Brigade had been milked of manpower to some extent over the previous two years. During 1940–41 each Gurkha regiment of two regular battalions had raised a new 3rd and 4th Battalion. Yet all three battalions of the 48th Brigade were fortunate as they had experienced recent active service in the North-West Frontier Province's Waziristan agencies for extended periods; Waziristan was the scene of an on-going tribal insurgency.[1] Drafts of recruits had been well absorbed into units that had a large and experienced cadre. The riflemen and light machine gunners of the brigade were as well prepared for war as could be expected in the circumstances of early 1942.

The Gurkhas' specialists, however, had to hastily acquire expertise with new types of equipment, as was the case in other formations. The 1/3rd Gurkhas had not fired their anti-tank rifles or two-inch mortars before sailing for Burma. Two-inch mortars would prove invaluable in jungle warfare given their portability, compact size and ability to give high angle support fire at close ranges. The three-inch mortar teams were only a little more advanced in their training; new wireless sets had to be mastered by the signallers. A Gurkha battalion, in common with other British and Indian units, comprised four rifle companies, a headquarters company and a transport echelon. The headquarters company was composed of six specialist platoons for signals, mortars, anti-aircraft machine guns, armoured Bren carriers, pioneers and administration. Apart from rifles and kukris, each battalion's armament included six three-inch mortars, four two-inch mortars, five anti-tank rifles, thirty-six Thompson sub-machine guns and thirty Bren light machine guns.[2]

The 48th Brigade, as was generally the case in Burma, had been converted to a scale of half-mechanical, half-animal transport. Each battalion possessed four armoured Bren carriers, eight lorries and one water tanker; fifty-two mules made up the other half of the transport.

The brigade's commander was Brigadier Noel Hugh-Jones. He was forty-seven years of age, and an officer of the Indian Army. Hugh-Jones had seen service in France and the Middle East during the First World War. After the armistice he saw further active service in the Third Anglo-Afghan war of 1919. Hugh-Jones later completed a Staff College course intended to prepare middle-ranking officers for senior staff and command postings. Most recently he had been mentioned in despatches for his role in 1936–37 chapter of the fighting underway in tribal Waziristan.

The 1st West Yorkshire and the headquarters of the 28th Mountain Regiment also reached Rangoon around this time. Burma Army now had two mountain regiments and a field battery of the Burma Auxiliary Force to meet the artillery requirements of the formations in the field. The West Yorks were sent to watch the coastline to the immediate east of Rangoon; India was being stripped of its last trained units.

At the start of February Allied air strength at Rangoon comprised thirty-five Tomahawks and Hurricanes. Many of the Hurricanes that had arrived in Burma less than a month before were already out of action. At Toungoo, to the north of Rangoon, were based a dozen Blenheim IV bombers of No. 113 Squadron and four remaining Buffaloes of No. 67 Squadron.[3]

In addition to aerial combat and bombing missions, aircraft were vital for flying Allied commanders across a theatre of war too vast for frequent long journeys by road or rail. On 2 February General Hutton set out on a flight to Lashio, a town north-east of Mandalay, to meet with Chiang Kai-shek.

Two Lysanders, a light aircraft often used for liaison flights, took Hutton and his aid, Lieutenant Nigel Chancellor, aboard at Mingaladon airfield. Hutton's aircraft was piloted by Flight Lieutenant E.W. Tate. The Lysander, however, developed engine trouble after darkness had fallen and the pilot became lost. When the aircraft ran out of fuel, Tate was obliged to make a forced landing alongside the railway line to the south-west of Lashio. A wing tip hit a tree. Tate was knocked unconscious in the resulting crash and the aircraft caught fire. Hutton, who was shaken but otherwise unhurt, tried to drag the pilot clear but Tate was jammed into his seat. The general was forced to desperately beat back the flames with his greatcoat until local villagers arrived on the scene to help pull Tate free of the wreckage. The badly injured pilot was taken to hospital and died a few days later.

After Hutton's aircraft was forced down, the pilot of the second aircraft, Flight Lieutenant A.S. Mann, decided to attempt a landing near the crashed Lysander. Mann suggested that Lieutenant Chancellor bale out beforehand. Chancellor made the plunge down into the darkness and managed to land safely in a tree. Mann's Lysander, which was also running short of fuel, crash-landed near the first aircraft.[4]

Hutton and Chancellor proceeded to the nearby railway and continued their journey to Lashio. On 3 February Burma Army's commander had profitable discussions with Chiang Kai-shek; Governor Dorman-Smith wired London that 'the meeting was a great success'. It was agreed that the Chinese 5th and 6th Armies should both enter Burma in the near future. The 6th Army was to take over responsibility for the defence of the Shan States; the 5th Army was to assemble at Toungoo. Once Chinese troops were in their new positions, the 1st Burma Division would depart the Shan States, and move southwards of Toungoo to establish direct contact with British troops in south-east Burma. Whether the Chinese would be able to live up to the promises made was another matter; but it was encouraging, nonetheless, to have a well-intended high-level arrangement with Chiang finally in place after the diplomatic stumbling of the previous couple of months. Hutton and Chancellor, to their great relief, had an uneventful return flight to Rangoon.

A few days later the Generalissimo, Madame Chiang and a small staff arrived at Delhi for a state visit to India of a week's duration. Chiang's public sympathy with Indian nationalist leaders was not to the taste of British officialdom. This was a reminder that the interests of Nationalist China and the British empire had little in common apart from a shared enemy.[5]

Martaban lay on the western side of the Salween estuary from Moulmein. The road and railway from Martaban ran north-westwards to Thaton and onwards to the Bilin and Sittang rivers. General Smyth advocated withdrawing from Martaban to Thaton. General Hutton, however, made it clear to Smyth that the line of the Salween river was to be defended, even though Moulmein was now in Japanese hands on the eastern side of the lower river's estuary.

The 17th Indian Division would have to defend over 100 miles of the Salween river stretching from Martaban to Papun. Eighty miles of coastline from Martaban to the mouth of the Sittang river would also need to be watched in case of Japanese amphibious landings. The division's operation instruction of 1 February stated: 'The Division will stop any further enemy advance from Moulmein. Any attempts to cross the Salween River or to land troops from the Gulf of Martaban will be dealt with by immediate counter-attacks.' A further divisional instruction ordered that key points on the Salween river such as Martaban, Pa-an and Papun were to be strongly defended and counter-attacked if lost.[6]

Shortly after Hutton's return to Rangoon, General Wavell made another brief visit to Burma. He reached Rangoon after the long flight from Java on 5 February. Wavell's visits resembled, in some respects, 'Jovian descents from Olympus'.[7] As Wavell's former chief of staff, Hutton took his superior's views very seriously. The Indian Army's newly appointed Commander-in-Chief, General Hartley, never visited Rangoon and was busy learning the ropes of his role. Wavell had flown to Burma in the hope of meeting Chiang Kai-shek at Lashio, but the Generalissimo did not receive sufficient warning of the timing of Wavell's arrival and the conference could not take place.

Instead, on 6 February Wavell visited the 17th Division's headquarters at Kyaikto with Hutton. Wavell tried to be upbeat with his subordinate commanders: 'We must allow the enemy no further advance. Offence is the best means of defence. We must eventually get back that part of Tenasserim we have lost.'[8] He noticed that the open paddy land to the west of the Sittang river would be good terrain for armoured vehicles in the dry season. Wavell recommended to his superiors that the 7th Armoured Brigade, which was en route to the Far East from the Nile delta, should be diverted to Burma instead of landing at Java. 'This should make Rangoon and Burma safe during the critical next few months before the monsoon, and may enable offensive to be taken and heavy defeat inflicted on the enemy.'[9] On the night of 6/7 February Wavell again boarded his aircraft to make the flight back to ABDA headquarters in Java. A few days later at Singapore, on the evening of the 10th, Wavell fell off a sea wall in the dark onto hard ground. Two small bones were broken in Wavell's back to leave him bed-ridden for almost a week.

Neither Wavell nor Hutton wanted any premature retreats by the 17th Indian Division towards Rangoon. Hutton later tersely stated: 'It is obvious that if he [Smyth] had been left a free hand he would have scuttled back across the River Sittang as quickly as possible, after perhaps a token resistance on the Bilin River.'[10] Rangoon was Burma Army's only port of reinforcement; there were no roads or railways running into Burma from north-east India; just a few rough tracks crossed the mountainous wilderness that lay astride the Indian-Burmese frontier. The only feasible strategy to defend Burma, in the opinion of Wavell and Hutton, was to hold the Japanese far enough from Rangoon to keep the port open to Allied shipping. Hutton was aware that considerable reinforcement was needed in Burma; he could see that Smyth's division was badly overstretched. At a meeting of Burma's Defence Council on 11 February Hutton said that 'nothing short of six divisions in addition to the Chinese will help save Burma in the present situation.'[11]

Behind the Salween river, the 17th Indian Division prepared for the next round of fighting, which was not likely to be long in coming. Smyth deployed his division in great depth, with one brigade behind the other, even though this left the front line along the Salween river dangerously thin.

On 8 February Smyth made the 46th Brigade responsible for defending the immediate line of the Salween river. The brigade was reinforced by the topi-wearing 2nd King's Own Yorkshire Light Infantry. The battalion had previously belonged to Scott's division in the Shan States. The Yorkshiremen's commanding officer, Lieutenant-Colonel Adrian Becher, was another of the many senior officers in Burma to have begun his career as a subaltern in France and Flanders. To watch the Salween river to the north of Pa-an, the 2nd Burma Rifles was detached and sent to Papun; a company each from the 4th and 8th Burma Rifles was also posted at Shwegun and Kamamaung respectively.

The 16th Brigade was in reserve behind the 46th Brigade. The 48th Brigade had come forward from Rangoon and was assembling at Bilin further to the rear.

The 2nd Burma Brigade had been sent to Kyaikto to re-group after the Moulmein action; Kyaikto was a village between the Bilin and Sittang rivers. The long railway bridge across the Sittang river was the most significant bottleneck between the Salween and Rangoon. To the west of the bridge the railway ran along a raised embankment across open paddy fields. 'Immediately overlooking the bridge [to the east]', Captain Lunt observed, 'was a hill crowned by a pagoda, and 500 yards further on was a large statue of the Buddha. From there, looking east, there seemed to be nothing but jungle.'[12]

Early in February, during the brief lull after the fall of Moulmein, General Smyth was visited at his headquarters by Major-General Treffry Thompson, Burma Army's chief medical officer. Thompson quickly saw that Smyth's health was poor and insisted that Smyth attend a medical board to assess his fitness to continue on active service. Smyth was undeniably in distress from his reopened anal fistula, which had turned septic. The medical board assembled on 11 February under the presidentship of Colonel MacKenzie, who was Smyth's chief divisional medical officer. According to Smyth: 'I had a word to him [MacKenzie] beforehand and begged him to let me carry on.'[13] The board recommended that Smyth take two months' sick leave when possible. The board did not recommend that Smyth be medically downgraded and no further action was taken by Burma Army headquarters at Rangoon. MacKenzie gave Smyth a course of strychnine and arsenic injections to keep him going.

In consequence of Thompson's intervention, Smyth also took the unusual step of writing to Hutton asking for sick leave once the current round of operations was completed. Smyth wrote:

> The wound only stopped bleeding ten days ago and is still discharging. I didn't feel too grand yesterday and your DDMS [Thompson] insisted that ADMS [MacKenzie] should have a look at me. He finds nothing organically wrong with me that a few months' comparative rest wouldn't put right. I should hate to go sick – it's a thing I've never done in the whole of my service. I feel if I could have a month off … and swap jobs with someone in a more sedentary job in India for a few months I should be absolutely OK for a command in the field again (if required) … Meanwhile I shall carry on, perfectly happily as long as you like. So sorry.[14]

What Hutton made of Smyth's communication remains unclear.

General Iida's XV Army held the initiative in southern Burma; the campaign would roll onwards at a time and place of the Japanese commander's choice. In preparation for the next phase of the offensive, Iida moved his headquarters forward to Moulmein, right behind the front line. The Japanese 55th Division was instructed to cross the Salween and capture Martaban; it was then to advance along the road and railway to Thaton and onwards to the Bilin river. The 33rd Division was to push up the east bank of the Salween to capture Pa-an, and then cross the river and advance westwards on the northern flank of the 55th Division. XV Army's supply of ammunition was dependent on a slender line of communication stretching across the Dawna hills to Thailand.

The Japanese had decided not to resort to amphibious operations along the coast as the risks of British naval intervention were too high. At this stage of the campaign Japanese warships had yet to penetrate the Java Sea and the waters around Singapore. The eastern Indian Ocean and the approaches to Burma were still in Allied hands. XV Army's commanders made a genuine effort to keep their soldiers under tight control as they wished to win the support of the Burmese people and create a loyal ally in the Burma Independence Army.[15]

Martaban was the rail and ferry terminus on the west bank of the Salween estuary from Moulmein. The 3/7th Gurkhas and a company of the 2nd KOYLI comprised the defending garrison under the command of the Gurkhas' Lieutenant-Colonel H.R. Stevenson. The 46th Brigade's headquarters was at Thaton, thirty-seven miles from Martaban, with the main body of the KOYLI. The Salween was a fine natural obstacle but only if the shore line was continuously defended. Martaban was shelled and bombed during the first week of February, and there were signs that the Japanese were preparing to cross the river.

On the night of 8/9 February a detachment of the 143rd Regiment moved upriver from Moulmein and landed on the west bank of the Salween at Hmawbi, eleven miles north of Martaban. These troops advanced inland and set up a road block eight miles behind Martaban. On 9 February the force at Martaban discovered that Japanese troops had cut the road to Thaton. The telephone lines from Thaton to Martaban had also been cut and wireless contact with the Gurkhas at Martaban failed. Stevenson sent a patrol up the road towards Thaton, but Captain Stourton and his force were killed in an ambush; only one man escaped to tell the tale.[16]

Brigadier Ekin had sent orders for the Martaban garrison to retreat but the message was lost in another ambush that killed the liaison officer. On the evening of 9 February British observers near Martaban saw Japanese troops advancing inland from the coast to the west of the town; this was a landing force of the 112th Regiment; a pincer operation was underway to surround Martaban. Stevenson decided to withdraw on his own initiative; his force retreated along a jungle track and reached Thaton on 11 February. The Gurkhas' rearguard company only appeared two days after that.

Twenty-five miles to the north of Martaban was Pa-an, a large village on the east bank of the Salween. Opposite Pa-an, on the west bank, was the small village of Kuzeik, which had been occupied by the 1/7th Gurkhas on 31 January. A ferry service ran between the two villages; the river was 800 yards across at this point.

Gurkha patrols were sent across the river to Pa-an. On 2 February there was a clash with Japanese troops entering the district; patrols clashed again in the days ahead. A group of Japanese were discovered on the west bank to the south of Kuzeik, and they were clearly scouting in preparation for offensive action. Gurkha patrols also noted enemy activity upstream of Pa-an. Japanese aircraft bombed Kuzeik, but on three occasions RAF Blenheim bombers struck Pa-an, flying low up the river, to inflict casualties on Japanese troops assembling in the jungle. The Gurkhas were relieved by the 7/10th Baluchis of the 46th Brigade on 8 February.[17]

The 7/10th Baluchis, a newly-raised wartime battalion, comprised two companies of Punjabi Muslims, one of Brahmin Dogras and one of Pathans. A Company's Pathans were commanded by Captain W.B. Cayley, a former tea planter in Bihar. C Company's Dogras were commanded by a fellow Brahmin Dogra, the regular-commissioned Captain Siri Kanth Korla. Korla had been promoted from the ranks and was the son of a havildar of the regiment. B and D Companies' Punjabi Muslims were led by 2nd Lieutenants John Randle and David Jarvis, both of whom had only left their public schools eighteen months before, and still lacked sufficient service to advance to the rank of 1st lieutenant.[18]

The Baluchis' main defensive position was a shallow perimeter in the rice fields facing the river just north of Kuzeik. The position was 600 yards across in a saucer of paddy with the edges of the saucer on higher ground facing dense jungle. The sepoys would have to defend the perimeter from slit trenches without the cover of barbed wire. The south side of the perimeter was skirted by the road running to Duyinzeik, a village ten miles to the west on the road to Thaton.

Lieutenant-Colonel 'Jerry' Dyer was ordered to deny the ferry crossing, and patrol the river bank ten miles to the north and five miles to the south. The Baluchis had been reinforced by a section of the 12th Mountain Battery; the rest of the battery remained at Thaton. In the event of a serious Japanese attack, the Baluchis at Kuzeik were to be reinforced by Lieutenant-Colonel H. Power's 5/17th Dogras at Duyinzeik. The Dogras, however, were deployed on both sides of the Donthami river, which was likely to retard rapid movement in either direction. The Dogras were instructed to patrol the road leading to the Baluchis at Kuzeik on a daily basis.

The Japanese 33rd Division was ordered to cross the Salween river in the vicinity of Pa-an. The 215th Regiment was assembling in the scrub and jungle near that village; the 214th Regiment was close at hand. The Japanese moved bullock carts and boats to the north of Pa-an as a ruse; but, four miles south of Kuzeik, near Pagat, Baluchi patrols encountered Japanese troops on the west bank of the river on the night of 10/11 February. The II/215th Battalion had crossed the river in small boats rowed by local Burmese. Japanese troops stormed the patrol base at Myainggale, where B Company had been in the process of relieving A Company. Platoons each from A and B Companies were overrun and it quickly became apparent that the Japanese had crossed the Salween in strength; Subedar Mehr Khan was amongst those Baluchis killed at Myainggale. The Japanese crossing place was just out of range of the mountain guns at Kuzeik.[19]

During the daylight hours of the following morning of 11 February the Baluchis' perimeter was subjected to dive-bombing. The troops took shelter in slit trenches. Duyinzeik was bombed as well. Patrols reported to Lieutenant-Colonel Dyer that the Japanese were definitely advancing on Kuzeik from Pagat. Dyer sent a message to the Dogras at Duyinzeik that evening saying he expected a strong attack during the coming night. The message was passed to brigade headquarters at Thaton. Brigade headquarters had already received an unusual message from Kuzeik during the afternoon reporting that the Japanese had been thrown back across the Salween river; this message was in all likelihood sent by Japanese signallers.[20]

In the Baluchis' perimeter C Company held the south-west flank; B Company held the western flank with only one platoon and a section of medium machine guns; D Company held the northern flank minus one platoon; A Company faced the river also without a platoon and supported by a section of medium machine guns. Battalion headquarters and the mountain gun section was behind A Company, near the track by the river bank. As well as the two platoons overrun near Pagat, other platoons were away from the battalion perimeter on patrol. The Baluchis could ill-afford to loose the services of so many riflemen at a crucial time.

After nightfall on 11 February the I/215th Battalion crossed the river at the same place where the II/215th Battalion had crossed twenty-four hours before. Japanese troops advanced northwards on Kuzeik across broken terrain. The plan was to take the defenders by surprise under the cover of darkness. The II/215th Battalion was to attack the Baluchis from the south-west, whilst the I/215th Battalion cut the road leading from Kuzeik to Duyinzeik. The road presented a clear assembly line from which to launch the attack on the Baluchis' perimeter.

About 2 a.m., as the moon was coming up, troops of the II/215th Battalion hurled themselves against the defences from the west and south-west shouting war cries, and with swords, bayonets and grenades at the ready. Flanking machine guns fired in support once the attack got underway. The Japanese advanced with unloaded rifles and bayonets smeared with mud to prevent them gleaming in the moonlight. The Japanese army devoted a lot of time to bayonet training as it was vital to the modern army's reinterpretation of the samurai tradition.[21]

The Baluchis were not taken by surprise and were awaiting the attack crouched or lying in weapon pits. Parachute flares shot skywards from the battalion's mortars; machine guns firing tracer ammunition sent streams of coloured light through the darkness. It proved difficult, however, for the section of mountain guns to fire in support of such a shallow perimeter. An outpost was quickly overrun and C Company, which was at the south-west corner of the perimeter, took the brunt of the initial assault. Before long B and D Companies also came under attack from the north-west. The Japanese advanced by short rushes, lying down when the defenders' fire became too heavy; when they were close enough they threw grenades; Japanese guns shelled the Baluchis from across the river.

B Company was commanded by Lieutenant John Randle. He recalled:

> That night we were attacked by 215 Regiment and pinned against the Salween. The CO had sent one of my platoons and a platoon from another company out on a patrol. God knows what for, so I was down to one platoon, and a section of MMGs … The Japs came in with no artillery support in what started as a silent night attack. When they got close, they screamed banzai and came charging in shoulder-to-shoulder. The Vickers [medium machine guns] fired across my front and caused heavy casualties to the Japs. They surged into Company HQ, I killed the chap coming for me (waving a sword). I was standing up firing my revolver, and missed first time. My CSM [Company Sergeant-Major] was grappling with a Jap. My batman was killed by a grenade.[22]

Naik Amir Khan of B Company would be awarded a posthumous Indian Order of Merit for his work with a sub-machine gun as the attackers closed in.[23]

Japanese troops infiltrated the defenders' perimeter through the gaps between company positions. Captain Suzuki Tadashi was at the forefront of the attack; his troops reached some tents within the perimeter:

> We advanced and stabbed a few men who were outside. When we entered a tent which looked like a combat headquarters I saw a wounded commander sitting upright with several of his men. He signed to us to shoot him and died in a serene frame of mind. His attitude really was in keeping with the honour of a military man. I sincerely respected him and wished I might do the same.[24]

The battalion's headquarters came under fire at close range; the pioneer platoon counter-attacked to temporarily restore the situation. Lieutenant-Colonel Dyer was wounded by bullets to the wrist, face and stomach. Lieutenant Charles Coubrough, the unit's signals officer, and a sepoy carried the mortally wounded Dyer to the bushes by the river bank. The remnants of battalion headquarters and A Company made a rush across the paddy to join what was left of C Company, which had held out since the fighting began. The survivors would speak highly of Captain Korla; he would be awarded the DSO for his inspirational leadership.

The headquarters of the 215th Regiment had advanced behind the battalion assaulting Kuzeik. At first light the regimental gun company, acting as infantry, skirted past and around the western flank of the Baluchis' perimeter to reach the river to the north of the field of battle. The company then attacked southwards along the river bank to overrun the last organised Baluchi posts. As the sun was rising Japanese light machine gun fire sprayed any sign of movement within the perimeter; sounds of battle began to die away and a Japanese officer stepped forward to call on the survivors to surrender. By 8 a.m. all resistance had come to an end. Indian soldiers still at liberty escaped as best they could. Lieutenant Coubrough took refuge in the surrounding jungle, but was captured by a Japanese patrol two days later.[25]

Captain Korla and Jemadar Anant Ram were captured and bound hand and foot, however, they managed to break free and escape; Major P.O. Dunn was also captured but escaped. The Baluchis' wounded are believed to have been 'butchered'. A rare exception was the unit's quartermaster, Captain Bruce Toothill. His party, which included the Subedar-Major, had escaped from the perimeter and plunged into the nearby jungle. The party reached the road three miles west of the river but were soon surrounded by Japanese troops. According to Toothill:

> The fight lasted a few minutes. Had they been Germans and better shots it wouldn't have lasted more than seconds. The first bullet got me through the leg just above the ankle, the second a couple of minutes later scraped my shoulder; the third knocked the smile off my face in no uncertain fashion, removing fourteen teeth and breaking my jaw prior to leaving via my left cheek. I am afraid I packed it in at that stage as I felt I had tried to kiss an express train.[26]

Subedar-Major Kirpa Ram Bahadur was bayoneted as he tried to throw a grenade. Toothill expected to be finished off when he saw a Japanese soldier looming above him, but for some reason he was spared and given rudimentary medical treatment. Toothill was carried across the river to Pa-an by other prisoners on a stretcher made of signal wire and bamboo; he was subsequently incarcerated in Moulmein's prison.

Lieutenant-Colonel Dyer, six officers and six VCOs were killed at Kuzeik; a further dozen VCOs would be posted missing. Lieutenant Randle, accompanied by two sepoys, took two days to reach safety after the battle. Randle commented: 'We were staked out there like a goat for the Jap tiger and sacrificed for no reason.' The battalion lost 289 dead at Kuzeik and Myainggale. The engagement had been a brutal hand-to-hand struggle by moonlight.[27]

The Baluchis had been overrun by a first-class, experienced opponent, without much support from either artillery or old-fashioned barbed wire. The I/215th Battalion had blocked the Baluchis' principal escape route along the road to Thaton and captured many prisoners; 235 Baluchi officers and men were rounded up.[28] Japanese troops referred to captured supplies of food

1. The spire of the Shwedagon Pagoda, Rangoon.

2. General Sir Archibald Wavell and General T.J. Hutton, March 1942.

3. Generalissimo Chiang Kai-shek, Madame Chiang and Lt-General Joseph W. Stilwell, Maymyo, Burma, April 1942.

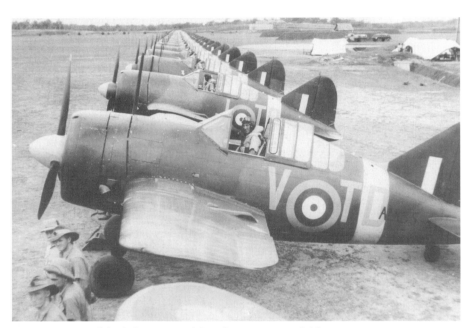

4. Brewster Buffalo fighter aircraft lined-up on an airfield.

5. Rangoon, 6 March 1942: smoke from demolitions rises over the city.

6. The battleship HMS *Warspite*, Indian Ocean 1942.

7. The aircraft carrier HMS *Hermes* sinking off the coast of Ceylon, 9 April 1942.

8. A view of the demolished Ava bridge in the Irrawaddy river near Mandalay.

and equipment as gifts from Mr Churchill. Japanese casualties amongst all units involved at Kuzeik were 100 killed and wounded.

Only five Baluchi officers and three VCOs escaped from the Kuzeik perimeter to rejoin the rest of the brigade at Thaton. Other escaping sepoys and detached patrols would bring the battalion up to a strength of 250, but that was less than a third of the unit's personnel present at the outset of the battle.

The Dogras had been ordered by brigade headquarters to march to the relief of Kuzeik during the night, but it took a long time to concentrate the battalion on the east side of the Donthami river. The advance from Duyinzeik only began after daylight and was halted soon after 11 a.m. on 12 February when it became apparent that the Baluchis had been overrun. Stragglers from Kuzeik told a dire story of their night's ordeal.

On 13 February Duyinzeik and its ferry were subjected to aerial bombing and an artillery and mortar barrage. The morale of the Dogras was shaken by the experience. The following day Brigadier Ekin at Thaton reported to divisional headquarters that the Japanese were probing past the northern flank of his 46th Brigade. The front along the Salween river had collapsed.

7

The Battle of Bilin River

A fresh face was about to take his place in the 17th Indian Division's command structure. Brigadier D.T. 'Punch' Cowan, formerly Director of Military Training at Delhi, had arrived in Burma and joined the division's headquarters. Cowan had been sent from India as a potential replacement for Brigadier Jones after his brigade's misfortunes at Kawkareik. Jones had managed to retain his command and General Smyth had Cowan appointed his chief staff officer, a post not usually held by a brigadier at a divisional headquarters. 'Punch' Cowan was a victim of army humour; he owed his nickname to a supposed resemblance to the puppet that featured in seaside Punch and Judy shows. Cowan was considered to be a safe pair of hands and he was alarmed by his first impressions at divisional headquarters. He later wrote that Smyth was in a 'very nervous and jittery state; not at all the Smyth I knew'.[1]

As the Japanese army was clearly across the Salween river in strength, Smyth sent Cowan to see Hutton on 12 February to seek permission to concentrate the division behind the Bilin river. Hutton would not agree to the proposal; on 13 February he signalled Smyth that he was to defend a line running from Thaton to Duyinzeik as long as was practical. That day Hutton also asked Wavell for the establishment of a corps-level field headquarters in Burma. Hutton was burdened with responsibilities to ABDA headquarters, India Command, the Burmese government, Burma's War Office, the Chinese expeditionary force, Royal Navy and RAF, all on top of the most immediate task of fighting the Japanese invaders. An extra lieutenant-general was needed in Burma to more closely direct the divisional commanders Smyth and Scott.

There was no Japanese attack on Duyinzeik on 14 February, but late in the day Smyth ordered his division to retreat to the Bilin river; he rightly feared that the Japanese were moving past the division's northern flank. Hutton was informed of this after the withdrawal was set in motion; he was displeased that Smyth had acted without prior authorisation. But there was the real danger that the division would be lost in penny packets, and Hutton later conceded that the withdrawal was well timed. Smyth's headquarters ordered the 46th Brigade to evacuate Thaton by dawn of 15 February; 400 vehicles were needed to help evacuate British forces from the town.[2]

The 2nd KOYLI was the rearguard at Thaton; they were to be collected by a train, but when no train arrived they marched north-westwards on foot. The train's crew were not informed of this; the train steamed through the new front line and headed to Thaton, oblivious to the war situation. The train reached Thaton before its crew realised what had happened, but managed to return unscathed to British-held territory a few hours later. Thaton had been deserted, however, the train rescued two Yorkshire soldiers who had been left behind after falling prey to the temptations of local liquor.

At Kawkareik, Moulmein, Martaban and Kuzeik isolated 17th Division brigades and battalions had fought the Japanese beyond the effective supporting distance of other units. The division would fight more effectively once it was concentrated behind the Bilin river. The 16th Brigade was to hold the line of the Bilin with the fresh 48th Brigade close at hand in reserve. The 46th Brigade crossed the Bilin and withdrew westwards to re-group at Kyaikto, which was midway between the Bilin and Sittang rivers and the location of divisional headquarters. The 2nd Burma Brigade was withdrawn across the Sittang to watch the river line to the north at Nyaunglebin. At this time the 2nd Burma Brigade comprised only the 3rd and 7th Burma Rifles. The understrength 3rd Burma Rifles was guarding the Sittang bridge.[3] Far to the north of Bilin, the 2nd Burma Rifles was still at Papun; companies each from the 4th and 8th Burma Rifles had also been detached from their parent units to occupy distant outposts.

The River Bilin was thirty miles east of the much broader Sittang. Smyth was later to write that the Bilin was impressive on the map but, 'at that time of the year, [it was] an almost dry ditch running through thick jungle country, which one could jump over'.[4] That was an exaggeration, though the Bilin was fordable in most places and only knee deep in the dry season. The river, however, had a broad sandy bed for long stretches that would provide a clear field of fire for automatic weapons, and an aiming point for artillery and mortars. The principal military value of the Bilin was that the estuary to the south, and the jungle-covered hills to the north, formed a bottleneck through which ran the road and railway from Martaban.[5] The local Bilin area was hilly, with patches of jungle and rubber plantation; the front to be held was fifteen miles of broken terrain.

The 16th Indian Brigade's commander, Brigadier Jones, was back at the centre of events for the first time since the confusion in the Dawna hills of the previous month. He made plans to deploy his brigade with – from north to south – the 2nd KOYLI, 8th Burma Rifles and 1/9th Jats holding the line of the Bilin river. The 1/7th Gurkhas were in brigade reserve. The 5/17th Dogras and a company of the 8th Burma Rifles was to hold an outpost line on the eastern side of the river, on high ground astride the road from Thaton.

These troops began to take up their positions early on 16 February. The 16th Brigade's supporting artillery comprised the 5th and 12th Mountain Batteries and two eighteen-pounders of the Burma Auxiliary Force. Fresh guns had been issued to the 5th Mountain Battery to replace those lost at Kuzeik. The headquarters of the 28th Mountain Regiment had joined Smyth's division to take command of all artillery units.

On 16 February Hutton visited the 17th Division's headquarters at Kyaikto; he made it clear to Smyth that there would definitely be no further retreat from the Bilin without the authorisation of Burma Army headquarters. The port of Rangoon had to be kept open by holding the Japanese as far to the east as possible. From his Java headquarters, Wavell reminded Hutton not to make any unnecessary retirements. He cabled Hutton:

> I do not know what consideration caused withdrawal behind Bilin River without further fighting. I have every confidence in judgement and fighting spirit of you and Smyth but bear in mind that continual withdrawal, as experience of Malaya showed, is most damaging to morale of troops especially Indian troops. Time can often be gained as effectively and less expensively by bold counter-offensive. This is especially so against the Japanese.[6]

Singapore had recently fallen to Imperial Japan. The shock of the capitulation was deeply felt across the British empire; particularly in territories of the region such as Burma and Australia.

The Japanese advanced swiftly westwards of the Salween river. The 33rd Division's 214th Regiment crossed the Salween eight miles north of Pa-an on the night of 12/13 February.[7] Advancing along good jungle tracks, by the evening of the 14th Japanese troops had almost reached the Bilin river about seven miles north of Bilin village. That night a company-strength force was sent across the river via a bamboo bridge into the village of Ahonwa. The following day, 15 February, the I/214th Battalion crossed the river and dug in on the west bank between the villages of Paya and Danyingon. The Japanese had managed to get a foothold in the Bilin line before retreating British forces could fully occupy that position.

Meanwhile the 215th Regiment, the 33rd Division's other regiment in Burma, had reorganised after the action at Kuzeik, and was advancing north-west towards the Bilin along tracks that also bypassed Duyinzeik to the north. The 55th Division was advancing from Martaban towards Thaton, though not with any urgency.

A track ran northwards from Bilin village along the western side of the river to Yinon. On the morning of 16 February a company of KOYLI was sent to Yinon to watch the ford over the river at that place. The main body of the

KOYLI, however, was to defend the river line from Paya to Danyingon. But when the Yorkshiremen marched across fields of paddy and six-foot sugar cane to establish a line of posts in their designated sector, they discovered that the Japanese had got there first. A small party of enemy troops was surprised washing near a village well and scattered, but they had strong support close at hand.

The village of Danyingon had been allotted to the KOYLI's D Company; the village was full of trees and surrounded by jungle. Captain E.D. Wardleworth rode forward on horseback to reconnoitre and confirm that the Japanese were in possession of the village. An attack was made on Danyingon supported by the battalion's three-inch mortars, but the Yorkshiremen made little progress in the face of a defiant Japanese defence in a dense strip of bamboo jungle.[8] The KOYLI settled down for the coming night in a line of posts west and south of Danyingon; the Japanese had a firm foothold in the 17th Division's proposed defensive line. At the southern end of the Bilin front there was some firing between Dogra and Japanese patrols on 16 February but little other contact.

That evening Brigadier Jones ordered his reserve battalion, the 1/7th Gurkhas, to march out and prepare to attack Danyingon at dawn on 17 February. The Gurkhas attacked the village at 8.20 a.m. supported by the 5th Mountain Battery. One company advanced on the northern side of Danyingon and two companies directly attacked the village. The assault was pressed with vigour but met a hail of machine gun and mortar fire; hand-to-hand fighting developed in places and the Japanese proved to be in greater strength than first realised. Major A.O.L. Burke and seventeen Gurkhas were killed, Captain Rae and twenty-five other ranks were wounded; another thirty Gurkhas were posted missing.[9]

General Smyth was keeping a close watch on proceedings. He detached the 1/4th Gurkhas from the 48th Brigade, and sent that unit to join the 16th Brigade to mount a further attack on Danyingon. At 5.30 p.m. the Gurkhas attacked, supported by mountain guns and mortars. A and D Companies assaulted Danyingon, whilst C Company advanced to cover the northern flank of those two companies. The troops attacking the village became caught up in bamboo jungle and were either halted by Japanese fire or lost direction. C Company successfully occupied a hill-feature named Point 313 without opposition; the hill was covered by dense jungle and afforded good views of the far side of the river. An artillery observation officer and his team set up a post on the hill.[10] After the attack was held up, the Gurkhas dug in for the night. The commanding officer of the 1/4th Gurkhas, Lieutenant-Colonel W.D.A. Lentaigne, a tall, thin, bespectacled man, did not intend to incur unnecessary losses on ground where a previous attack had failed.

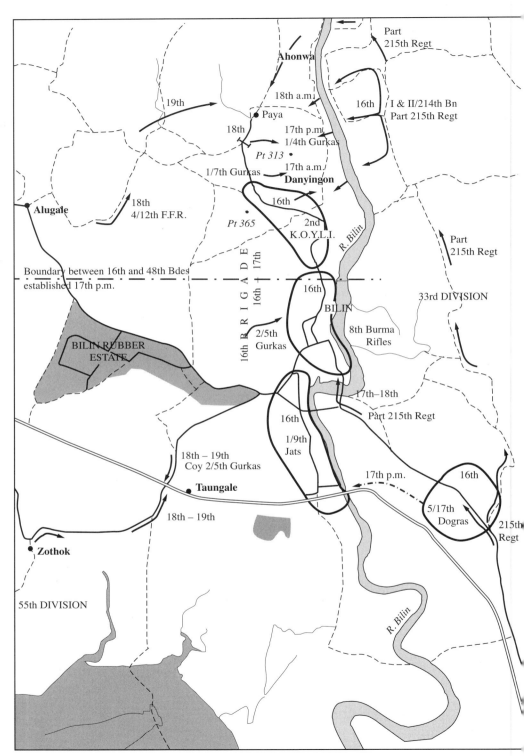

Map E The Action on the Bilin River

Further north, a second Japanese battalion crossed the river that day and cut the road on the west bank leading to Yinon. Armoured Bren carriers sent to investigate were driven off by machine gun and mortar fire. The II/214th Battalion took up station on the northern flank of the I/214th Battalion.[11] The remainder of Colonel Sakuma's 214th Regiment was close at hand.

Meanwhile, at the southern end of the front, the 215th Regiment was marching towards Bilin village. At 1 p.m. on 17 February the 16th Brigade's headquarters ordered the 5/17th Dogras to withdraw from their outpost positions astride the main road on the exposed eastern side of the river. During the morning patrols had sighted Japanese troops a few miles north-east of Bilin village. The Dogras began to pull out at 2.15 p.m., but subsequent events did not go to plan. According to the unit's war diary:

> Japanese parties approaching from north got astride the road between the Battalion's position and the bridge and captured five trucks. The Battalion's line of withdrawal was now altered to the railway bridge south of the road bridge and the ford farther east. The withdrawal was, however, closely followed by the Japanese, who opened up accurate mortar fire from high ground to the north of the Battalion position.[12]

As the Dogras headed rearwards the mortar fire caused a collapse in morale and a panicked flight. The Jats' war diary frankly stated that the Dogras retreated 'in complete disorder, without rifles, automatic weapons and in some cases boots'.[13] The Dogras streamed across the Bilin and were sent to the rear to gather breath. A party of Dogras and 8th Burma Rifles was left behind on the far side of the river; many of these troops were overrun by the advancing Japanese of the I/215th Battalion.[14]

Lieutenant-Colonel B.R. Godley had taken command of the Jats on the eve of the Bilin action after a briefing from General Hutton to restore morale in the unit. The Jats' three-mile front stretched from the road bridge just south of Bilin village southwards to the railway bridge at Hninpale. The river's sandbanked bed was up to 150 yards across at this point. Sappers blew-up the road and rail bridges at 5 p.m.; the Jats were holding the front with three rifle companies in the line and the fourth in reserve. The sepoys crouched or lay in cramped weapon pits; a lack of signalling equipment hampered command arrangements within the battalion's sector. The Japanese, however, did not follow up the Dogras in strength, and the Jats only came under sporadic rifle and mortar fire.

After darkness fell the II/215th Battalion sent a strong patrol across the river into Bilin village and panicked the defenders of the 8th Burma Rifles, who were bundled out of their forward line of posts. The left flank company of the Jats reported to battalion headquarters that the Japanese were in the village. But the crisis soon passed as the Japanese withdrew from Bilin village of their own accord. General Sakurai, the 33rd Division's commander, could see greater opportunities for his troops at the northern end of the battle front.[15]

Given the scale of the battle underway, General Smyth decided to divide the Bilin front into two sectors. The 48th Brigade would take over the line from Bilin village southwards; the 16th Brigade would retain control of the northern half of the front. During the night of 17/18 February the 48th Brigade's headquarters and the 2/5th Gurkhas took up positions to the west of Bilin village. Brigadier Hugh-Jones took command of the 8th Burma Rifles and the Jats. The 1/3rd Gurkhas had remained at Thebyuchaung – 'river of white sand' – to guard the bridge at that location.

During the morning of 18 February the 2/5th Gurkhas moved forward to the river to fill the gap on the left flank of the Jats and secure Bilin village.[16] The 8th Burma Rifles was reorganised to the north and west of Bilin village.

Smyth visited the front on the morning of 18 February; he returned to Kyaikto and sent a message to Hutton in the afternoon. Smyth reported that the 16th Brigade had been 'fought to a standstill' and the Japanese seemed to be gathering in greater strength than first appreciated.[17]

The 16th Brigade's outpost line around Danyingon changed little on 18 February. From Point 313 British observers directed artillery fire on Japanese positions; two flights of Blenheim bombers hit targets near the river. Little was seen of the Japanese air force. Armoured Bren carriers made another attempt to reach Yinon to pick up the KOYLI's detached company, but Major Houghton was killed by a mortar bomb and his detachment was unable to break through a road block. Brigade headquarters had a message dropped by aircraft to the troops at Yinon; the container was rescued from a sandbank in the river. The KOYLI company was ordered to withdraw to Thebyuchaung.

During the night of 18/19 February a Japanese bombardment near Danyingon interrupted the snatches of sleep of exhausted men. Exploding mortar rounds and vivid red tracer ammunition lit up the darkness and provoked a lot of retaliatory fire from Lentaigne's Gurkhas. The Japanese were said to have used Chinese crackers amid the shelling. 'These crackers [noted the regimental history of the 4th Gurkhas] are more alarming than they sound. They are probably attached to mortar bombs or other missiles, and burning off in flight, fizz and crackle far behind the forward defended localities and make it appear that the enemy are through or behind our positions.'[18] Japanese infantry advanced behind the bombardment but hit thin air as Lentaigne had pulled back his forward companies after dark; the Japanese were mortared on the ground they had occupied.

At the southern end of the front there was also skirmishing with Japanese troops during the night of 18/19 February. There was a lot of firing by riflemen of the 2/5th Gurkhas at shadows and figures flitting through the darkness near the river bank. At one place the Japanese drove a herd of cattle towards the river; the Gurkhas held their fire until they saw through the ruse.

During the night troops belonging to the Jats returning from patrol were fired on by Gurkhas who believed them to be Japanese. The Jats lost five dead, eight wounded and two missing in the brief firefight. This skirmish caused Lieutenant-Colonel Godley to believe that Japanese troops were within his unit's position. Elsewhere on the Jats' front a clash with a Japanese patrol caused several men to retreat in panic; the next morning Godley inflicted corporal punishment on the men with a bamboo cane in the presence of his approving Subedar-Major and two other VCOs.[19]

Whilst Japanese troops of the 33rd Division were engaged with Smyth's division at the Bilin river, the 55th Division had been advancing along the coast from Martaban. The 55th Division's 112th Regiment had been detached and left in Moulmein to establish order in the town. The division's other regiment, the 143rd Regiment, advanced along the railway and road from Martaban to occupy Thaton. Troops of this regiment marched westwards, and then crossed the Bilin estuary in boats to land on the south coast at Zokali on the evening of 18 February. The 17th Division's position behind the Bilin was in danger of being outflanked from the sea to the south.

When Smyth's headquarters received a report of a Japanese landing on the coast, B Company of the 2/5th Gurkhas was dispatched to investigate. On 19 February the Gurkhas skirmished with Japanese troops near Taungzun station. A second company of the 2/5th Gurkhas – A Company – was also dispatched to patrol the coastal flank. As A Company approached the village of Taungale they came upon a large tree fallen across the road. In the firing that followed Subedar Narainsing Thapa was killed. A message was sent to battalion headquarters and the unit's commander, Lieutenant-Colonel R.T. Cameron, soon arrived with a three-inch mortar detachment and two Bren gun teams. Cameron was 'a tall, wiry, hard, tough bachelor and a man of high physical and moral courage. A red face, a sharp temper and a fondness for whisky concealed a naturally sympathetic nature.'[20] He had first seen action in the Gallipoli campaign.

Cameron organised an attack to clear the road and capture parts of the village of Taungale, which was on the railway to the east of Taungzun. Platoons advanced swiftly to the left and right of the road to force the Japanese back. The battalion's war diary recorded that the section commanders of one particular platoon 'each played away with their Tommy Guns and set a magnificent example of fearless leadership to which their young soldiers were quick to respond'.[21] At 4 p.m. Cameron ordered his men to pull back to the battalion's headquarters harbour. The following day the Japanese were very quiet on the coastal flank; the Gurkhas had made their presence felt.[22]

In the northern sector the Japanese remained securely dug-in on the western bank of the Bilin river. The KOYLI's casualties so far had amounted to fifteen killed and 114 wounded. Smyth had sent the 4/12th Frontier Force from divisional reserve to reinforce the northern portion of the line. The Frontier Force was given orders to counter-attack the Japanese who were threatening to outflank the 16th Brigade. On the afternoon of 19 February two companies advanced to drive the Japanese off a jungle-covered ridge overlooking Paya. The weather was hot and thirst was a constant problem. Skirmishing and steady Japanese mortar fire caused many casualties; the Frontier Force's losses were twelve killed, forty wounded and three missing.[23]

General Hutton was following the Bilin engagement from his Rangoon headquarters. He summarised the situation for General Wavell and the War Office as follows:

> Present situation is that 17 Div. is holding line of Bilin River and has inflicted severe check on enemy which may hold him up for some time unless he has fresh troops available which appears probable. 17 Div. are mostly tired and have suffered a good many casualties. In event of fresh enemy offensive in the near future I cannot be certain of holding present positions though every effort will be made to do so. If this battle should go badly enemy might penetrate line of River Sittang without much difficulty and evacuation of Rangoon would become imminent possibility ... Probably the best that can be hoped for is that we shall be able to hold line of River Sittang possibly with bridgeheads on east bank.

Hutton added that to hold the Sittang line permanently, or to undertake an offensive, five divisions would be needed in Burma, as well as any Chinese forces present in the colony.[24]

Japanese commanders were also assessing the situation. On the whole the Japanese were impressed that their enemies were able to maintain a front at the Bilin river. General Iida wrote: 'Around Bilin we received strong and firm resistance by troops from the British mainland, King's Own Yorkshire, who fought fiercely.' The regimental history of the 214th Regiment wrote of the Bilin action:

> Soldiers of 214 Regiment, who had been fighting against the Chinese army, were for the first time attacked by aeroplanes and fought against an army with modern equipment ... Repeated training in close quarter attack on tanks and armoured cars proved fully effective and so they did not find them too frightening. What

really surprised them was the vast amount of shelling and the amount of British small arms fire. This was something they had never experienced or imagined. The Japanese army stressed saving ammunition. Even the artillery tried to hit its target with only one shell. In contrast the British fired a barrage which was like ploughing the land with shells.[25]

Western armies had come to rely on firepower to a far greater extent than the bayonet.

General Sakurai continued to drive forward his 33rd Division in a manner that bordered on recklessness. On the morning of 19 February the division's 214th Regiment was in action at the northern end of the front around Paya and Danyingon. The 215th Regiment had a detachment near Bilin village; the rest of the regiment was in reserve. But after the 55th Division began to arrive on the coastal flank, Sakurai ordered the main body of Colonel Harada's 215th Regiment to march northwards. The regiment was ordered to cross the river to Ahonwa during the night of 19/20 February, and take up station on the northern flank of the 214th Regiment. This manoeuvre would turn the left flank of the British force at Bilin.[26]

It was clear to British commanders that the Japanese were threatening both flanks of the 17th Division. If the division remained in position along the Bilin, there was the risk of the Japanese cutting the line of retreat. General Hutton visited divisional headquarters at Kyaikto early on 19 February; he gave Smyth permission to retire westwards to the Sittang river. The Sittang was thirty miles west of the Bilin river. On the evening of 19 February Smyth ordered a withdrawal to Kyaikto, seventeen miles to the rear, for the following day. Preparations to retreat began that evening. This was to be the first phase of a two-step retreat to the Sittang.

The 48th Brigade was to be the 17th Indian Division's rearguard; it was to cover the retreat from the line of the Thebyu river. The 16th Brigade was to withdraw first and march or motor to Kyaikto, where the 46th Brigade was located. The Japanese may have intercepted the wireless orders for Smyth's division to withdraw from the Bilin river, but, nevertheless, the 16th Brigade successfully broke contact with Japanese forces during the hours of darkness and set out for Kyaikto. The transport and wounded pulled out at 2 a.m. on 20 February; the infantry began to depart at 4.30 a.m. The 16th Brigade reached its destination near Kyaikto after a long march; weary soldiers rested as best they could under the rubber trees of the Boyagyi estate.[27]

A heavy mist had risen near the coast during the night and this helped the troops of the 48th Brigade get clear of the Bilin river the following morning. The 8th Burma Rifles was first to depart and pulled out before dawn. The retreat of the Jats, however, was a more difficult affair. At 3 a.m. a Bren carrier had arrived at the Jats headquarters with orders for Lieutenant-Colonel

Godley to report to brigade HQ to discuss preparations for the retreat. Godley declined to attend as his battalion had been probed earlier in the night by Japanese patrols that had crossed the river near the demolished bridge. Radio failures meant that the finalised brigade plan for the scheduled retreat did not reach Godley until about 10 a.m. in the morning. The Jats only got clear of the Bilin front around midday. RAF Blenheims and Hurricanes bombed positions near the river and inflicted a small number of friendly casualties.[28]

The rest of the 48th Brigade had waited for the Jats at the shallow Thebyu river. In the early evening Brigadier Hugh-Jones received a letter from Smyth:

> You know best the condition of your troops and the local situation. I leave you therefore a free hand to harbour for the night wherever you wish. I think however you should make a big effort to get west of the Thebyuchaung River before dark if you can. I have sent you some M.T. [motor transport] to assist. The sooner you get into Kyaikto the better I shall be pleased, as we have still unlocated parties of Japanese in the coastal area and there may of course be other parties working round the flanks. When we do get you right back, I hope very much to be able to give you a little rest.[29]

A detachment of the rearguard on the railway was involved in a skirmish with Japanese troops before pulling out. Near Thebyuchaung there was another brush involving Hugh-Jones and his brigade-major when they tried to retrieve a lost map case. The bridge over the Thebyu river was blown by sappers; the troops marched or motored westwards.[30] The 2/5th Gurkhas arrived at Kyaikto at 2 a.m.; the 8th Burma Rifles and 1/3rd Gurkhas marched in shortly after that time.

On 20 February Hutton reported to Wavell: 'After further severe fighting have had to order withdrawal 17th Division behind River Sittang which will be difficult operation. Troops very tired, have had heavy casualties, and most have fought well.'[31] The Bilin engagement had held up XV Army's advance for four days. It was in many respects a fine rearguard action, despite the alarms and muddle that a fighting retreat inevitably involves. With one exception, all of the 17th Division's battalions had fought well against both regiments of the Japanese 33rd Division and one of the 55th Division's regiments.

Burma Army's casualties at the Bilin river had been within reason for a divisional-scale battle; for instance the heavily engaged 1/4th Gurkhas had only lost seven dead. Casualties in Smyth's division added up to roughly 350 killed, wounded and missing. For the main Japanese units engaged, the 214th Regiment lost twenty-five killed, including the commander of II Battalion; fourteen were counted dead in the 215th Regiment; the casualties of the 143rd Regiment and other units are unknown.[32]

The Japanese did not aggressively pursue Smyth's rearguard during 20 February, which made a difficult retreat on a typically humid Burmese day a good deal easier. But the danger for the 17th Indian Division had by no means ended. Once it was clear that the British were retreating from the Bilin river, Sakurai ordered his 215th Regiment to set out directly for the Sittang bridge by way of tracks through the jungle. The main body of the 214th Regiment was to advance westwards from Bilin to Kyaikto as quickly as possible. By nightfall of 20 February Sakurai's advance guard was on a track only a few miles north-east of the rearmost troops of their opponent. On the railway Japanese troops of the 55th Division with elephants carrying baggage were spotted by airmen three miles north-west of Taungzun.[33]

On 20 February, whilst the 17th Division was withdrawing from Bilin to Kyaikto, General Hutton held a conference at Rangoon. Governor Dorman-Smith and Air Vice-Marshal Stevenson were amongst those in attendance. Hutton told the conference that the situation was crumbling east of the Sittang river; a renewed enemy offensive might cause the defence to collapse and place Rangoon in jeopardy.

The convoy carrying the 7th Armoured Brigade was due at Rangoon the following day. This was a cause for optimism amid the gloom of constant retreat. The armoured brigade would give British commanders in the field a mobile force with which to parry the thrusts of the fast-marching Japanese light infantry. Hutton, however, believed this fresh reinforcement would probably bring about no more than a temporary stabilization of the front. The conference agreed to accept the part of the convoy carrying fighting units, but turn back those ships on which administrative units were embarked. Stevenson added that the redeployment of RAF units to eastern India and central Burma was under consideration. The airfields near Rangoon would then be used as advanced landing grounds.

General Wavell at Java, the War Office in London, and India Command in Delhi were sent cables by Hutton informing them of the views he had expressed at the conference. Hutton added that he had begun to evacuate Rangoon; the scheme of demolitions planned for the city's key installations and the oil refineries was ready for activation.[34]

8

Confusion at Kyaikto

By the early hours of 21 February all three brigades of the 17th Indian Division were in the vicinity of Kyaikto. The retreat from the Bilin river to Kyaikto had been exhausting, and the weary troops spent what remained of the night bivouacked amid rubber and jungle around the village.

The previous evening the 2nd Battalion Duke of Wellington's Regiment had arrived at Kyaikto to join Smyth's division. The Yorkshiremen of the Dukes had only landed at Rangoon six days earlier, after a hasty mobilisation for overseas service at Peshawar, a military station near the Khyber pass in north-western India. A week-long rail journey had been needed to reach Madras, after which it had taken another week to sail to Rangoon. On the voyage from Madras soldiers fired anti-tank rifle rounds into the sea to practice with an unfamiliar weapon. News of Singapore's fall was broadcast on the ship's radio at sea. From Rangoon the Dukes were sent to a hutted camp at Mingaladon, alongside which Tomahawk fighters used the main road as an auxiliary landing strip. Jeeps for the battalion were obtained from Lend Lease stocks.[1]

After the Dukes' arrival at Kyaikto from Mingaladon, Captain A.D. Firth, the battalion's signals officer, observed:

> Around us there was incessant small-arms automatic fire, probably nothing at all. I was sent, in my new jeep, to brigade headquarters to report our arrival. There was a steady stream of transport passing through westwards toward the Sittang River bridge. It was nearly dark. I asked this officer in front of a truck if I was now near the front line. His tired answer was: 'My dear chap, this convoy is the front line.'[2]

The Dukes joined the 46th Brigade, though one rifle company was detached to help guard the Sittang bridge. There would be a certain amount of hindsight criticism that the whole battalion might best have been employed in a bridgehead position on the eastern bank of the river.

General Smyth's headquarters now had to plan the next stage of the retreat to the Sittang river. The all-weather road from Tenasserim ended at Kyaikto. The fifteen-mile track from Kyaikto to Sittang village ran across paddy for a couple of miles and then skirted the northern side of Boyagyi rubber estate, which was situated between the track and the railway to the south. The track then penetrated dense jungle until reaching the village of Mokpalin. A trace had been cut through the thick jungle with the future intention of constructing a finished road. Scrub and trees were cleared to either side of the rough, forty-yard-wide trace.[3] There was little water along the route and the track was inches deep in loose dirt. Marching men and vehicles would inevitably beat up clouds of dust that would be visible to marauding airmen with hostile intentions.

The railway line from Bilin followed a coastal route and only joined up with the road at Mokpalin; from that village, after continuing a mile to the north, the railway turned west and ran through a cutting towards the bridge over the Sittang. The road also headed north from Mokpalin, and looped to the north-east around a ridge to reach Sittang village on the north side of the ridge. A power-driven ferry service operated just north of the bridge near the village.

To the immediate south of Sittang village, and east of the bridge, was a 500-yard ridge line surmounted by a pagoda at the western end, and a great image of Buddha at the eastern end. The Sittang railway bridge had eleven spans and did not carry a separate roadway for vehicles. The river's bed was particularly wide to the immediate north and south of the bridge. The river current was strong in the rainy season but relatively sedate in the dry season. The eastern and exposed end of the Sittang bridge was defended only by the 3rd Burma Rifles, which was 250 strong, and the detached company of Dukes.

There was the obvious risk that the Japanese might push past the northern flank of the retreating 17th Division and head straight for the vital bridge. Brigadier Ekin, who had been at Kyaikto for a number of days, had suggested to Smyth during 20 February that his 46th Brigade should hasten back to cover the relatively unguarded bridge. Ekin had received vague reports that there were Japanese somewhere in the jungle to the north-east. Ekin's battered but rested brigade had not been involved in the recent round of fighting. Smyth disagreed – according to Captain Lunt: 'He [Smyth] said he must hold Kyaikto as a firm base until both the other brigades were through. He agreed with Ekin that the enemy might well try to outflank him on the north but he had sent out reconnaissance troops to provide him with prior warning of any such attempt.'[4] Smyth wanted to know if the force retreating from Bilin was being closely pursued before firmly deciding what to do next. As a precaution, late on 20 February Smyth ordered the 4/12th Frontier Force and a field company of sappers to head back and reinforce the Sittang bridgehead the following morning.

The troops that Smyth had dispatched to keep watch in the jungle to the north of Kyaikto belonged to the Burma Frontier Force. Two company-strength columns of BFF were deployed along a track running north-eastwards from

Kyaikto to the hamlet of Kinmun, which was six miles north-east of Kyaikto. The BFF's orders were to remain on that line for two days, after which they were to withdraw along jungle paths towards Mokpalin whilst continuing to patrol the jungle north of the Kyaikto-Sittang track.[5]

Before the main body of the 17th Division could cross the Sittang river, it would be necessary to send the division's motor transport across the bridge. This was easier said than done as the railway bridge had yet to be converted to carry motor vehicles.[6] Some transport could be back-loaded on the power ferries near Sittang village, but most vehicles would need to use the bridge. It was an oversight to leave the task of converting the bridge until the eleventh hour, but until someone in authority made the decision to stop running trains across the bridge to Kyaikto the engineers could not set about the task.

At this time the divisional CRE (Chief Royal Engineer), Colonel A.E. Armitage, had a number of pressing tasks on hand. The 60th Field Company had already been sent back across the Sittang to work on a bridge over the Waw canal in anticipation of the arrival of the tanks of the 7th Armoured Brigade. The 24th Field Company had orders to cross the bridge and gather together all civilian boats and sampans on the river. The 1st Burma Auxiliary Force Artisan Works Company was given the difficult task of converting the bridge from rail to motor traffic. It was planned to bolt sleepers either side of the rail lines to create parallel pavements wide enough for a vehicle's wheels to drive along with care. This vital task was not likely to be completed for another twenty-four hours.

The new day of 21 February was to be full of drama. About dawn advanced divisional headquarters at Kyaikto came under sniper fire, which served as a reminder that the Japanese were not far away. The troops bivouacked around Kyaikto had sunk down to sleep knowing little of the locations of neighbouring units. Japanese patrols, yelling wildly, fired into the camp from the east and south. These Japanese were from the I/143rd Battalion, which was advancing along the coast from the mouth of the Bilin.[7] Captain A.H. Macrae of the 1/3rd Gurkhas recalled: 'We were roused by machine-gun fire nearby. In a few seconds there was pandemonium. Some over-zealous, trigger-happy sentries opened up with Brens, not realising that we were inside a harbour protected by other troops. Bullets were flying about in all directions.'[8] Panicked soldiers sent coloured tracer flickering wildly into the jungle around Kyaikto. The Japanese raiding party withdrew. Macrae found that his senior VCO, Subedar Amar Singh, had been wounded in the leg and would require evacuation.

After order was restored, the 4/12th Frontier Force departed for the bridge in motor transport. This was in accordance with plans made the previous evening. The Frontier Force was followed at 10 a.m. by Smyth and his advanced headquarters, which was to halt near Mokpalin Quarries, where the depleted Baluchis were guarding a ration dump and the rear echelon of divisional headquarters. Mokpalin Quarries was still five to six miles short of the bridge. The Malerkotla Field Company and divisional supply and transport troops followed behind Smyth's headquarters group. The leading battalion of the 48th Brigade was also ordered to march for Mokpalin Quarries. The rest of the brigade would march part of that distance.

The 46th Brigade became the division's rearguard at Kyaikto. The brigade's infantry and supporting mountain batteries adjusted positions to cover the line of the Kadat Chaung and watch for pursuing Japanese troops. The Kadat Chaung was a stream on the western fringe of Kyaikto. The 16th Brigade was to spend 21 February in Boyagyi rubber estate, three miles north-west of Kyaikto. The divisional plan was for all three brigades to cross the Sittang river the following day of 22 February. But, in the meantime, two of the division's brigades would remain mostly stationary during 21 February, whilst the other brigade – the 48th Brigade – made only a relatively short march westwards. The coastal railway route was ignored as motor transport would not be able to cross the mouth of a small stream to the south of Mokpalin Quarries.

It is remarkable that at least one brigade did not march the full distance from Kyaikto to the Sittang bridge on 21 February to form a stronger bridgehead garrison. Smyth may have been discouraged from ordering a more rapid retreat as the engineers were still working to convert the Sittang bridge to carry road traffic.[9] According to the regimental history of the KOYLI: 'This halt at Kyaikto astonished and worried officers. With the Japanese moving steadily round the inland flank by jungle paths they felt it was vital to get back to the Sittang as quickly as possible, moving by night as well as day.'[10] The failure of the Japanese to quickly pursue the division along the main Bilin-Kyaikto road seems to have lulled Smyth and his staff into thinking there was no need for haste in the final leg of the march to the Sittang bridge.

Meanwhile the Japanese were busy laying their own plans for the next stage of the campaign. General Sakurai's 33rd Division was the force detailed to capture the Sittang bridge. The 214th Regiment's I and II Battalions were ordered to push westwards on the road from Bilin to Kyaikto; they had borne the brunt of the Bilin engagement, and were making slow progress for that reason. The III/214th Battalion and 215th Regiment were relatively fresh, and the most immediate threat to Smyth's division. These troops were moving along tracks to the north of the main Bilin-Kyaikto road. The 215th Regiment was marching via Kinmun and intended to thrust straight for the bridge. The III/214th Battalion was planning to cross the track running from Kyaikto to

Kinmun, and hook down to cut the track midway between Kyaikto and the bridge. The flanking movement by these Japanese troops in the jungle was not due to strike until the morning of 22 February. On the coast the leading regiment of the 55th Division continued its slow but steady march westwards.

At 9 a.m. on 21 February Brigadier Hugh-Jones of the 48th Brigade held a conference for the commanders of his units to plan the day's march. After some discussion it was decided that the 1/4th Gurkhas would lead out the brigade's march to Mokpalin Quarries; the 2/5th Gurkhas were to follow and halt for the night four miles short of the quarries; the rear battalion, the 1/3rd Gurkhas, was to bivouac seven miles short of the quarries. Lack of water along the track was the reason for spacing out the units. The 12th Mountain Battery, brigade headquarters and brigade transport accompanied the infantry columns.[11]

The brigade marched out at 11 a.m. The day was hot and dry; lorries jerked forward in low gear; marching troops wrapped pugarees or clothing around their heads to keep the dust out. Refugees were on the track in places and bullock carts had to be pushed aside to make way for the military columns. Where the jungle encroached upon the track the airless humidity of the climate bore down oppressively on man and beast; a shortage of water caused constant thirst. The dust clouds beaten up by men, animals and vehicles were clearly visible from the air.

The first mile leading north-westwards from camp was over paddy plain. The 1/4th Gurkha Rifles was strafed by four aircraft whilst crossing the rice fields soon after the march started; these were Japanese aircraft.[12] The troops and mules marched on along the red, dusty track. During the afternoon the Gurkhas were strafed by three fighters with American Volunteer Group markings. At 5.30 p.m. the battalion finally reached Mokpalin Quarries; divisional headquarters was nearby. Lieutenant-Colonel Lentaigne reported the attacks by Allied aircraft and had as evidence a cannon shell of American manufacture ejected from a fighter on a strafing run. The air liaison officer was sceptical; he suggested that the Japanese might be using RAF aircraft captured in Malaya, or Thai aircraft with which the troops were unfamiliar.[13]

The 2/5th Gurkha Rifles was the next battalion in the column; the unit first came under air attack at midday and then at intervals for the rest of the afternoon. Some of the aircraft had British markings. Tree-top level strafing halted the battalion's column from time to time; streams of tracer bullets scythed through branches to send men scurrying to shelter in ditches or behind the base of trees. Major E.F. Townsend and Captain A.C. Bird were wounded and eight Gurkha other ranks were killed or wounded by the air attacks.[14]

At the rear of the brigade column came the 1/3rd Gurkhas. According to Captain Macrae:

> Progress was slow and tedious. The road was deep in dust and the outskirts of Kyaikto were in ruins and still burning. After a while we came out of the jungle and spread out over a plain about a mile wide before returning to the road, which then wound through scrub jungle. Whilst crossing the plain, we watched dog-fights between our own and enemy planes. The Japs soon made off. For an hour or so things were quiet. The column plodded on. It was very hot. Then came the sound of aircraft. They were British – at least, they had British markings – but a few moments later they opened up on the column with everything they had ... The rest of the day was hell – every few minutes aircraft would appear and shoot up the column, which would halt and take cover in the jungle, firing at the planes with rifles and Brens.[15]

Captain B.G. Kinloch of the 1/3rd Gurkhas wrote of the air attacks:

> The earth heaved and shuddered under the muffled thud and roar of fragmentation bombs. The screams of injured mules ripped and torn by broken pieces of flying steel mingled with the groans and cries of sorely wounded and dying men. An ambulance was burning fiercely nearby, the Sikh driver cut in half by a machine gun burst, the occupants dead. Two young Gurkha soldiers were standing solidly in the open behind the funeral pyre of the ambulance manning a tripod-mounted Bren gun and sending a steady stream of bullets into the flickering guns of the howling fighters.[16]

Air attacks caused mules to bolt, along with the rations, mortars and wireless sets they were carrying. The civilian drivers of the motor ambulance convoy fled into the jungle; the keys to the ignitions of the loaded ambulances vanished with them.

Whilst the 48th Brigade marched westwards, the 16th Brigade spent the day at Boyagyi estate and also suffered from friendly fire delivered down from the sky. The regimental history of the 7th Gurkhas noted: 'At first we thought that they were Thai planes whose markings were similar to ours: then, when Blenheims joined in the attack, we thought they must be planes captured by the Japanese at the fall of Singapore.' The strafing and bombing by the RAF was 'totally beyond the comprehension of our discouraged men'.[17] Lieutenant D.H. West of the 1/7th Gurkhas stated:

> It is impossible emphasise the effect these attacks had on the Indian [and Gurkha] troops. They had reached a stage where they could identify both our planes and the Japs and to be fired upon by planes bearing our markings completely shattered their convictions, the more so since the British officers were at a loss to give a satisfactory explanation.[18]

According to Captain Firth of the 2nd Dukes: 'My baptism of fire in World War II was from the front end of a Wellington [Blenheim] about two hundred

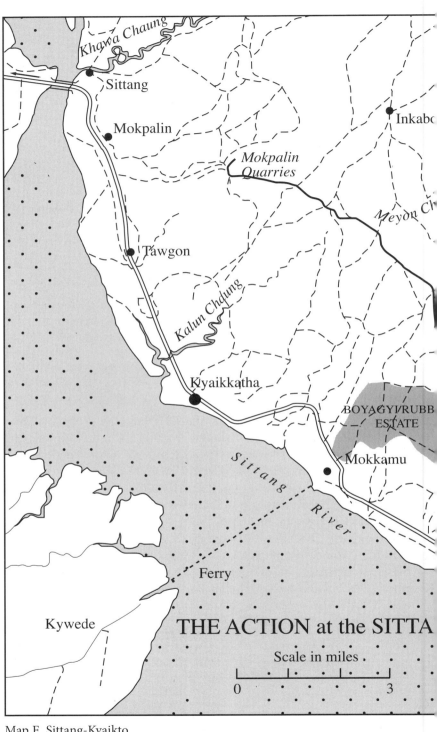

Map F Sittang-Kyaikto

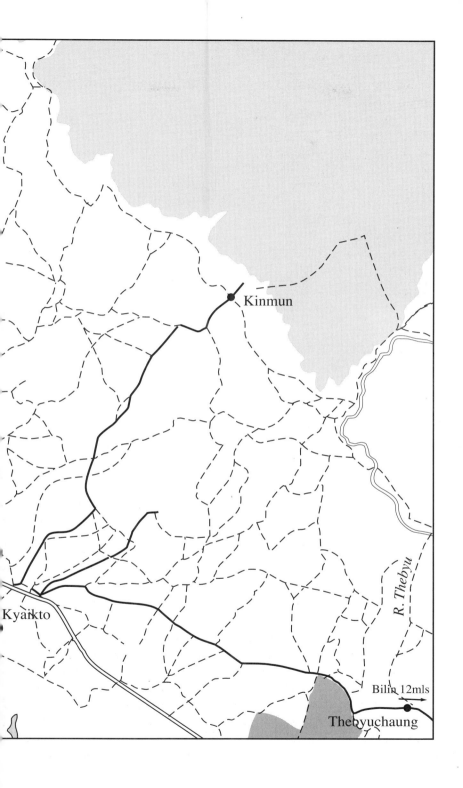

Kinmun

R. Thebyu

Kyaikto

Bilin 12mls

Thebyuchaung

feet above me and coming straight at me with guns blazing.'[19] At nightfall the air attacks on the 17th Division came to an end.

The bombing and strafing of Smyth's division by Allied aircraft was a tragic set of events. What had gone wrong? It had certainly not helped that the troops on the ground had no direct radio contact with Allied aviators. Army officers had used the railway telephone to try to tell RAF headquarters that their aircraft were attacking friendly troops, but the message did not get through to those who mattered. It was speculated that the pilots had been ordered to attack anything moving to the east of the Sittang river? Or perhaps the RAF had been given information that the army was moving along the coast, and the Japanese were using the roads and tracks inland? When returning aircrew commented that the transport had looked suspiciously British they were told it had probably been captured by the Japanese earlier in the campaign.

What had transpired was that an aerial reconnaissance report had been received by British commanders that a column of 300 enemy vehicles was on a track leading north from Kyaikto to Kinmun. The 17th Division's headquarters accepted the report and requested a RAF air strike. Air-Vice Marshal Stevenson responded willingly and all available fighters and bombers were sent out on the strike. Aircrew were instructed to attack targets to the east of a north-south bomb-line drawn on maps. The bomb-line was close to Kyaikto but east of the village.[20]

In practice, however, it was too difficult for low-flying pilots travelling at 300 miles per hour to tell friend from foe in a jungle-covered landscape, especially when they were constantly scanning the skies above for Japanese fighters. The jungle between the Bilin and Sittang rivers all looked much the same. Twin-engine Blenheim bombers escorted by Hurricanes and Tomahawks had mistakenly attacked Smyth's division on the march towards Mokpalin Quarries, or sheltering in Boyagyi rubber estate, at regular intervals during the afternoon. The eight machine guns mounted by a Hurricane made it an effective ground attack aircraft. After the aircraft returned to base from the initial mission, they were re-armed and re-fuelled for further attacks on the jungle around Kyaikto.

One particular Allied fighter pilot took part in three sorties against traffic on the roads between the Sittang and Bilin rivers. Japanese aircraft interfered with the first sortie; fifty trucks were strafed on the second trip. On the third sortie, 'I headed north to the main road on which I had seen so many trucks in my previous mission. This time I was at treetop level, and then I found the Japanese [British-Indian] motorised column. I strafed it from one end to the other. Some vehicles already were on fire and bombed out from the previous RAF bombing.' The troops on the ground returned fire and many British and American aircraft returned to base peppered with bullet holes. For the soldiers the experience was terrifying and memorable.

Air Vice-Marshal Stevenson was at first inclined to disbelieve reports of air attacks on Allied troops. He later wrote in his dispatch on the campaign: 'After an exhaustive enquiry I have failed to reach a firm conclusion that our aircraft did, in fact, bomb our own troops at this time and place.' It was suggested in RAF circles that the army had confused Japanese Ki-21 Mitsubishis for Blenheims.[21] But the original report of transport in the Kyaikto area could only have been sightings of British traffic. At this time there were no Japanese motor vehicles forward of Bilin. Indeed, there were few Japanese lorries west of Moulmein, apart from captured transport, due to the difficulties of the road stretching back into Thailand.

During the afternoon of 21 February, whilst the air attacks were underway, important developments overtook the detachment of Burma Frontier Force sent by Smyth into the jungle north of the track from Kyaikto to Mokpalin. As described earlier, the BFF detachment, which was divided into two company-strength columns, had been deployed on a track that ran north-eastwards from Kyaikto to Kinmun on 20 February. The first column was between those two places; the second column was in the jungle to the north of Kinmun. The BFF commander had orders to remain in position till the afternoon of the 22nd and then withdraw towards Mokpalin. The southern column, however, was heavily engaged by Japanese troops about 2.30 p.m. on 21 February; the northern column also clashed with Japanese patrols around that time. Both columns retired independently along jungle paths, only to again collide with Japanese forces near Mokpalin the following day. The BFF detachment then veered north to cross the Sittang seven miles north of the bridge and head onwards to Pegu. Meaningful reports of these clashes were slow to reach divisional headquarters; only late in the evening of 21 February was something learnt about what had happened.[22] Such a vital task might best have been given to regular troops in the first place.

By dusk of 21 February divisional headquarters, 48th Brigade headquarters and the 1/4th Gurkhas had joined the Baluchis at Mokpalin Quarries. The 1/3rd and 2/5th Gurkhas had also successfully completed the short marches planned for the day despite the air attacks. More importantly, the 4/12th Frontier Force and the Malerkotla Field Company had reached the Sittang bridge; these troops joined the slender bridgehead held by the 3rd Burma Rifles and the detached company of Dukes.

Lieutenant-Colonel Edward of the Frontier Force had gone ahead of his battalion to reconnoitre the east bank of the river near the Sittang bridge. Upon arrival at the bridge, Edward was disheartened to find there were no prepared defences, however, he made plans to put his troops on the Pagoda-Buddha ridge adjacent to the eastern end of the bridge. This plan made good sense, but it was not put into practice as the Frontier Force column had been badly delayed by the air attacks on the track between Mokpalin and Kyaikto. The air attacks and roughness of the track caused the march to take much longer than expected. In consequence, darkness fell before the Frontier Force battalion could be sited on the Pagoda-Buddha ridge. Local commanders decided to leave the detachment of 3rd Burma Rifles on the ridge overnight; the troops of the Frontier Force could move onto the feature sometime the following morning.[23]

At 7 p.m. Colonel Armitage, the divisional Chief Royal Engineer, instructed the Malerkotla Field Company, a unit of the Indian States Force, and the only field company still east of the river, to prepare the Sittang rail bridge for demolition. Malerkotla was a princely state in the Punjab. The sappers marched towards the bridge in the darkness of early evening.[24] The divisional transport was gathered on the road between the bridge and Mokpalin village.

At Rangoon General Hutton reported to Wavell on 21 February: 'Withdrawal from Bilin line was carried out without being heavily pressed. That severe casualties inflicted on enemy evidenced by tentative way enemy followed up.' But this was only one of several important cables flying backwards and forwards between British headquarters at this time. At Java Wavell had been surprised to receive Hutton's gloomy message of the previous day warning of the possible loss of Rangoon. Wavell had replied early on the 21st, 'why on earth should resistance on the Sittang River collapse ... What is the matter that these sudden pessimistic reports are given'. Later in the morning Wavell signalled Hutton:

> There seems on surface no reason whatever for decision practically to abandon fight for Rangoon and continue retrograde movement. You have checked enemy and he must be tired and have suffered heavy casualties. No sign that he is in superior strength. You must stop all further withdrawal and counter-attack whenever possible. Whole fate of war in Far East depends on most resolute and determined action. You have little air opposition at present and should attack enemy with all air forces available.[25]

Furthermore, Wavell signalled Hutton that evening:

> You should draw up at once plans for counter-offensive with Armoured Brigade and all available troops. If at all possible Sittang River must be crossed and counter-offensive be made east of river. In any event plans must be made to hit enemy, and hit him hard, if he ever succeeds in crossing. He will go back quick in face of determined attack.[26]

Wavell was desperate to keep the port of Rangoon open to receive whatever reinforcements could be scraped together for Burma.

In London the Chiefs of Staff had also been reading Hutton's reports. On 21 February they directed that Rangoon should be held only as long as it helped keep open the supply route to China; if Rangoon became isolated, the garrison was not to be sacrificed merely to delay the Japanese. The Chiefs of Staff also ordered that Burma be transferred from ABDA Command to India Command; the Chiefs felt that Wavell was too isolated at Java to continue to manage a fast-moving campaign 2000 miles away in Burma.[27]

Hutton's cabled assessments of the situation over the previous fortnight had made depressing reading. Back on 18 February the Viceroy of India, the Marquess of Linlithgow, had cabled the Secretary of State for India, Leo Amery: 'Our troops are not fighting with proper spirit. I have not the least doubt that this is in great part due to lack of drive and inspiration from the top.' In response Amery cabled Governor Dorman-Smith: 'Have heard doubts cast of Hutton's quality as fighting leader. Have you any misgivings as to his being the right man?'

Prime Minister Churchill also read a copy of the Viceroy's telegram to Amery. Churchill passed a copy by cable to Wavell and asked: 'The Chief of the Imperial General Staff [General Sir Alan Brooke] wants to know what you think. If you concur with the Viceroy, he will send [Lieutenant-General Sir Harold] Alexander at once.'[28] Alexander was GOC Southern Command in England and a personal favourite of the Prime Minister.

Wavell immediately replied to Churchill that the poor performance of Burma Army was of great concern to him:

> Leaders of real drive and inspiration are few ... Hutton has plenty of determination behind quiet manner and will never get rattled but lacks power of personal inspiration. At time I selected him reorganization of whole military machine in Burma was imperative, I knew he would do this excellently and considered also he would be resolute and skilful commander. I have no reason to think otherwise but agree that Alexander's forceful personality might act as a stimulus to troops. Dorman-Smith when I last visited Rangoon spoke well of Hutton and said he had impressed his ministers.[29]

At first Wavell was reluctant to replace Hutton; but after re-reading Hutton's recent reports Wavell agreed it would be best to install Alexander at Rangoon. It would, however, take a journey of many days to get Alexander from wartime Britain to South-east Asia.

Wavell sent his recommendation to London on 21 February and this cable crossed a message from the War Office informing him that Alexander had already received his orders to depart for Burma. Churchill later conceded, 'if we could not send an army we could at any rate send a man'. Hutton was to be superseded as he appeared to his peers to be overly pessimistic, and that might adversely affect the morale of his army. Hutton was to remain in Burma as Alexander's Chief of Staff, which was a recognition that there had been no specific failure by Hutton in his conduct of operations.[30]

At this time General Hutton was unaware that his position was under review. On 21 February Hutton flew to Lashio, in north-east Burma, for another meeting with Chiang Kai-shek. Hutton's extensive responsibilities stretched to conducting high-level inter-Allied negotiations with minimal direction. Hutton was eager to hasten the arrival of Chinese forces to relieve the pressure on his army. He had received news that Chiang was likely to land at Lashio on a return journey from India. The twenty-four-hour period during which Hutton would be absent from his headquarters proved to be a vital one.[31]

9

The Sittang Bridge

Night fell on 21 February with the bulk of the 17th Indian Division not much closer to the Sittang river than when dawn had broken at the start of the day. In stark contrast Japanese forces had spent the day marching rapidly through the jungle to the north of the Kyaikto-Sittang track. Smyth's division was in considerable danger: the 48th Brigade was strung out along the track between Mokpalin Quarries and Boyagyi rubber estate; the 16th Brigade was at Boyagyi; the 46th Brigade was still on the western outskirts of Kyaikto. The divisional plan was for the infantry brigades to close up to the bridge during 22 February; they would cross the bridge once the transport had passed safely to the western side of the river. It was expected that the conversion of the Sittang rail bridge to carry road vehicles would be completed during the night of 21/22 February.

After nightfall Smyth was visited by a staff officer from Army Headquarters. Smyth recalled that the officer had 'important news … [Army Headquarters] had received information that the Japanese might make parachute landings early next morning on the open ground to the west of the river to try and take the bridge from that side.'[1] Smyth was also informed that the 7th Armoured Brigade was disembarking at Rangoon.

The staff officer who spoke to Smyth was probably sent by Brigadier H.L. Davies, who was Chief of Staff at Hutton's Rangoon headquarters. There had been reliable reports of Japanese parachute troops in Thailand and a warning to Smyth was a sensible precaution. The parachute regiment allocated to XXV Army in Malaya had been profitably dropped on Palembang in Sumatra a week previously. XV Army's parachute regiment, however, was sunk in the South China Sea after an explosion on board the ship. The troops were rescued and taken onwards to Bangkok, but their parachutes were lost in the accident and no replacements were available.[2]

The headquarters of the 48th Brigade and the 1/4th Gurkhas had halted for the night at Mokpalin Quarries, close to divisional headquarters. Smyth sent for Lieutenant-Colonel Lentaigne of the Gurkhas. Lentaigne's unit was ordered to hasten westwards and cross the river to protect the bridge from parachute assault.[3] The Gurkhas marched at 4 a.m.; Lentaigne was to take the company of Dukes under command after they had crossed the bridge.

At Boyagyi rubber estate Brigadiers Jones and Ekin had met the previous evening to discuss the situation. A number of senior officers of the 16th and 46th Brigades were keen immediately to press on for the Sittang. The 48th Brigade, however, was blocking the track ahead; the 46th Brigade was also the designated divisional rearguard and could not cast that duty aside. Definite instructions had not been received from divisional headquarters. The brigadiers decided to maintain their positions during the night. The transport and armoured Bren carriers would leave camp before dawn, and be followed by the 16th Brigade at 6 a.m. and then by the rearguard 46th Brigade.

At 1 a.m. on 22 February Brigadiers Jones and Ekin received a radio message from divisional headquarters that a strong Japanese force was moving through the jungle past their northern flank. The news had belatedly reached the divisional staff of the BFF detachment's collision with the Japanese in the jungle to the north of Kyaikto the previous day. Jones and Ekin were advised to set out for the Sittang as soon as possible. But the brigadiers at Boyagyi estate decided there was little to gain from a change of plan on a dark night given the confusion that would cause; they decided to wait the few extra hours for daylight.[4]

At the Sittang bridge motor transport driving without lights finally began to roll across the converted structure at 2 a.m. Proceedings went well at first but an accident occurred a couple of hours later. A three-ton lorry ran off the bridge sleepers and became jammed in the girders. The high girders of the bridge meant that the vehicle could not be swiftly tipped into the river. The sappers worked by lamp and moonlight to clear the blockage under the supervision of Colonel Armitage; this delay cost a further two hours of valuable time.[5]

As the eastern horizon was colouring with the light of dawn, Lentaigne arrived at the bridge with his Gurkhas. One Gurkha company, however, had lost its way in the darkness and was yet to arrive. Brigadier Cowan told Lentaigne: 'Thank God you've arrived. Get over the bridge as quickly as possible.'[6] There was a narrow catwalk on the north side of the bridge outside the girders. The Gurkhas crossed by the catwalk and joined the company of Dukes that had already crossed to the west bank. This meant that the slender bridgehead on the east bank was held only by the 4/12th Frontier Force and 3rd Burma Rifles.

Full daylight on 22 February revealed a long line of motor traffic waiting to cross the Sittang bridge. At 6.30 a.m. the bridge was cleared of the crashed lorry and reopened to traffic. An officer described the scene between Mokpalin and the river: 'Vehicles of all sorts including carriers and of many different units were all mixed up together. They were head to tail in a defile and in many cases had double banked on the road.'[7] The vehicles from Boyagyi began to arrive to join the jam, many vehicles overloaded.

After dawn General Smyth crossed the bridge to the west bank 'to have a look at the 1/4th Gurkha's anti-parachute positions and select positions for the brigades when they arrived'.[8] Divisional headquarters soon crossed the bridge as well. The headquarters of the 48th Brigade crossed at 8 a.m.[9]

Unbeknown to General Smyth, the Japanese scheme to cut off the 17th Indian Division from the Sittang bridge was on the verge of success. At this time the 33rd Division's 214th Regiment (less III Battalion) was taking the main road from Bilin to Kyaikto; from there the regiment was planning to march onwards to Mokpalin. The III/214th Battalion was marching through the jungle with the intention of blocking the track between Kyaikto and Mokpalin. On the coast the 55th Division's 143rd Regiment was advancing along the corridor formed by the railway line.

The direct thrust on the bridge, however, was in the hands of the 215th Regiment. By the early hours of 22 February an advanced guard comprising the I/215th Battalion and supporting artillery and engineer detachments had reached the village of Pyinkadogon, four to five miles to the east of Sittang village. The battalion's commander, Major Mugita, decided to swoop on the bridge without delay; he gave orders for his troops to press onwards without waiting for the rest of the regimental column.

Sittang village was to the immediate north-east of the bridge and to the north of Pagoda and Buddha Hills. When Japanese troops advanced on Sittang village they were met by hostile fire. Lieutenant Hashimoto's No. 1 Company veered southwards onto the slopes of Buddha Hill and swiftly took the feature against light opposition. Troops of the 3rd Burma Rifles on Buddha Hill collapsed in the face of the unexpected Japanese assault. Japanese troops pressed on to also gain footholds on parts of Pagoda Hill.[10]

At the Sittang bridge one of the next units waiting to cross was the 7/10th Baluch. At 8.30 a.m. the Baluchis were marching through the railway cutting towards the eastern end of the bridge when a burst of firing came from the jungle to the north-east.[11] Some of the Baluchis were hit; others scattered in all directions; the rest headed towards the river and made their way along the bank to the bridge. The machine gun fire seemed to have come from the slopes of Pagoda Hill, near the eastern end of the bridge. This meant that Japanese troops were on that vital feature. Lieutenant Randle of the Baluchis reported to the Frontier Force's commanding officer at the bridge. Randle was unimpressed that so little had been done to build up a prepared position to cover the division's jugular vein.

The Pagoda-Buddha ridge line overlooked Sittang village from the south. Japanese troops of the I/215th Battalion successfully attacked the village from the ridge, and swept onwards around the base of Pagoda Hill towards the bridge. A dressing station of a field ambulance was quickly overrun and startled soldiers rushed for the bridge ahead of the Japanese. Colonel MacKenzie, the division's chief medical officer, his deputy, Major McLeod, and a number of others were taken prisoner. MacKenzie recalled that he was taken prisoner by a Japanese lieutenant, brandishing a revolver, who shouted in good English: 'Hands up. Keep them up. Come here.'[12] Smyth had been talking with MacKenzie only minutes previously; the general had declined a cup of tea and was half-way across the bridge when the firing broke out.[13] The advancing Japanese almost reached the bridge but were shot down or driven off by Indian soldiers firing automatic weapons.

The Japanese attack put out of action the motor ferry service at Sittang village by rendering the east bank landing stage unusable. A section of the 12th Indian Mountain Battery had just crossed the river in a small steamer when the Japanese attacked. As the vessel reached the west bank it came under small arms and mortar fire that set it ablaze. The gunners rescued their loads and carried them into the jungle. A naik was later awarded the Indian Order of Merit for his bravery, though he died three days later from injuries incurred in the engagement.

British officers had planned the previous evening to send the 4/12th Frontier Force onto the Pagoda-Buddha feature in the morning, but that had not happened in time to prevent the sudden loss of the ridge. The Frontier Force, however, was nearby and ready for action; A and B Companies were ordered to counter-attack the ridge and regain the ground recently lost by the 3rd Burma Rifles. The Indian troops advanced rapidly, supported by the fire of three-inch mortars. Captain S.H.J.F. Manekshaw was seriously wounded at the head of A Company. He was hit in the stomach by a burst of machine gun fire and in danger of death. Manekshaw was awarded the Military Cross by a senior officer prior to his medical evacuation. In the fullness of time he would become a field-marshal of the Indian Army. The Frontier Force lost fifty casualties in the course of retaking Pagoda Hill. An attempt by the Frontier Force to push onwards to Buddha Hill broke down as by now three companies of Japanese troops, supported by two medium machine gun platoons, were ensconced on the feature.[14]

At 10 a.m. Brigadier Hugh-Jones of the 48th Brigade was ordered by Smyth to take command of all bridgehead troops. The main body of divisional headquarters moved rearwards to Abya to better maintain communications with Rangoon. Hugh-Jones deployed the units under his command to cover the eastern end of the bridge. The Frontier Force dug in on Pagoda Hill; D Company of the Dukes was ordered to occupy Bungalow Hill, to the south-east of the bridge; the bewildered 3rd Burma Rifles and Baluchis were re-assembled into some sort of order near the river bank. The missing C

Company of the 1/4th Gurkhas reached the bridge during the morning along the river bank from the south.

The previous day 300 sampans and local boats had been collected on the west bank of the river to stop them falling into Japanese hands. Late in the morning most of these boats were destroyed on the orders of the exhausted chief divisional engineer, Colonel Armitage. Troops used pickaxes to hack in the bottoms of the craft. Engineers were also busy setting explosive charges on the bridge.[15]

In the meantime more Japanese troops were approaching the bridge. The II/215th Battalion had reached the village of Pyinkadogon and was ready to support the I/215th Battalion, which had seized Buddha Hill. No. 8 Company was held back in reserve but the rest of II Battalion headed south-west through the scrub jungle towards Mokpalin.[16] Later in the day No. 8 Company was committed on the right flank of its parent battalion.

As the Japanese attack on the bridgehead was getting underway, on the track leading north-westwards from Kyaikto the nearest units were the 2/5th Gurkhas and 1/3rd Gurkhas. Lieutenant-Colonel Cameron's 2/5th Gurkhas had broken camp by 5 a.m.; the unit's motor vehicles drove on ahead of the marching column and crossed the bridge after daylight. The 1/3rd Gurkhas marched behind Cameron's unit along a track inches deep in dust. Cameron, mounted on a bicycle, rode ahead of his marching Gurkhas with a small escort. He found a column of vehicles stationary near Mokpalin; the road seemed to have been cut by the Japanese somewhere up ahead. There was no sign of the 48th Brigade's headquarters or the 1/4th Gurkhas. The main column of the 2/5th Gurkhas reached Mokpalin station; this was only two to three miles from the Sittang bridge.[17]

Cameron decided to secure Mokpalin and the patches of scrub on the high ground to the east of the village. The Gurkhas lacked mortar support as the mules carrying that equipment had stampeded into the jungle in an earlier incident. It was unclear how many Japanese troops were nearby. B Company was first into action; Jemadar Ranbahadur Gurung was killed at the head of his platoon as the village of stockaded houses and compounds was swiftly taken. The Gurkhas pushed onwards to reach a feature to the north of Mokpalin that became known as Outpost Hill. Beyond Outpost Hill was undulating, scrub-covered country leading to a ravine in front of the southern slopes of Pagoda and Buddha Hills. A and C Companies were directed at the ravine, but the companies soon lost touch with each other in the thick scrub. The Gurkhas were halted by Japanese mortar bombing and small arms fire.

The 1/3rd Gurkhas reached Mokpalin railway station later in the morning, along with two and a half mountain batteries. Lieutenant-Colonels G.A.

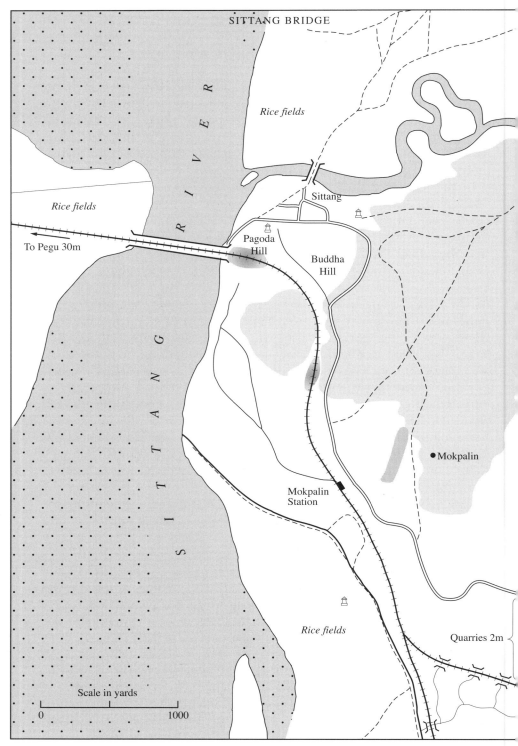

Map G Sittang Bridge

Ballinger and Cameron conferred on Outpost Hill at 10.30 a.m. It was clear by now that the Buddha Hill feature was in Japanese hands; the road to the bridge was definitely cut. In reality Pagoda Hill was held at this time by the Frontier Force, but Ballinger and Cameron knew little about the precise geography of the landscape; they were also unaware that Bungalow Hill, up ahead to the west of the road, was in the hands of a company of Dukes. Ballinger and Cameron decided that the 1/3rd Gurkhas would take over the attack towards the thickly scrubbed ridge line up ahead. The 2/5th Gurkhas were to regroup and cover the right flank facing the jungle north-east of Mokpalin.

The two and a half batteries of mountain artillery east of the river had taken up a firing position near Mokpalin station; the gunners fired a twenty-five-minute barrage-concentration from 11.30 a.m. at Pagoda and Buddha Hills to support the Gurkhas' next advance. Ten guns from the 5th, 12th and 28th Mountain Batteries were in action. Colonel MacKenzie and Major McLeod, the British medical officers captured earlier in the morning, had been sent under escort to the Japanese-held feature overlooking Sittang village. According to MacKenzie, when the mountain guns started firing, 'One [shell] exploded uncomfortably close to us and killed two Japs and wounded two more. McLeod had a surgical haversack with him and we were ordered to attend the wounded. We gave first aid to them both and found that one had his right arm very badly smashed.'[18] The wounded were carried off on stretchers and the dead hastily buried. During the afternoon MacKenzie and McLeod had to take cover on several occasions to avoid bullets from fighting underway nearby.

Meanwhile the 1/3rd Gurkhas had advanced behind the barrage; B Company made for Pagoda Hill; C Company set out for Buddha Hill; D Company moved in support; battalion headquarters and A Company remained on Outpost Hill to the rear. Captain Kinloch, the adjutant, recorded:

> Through the roar and crash of the shells and the drifting smoke came the stutter of light machine guns and the yells of our Gurkhas as following the barrage they found the Japs in slit trenches on the forward slopes and killed them or drove them back with bayonet and kukri. But when they reached the top of the feature they were held up by heavy automatic fire from Japs well dug in on the reverse slope.[19]

Lieutenant Fay's C Company reached the top of the ridge near the stone statue of Buddha, but the crest was swept by Japanese machine gun fire. Fay was wounded and would require evacuation. Captain Peter Stephens' D Company had followed the leading pair of companies into the attack; D Company moved up to join those Gurkhas already pinned down below the

ridge's crest. Stephens led a further assault to capture the northern side of the
hill; he was killed firing a Bren gun from the hip and the attack ground to a
halt.[20]

As the Gurkhas were attacking northwards from Mokpalin, British
commanders at the bridge were unsure of what was happening beyond
their immediate perimeter. Brigadier Hugh-Jones of the 48th Brigade and
Lieutenant-Colonel Lentaigne, CO 1/4th Gurkhas, had met on the west
bank and decided to cross the bridge for a reconnaissance of the east bank
bridgehead. The two officers were three-quarters of their way across the
bridge when a salvo of shells landed on a small sand-bagged redoubt thirty
yards from the eastern end of the bridge above the railway cutting. Further
shells followed and there was a panicked flight of troops towards the bridge.
The shelling was the fire of the mountain guns supporting the advance of the
1/3rd Gurkhas. The gunners were unaware of the location of friendly troops
up ahead near the bridge. As a consequence of the shelling, Hugh-Jones
ordered the troops in the bridgehead and on Pagoda Hill to withdraw across
the bridge to the west bank. The bridge was to be held by covering fire from
across the river.

In preparation for this withdrawal Captain Attiqar Rahman of the Frontier
Force was instructed by Hugh-Jones:

> to go back and recce out some positions on the west bank and I remember going
> back with the Adjutant of the 1/4th Gurkhas and we ran into Jacky Smyth who was
> waving a pistol at us as he thought we were running away from the other side of
> the bridge. It took us some time to convince him but he was in a roaring temper.[21]

To complicate matters further, the Japanese soon mounted another attack on
the bridge from their position on Buddha Hill. A small force of infantry and
engineers attempted the assault, but as they moved over open ground they
were caught by the fire of the mountain guns shelling Pagoda Hill. Shells
exploded when they hit trees to shower shrapnel over the troops below.
When the shelling lifted the Japanese advanced again, only to clash with
soldiers of the 1/3rd Gurkha's B Company, which had approached Pagoda
Hill from the south-east behind the cover of the barrage. The Indian Army's
history recorded of B Company's thrust: 'In the small actions that went on in
this area, Jemadar Gangansing and Havildar Sulbahadur Rana were particularly outstanding for their cool behaviour.'[22] The Japanese were repelled and
two platoons of B Company reached the eastern end of the bridge, only to
find the vicinity deserted of British troops.

After the crisis had passed, at 3.30 p.m. Smyth ordered that the bridgehead
be re-established on the east bank of the river. Two companies of the 1/4th

Gurkhas doubled over the bridge and pushed up onto Pagoda Hill; they ran headlong into Japanese troops again advancing from the opposite direction. The Japanese were driven off and the Gurkhas gained a firm footing on Pagoda Hill. There seems to have been some firing between troops of the 1/3rd and 1/4th Gurkhas around this time. The bridgehead was re-organised with the company of the Dukes again placed on Bungalow Hill. The Frontier Force and 3rd Burma Rifles formed an inner perimeter behind the Gurkhas on Pagoda Hill. Divisional headquarters was still out of touch with the brigades believed to be marching towards the bridge from Kyaikto.

To the north of Mokpalin the headquarters group of the 1/3rd Gurkhas on Outpost Hill waited for news of the progress of the battle to seize the ridge line up ahead. Captain Kinloch recalled:

> Colonel Ballinger suddenly turned to me and said, 'Bruce, I would like you to go forward and try and find out what is happening to the forward companies.' I thought, well this is it, this is the end, literally a sentence of death, because I knew the whole jungle between us and the forward companies was crawling with Japanese. I tried to keep my emotions under control and I saluted and said, 'Yes, sir, certainly.' I had only gone a few paces when Colonel Ballinger called me back. 'I've changed my mind. I think it would be better if I went along with the Intelligence section. I'd like to see what's happening myself anyway.'[23]

About 2 p.m. Ballinger and Subedar-Major Gagan Sing Thapa set out with a small party. The first friendly troops they encountered was B Company's reserve platoon. According to the regimental history:

> Although advised by the platoon commander that the way ahead was covered by automatic fire the C.O. [Ballinger] took the shortest route and ordered the platoon and his escort to advance. After a short distance they came across some Japs who held up their hands in surrender. Telling the men not to fire, the C.O. advanced to take the Japs prisoners. As he did so they fell on their faces and LMGs from behind opened up, killing the C.O. and many of the men with him. The remainder scattered and returned to Battalion H.Q. under the Subedar-Major.[24]

Ballinger's party had clashed with Japanese troops probing the scrub country south of Buddha Hill.

Major F.K. Bradford took over as commanding officer after Ballinger's death. He had A Company and Headquarters Company of the 1/3rd Gurkhas and two platoons of the 2/5th Gurkhas at Outpost Hill. When C Company's commander, Lieutenant Fay, was carried to the rear wounded he brought the news with him that the Gurkhas held part of Buddha Hill, but the Japanese remained firmly in possession of the northern slope. Bradford went by Bren carrier to Mokpalin station to confer with Lieutenant-Colonel Cameron.

There were few working radio sets in the division that day. To the south of
Outpost Hill the railway station area was jammed with transport. Occasional
shells fell amongst the vehicles and some were on fire.

On the north-eastern flank of Mokpalin the 2/5th Gurkhas were closely
engaged throughout the afternoon. Japanese pressure increased as the day
wore on. About 1.30 p.m. heavy mortar fire scored a direct hit on the
regimental aid post; B Company's Jemadar Nandalal Ghale was seriously
wounded. Late in the afternoon troops of A and C Companies counter-
attacked to keep the Japanese at bay; the battalion was hard pressed to hold
its ground.

As the battle raged around Sittang and Mokpalin, the brigades that had spent
the night near Boyagyi rubber estate, to the north-west of Kyaikto, were
making their way along the track to rejoin the rest of the division. The 16th
Brigade had marched out first at dawn. The troops made slow progress along
the rough track, but the brigade reached Mokpalin during the afternoon.
The 8th Burma Rifles arrived first, followed by the Jats, KOYLIs and 1/7th
Gurkhas. Sounds of firing had indicated that a battle was underway ahead;
the last section of the route was carefully picqueted to avoid ambush.

The 16th Brigade was followed by the 46th Brigade. When the order came,
troops of the 46th Brigade left positions held the previous night along the
Kadat stream. The march was led by the 3/7th Gurkhas, which was followed
by the 5/17th Dogras and the main body of the 2nd Dukes. The 4th Burma
Rifles marched by a separate route along the railway, beyond the left flank of
the main brigade column. A fifteen-mile march was planned for a warm day,
along a dusty track flanked by undergrowth and jungle.

Shortly before 9.30 a.m. the 46th Brigade was halted as the Dukes had
been delayed by a missing detachment. At this time the troops were roughly
halfway along the track from Kyaikto to Mokpalin. The 16th Brigade had
marched on and this allowed a gap of a mile to open up between the two
brigades. In the gap the enterprising Japanese swiftly built a road block
composed of tree trunks. The III/214th Battalion had used jungle paths to
swoop down on the track from the north. The road block was manned by a
Japanese company. The other companies of the battalion took up positions to
ambush the flank of troops marching towards the barricade.

The leading troops of the 3/7th Gurkhas came under fire when they
marched into the ambush zone. The Gurkhas swiftly deployed to attack the
road block from front and flank. The confused fighting that followed broke
up the battalion into several detachments; Lieutenant-Colonel Stevenson
was cut off in the chaos and only rejoined British forces days later; Captain
C.D. Carver was killed. The block was captured by the Gurkhas only for

more Japanese opposition to be encountered further along the track. Captain Harris' D Company headed westwards through scrub towards the river, and from there marched along the river bank to reach the bridge late in the afternoon.[25]

Japanese troops shot up and mortared the rest of the 46th Brigade's column from the northern jungle flank. The column split up and entered the jungle beside the track to get past the block. Brigadier Ekin and a party only reached Mokpalin station after nightfall; Brigade-Major Guy Burton led a separate party northwards and crossed the Sittang river by boat north of the bridge. According to Captain Firth of the Dukes: 'It was a fearsome march to Mokpalin village … no food, no water, and a heavy load of weapons and ammunition, hot sun and dust, and quite a lot of pellets flying around.'[26] The 4th Burma Rifles marched along the railway and arrived safely at Mokpalin. During that day there were no reports of air attacks by Allied airmen on Smyth's division. A Hurricane was shot down into the Sittang river by troops of one or other of the combatants; Pilot Officer Dunsford-Wood survived unhurt.[27]

After the 46th Brigade had dispersed, the Japanese III/214th Battalion also withdrew from the track to re-group in the jungle. The Japanese battalion had lost forty-one killed and 100 wounded in the action; the close-quarters fighting had been fierce.[28] Once the track was clear of Japanese troops, groups of British, Indian and Gurkha soldiers re-emerged from the scrub and continued directly along the track towards Mokpalin.

The main body of the Japanese 214th Regiment had reached Kyaikto by this time. At some point during the day this regiment clashed with troops of the 46th Brigade, after which the Japanese marched onwards by a separate route through the jungle and lost contact with the battle.

The Dukes' Lieutenant-Colonel H.B. Owen and a small group were separated from their unit during the retreat and headed directly for the river thinking that British forces would soon be crossing the bridge. The men crossed the river after nightfall and Owen and his batman sought shelter in a nearby village. They were subsequently attacked by Burmese. Owen was killed and his batman only escaped after loosing the fingers of one hand to a machete slash.

When Brigadier Jones had reached Mokpalin with his 16th Brigade in the afternoon he became the senior officer present and gave orders that Outpost Hill be firmly held. An officer of the 8th Burma Rifles recorded:

We arrived at Mokpalin, from the south … There were masses of troops but no staffs … We were at the south of the railway station but west of the line, and throughout the day the Japs were attacking on the other side of the line … After a bit the Kawkareik Brigadier [Jones] turned up … and really did get things organised. We were very glad to see him. We were to form a box round Mokpalin, we being in the S.W. corner.[29]

The forward companies of the 1/3rd Gurkhas remained isolated on and around the southern slopes of Buddha Hill. The Gurkhas were short of water, food and ammunition; the wounded suffered terribly.

Brigadier Jones knew little of the situation at the Sittang bridge. He was unable to establish radio contact with divisional headquarters, but the news reached Mokpalin that the 46th Brigade had been broken up in heavy fighting on the track to the south-east. Jones decided to form a night perimeter around Mokpalin. Units from all three of the division's brigades had to be hastily rearranged as night was falling. The 2/5th Gurkhas held the east flank of the perimeter on the ground they had fought over during the day; the 8th Burma Rifles was astride the road and railway 400 yards south of Mokpalin station; the KOYLI were behind an embankment alongside the 8th Burma Rifles; the 4th Burma Rifles were on the western flank of the perimeter; the Jats were on ground south-east of Bungalow Hill; the headquarters of the 1/3rd Gurkhas continued to hold Outpost Hill; the 1/7th Gurkhas and two companies of the Dukes were in reserve near Mokpalin station. Other parties to reach Mokpalin were added to the southern side of the perimeter. Jones' provisional plan that evening was to resume the attack towards Buddha and Pagoda Hills at first light.[30]

General Hutton spent most of 22 February far from the dramatic events unfolding around the Sittang bridge. He had flown to Lashio for a meeting with Chiang Kai-shek. The conference, however, had not taken place as the Generalissimo's planned stop-over at Lashio was cancelled at the last moment. Hutton returned to Rangoon by air in the evening. Upon arrival he received a signal from Wavell with the covering instruction that he was to personally decipher the message. The signal read: 'War Cabinet has decided in view large proposed increase army in Burma that General Alexander should be appointed C-in-C Burma. You will remain Chief of the General Staff in Burma after his arrival. Otherwise keep appointment secret till arrival Alexander.' This message was a surprise and a considerable blow for Hutton, but – given the length of time it would take Alexander to reach Burma – he was likely to remain Burma Army's commander for some days yet.

On 22 February Burma Army reverted to the control of Delhi in yet another re-shuffling of the deck of poor cards available to the Allies in the Far East. Wavell signalled London, Delhi and Rangoon: 'I have no longer responsibility for Burma … Neither Rangoon nor Burma will be held by defensive methods and maintaining a front. Only prospect of success is vigorous counter-offensive at early date for which 7th Australian Division is required as well as 7th Armoured Brigade.' Wavell went on to say, 'Surely our Eastern Fleet can prevent Japanese singeing our beard at Rangoon … We have got to fight these Japs some time somewhere. Burma not ideal geographically but represents almost our last chance to show the Japs and the world that we do mean to fight.'[31] The Allies had been in constant retreat since the outbreak of the war against Japan.

A pile of cables and reports had gathered for Hutton at Rangoon whilst he was absent in Lashio. The mass of paperwork included a report from Smyth timed at 2 p.m. that day:

> Heavy fighting going on East side Sittang River. Enemy shelling our bridgehead with quite heavy guns and appears to be attacking strongly. So far have only got 1/4th G.R. over complete but oddments of other battalions are trickling in. Situation appears to be serious. Have no communication either 16th Infantry Brigade or 46th Infantry Brigade, but they are obviously very strongly engaged.[32]

Hutton telephoned Smyth's headquarters to arrange a meeting for 11 a.m. the following day on the road from Pegu to Waw, some miles to the west of the bridge.

10

The Demolition of the Sittang Bridge

After nightfall on 22 February General Smyth left the Sittang bridge for divisional headquarters at Abya, seven miles west of the bridge. He was due to meet Hutton near Pegu the following day. Brigadier Hugh-Jones was put in command of the bridgehead; he was given orders that the bridge was not to fall into Japanese hands. Brigadier Cowan, Smyth's chief of staff, remained at the bridge for a while after Smyth's departure. Later in the evening he was relieved by Lieutenant-Colonel F.C. Simpson, the 17th Division's GSO 1 (chief operations staff officer). Cowan went to join Smyth at Abya. Smyth had slept very little in the previous three days and was exhausted.

Major Richard Orgill's company of Malerkotla sappers and miners was responsible for setting demolition charges on the bridge. At 6 p.m. Orgill reported that two spans of the bridge were prepared for demolition. A third span was also ready to be blown, though a lack of stores had prevented this span's full preparation. In total the bridge had eleven 150-foot spans.

Hugh-Jones had only limited information as to how the battle was faring to the east of the Sittang bridgehead; he was unable to make radio contact with the headquarters of either Brigadier Jones or Ekin. Captain Macrae of B Company of the 1/3rd Gurkhas, which had fought its way into the bridgehead during the day, was able to tell something of the engagement around Mokpalin. Likewise, when Captain Harris of the 3/7th Gurkhas reached the bridge with his company he was able to tell what he knew of the ambush of the 46th Brigade; other stragglers reached the bridgehead with their own grim stories of desperate encounters.

In reality the forward companies of the 1/3rd Gurkhas were no more than a few hundred yards away to the east on the slopes of Buddha Hill. The night position of the 1/9th Jats was probably just as close to the Dukes on Bungalow Hill. Captain Bishop of the 1/3rd Gurkhas had arrived at the bridge during the day on his way to rejoin his unit from hospital in Rangoon. He offered to lead a patrol into the darkness to find his unit, which seemed to the clear-headed likely to be not far away. Hugh-Jones rejected the request and did not arrange for other patrols to be sent out.[1] The commanders at Mokpalin were also strangely incurious as to the lie of the land between their posts and the bank of the river, which could be followed northwards to the bridge. By this stage of the battle the participants were suffering badly from a lack of sleep, food and water and the draining heat of a humid, tropical climate.

At 2 a.m. on 23 February Hugh-Jones asked Orgill whether his engineers could guarantee the demolition of the bridge by daylight if the Japanese brought the structure under direct fire from the east bank. Obviously Orgill could not give guarantees that were contingent on the actions of hostile forces. According to the history of the Frontier Force Regiment: 'The enemy did not press hard against the bridgehead that night, but menacing incidents were continuous. One of these was a Japanese machine-gunner who infiltrated in the darkness through to the railway cutting east of the bridge and fired bursts down its length.'[2] This took place at about 3.30 a.m.; showers of sparks were caused by ricocheting bullets striking the girders. When the bridge seemed to come under direct fire, this caused further anxiety in the minds of weary senior officers. It was not in Japanese interests to bomb the bridge from the air, but small arms or even mortar fire could not do much structural damage.

In the depths of that night, during the hours before dawn, the proverbial fog of war was very thick.[3] At 4.15 a.m. Hugh-Jones held a conference on the west bank. He consulted with the commanding officers of the 1/4th Gurkhas and Frontier Force, and then decided it was time to request permission of Smyth to blow up the bridge. Hugh-Jones had formed the impression that the 16th and 46th Brigades were too broken up to fight a way through the Japanese force blocking their progress. The bridgehead might collapse suddenly if hit by a strong attack at dawn. As there was no guarantee of holding the bridgehead, or blowing the bridge by daylight, Hugh-Jones felt the bridge would need to be demolished before dawn.[4]

At 4.30 a.m. a staff officer from the 48th Brigade's headquarters rang divisional headquarters at Abya to ask for permission to wreck the bridge. The staff officer spoke to Cowan, who recalled:

Hugh-Jones had a conference with Lentaigne and Edward, and it was their considered opinion that the bridge should be blown because they did not consider the troops would 'stand up' to a Jap attack of any intensity. Furthermore they considered that all officers and other ranks who could get over the bridge had already done so. All this information was given to me over the telephone by an officer deputed by Hugh-Jones, as the latter had gone forward to arrange for evacuation of the bridgehead troops.[5]

Smyth's recollection of events was as follows:

At 4.30 a.m. Punch Cowan woke me up. Brigadier Hugh-Jones was on the phone. During the night pressure on the bridgehead troops had increased. After a consultation with his COs he had decided that he could not guarantee to hold the bridgehead against a dawn attack and if the bridge was not blown under cover of darkness he couldn't be sure he would be able to blow it at all. He therefore wanted my permission to withdraw the bridgehead troops and blow the bridge immediately.[6]

Smyth took less than five minutes to make up his mind, and gave his permission for the bridge to be wrecked. He later rationalised: 'If we did not blow a complete Japanese division could march straight on Rangoon.' Smyth and Cowan may have believed that a greater part of their division had crossed to the west bank than was actually the case.

At 5 a.m. Hugh-Jones gave orders for the bridgehead to be evacuated. The company of Dukes on Bungalow Hill joined the troops heading for the bridge through the darkness. They had suffered only two casualties in the course of their relatively uneventful vigil on that feature, more or less ignored by both friend and foe.[7] The Frontier Force and 1/4th Gurkhas withdrew across the bridge as well. Edward of the Frontier Force gave the order at 5.20 a.m. for the sappers to make their final preparations to fire the demolitions. The last troops to cross the bridge was a group of headquarters staff armed with Tommy Guns. One of that party wrote:

> At the western end we collected in the sandbagged redoubt. A series of terrific explosions, a blinding flash, a blast of hot air and a shower of fragments brought down the curtain on that act. Complete silence followed and the noise of all firing ceased. The clang of nailed boots on the steel-work as a few of us went forward to the gap to see if it was well and truly blown sounded as if all the world could hear. As far as we could see, two spans were down but tops of girders showed above the swirling tide.[8]

Two spans were blown down into the river and a third damaged. The charges on the three spans had been connected with detonating cord for simultaneous explosion; a reserve safety fuse was lit beforehand. The man who pressed the plunger on the exploder box was Lieutenant Bashir Ahmed Khan. 'After lighting the safety fuses I jumped into the firing pit and exploded electronically. The electric circuit worked. The explosions were enormous and nearby trees lost their leaves and our little foxhole was filled with earth.'[9]

About dawn, half an hour after the demolitions had been blown, Cowan left divisional headquarters and went to the bridge; he met with Hugh-Jones and Lentaigne on the river bank. Shortly after, Hugh-Jones was given a message carried by Subedar Maya Singh of the Jats. The Subedar had volunteered to swim the river with the message and had managed to find a small boat. The message was in code and marked 'Jonah to Punch'. The message said, 'I am attacking the bridge at first light.' During the night Brigadier Jones had decided to abandon his transport and head westwards through the scrub from Mokpalin to the bank of the river; from there the troops could move north along the river bank to the bridge on foot. Earlier in the night Cowan had sent the cut off units a radio message in uncoded Morse: 'Friends waiting to welcome you at the east gate.' Hugh-Jones was horrified to receive the Subedar's news and collapsed and staggered down the bank. According to Cowan: 'When Brigadier Hugh-Jones read the signal he broke down and I then put Lentaigne in temporary command of all troops on our side of the Sittang.' Lieutenant Randle passed the brigadier near the river bank later in the day:

> [He was] ashen-faced and in a state of collapse, being physically supported by Lieutenant-Colonel Donnie Edward of the 4/12th Frontier Force Regiment. Three weeks later I was in a hospital ship going up the Irrawaddy and I saw Brigadier Hugh-Jones again – his hair had gone white with the shock of it all.[10]

News of the bridge's demolition was signalled to Hutton's headquarters. After daylight the 1/4th Gurkhas and Frontier Force took up defensive positions along the western river bank either side of the ruined structure.

During the hours of darkness, before the bridge was blown, there had been occasional Japanese mortar and small arms fire into the perimeter at Mokpalin. On the south side of the perimeter the Yorkshiremen of the KOYLI were probed by a Japanese bicycle patrol. During the night Japanese patrols also approached the south-east flank of the perimeter.[11]

Captain Bruce Kinloch of the 1/3rd Gurkhas recalled that after a tense night,

> as the first light of dawn appeared in the eastern sky, from the direction of the river came the reverberating roar of three enormous explosions, and on the instant we realised that the bridge had been blown and our lifeline cut. As the chaos died away, there was complete silence. All firing ceased, and every living thing seemed to be holding its breath. Then the Japanese, like a troop of excited monkeys, broke into shrill chattering. Believing that everyone else had crossed over and abandoned us to our fate, we were filled with anger.

Kinloch commented in another interview: 'My own fury was not directed at the enemy but at our own senior commanders who had been responsible for blowing the bridge. We felt the senior commanders had panicked and let us down.'[12] Many troops in the jungle around Mokpalin heard the explosions and, in some cases, saw flashes in the sky.

At 7.30 a.m. Kinloch's position at Outpost Hill was approached by a detachment of Japanese troops marching southwards along the railway, oblivious to the presence of hostile forces. Bren gun fire swiftly dispersed the Japanese and left a number of crumpled figures on the railway. Kinloch's eventful morning was not over yet:

Soon after a Jap reconnaissance plane flew slowly over us, so low that I could distinctly see the pilot's goggled face peering down. Everyone opened up on it, and I emptied a full drum of my Tommy gun. We could see the bullet strikes on the fabric, and over the station the plane suddenly banked and dived to the ground, exploding in a ball of flame. A great cheer went up, like a football crowd applauding the winning goal.[13]

Troops belonging to a number of units claimed to have fired the fatal shots.

The sound of the fierce explosions that wrecked the Sittang bridge had also been a surprise to the Japanese. The two battalions of the 215th Regiment that had attacked the bridgehead and Mokpalin the previous day had suffered many casualties, lacked ammunition and were reeling from the same level of exhaustion and thirst that afflicted British forces. The Japanese had no plans to attack the bridgehead on the morning of 23 February. Colonel Harada had given the I/215th Battalion orders to maintain its position on Buddha Hill; part of the II/215th Battalion was withdrawn to Pyinkadogon to regroup, though two companies remained in position near Mokpalin.[14] A renewed attack on Mokpalin was planned for after nightfall that evening.

Brigadier Jones at Mokpalin had received no warning that the bridge was to be blown. Once he realised that the bridge had been wrecked, Jones decided that his force had best maintain their positions during the day and attempt to cross the river after dark. The Sittang was over 1000 yards wide to the immediate south of the bridge, but – in the dry season – less than half as wide further south, to the west of Mokpalin.

Troops of the 1/3rd Gurkhas were still clinging to posts on the scrub-covered southern slopes of Buddha Hill. As the morning wore on their position became untenable. The Gurkhas withdrew towards Outpost Hill, but were ambushed and scattered by machine gun fire; few of these men rejoined their unit.[15]

At Mokpalin small arms and mortar fire was intermittently directed at the perimeter by Japanese troops in the scrub nearby. The 4th Burma Rifles collapsed and many men headed for the river. The commanding officer of the KOYLI, Lieutenant-Colonel J. Keegan, was seriously wounded by a mortar bomb. Around midday RAF Blenheims dropped bombs around Mokpalin and Outpost Hill to cause further casualties.[16] Later, in a separate incident, an ammunition dump was set on fire. The fire spread to the jungle and vehicles near the roadway. There were further explosions as some of the lorries were carrying ammunition.[17]

About 2 p.m. Brigadier Jones ordered a withdrawal to the river; there was no longer any good reason to wait for nightfall. This was the last order received by many units from Jones' headquarters. Brigadier Ekin was also at Mokpalin, though he had few organised troops to command. Wooden houses near the railway station were set on fire to cover the troops' retreat to the river. The gunners and drivers of the mountain artillery rendered their equipment useless, and released the mules to fend for themselves. The mortars fired off their remaining ammunition; the transport was abandoned.

The troops moved through scrub and patches of jungle to reach the river on a wide front. Some wounded men were carried or limped to the river bank. The wounded who had shattered limbs and gaping holes in their bodies could not be moved; these soldiers stayed behind near Mokpalin in ambulances or aid posts and were seldom heard of again. In general the Japanese shot or bayoneted wounded or exhausted prisoners who could not march.[18]

Japanese troops were not present near the river bank south of the bridge on 23 February, nor during the following night. This made an improvised crossing of the river a good deal easier than might otherwise have been the case. But there was no prospect of a Moulmein-style evacuation as there were no boats on hand to ferry the troops. The river, however, was relatively tame in the dry season. The Sittang was at its worst during the monsoon period of May to October, when the waterways of Burma became raging torrents. Nonetheless, though the surface of the Sittang was smooth, the current underneath was enough to put a man in danger.

At the river bank there was in many places a narrow beach on which troops could gather. Low cliffs provided the bank with a degree of shelter. The more enterprising men set about building rafts, upon which the injured were given priority. Bamboo floated well, as did doors, furniture and thatch taken from the houses of Mokpalin. Those who could swim attempted the crossing; some drowned; Gurkhas from the mountains of Nepal were especially likely to be non-swimmers. It was a slow and laborious crossing even for strong swimmers. Petrol tins were an effective flotation device; some men tied them to their chests with puttees. Many soldiers discarded their boots before entering the water.

Brigadier Ekin recorded the scene at the river bank.

> Here there was chaos and confusion; hundreds of men throwing down their arms, equipment and clothing and taking to the water … some bringing their arms with them on improvised rafts … As we crossed, the river was a mass of bobbing heads … Although it was a disastrous situation there were many stout hearts and parties shouted to each other egging on others to swim faster with jokes about the [Oxford and Cambridge] boat race.[19]

Ekin crossed at about 3 p.m. and Jones an hour later. The KOYLI's wounded CO was given a place on a raft built under the supervision of Lieutenant Sundaram, the medical officer of the 2/5th Gurkhas. Lieutenant-Colonel Cameron could swim and accompanied the raft across. Hastily built rafts might suddenly break up mid-stream with comic or tragic results. On the far side exhausted swimmers emerged from the crossing half-naked, unarmed and unshod. The occasional small arms or mortar round landed in the water or near the river bank. These were 'overs' from the sporadic skirmishing still underway in the vicinity of Mokpalin.

Some men on the south face of the Mokpalin perimeter did not get the order to retreat. Sub-units of the KOYLI and 8th Burma Rifles clashed with Japanese soldiers advancing along the railway; eventually it became obvious that a retreat was underway, and they joined the exodus in the early evening.[20] Those troops left behind in the Mokpalin perimeter unintentionally screened the departure of the rest of the force.

The Gurkhas at Outpost Hill also did not receive the order to retreat, but once it became clear that Mokpalin was to be abandoned, Major Bradford and Captain Kinloch took what remained of the 1/3rd Gurkhas westwards to the river. They reached the bank 800 yards south of the bridge. Nearby some wounded men lay on the sand. Kinloch headed north along the bank to have a closer look at the bridge and the slopes of Pagoda Hill; he reached within 100 yards of the bridge but only narrowly escaped from an encounter with Japanese troops. Kinloch returned with some Dukes, but this probe found the Japanese firmly established on Pagoda Hill. Kinloch and some British soldiers later swam the river and found a sampan on the far side, which was used to ferry more troops across.

Each detachment had its own story to tell. Captain Firth of the Dukes recalled:

> About 4 p.m., with a lance corporal called Burns, I walked down to the river, about 600 yards away, carrying a private soldier with his knee smashed by a mortar. We loaded him on a banana trunk raft, where he lay comfortably enough and secure. Burns and I stripped off, except for my .45 Webley round my neck, and swam gently across in warm sunshine for 800 yards, pushing the raft along. At this point there was no one else in sight. On the other side, we discovered a bullock cart ... Our wounded man was made room for.[21]

Firth walked to Waw railway station. In a rail carriage he found the commanding officer of the Jats wrapped in a blanket and shivering with fever.

The Dukes' Captain Simonds and his B Company headed north through the jungle from Mokpalin; they managed to evade the Japanese and crossed the river to safety by ferry well to the north of the site of the wrecked bridge. Captain Mason and what remained of A Company were overrun and taken prisoner. Major Jack Robinson and some men of his C Company reached the eastern end of the bridge about 4 p.m.; they were forced to take shelter as Japanese troops on Pagoda Hill fired at any movement near the bridge. After dark Robinson, and the KOYLI's Corporal A. Fox and Lance-Corporal R. Roebuck, swam the river alongside the bridge span and slung out a line across the gap in the structure. Three hundred men managed to cross the bridge by scrambling over the fallen sections; these men included some Dukes, thirty men of the KOYLI and many Indians and Gurkhas.[22] Robinson, Fox and Roebuck would be commended for their work; Robinson received the Military Cross and the other two men the Military Medal.

The 17th Division's headquarters was relocated to Waw that day. Smyth had met Hutton late in the morning and told him further of events surrounding the decision to destroy the bridge. According to Smyth, Hutton 'took my unpleasant news with commendable sangfroid'.[23] The commanders of the 2nd Burma Brigade and the recently landed 7th Armoured Brigade were also present at the conference. An observer noted that Smyth seemed to be the most upbeat of the assembled officers. Brigadier Ekin would say of Smyth: 'The trouble with Jacky was that he always looked so damned cheerful, however badly he might be feeling. The night I saw him after swimming the Sittang, he seemed to be his same old cheerful self.'[24] The division's position on the west bank alongside the wrecked Sittang bridge was abandoned at midnight on 23/24 February; the 1/4th Gurkhas withdrew westwards along the railway towards Waw.

On the morning of 24 February, after the sun had dispersed the mist, the Japanese came out of the jungle to sweep the river bank south of the bridge and round up the last groups still on the eastern side of the Sittang. The remnants of D Company of the 2/5th Gurkhas and A Company of the 1/3rd Gurkhas were taken prisoner. Major Bradford's headquarters group was also overrun in a dramatic fashion. The regimental history of the 3rd Gurkha Rifles records the following:

> To accept Major Bradford's surrender, a Japanese officer came forward, but Subedar-Major Gagan Sing Thapa, after refusing to surrender, fired his pistol at the Jap and then shot himself through the heart. The Jap officer who had received Bradford's pistol, on being shot at, fired at and mortally wounded Bradford. Immediately a Naik then shot the Jap through the head.[25]

The Subedar-Major had joined the army in 1912; he saw active service in France in the First World War and in a generation's worth of campaigning on the North-west Frontier.

On the western bank of the river Kinloch heard the story of the loss of Bradford's headquarters and set out towards Waw with a detachment of Gurkhas to make contact with friendly forces. They eventually met a British patrol; Kinloch would be awarded the Military Cross for his exploits in the Sittang battle.

Once troops had crossed the river they tramped westwards across paddy fields alongside the railway line. Stragglers with haggard, unshaven faces and sunken eyes gathered at Waw station and were sent onwards by motor transport or train to Pegu. At evening roll call on 24 February the 17th Indian Division's infantry comprised just eighty officers, sixty-nine VCOs and 3335 other ranks. The soldiers had 1420 rifles between them; many had no boots. Only fifty-six light machine guns and sixty-two Thompson sub-machine guns were counted; about half of those were in the possession of the 1/4th Gurkhas.

Few of the infantry battalions had more than half their authorized strength. The 1/4th Gurkhas had 680 all ranks present and the 4/12th Frontier Force 502. Those two battalions, however, had crossed the bridge before it was blown. The units cut off on the east bank were shattered and grossly under-strength: 1/3rd Gurkhas 107 all ranks, 1/9th Jats 568, 5/17th Dogras 104, 3/7th Gurkhas 170, 8th Burma Rifles 96, 1/7th Gurkhas 300, 2/5th Gurkhas 227, KOYLI 206, Dukes 316, 4th Burma Rifles – unknown.[26] The division urgently needed reorganization; as a first step, the 46th Brigade was disbanded.

In the days ahead, small groups from the Sittang debacle straggled back to friendly lines equipped with little more than khaki drill shorts and shirts stained black with sweat. B Company of the Dukes arrived on 25 February; two days later a platoon from the 1/3rd Gurkhas led by Jemadar Birta Sing Gurung turned up. By 27 February the 2/5th Gurkhas and 1/3rd Gurkhas had risen in strength to 389 and 200 officers and men respectively. The 5th Gurkha's regimental history records that an extra forty survivors of the Sittang battle would rejoin the battalion eventually, but that was only a small part of those missing.[27] Some stragglers headed northwards up the Sittang valley. At Nyaunglebin Captain Lunt noted that small groups and individuals arrived, mostly by train. 'I pulled a complete platoon of 4/12th Frontier Force Regiment off one train. They were in good heart but totally lost.'[28] By 27 February stragglers and available reinforcements had added another 800 officers and men to the 17th Division's mournfully low tally of three days before.

The 17th Division's casualties in the Sittang battle had been heavy and few units were spared. The 1/4th Gurkhas lost eighteen dead and could consider themselves fortunate. The two battalions of the 7th Gurkhas are believed to have lost 350 dead between them. After the postwar recovery of POWs, the 1st Battalion had 130 missing presumed dead and 3rd Battalion 170. The five Gurkha battalions of the division lost 800 dead. The Japanese estimated total enemy dead as 1300; about 1100 prisoners were taken, of whom 120 were Europeans.[29] Lieutenant-Colonel Henry Power of the Dogras was the most senior infantry officer to be made prisoner.

Japanese casualties in the Sittang battle were not severe. The 215th Regiment lost twenty-nine killed and sixty wounded around Buddha Hill and Mokpalin; there were additional losses amongst the artillery and engineer detachments with the 215th Regiment. The III/214th Battalion lost forty-one killed and 100 wounded on the track between Kyaikto and Mokpalin; the 143rd Regiment posted losses of four dead and eight wounded.[30] The Sittang battle cost the Japanese 400 killed and wounded; this was a modest price to pay given the scale of the victory.

After the engagement, Colonel MacKenzie was taken back along the track from Sittang to Kyaikto and onwards to initial internment in Moulmein Jail:

> We passed the ambulances of the Rangoon motor ambulance convoy exactly where the drivers had abandoned them, when they took to the bush. We saw mules with their legs in the air, their bellies distended through decomposition and on the point of bursting. Many dead Indian soldiers could be seen lying at the side of the road, dead in their equipment, as they had fallen.

MacKenzie passed the vehicles of Ekin's headquarters. 'Some vehicles were ditched; some had been set on fire but were in comparatively intact condition, whilst others were completely burnt out.' MacKenzie spotted the brigadier's station wagon with a flag still flying.[31]

The opening phase of the battle for Burma had been a debacle for British forces. This came hard on the heels of the failed campaign for the Malayan peninsula and Singapore Island. On 23 February Hutton reported to the War Office that the Japanese had employed one division in a flank attack against the Sittang bridgehead, whilst a second division had advanced along the road leading westwards from the Bilin river. On 24 February Hutton cabled a fuller account to Delhi of the events of the past week:

> I instructed Smyth to make all arrangements for withdrawal and go back if he felt it necessary, getting as much possible of his transport back early. Air reconnaissance appeared to show enemy greatly reinforced. At great risk 1 D.W.R. [Dukes] from the defence of Rangoon was sent up to help division get back. A bridgehead was organised at Sittang and withdrawal commenced early on 20th February, by which time it was clear that Bilin position could no longer be held. Intelligence reports since received confirm attack on bridgehead from the north was carried out by a fresh enemy division brought up for the purpose. Area is thick jungle and, although we had columns operating wide on the northern flank, it was not detected. I accept full responsibility for decisions taken and Smyth is not in any way to blame.[32]

Hutton later stated in his campaign despatch: 'There is no doubt that the battle of the River Sittang was nothing less than a disaster.' Wavell also succinctly commented: 'From reports of this operation which I have studied I have no doubt that the withdrawal from the Bilin River to the west of the Sittang was badly managed by the headquarters of the 17th Division, and that the disaster which resulted in the loss of almost two complete brigades ought never to have occurred.'[33] Regiments drawn from two Japanese divisions were employed in the Sittang battle, but the 17th Indian Division had enjoyed a numerical superiority in most local engagements.

There were conflicting opinions in respect to the Sittang action. Smyth's chief of staff, Brigadier Cowan, wrote to his former commander in 1955:

> I think it would have been wise to have sent Ekin's brigade back to the bridge the day before we commenced our withdrawal. You will remember Ekin pressed for this. It meant taking a chance at Divisional Headquarters till the 16th and 48th Brigades joined us. However, that is being wise after the event.

Smyth replied that it was unclear if the Japanese were closely following the 16th and 48th Brigades as they retreated from the Bilin. He had wanted to keep the 46th Brigade at Kyaikto in case the other brigades got into trouble. Burma Army's chief staff officer at Rangoon, Brigadier Davies, had some sympathy with Smyth insofar as the latter was compelled by Hutton to fight a protracted battle at the Bilin river, but he still thought that the retreat to the Sittang was 'disgracefully mismanaged'.[34]

General Hutton had given permission for Smyth's division to withdraw from the Bilin on 19 February. He subsequently felt, not unreasonably, that it should have been possible to manage a thirty mile retreat by 5.30 a.m. on the 23rd, when the bridge was blown. The cause of a great deal of what went wrong for British forces can be sheeted home to the fact that most of the 17th Division was stationary near Kyaikto on 21 February, the vital day during which the Japanese slipped past Smyth's northern flank. The delay at moving the division's transport back across the bridge, as it was converted from rail to road traffic, need not have prevented the infantry from attempting to fall back into a bridgehead position. The Allied air attacks on 21 February interfered with the manoeuvre of units, but did not prevent movement on the ground. There was no sense of urgency on either the 20th or 21st to build up a bridgehead force to cover the eastern end of the vital bridge.

Once the main body of the division was cut off on the morning of 22 February, divisional headquarters let matters drift further. No attempt was made to send patrols to regain contact with Ekin's and Jones' brigades. Neither Smyth nor Cowan were at the bridge when it was blown. An enormous responsibility was thrown onto the shoulders of Hugh-Jones, who had little part in creating the crisis in the first place.[35] Even at the last minute Smyth could have refused permission to blow the bridge and further investigated the situation. The extent of the debacle made it abundantly clear that Burma Army needed a corps commander to more firmly supervise front-line operations.

Junior officers present at the Sittang battle were not impressed when they more fully understood what had happened. Lieutenant Randle of the Baluchis wrote:

> Jackie Smyth took no proper steps to defend the bridge. There was no close bridge garrison, no proper fire plan, no proper defence. This bridge was the jugular of the Division. The Japs were just probing at the first stage. They used to take a commanding bit of ground and sit to see what we would do about it. We would attack and take heavy casualties. By holding Pagoda Hill they had a key feature overlooking the bridge and approaches to it. Smyth lacked moral courage, he should have pushed 1/4th Gurkhas across and dug in a proper position in depth. I didn't know all this at the time. I didn't know what the hell was going on in my own little world.[36]

According to Captain Attiqar Rahman of the Frontier Force, Smyth was wrong 'to command when he was so ill. Everyone knows that he was a very brave soldier but unless a divisional commander, especially in the jungle, is 100 per cent fit, I think it is very unfair on his troops.'[37] A general from a later generation – Julian Thompson – observed: 'The arrangements, or lack of them, for the proper conduct of the close bridge garrison at the Sittang [would be] … studied at the British Army Staff College at Camberley … as an example of how it should not be done.'[38] The brilliant performance of General Sakurai's 33rd Division ruthlessly punished the mistakes made by Allied commanders.

Smyth resolutely and consistently defended himself from criticism in the years ahead. He always blamed Hutton and Wavell for ordering his division to fight in exposed locations at Moulmein and behind the Salween and Bilin rivers. Those engagements, in Smyth's view, played a decisive part in preventing his division from crossing the Sittang in a timely fashion. Smyth wrote of Wavell's and Hutton's strategy for southern Burma:

> I quite understood General Wavell's reasoning with regards to this forward defence. It was comforting for Winston Churchill and the Chiefs of Staff in London, for Generalissimo Chiang Kai-shek, for the Viceroy of India and for the Governor of Burma, to see each morning the red line on the map depicting the position of the 17th Division as far in front of Rangoon as possible: but this was a political defence plan, not a military one.[39]

The straightforward retort to that argument is that Rangoon was the only possible reinforcement route. The need to keep the port open was based on dire military necessity.

The seriousness of Smyth's ill-health could not be over-looked for much longer. On 25 February Smyth wrote to Hutton requesting the two months' sick leave his medical board had recommended earlier in February. The letter went as follows:

> My dear General, The medical board held on me on 11.2.42 whilst agreeing that I was quite fit to carry on, recommended that I should be given two months' leave as early as I could be spared. As my division has now been so much reduced in numbers … I am writing to ask if I could have that leave as early as you could spare me. I should have hated to have asked for it whilst active operations were in progress or had there not been a really efficient substitute in Punch Cowan ready to step into my shoes. I have, however, had rather more than an ordinary strain and do feel very much in need of a rest. I have also had to conduct a series of withdrawals since I have been in command of the division which are always lowering to the morale of troops and I feel they would perhaps do better under new management. The war is going to be a long one and I hope that you may, if you do not think I have done too badly, change me for someone in India where I can have a bit of a rest and be ready for an active command again.[40]

Hutton subsequently signalled the Military Secretary at India Command:

> I visited him [Smyth] yesterday and he appeared well and cheerful. I made no suggestion that he was to blame for recent reverses. This is not the moment to spare people to proceed on leave and I must assume that he has lost confidence in his ability to command and should be relieved. Propose to appoint Cowan and despatch Smyth to India forthwith.[41]

The exact state of Smyth's health during the Sittang battle is a matter for speculation. Hutton would later write on this subject:

> His [Smyth's] state of health must have been known to a number of senior officers in India, including General Hartley, the Army Commander-in-Chief, and possibly to some of my own staff, though nobody felt it was his duty to tell me. It seems extraordinary that he was ever allowed to go to Burma by GHQ India. I have since heard, unofficially, that once or twice during the campaign he was virtually in a state of collapse.[42]

Hutton's own tenure as a commander was also drawing to a close. He was a caretaker awaiting General Alexander's arrival. The journalist, James Hodson, arrived at Rangoon on 27 February and had an interview with Hutton not long afterwards. 'Hutton looked as much like a university professor as a general. He sat at a roll-top desk, looked at us over his spectacles and, answering a telephone from time to time, talked of the military situation. It is grim.'[43] Hutton's lack of charisma was often commented upon at a time when people were looking for extroverted leadership to turn around a failing cause.

11

Rangoon in the Front Line

As the Sittang battle was unfolding, tense negotiations took place between Prime Minister Churchill and the Australian government to decide whether or not the 7th Australian Division should be landed at Rangoon. It was vital to hold Rangoon open as a viable port until those discussions were resolved. The 7th Australian Division, with the 6th Australian Division following behind, had been embarked on transports in the Nile delta to sail for the new war against Japan. The 7th Division was the first complete Allied division to reach the Indian Ocean from the Middle East. As long as Singapore was in British hands, that fortress had priority to receive army reinforcements at sea in the Indian Ocean; but, after the capitulation of Singapore on 15 February, Rangoon became the most important port in the Far East.[1]

There had been some thought of landing the 1st Australian Corps at Java. The fast liner *Orcades* raced ahead of the main 7th Division convoy and landed 3400 troops in the Dutch East Indies. But Wavell advised that there was no point landing a large force of Australian troops in the East Indies for almost certain capture; Burma or Australia would be better destinations.

Wavell subsequently sent a message to Churchill recommending that at least one Australian division should be diverted to Burma. The London-based Pacific War Council considered this recommendation on the evening of 17 February and supported the proposal. Sir Earle Page, Canberra's envoy in London, cabled the Australian government his endorsement. The Australian High Commissioner, S.M. Bruce, also cabled his approval.[2] Page and Bruce were both former prime ministers. Churchill wrote to the Chiefs of Staff on 17 February that the 'best course' would seem to be the landing of the 7th Division at Rangoon, providing that the 6th and 9th Australian Divisions were swiftly returned to Australia.

The 7th Australian Division had recently fought a short but tough campaign against Vichy French colonial forces in Syria and Lebanon. That experience of war would stand them in good stead against the Japanese. The 7th Division's infantry battalions were 900–1000 strong, which meant that the division had almost as many infantry as the 17th Indian and 1st Burma Divisions combined. The 7th Division's seventy-two field guns had more firepower than the artillery of Hutton's and Iida's armies put together.

In Australia, however, Singapore's capitulation on 15 February had caused great alarm. With the fall of Singapore, British strategy in the Far East was in ruins; the Japanese blitzkrieg was sweeping all before it. On 16 February the Australian Chiefs of Staff recommended that, 'if possible, all Australian forces now under order to transfer to the Far East from the Middle East should be diverted to Australia'.[3] The Australian War Cabinet confirmed this decision the following day. Prime Minister John Curtin requested of London that the Australian force in transit from the Middle East sail onwards to Australia.

The bombing of Port Darwin, in northern Australia, only hardened the resolve of the Australian government. Darwin was raided on 19 February by the Japanese aircraft carrier task force that had pounded Pearl Harbor. Darwin was a supply base for Allied forces still in the East Indies, and was also raided to cover Japanese landing operations planned for Timor. Four fleet carriers were supported by two fast battleships and a host of smaller warships.

At dawn on 19 February Admiral Nagumo's strike force of eighty-one aircraft was launched in the Timor Sea about 220 miles north-west of Darwin. Commander Fuchida wrote of the air strike:

> As at Rabaul, the job to be done seemed hardly worthy of the Nagumo Force. The harbour, it is true, was crowded with all kinds of ships, but a single pier and a few waterfront buildings appeared to be the only port installations. The airfield … had no more than two or three small hangers, and in all there were only twenty-odd planes of various types scattered about the field.

The Japanese aircraft devastated Darwin's port facilities, airfield and shipping in the harbour. About midday fifty-four land-based bombers raided the aerodrome to add to the tumult. Approximately 250 people were killed in the attack.[4] Nagumo's carriers returned to Starling Bay in south-west Celebes; the invasion of Timor went ahead on 20 February.

In the meantime Churchill's patience gave out. At 9 p.m. on 20 February he ordered the Admiralty to divert the 7th Division's convoys to Rangoon. He cabled Curtin to seek his support for the diversion without clearly indicating it had already been ordered. Churchill told Curtin that the 7th Division was 'the only force that can reach Rangoon in time to prevent its loss and the severance of communication with China'. Churchill pleaded that 'a vital war emergency cannot be ignored'.[5] The British Prime Minister also asked President Roosevelt to intervene and support the request, which the later did. On 20 February the headquarters of the 7th Division and the 25th Brigade were at Colombo; the 18th Brigade was at Bombay; the 21st Brigade was at sea to the east of Ceylon. If the diversion was carried through, the leading Australian brigade could reach Rangoon about 26 February, and the second brigade convoy a few days after that; the third and final brigade might arrive by 6 March.[6]

On 21 February the Australian War Cabinet reconfirmed their decision; troops were not to be landed at Rangoon. This information reached Churchill on the morning of the 22nd. Curtin cabled Churchill that his government had no desire for a 'recurrence of the experience of the Greek and Malayan campaigns'.[7] Curtin's signal added that given the contribution to Far East defence Australian forces had already made and the services the AIF had rendered in the Middle East:

> we have every right to expect them to be returned as soon as possible, with adequate escorts to ensure their safe arrival. We assure you, and desire you so to inform the President, who knows fully what we have done to help the common cause, that if it were possible to divert our troops to Burma and India without imperilling our security in the judgement of our advisers we should be pleased to agree to the diversion.[8]

The fiascos at Crete and Singapore had been grievous blows to Canberra's confidence in the judgement and commitment of the London government to the empire.

There was further discord between Canberra and London when it was revealed that the convoys had already been diverted pending Canberra's acquiescence. On 23 February the Australian government signalled that it was 'quite impossible to reverse a decision which was made with the utmost care and which we have affirmed and re-affirmed'. Churchill backed down and signalled Curtin on 23 February: 'Your convoy is now proceeding to refuel at Colombo. It will then proceed to Australia in accordance with your wishes.'[9] Churchill would concede in his memoirs that, 'whereas the advance of Japan made no difference to the safety of the British Isles, it confronted Australia with a mortal danger'.[10]

Australian troops would doubtless have been a valuable improvised addition to Burma Army. But at some point the Australian government had to allow self-interest to take precedence over the conflicting desires of a British government for whom the war in the Far East was not a high priority. Once the Japanese had overrun the Dutch East Indies, landings in the Darwin area or at Port Moresby in Papua New Guinea became definite possibilities; Allied support in North America and India was thousands of miles away.

In the short term, many of the worst fears of Canberra seemed to come true in the period after the loss of Singapore. The Japanese promptly took advantage of their newly won control of the shipping channels that lead into the heart of the Dutch East Indies. Palembang on Sumatra, the location of a large oil refinery, swiftly fell into Japanese hands. Wavell ordered Allied forces on Sumatra to withdraw to Java. Japanese troops also landed on Bali, to the east of Java. The island of Java was the archipelago's principal body of wealth and population.

Wavell warned his superiors that Java was likely to be invaded before the end of February. On 20 February the Combined Chiefs of Staff in Washington issued orders to resolutely defend Java. 'Every day gained is of importance. There should be no withdrawal of troops or air forces of any nationality and no surrender.' The following day Wavell was instructed to shut down ABDA Command headquarters and leave Java, which he did a few days later.

The Dutch Vice-Admiral C.E.L. Helfrich remained as CIC at Java after Wavell's departure. Major-General Hein ter Poorten was commander of Allied land forces, which comprised 25,000 Dutch troops, 40,000 poorly-armed local militia and small British, Australian and American contingents. Allied naval forces at Java included eight cruisers and twelve destroyers; Helfrich divided his fleet between the ports of Batavia and Sourabaya, which were on the north-western and north-eastern coasts of Java respectively.

The Japanese were planning to make amphibious landings at both ends of Java. Invasion convoys had been assembled in the Philippines and Indochina. The convoys would be escorted by a large force of cruisers and destroyers; almost 100 transports would embark the troops and equipment of XVI Army. Admiral Nagumo's aircraft carriers and battleships were also at sea to provide the invasion fleet with protection from any Allied naval forces at large in the Indian Ocean. Java was effectively isolated from the rest of the Allied world.

On 24 February Helfrich received information that a Japanese convoy and escort was sailing southwards down the Macassar Strait, on the eastern flank of Borneo. The following morning the report was confirmed and he ordered all available warships at Tanjong Priok, the port of Batavia, to join Rear-Admiral Karel Doorman at Sourabaya to form a 'Combined Striking Force'. Doorman's fleet, after this reinforcement, comprised two heavy cruisers, three light cruisers and nine destroyers. This was of similar strength to Rear-Admiral Takeo Takagi's task force sailing with the invasion convoy bound for eastern Java. Takagi had at his disposal two heavy cruisers, two light cruisers and fourteen destroyers. The Japanese fleet formed a coherent fighting force, but the Allied fleet was of several nationalities and had many ships of older vintage. An officer in the destroyer HMS *Electra* commented: 'We were committed to fight in the worst possible conditions; to manoeuvre against a superior enemy in what was practically a land-locked sea. The shores were his, with the exception of Java.'[11] Allied naval forces could count on little in the way of aerial support.

After an uneventful sweep of the seas north of Java during the night of 26/27 February, Doorman's fleet was returning to Sourabaya harbour at 3 p.m. the following afternoon when the admiral received a report from Helfrich that enemy convoys had been sighted. The Combined Striking Force headed out to sea again half an hour later. The weather in the Java Sea was typically sunny that day; the seas were calm; the visibility under a blue sky was excellent.

The disastrous battle of the Java Sea – from the Allied viewpoint – got underway on the afternoon of 27 February. Early in the engagement the heavy cruiser HMS *Exeter* was damaged by shell fire and dropped out of action. Before long a British and a Dutch destroyer were sunk by mine and torpedo respectively. The principal Allied losses in the action, however, were the Dutch light cruisers *Java* and *De Ruyter*, both of which were fatally damaged by Long Lance torpedoes. The two ships sank at night with a combined loss of 854 Dutchmen, including the fleet's commander Admiral Doorman. The surviving Allied warships beat a hasty retreat; the victorious Japanese fleet also retired to cover the final approach of the troop convoy destined to invade eastern Java.

There were further Allied warship losses over the next two days when attempts were made to escape from Java to ports in Ceylon and Australia. On the night of 28 February HMAS *Perth* and USS *Houston* made a run for Sunda Strait between Java and Sumatra, only to plough into the anchored transports of General Imamura's western invasion convoy in Banten Bay. The convoy's naval escort sent the Allied cruisers to the bottom after a fast and furious night action that cost the lives of 1056 American and Australian seamen. Several Japanese transports were sunk or damaged in the engagement, including the headquarters ship of General Imamura. The general was amongst those who jumped into the water; he floated on a piece of wood for twenty minutes before a boat rescued him and took him ashore. Later in the night Imamura's aide came ashore and found the general 'sitting on a pile of bamboo about a hundred metres away. Dispiritedly I limped over to him and congratulated him on the successful landing. I looked around me. Everyone had a black face [from the oil in the water] including the commander.'[12] Japanese generals were at the forefront of the action right across South-east Asia.

The Imperial Japanese Navy lost no ships in the Java Sea battles; the Allies lost five cruisers and six destroyers (the fifth cruiser was HMS *Exeter*). A long list of additional Allied warships and merchantmen were also sunk fleeing from the East Indies. The Japanese Navy's use of aircraft, torpedoes and gunnery had been outstanding. Vice-Admiral Sir Geoffrey Layton, Eastern Fleet's commander at Ceylon, wrote to Admiral Sir Dudley Pound, First Sea Lord at the Admiralty:

the handling of the ships in the Java Sea battle during the day action and subsequent night action was nothing short of deplorable ... I only wish we had been able to withdraw all our surface forces to the south of Java when the attack on Java became imminent, as we have lost valuable ships now with no corresponding advantage.[13]

Pound could only agree with Layton's assessment.

The Java Sea battles caused the Japanese invasion convoys to be delayed by only twenty-four hours; both the eastern and western landings went ahead on the night of 28 February/1 March. General Imamura's XVI Army made quick progress inland and the end of the campaign in Java was not long in coming. The Dutch General ter Poorten signalled to his scattered forces on the morning of 8 March that they should lay down their arms. In the days ahead, 12,500 British and Australian soldiers, airmen and sailors were amongst those who went into captivity.

By this time the Japanese had already taken Rabaul and occupied Salamaua and Lae in eastern New Guinea. In the Philippines over 100,000 Filipino and American servicemen and civilian refugees had been trapped in the Bataan peninsula. The neck of the peninsula, only fifteen miles wide, was dominated by jungle-covered mountains. The beleaguered garrison suffered from lack of food, malaria and dysentery, and could only be expected to hold out for a finite period.

The Japanese conquest of the Dutch East Indies, hard on the heels of the fall of Singapore, opened the sea route into the Indian Ocean for Japanese naval forces. Japanese shipping could now pass either side of Sumatra through the Malacca or Sunda Straits. It was now possible for Japanese commanders to plan amphibious operations against southern Burma with army divisions made available by the general success of operations across South-east Asia.

The British colonial regime in Burma was in great peril. The government at Rangoon, however, was slow to pass on bad news for fear of alarming the civilian population. The Daily News Bulletin on the front page of the *Rangoon Gazette* for 18 February told its readers: 'Well informed quarters are not inclined to admit any question of an immediate evacuation – or even a distant threat to Rangoon at present ... Our forces are in very good heart and are only anxious insofar as they are counting the days until the time comes for an advance.' In the same issue of that newspaper nine banks announced that they were closing in Rangoon the following day and would reopen in Mandalay.[14]

The crisis of the Japanese invasion had placed enormous strain on Burma's administration, though relations between Governor Dorman-Smith, General

Hutton and Burmese holders of ministerial office remained cordial. The first stage of a three-phase evacuation of the government from Rangoon began on 20 February. The main hospital was evacuated to Mandalay over the following two days. By this time Rangoon's peacetime population of almost half a million had shrunk to 150,000. A mass exodus of Indians from southern Burma had been underway for the past several weeks. Over 60 per cent of Indians resident in Burma were Indian-born, and it was natural that in a crisis many would look to return to the land of their birth. Thousands of refugees were evacuated by sea on ships making a six-day journey to Madras or Calcutta. The rest of the Indian community headed northwards by road, mostly on foot.

The 7th Australian Division would not make landfall in Burma, but other reinforcements were en route. A convoy carrying the 7th Armoured Brigade and 1st Cameronians arrived at Rangoon on 21 February. The convoy had ploughed and rolled eastwards across the empty seas of the Bay of Bengal. When the transports reached the mouth of the Rangoon River the clear waters of the bay turned brown. The city was twenty-five miles up-river; the Shwedagon Pagoda continued to loom over Rangoon, the sun's rays sparkling on the golden shrine.

The 7th Armoured Brigade arrived at Rangoon in two transports. Outward bound RAF personnel and other evacuated civilians passed by on ships sailing in the other direction. Mocking cries of 'You're going the wrong way' were helpfully directed at the inbound transports.[15] Air raid sirens wailed though there was no air attack underway. Brigadier J.H. Anstice had flown to Burma ahead of his brigade and was waiting for the ships on the quayside. During the First World War Anstice had served with the 5th Inniskilling Dragoons; he had recently been awarded the DSO for his role in the Dunkirk campaign. L.E. Tutt of the 414th Battery wrote of the convoy's disembarkation at the waterfront.

> Our arrival was largely unsung. The smell of disaster was everywhere. There were no dock gangs to take our hawsers and to help us berth. There were no stevedores to help us unload, no crane operators, no one. We understood now why some of the ships we had passed going the other way and packed with civilians had saluted us on their sirens and the passengers' cheers. We must have seemed to be sailing right into the arms of the Japanese. Over the city there was a dense pall of smoke, the sound of demolitions and rifle fire ... We were not heartened when a boat, already there when our convoy arrived, suddenly slipped her moorings and made for the open sea, churning the harbour water into a froth with the speed of her departure.[16]

An official reported: 'From the time when the E [Evacuation] signal was given, law and order broke down in Rangoon. Nearly all the police had evacuated ...

Looting went on all over the city and its suburbs, in shops and private houses; highway robbery and murder were rife.'[17] Burman gangs violently settled scores with Chinese and Indian merchants. The bodies of bomb victims still lay in the streets where they had fallen. Kites – a kind of vulture – tore at the corpses to the disgust of onlookers. Tutt saw disturbed kites rise 'with slow, laborious wing flaps as we passed. They were so sated that they could hardly get off the ground, and as they moved off, the dogs came in.'

The 7th Armoured Brigade arrived at Rangoon too late for the Sittang battle, but would play an important role for the remainder of the campaign. The brigade comprised two of its usual three armoured regiments: the 7th Hussars and 2nd Royal Tank Regiment. The third armoured unit had been left behind in the Middle East. The brigade had fought against the Italians at Sidi Barrani and Beda Fomm and the Afrika Korps' panzers at Sidi Rezegh outside Tobruk. The brigade's two armoured regiments represented the two wings of the Royal Armoured Corps, namely the traditional cavalry regiments and the more recently founded Royal Tank Regiment. Across the interwar period relations between these modern equivalents of the Cavaliers and Roundheads of the English Civil War had been marred by rivalry and mutual suspicion, but by 1942 shared experiences in war had brought about a unity of outlook hitherto absent.[18] The 414th Battery Royal Horse Artillery (Essex Yeomanry) and A Battery 95th Anti-Tank Regiment disembarked with the armoured regiments.

Anstice's brigade was equipped with mechanically reliable American Stuart light tanks, which were armed with a thirty-seven millimetre cannon that fired solid shot, and two Browning machine guns. Stuarts carried a four-man crew, weighed thirteen tons and were powered by a modified aero-engine; they were thinly armoured by the standards of North Africa, but would prove to be more than a match for Japanese anti-tank weaponry. Japanese troops, however, would learn to use mortars to lob bombs onto the top of a tank where the armour was thinnest. The brigade arrived at Rangoon with its own workshops and transport echelon; each regiment had fifty-two tanks. Surprisingly, the tanks would be confined to roads and tracks in Burma to a greater degree than expected as the *bunds* – low mud walls – that divided paddy fields baked rock hard during the dry season and were difficult even for a tank to drive over or through. The heat of the tropics made life inside the iron box of a tank difficult – at times the exterior surface of a metal vehicle was too hot to touch.

The last formations to land at Rangoon were able to help themselves to American Lend Lease supplies warehoused for shipment to China. British forces took possession of 300 Bren light machine guns, 1000 sub-machine guns, 260 jeeps and 680 trucks, all of which was desperately needed by

Burma Army. But, apart from this sort of officially-sanctioned looting, commercial life in Rangoon had ground to a halt. Heavy vehicles, buses and taxis had disappeared; street lights and electric signs went off; the sweepers fled and restaurants and newspapers closed. The American Volunteer Group's Paul Frillman observed: 'Each day the emptying streets slipped back a little further toward jungle.'[19]

Burma Army headquarters had left for Maymyo and only an advanced headquarters remained in the capital. The Judicial Secretary ordered that the convicts and inmates of Rangoon's prison and lunatic asylum be released as the warders were no longer on duty to supervise their maintenance. This added to the chaos in the doomed city. An official report concluded: 'Many looters were shot but it is feared that some of those shot at night were unfortunate lunatics, who, released from the asylum, were wandering about the streets looking for food and shelter.'[20] On a lighter note, Captain the Reverend N.S. Metcalfe of the 7th Hussars went to the Rangoon Zoo with a transport officer to retrieve some abandoned vehicles:

> Fortified by the report that all the animals of a dangerous nature had been destroyed, we made our entry only to discover that some were very much alive, and outside their cages! There was a tense moment when it was discovered that a 'tree trunk' was really a crocodile, and a 'rope' hanging from a tree was a full size boa constrictor![21]

An orang-utan was also loose; he was rumoured to be living it up downtown.

The front in south-east Burma urgently needed reinforcement in the aftermath of the Sittang debacle. News of the non-arrival of the Australian division was slow to reach the Rangoon authorities. On 24 February Dorman-Smith signalled London: 'If we can get the Australians here we might well effect a radical change for the better. Obviously it will be an anxious business getting them here, but I feel that it is a risk well worth taking as otherwise Burma is wide open for the Japanese.'[22] A signal Hutton sent Delhi that day also mentioned the expected arrival of the Australian division, 'which may just save the situation'. Hutton was angered that his willingness to resolutely defend Rangoon had been doubted in India. He cabled General Hartley, CIC India Command: 'The possibility of offensive action has always been in my mind but it is impossible to ignore the realities of the situation … Practically everything I have said has been actually borne out by events, but the unpleasant truth is never popular.'[23] During the night of 25/26 February Dorman-Smith cabled London asking if the Australian division was actually on its way. The reply came: 'Prime Minister [Churchill] to Governor of Burma. We have made every appeal, reinforced by President, but Australian Government absolutely refuses. Fight on.'[24]

Heavy Japanese air attacks on Rangoon on 25 and 26 February involved 170 aircraft across the two days. After a string of dog-fights Hurricane and Tomahawk pilots claimed to have inflicted heavy losses to the raiders. There was little further Japanese aerial activity over Rangoon whilst the city remained in British hands. Air Vice-Marshal Stevenson wrote in his despatch:

> Such a wastage had been inflicted on the enemy that thereafter he never attempted to enter our warning zone round Rangoon, until the city was captured and the air bases in his hands ... This had a critical influence on the course of our land operations and on the security of our convoys bringing in final reinforcements.[25]

In reality Japanese losses in the air had not been heavy. As the Japanese wanted to capture Rangoon port intact, they had little incentive to bomb the city any further. General Iida wrote in his diary of this period:

> We now saw little of British aircraft. The constant air attacks that we had suffered up to the battle of the Sittang were drastically reduced as the Japanese gained control in the air. Until then even a single soldier was conscious of danger in walking along a road in daytime but now worry about enemy aircraft became unnecessary.[26]

The RAF and AVG were hard pressed to defend their own bases, and were no longer in a position to influence the ground war.

Delhi had hastily assembled a brigade group at Madras to reinforce Burma at the eleventh hour. The brigade's vehicles and heavy equipment would sail from Calcutta. General Hartley cautioned Hutton: 'I have accelerated dispatch of 63 Brigade but point out that it requires a lot more training. It will be a good brigade but be under no illusion about its present position.'[27] The 1st Indian Field Regiment was to sail from Calcutta as well.

The 63rd Brigade sailed on 26 February from Madras, but that day Hutton recommended that no further troops be landed at Rangoon. Governor Dorman-Smith was in agreement. On 27 February he wrote, 'I went round the city last night. Saw no looting, perhaps because there is but little left to loot.'[28] The Governor signalled London : 'I can see nothing in sight which can save Rangoon.' On 28 February Hutton ordered the convoy carrying the 63rd Brigade to return to India. At Delhi, Hartley was in agreement. On that day Hutton also ordered the complete evacuation of Rangoon; he informed India that, unless he received instructions to the contrary, the final demolitions would take place on 1 March.[29] That afternoon, however, a signal arrived from General Wavell ordering that the demolitions be postponed. Wavell had just resumed his post as the Indian Army's CIC after returning from his ill-fated mission to Java and ABDA Command.

The night of 28 February was to be Dorman-Smith's last at Government House in Rangoon. The Governor and his personal staff dined in reduced circumstances. A bodyguard of military police remained on duty. Dorman-Smith recalled:

> After we had eaten, we went across to the billiard room. There we played a haphazard game of billiard-fives, while the past Governors of Burma, whose enlarged photographs lined the wall, looked down on us with bland expressions. To them such a last supper would have been unthinkable. They seemed to irritate Eric Battersby. [Dorman-Smith's ADC] 'Don't you think, H.E., that we ought to deny them also to the Japs?' he asked and took a billiard ball in his hand. I ought, I suppose, to have told him to put it down, but didn't and he let fly. The others joined in. It was a massacre.[30]

At dawn on 1 March Dorman-Smith left Government House for the airfield. The aircraft was bound for Magwe in central Burma to meet with Wavell and other military commanders.

12

Wavell Takes Charge

On 28 February General Wavell resumed his old post as Commander-in-Chief of the Indian Army. General Hartley was relegated to a deputy's role. Japanese forces were poised to advance on Rangoon and quick decisions had to be made. Wavell postponed Hutton's provisional order to evacuate Rangoon; he immediately flew to Burma to investigate the situation for himself. Wavell met Hutton, Dorman-Smith and Air Vice-Marshal Stevenson at Magwe on 1 March, 250 miles north of Rangoon. Hutton recalled:

> Wavell's feelings were manifest when I met him at Magwe on 1st March. He stormed at me in front of the Governor, the AOC [Stevenson] and a number of officers and civilians in a most excited way and I felt the only dignified thing to do was to make no reply … It was the one occasion I know of on which Wavell's imperturbability failed him.

The usually taciturn Wavell was possibly still in pain from his back injury; it is difficult to know the exact lingering impact of his accident at Singapore.

Wavell had no intention of letting the Japanese surround and cut off the garrison of Rangoon, but he was keen to land the 63rd Indian Brigade whilst that was still possible.[1] He later wrote of this time: 'There was no evidence of any great enemy strength west of the Sittang, 7th Armoured Brigade was still intact, and Chinese troops were moving down towards Toungoo.' The convoy carrying the 63rd Brigade was ordered to turn around again and head for Rangoon; the city was not to be evacuated until the reinforcements at sea were landed. The convoy carrying the 1st Indian Field Regiment was due on 3 March. The regiment was equipped with sixteen twenty-five-pound field guns organised in two batteries.[2] If the 7th Australian Division had been permitted to land at Rangoon the leading brigade would have arrived on 26 February, the second brigade a few days later and the last brigade about the time of the 63rd Brigade's scheduled arrival on 5 March.

After Wavell's stormy interview with his commanders at Magwe, he flew on to Mingaladon airfield with Hutton. The generals drove out to the 17th Division's headquarters at Hlegu that day. Hutton had yet to finalise Smyth's relief, but Wavell wasted no further time and dismissed him on the spot. Wavell commented that Smyth was a 'definitely sick man'. Brigadier Cowan

Map H Rangoon area

took over as divisional commander. Smyth had got away with hiding his ill health for weeks but the game was up; Headmaster Wavell had finally caught up with him.[3] Wavell had seen Smyth in private. Cowan later found Smyth sitting with his head in his hands and shaking. Smyth said: 'My career is finished.' He also said of Wavell, 'that man wouldn't forgive his own son.'[4] Wavell drove onwards to visit Pegu and gave orders that the town be held. On 2 March Wavell flew in a Blenheim bomber to Lashio to meet with Chiang Kai-shek and discuss the role of Chinese troops in Burma.

By 3 March Wavell had flown back to Calcutta. Smyth was travelling on the same flight and Wavell ignored him. Cowan later said that, 'Wavell remained mute because he was disgusted with Smyth and thought he had let the side down.'[5] Smyth was swiftly retired from the army and would spend long periods in hospital recovering his health. He was to reflect: 'It is always easy to be wise after the event, and looking back on this moment of my life now, it would obviously have been wiser to have declined the appointment [to 17th Division] on health grounds.'[6] A medical board found that Smyth had paroxysmal tachycardia, acute dyspepsia and malaria. He conceded: 'I realise now that I was as ill as my ADMS said I was in Burma and a great deal worse than I myself realised.'[7] Smyth sailed for England from Bombay late in 1942. The following year he began to work as a military correspondent for a newspaper in London. Smyth was not the only officer from the 17th Division's headquarters to be replaced. The Chief Royal Engineer, Colonel Armitage, was evacuated sick to India. The GSO 1, Lieutenant-Colonel Simpson, was relieved by Major Guy Burton.[8]

Wavell met General Alexander's incoming flight at Calcutta airfield. To hasten his arrival in Burma, Alexander had flown from England to Egypt across occupied France at high altitude.[9] Alexander, the debonair third son of the Earl of Caledon, had begun his military career in the Irish Guards just before the First World War; he had a brilliant war in France and Flanders and rapid promotion had followed in the interwar period. Alexander had experience of the Indian Army as he had commanded a brigade at Nowshera on India's North-west Frontier in the mid to late 1930s. He subsequently commanded a division and the rearguard at Dunkirk. It might be said that Alexander was handed a poisoned chalice in the form of command of Burma Army, but that was equally the case for all ranks of British forces in the Far East.

Wavell told Alexander in their brief interview at Calcutta: 'The retention of Rangoon is a matter of vital importance to our position in the Far East and every effort must be made to hold it.'[10] Alexander was also ordered not to let the Rangoon garrison be cut off if the city could not be successfully defended. How Alexander was to juggle those two conflicting priorities was easier said than done. His outward serenity and good sense would be sorely tested in the days ahead. Wavell felt it necessary ruthlessly to impose leadership upon his subordinates. A more measured review of the situation could take place once the front had been stabilised.

Whilst Alexander was making the final stage of his long journey to Burma, the fighting continued to the north-east of Rangoon. General Hutton had ordered the 7th Armoured Brigade to hold Waw, which was a village of lightly constructed buildings between Pegu and the Sittang river. A canal ran through the village from north to south. Tanks could not cross the flimsy canal bridge and were confined to the west bank.

The armoured brigade provided a screen behind which the 17th Indian Division could prepare for its next battle. The ordnance dump at Pegu contained clothing and arms, but other types of equipment were in short supply. The 48th Brigade was located at Pegu; the 16th Brigade and the headquarters of the 17th Division were located at Hlegu, a village on the road from Rangoon to Pegu.[11]

By this time Chinese troops had relieved the 1st Burma Division in the Shan States. Scott's division had begun to transfer southwards. The 1st Burma Brigade was now fifteen miles north of Nyaunglebin; the 13th Indian Brigade was in the Karen hills covering a crossing of the Salween river near Kemapyu and Mawchi. The 2nd Burma Brigade would also be placed under Scott's command; this brigade was at Nyaunglebin, thirty-five miles to the north of Waw.

The 1st West Yorkshire and the newly disembarked Cameronians were sent forward from Rangoon to fight with the 7th Armoured Brigade. The Cameronians, many of whom haled from Glasgow and the towns of Lanarkshire, had left Secunderabad in India with newly issued mortars, armoured Bren carriers and motor vehicles only ten days before. The West Yorks had started the year at the Indian station of Barrackpore. The Cameronians and West Yorks had been in India since the early 1930s and were amongst the oldest regiments in the army. The Cameronians (26th Foot) had been on the field at Blenheim in 1704; the West Yorks (14th Foot) had fought at the 1695 siege of Namur.

Hutton was concerned that the Japanese might cut the main road heading north from Rangoon to Prome in the Irrawaddy valley; he sent a squadron of 7th Hussars and a company of West Yorks to patrol the road. If Rangoon was evacuated, Hutton's plan was for the 17th Division and the armoured brigade to retire on Prome; the 1st Burma Division would cover the arrival of Chinese forces in the upper Sittang valley.

Whilst Burma Army was trying to rebuild a viable front between Pegu and the Sittang, Japanese troops were busy heading northwards along the east bank of the Sittang with the intention of crossing the river at Kunzeik. XV Army relied on animal transport and could make do without a bridge for motor vehicles. Repair work on the wrecked Sittang bridge was not a priority.

Japanese detachments crossed the river by ferry at Kunzeik and fanned out into the countryside on the west bank. On 27 February a standing section patrol of the Cameronians was surprised by Japanese and wiped out; the bodies were found full of bayonet punctures. Reverend Metcalfe officiated at the burial service. The following night the bridge over the canal at Waw was destroyed as Japanese patrols were reported to be in houses on the far bank. British troops evacuated Waw on 1 March.

General Iida ordered the main body of the 55th Division to cross the Sittang river on the night of 3/4 March and capture Pegu. The 33rd Division was to follow the 55th Division and then swing westwards across the hills towards the road and railway that ran northwards from Rangoon to Prome. For the 55th Division's attack on Pegu, the 143rd Regiment was to attack the town from the west, whilst the 112th Regiment hooked past the western side of the town to block the road to the south of Pegu. The II/143rd Battalion was detached to watch the road heading northwards along the Sittang valley to Toungoo. The I/112th Battalion was also detached and sent down the coast with orders to capture the Syriam oil refineries.[12]

General Alexander landed at Magwe airfield late on 4 March. On the morning of 5 March Hutton, unsure exactly when Alexander would appear at Rangoon, ordered the 48th Brigade to withdraw from Pegu towards the capital. Hutton and Cowan agreed that the retreat should begin that night. But at 1 p.m. that afternoon Alexander reached Rangoon and took command of Burma Army. The cool-headed and well-turned-out Alexander radiated a quiet optimism. He cancelled Hutton's order and instructed Cowan's 17th Division to make a stand at Pegu in accordance with the spirit of Wavell's orders to keep the port of Rangoon open as long as possible.

On 5 March the convoy carrying the 63rd Indian Brigade docked at Rangoon. The brigade had been taken from the 14th Indian Division, which was one of several semi-formed divisions of the field army in India. The brigade comprised the 1/10th Gurkhas, 1/11th Sikhs and 2/13th Frontier Force Rifles. In theory these were regular units but they had been thoroughly milked of experienced soldiers to help create or reinforce other battalions. The Sikhs had taken on 400 recruits with five months' service to make the unit up to strength. On the voyage across the Bay of Bengal troops practised with newly unpacked weaponry by firing them over the stern. As the ships approached the docks at Rangoon not a sound could be heard in the empty city beyond. Sepoys of the Sikhs noted a covey of vultures circling ominously over the doomed metropolis. After the brigade had disembarked they would be available to reinforce the troops at Pegu.

At dawn on 6 March Japanese troops of the 143rd Regiment attacked Pegu from the west. This took the garrison by surprise as an attack had seemed more likely from the north or north-east. The West Yorks were compelled to give ground near the rail station; the Japanese captured the station and parts of western Pegu, though the Cameronians held on to the vital bridges in the town over the river and railway. Japanese aerial bombing of Pegu caused fires that spread into the surrounding jungle. A counter-attack by troops of the 48th Brigade at midday restored the situation. During the afternoon the town was cleared of Japanese and the station recaptured.[13]

As the Japanese attack on Pegu was getting underway that morning, tanks of the 7th Hussars had advanced up the main road leading northwards from Pegu on a routine patrol. The mist was heavy and the tanks were ambushed by a Japanese battery of thirty-seven-millimetre anti-tank guns. Tracks were blown off a couple of tanks, but when the mist lifted a counter-attack by the Hussars and a supporting company of West Yorks overran all four guns of the battery and killed many of the gunners. Japanese anti-tank guns were unable to penetrate the armour of the Stuarts. Shortly afterwards the Hussars added to their laurels by knocking out three Japanese seven-ton light tanks. The Japanese tanks belonged to the 2nd Tank Regiment and had entered southern Burma by the overland route from Thailand – a fourth tank had been lost when it slid off a ferry into the Sittang river.[14]

Burma Army headquarters intended to quickly send the disembarked 63rd Brigade from Rangoon to reinforce the defenders of Pegu. The Japanese, however, struck a terrible blow against the brigade when its commander, Brigadier J. Wickham, and all three battalion commanders were killed or wounded in an ambush to the south of Pegu on the morning of 6 March. The party of commanders had driven to Pegu the previous evening to discuss their brigade's future deployment in the vicinity. The following morning they set out on the return journey in a convoy of armoured vehicles. The commander of the 1/10th Gurkhas, Lieutenant-Colonel R.G. Leonard, recalled when the Bren carrier in which he, the brigadier and brigade-major were travelling passed a tree:

> There was a harsh rattle of a light automatic. I felt as if a heavy draught horse had kicked me on the knees. I saw John Wickham and Ian slump towards each other and the carrier slithered to a stop. A moment later another burst followed the first and my left arm, by which I was bracing myself, was flung aside and I fell forward in time for my head to be missed by the third burst which, ricocheting off the back-plate filled the carrier with further splashes of lead.[15]

Brigadier Wickham was badly wounded in the ambush. The machine gun fire was thought to have come from an ambusher up in a tree. In a separate incident, grenades were pitched into another Bren carrier to kill both the commanding officers of the Sikhs and Frontier Force Rifles. It was later ascertained that the ambush had been set by men of the Burma Independence Army with the assistance of Japanese troops.

After taking command at Burma Army headquarters, Alexander soon came to realise the full extent of the danger British forces faced. He reversed his previous policy and ordered the evacuation of Rangoon. At 8 p.m. on 6 March British forces were ordered to pull out of Pegu the following day and retire to Hlegu, twenty-one miles back along the road to Rangoon. The 48th Brigade and 7th Armoured Brigade formed a close perimeter at Pegu for the night of 6/7 March. Plans were drawn up to attack the road block known to be somewhere on the road between Pegu and Hlegu.

After first light on 7 March the tanks and Gurkha battalions led the force southwards from Pegu; the West Yorks and Cameronians formed the rearguard. The tanks and transport were drawn up on the road with the infantry in columns on either side. The demolition of the bridges in Pegu alerted the Japanese that something was up, but heavy morning mist covered the retreat at the outset. As expected, a defended Japanese road block was in place to the south of Pegu. Infantry of the 112th Regiment had marched around the western side of Pegu through jungle-covered hills.

The tanks of the 7th Hussars attacked the block at 8.30 a.m. after a brief artillery bombardment. The lead tank was disabled ramming the block, but the rest of the Hussars, the 414th Battery and some vehicles drove through the block and onwards to Hlegu.

After the tanks had gone, the Japanese closed in again to block the road and halt the rest of the column's progress. The Gurkhas became involved in confused fighting with Japanese in the jungle and gardens flanking the main road. Some of the stationary vehicles were peppered with small arms fire and set alight. Lieutenant-Colonel White of the 7th Gurkhas was killed; Cameron of the 5th Gurkhas was wounded in the leg by a sniper.[16] The Japanese suffered heavy losses when two companies of the 1/4th Gurkhas counter-attacked to clear an orchard and compound near the village of Payathonzu.

As a result of the fighting, the Japanese II/112th Battalion was thrown back into the jungle and the transport column was able to drive down the road to Hlegu. Isolated detachments of Gurkha and British infantry had to march cross-country around the block-site to rejoin the road. A party from the 1/4th Gurkhas marched by a separate route and collided with the 214th Regiment's mounted infantry platoon. The Japanese horsemen charged the Gurkhas, who emptied several saddles with rifle fire before calmly proceeding on their way again.

For British, Indian and Gurkha troops, the fighting around Pegu provided further evidence of the indestructible morale of the Japanese soldier. The story did the rounds of a Japanese officer on a white horse who charged a tank of the Hussars. He dismounted to scramble aboard the vehicle and hacked with a sword at the tank's commander, who defended himself with a hammer. The Japanese officer fell off the tank, which ran over his legs, only for the officer to draw his revolver to fire at the tank.[17] Whether apocryphal or not, those who fought the Japanese did not doubt their devotion to duty. When a soldier of the 2nd Royal Tanks was asked how warfare in Burma compared with North Africa, he replied: 'Much the same amount of shit flying around, but the trouble with these Japanese bastards is that they don't run away like the Italians.'[18]

Corporal Alexander Morrison was a driver with the armoured brigade's transport. At Pegu the medical staff had gathered together the wounded in a plantation until the time came to evacuate:

> The final vehicle was being loaded with the last of the wounded who stood any chance of surviving the rough journey ahead. All that were left were the dying and the immovable, the hopeless cases, rows of them. The medical officer was going round giving each man an injection of morphine. On one side of the clearing lay half-a-dozen corpses and as I watched about a dozen large vultures, massive birds, over three or four feet high, were tearing them apart and eating them. Four medical orderlies drew lots to see who would remain behind with the wounded and await his fate at the hands of the Japs.

Morrison glanced back as his vehicle drove away. 'We left one lone figure, a young medical orderly, who stood to attention and saluted us.'[19]

The fighting around Pegu was another setback for Burma Army, though for the first time in the campaign the losses in the engagement may have been higher for the Japanese. The 1/4th Gurkhas had been heavily involved and lost thirty-six dead on 6–7 March; the West Yorks suffered twenty-two killed and forty-five missing; the Cameronians ten killed and seventy-five missing. Many of the missing, however, would eventually rejoin their units. The Japanese III/112th Battalion lost three officers and seventy-nine other ranks killed at Pegu. Losses in the II/112th Battalion and 143rd Regiment are not recorded, but those units were also roughly handled. After Pegu was captured, the 143rd Regiment turned back northwards to advance up the Sittang valley, whilst the 112th Regiment pushed on towards Hlegu and Rangoon.[20]

By this time colonial Rangoon was a dead city. The Shwedagon Pagoda gleamed gold against the black clouds of smoke billowing skywards; dogs howled in the distance; vandals and looters roamed the streets. Detained miscreants were shot in moderation by security troops to restore an uneasy and tense calm.[21] Unwanted Lend Lease stores were set on fire. An eyewitness recalled that:

> the docks were in a state which it was hardly believable could have existed in any British possession. Apart from our small party, I do not think there was one sober man anywhere. The crews of the ships alongside, and the troops, had looted cases of liquor and were rolling about the place in the last stages of drunkenness. We interviewed several ships' officers, who were quite powerless to take any action, as there were no forces of law and order to assist them.[22]

Professor Pearn wrote of his evacuation from the city:

> As the launches passed down the Rangoon River against a strong flood-tide, a strange spectacle was presented to the eyes of the weary passengers. A heavy pall of smoke hung over the town, but a light southerly wind kept the smoke off the foreshore ... The electric power station was ablaze; ... the port warehouses were blackening skeletons; ... on the jetties the cranes, damaged by dynamite, leant over at a drunken angle ... All along the normally thronged foreshore not a sign of human life was to be seen. By the time that Syriam was abeam, it was almost dark and the flames, topped by columns of dense black smoke rising thousands of feet into the air from the oil refineries, presented an awe-inspiring sight; and as the night fell the whole sky was lurid with the glare of that inferno.[23]

Rear-Admiral Cosmo Graham was commodore of naval forces in southern Burma, though his handful of motor-launches and auxiliary craft of the Burma Royal Navy Volunteer Reserve had given him little to work with. Remarkably, no large transports were lost to air attack during the evacuation of Rangoon, nor during the last ditch attempts to reinforce southern Burma.[24]

The civil engineer Leslie Forster was in charge of the demolitions at the installations of the Burmah Oil Company, down river from Rangoon at Syriam. Forster was aided by a team under the command of a twenty-three-year-old Royal Engineer, Captain Walter Scott. The refinery, power-house, workshops and tank farm covered several square miles; 150 million gallons could be stored in giant tanks. Seven-hundred separate explosive charges had been laid. The oil tanks were opened and a great black cloud of vapour formed over the refinery. At 2 p.m. on 7 March, after Scott had received the coded signal 'Red Elephant', the charges were detonated. The sound of great explosions rent the air. Thick black smoke, lit by pillars of fire, billowed to over 20,000 feet and the fires at Syriam burnt for weeks.[25]

The last train left Rangoon on the evening of 7 March at 7.30 p.m.; the last shipping sailed in the early hours of the following morning. Graham and his naval detachment left Rangoon by sea for Akyab. The Danish steamer *Henrich Jessen* was moored ten miles downstream of the city. The last parties, including a company of the 1/9th Jats, were taken to the ship by launch, which sailed for Calcutta at 3 a.m. on 8 March.

As the last demolitions took place in the colonial capital on 7 March, Alexander's Rangoon garrison set out northwards along the road to Prome. Lend Lease stores warehoused at the docks had been used to re-equip units for the journey. The Glosters now possessed over 120 lorries and motorcycles. The first vehicles left Rangoon at dawn. To the north of Mingaladon airfield large rubber estates stretched to the vicinity of the Taukkyan cross-roads, twenty-one miles north of the capital. At Taukkyan the road bifurcated to the north-west and north-east. The north-western arm ran to Prome; the north-eastern arm ran to Hlegu and Pegu. The 17th Indian Division and 7th Armoured Brigade had orders to fall back upon Taukkyan from Hlegu to meet the column heading north from Rangoon. The combined force would then take the road heading to Prome.

Meanwhile General Sakurai's 33rd Division was advancing through the hills north of Rangoon with the intention of reaching the rail and road routes that ran from Rangoon to Prome. The leading unit of Sakurai's division, the III/214th Battalion, had reached the small village of Yetho, two miles to the east of the Rangoon-Prome road; Yetho was to the north of the Taukkyan cross-roads.

On the morning of 7 March Lieutenant Tatumi Shiotubo's platoon of the III/214th Battalion was keeping the Rangoon-Prome road under observation from posts near the village of Satthwadaw. Shiotubo watched as a 'column of tanks, armoured cars, guns and trucks fully loaded with soldiers holding rifles and looking out both sides, passed by the village. It was really impressive to see them from so close.'[26] This was the advance guard of Burma Army's column leaving Rangoon.

The advance guard comprised the combined KOYLI and Dukes battalion, a troop of the 2nd Royal Tanks and a battery of the 1st Indian Field Regiment. This column of vehicles passed safely up the road to reach Tharrawaddy. Upon arrival the column's commander, Lieutenant-Colonel Tynte, received news that Japanese troops had been sighted to the south near the road they had just traversed.[27] Tynte and a party set out to investigate.

In the meantime Shiotubo's platoon had taken up ambush positions by the road, and intended to fire on the next Allied vehicles to appear. After a while a truck came down the road from the north at high speed. This truck was carrying Lieutenant-Colonel Tynte's reconnaissance party and was promptly shot up. Tynte was mortally wounded. Some panicked men leapt out of the vehicle and ran into the nearby jungle. The damaged truck headed back north again. A black saloon car later arrived down the road from the north; it was halted by firing and all the occupants were killed in the subsequent melee; the car was pushed off the road and out of sight. Soon a motorcyclist also fell victim to the ambush.

The charmed life of Shiotubo's platoon could not last forever. Japanese scouts brought news of another large motorised column rumbling up the road from Rangoon. A runner was hastily sent to the III/214th Battalion's headquarters. The unit's commander, Major Takanobe, dispatched reinforcements that included the regimental gun company and its pair of seventy-five millimetre mountain guns. Takanobe sited a road block near Satthwadaw, sixty yards north of a bend in the road. Dense jungle stretched to the west of the road; the landscape was more open to the east. The mountain guns were sited in the monsoon ditches on the sides of the road, one gun facing northwards and the other southwards. A low sandbag wall was built to shield the gunners; a company of infantry was sited on each side of the block.

The first British vehicles to approach the road block from the south were tanks of the 7th Hussars. The Japanese claim to have scored hits on the first two tanks, one of which was set on fire; the next pair of tanks drove through the block and onwards to the north. Following behind the tanks was Lieutenant-Colonel Bagot's Glosters. This battalion was ordered to attack the block at about 3 p.m. The bulk of the Glosters, however, were still at the rear of the long column leaving Rangoon. The troops at Bagot's immediate disposal were B Company, most of Headquarters Company, a platoon of C Company and two armoured Bren carriers.

Bagot, a stocky man with a red face, sent his B Company and the two armoured carriers to clear the block, which was built from branches and barrels. Withering Japanese machine gun fire forced the infantry to take cover. Of the carriers, one was hit by a mortar shell ten yards from the block and the crew killed. The other carrier was driven by Private V.V. Phylatoff, a Russian exile from Shanghai, and was knocked out by close range gunfire. The Dukes' Captain J.A.A. Christison, the son of an Indian Army general, was amongst the dead with the carriers. Bagot led forward the Glosters for another assault on the road block, but this movement failed as well and he was wounded in the leg.[28] The Glosters casualties for the engagement were three officers and seventeen other ranks killed, and three officers and twenty-three other ranks wounded.[29]

Major Takanobe's III/214th Battalion was proving to be a formidable adversary. The 2/13th Frontier Force Rifles (less two companies) and a squadron of the 2nd Royal Tanks came to the head of the column for another attack on the road block. The Frontier Force attacked on either side of the road but found the Japanese strongly posted in the jungle to the west of the block; medium machine guns commanded the open paddy to the east of the road. The Japanese held their ground till darkness fell.

British forces formed unit perimeters that evening 500 yards south of the road block. At about 10 p.m., the Japanese attacked the perimeter of the Frontier Force Rifles. Japanese rushed out of the darkness from the eastern flank; the sounds of machine gun fire, grenade bursts and screaming shattered the night. The intruders reached battalion headquarters; a Japanese officer attacked the chief clerk, but Captain Rahim Khan shot him with his revolver at the sixth attempt. The brief but furious action ended when the Japanese retreated into the night leaving their dead behind; the Frontier Force lost twenty-one killed and fifty-four wounded.[30]

The situation seemed dire for Alexander's Burma Army during the night of 7/8 March. The 55th Division was advancing on Rangoon down the road from Pegu; now it seemed that the 33rd Division had blocked the road from Rangoon to Prome. The 17th Indian Division and 7th Armoured Brigade had joined the Rangoon garrison, and over a thousand vehicles were assembled in the rubber plantations and scrub near the Taukkyan cross-roads. The traffic jam was compared to 'Piccadilly Circus on Coronation night'.

Alexander's troops prepared for another attack on the road block at first light on 8 March. The 63rd Brigade was to lead the assault. The 2/13th Frontier Force was to advance again astride the road, supported by tanks. The 1/10th Gurkhas were to advance to the west of the road and the 1/11th Sikhs to the east. The later two units had to make difficult night marches to their assembly positions. A brief artillery bombardment was to precede the advance of the infantry. After the plans for the attack had been decided, Alexander sent an instruction to all units announcing that, 'the attack on the road block today has failed. Another attack will be made tomorrow morning. If that fails units are to split up into small parties of twelve men who are to make their own way to India independently.'[31] That was not an appealing prospect.

After daylight on 8 March, L.E. Tutt of the 414th Battery watched proceedings get underway:

> Some of the tanks went off in advance to spearhead the attack on the road block. We followed at a more sober pace but were in time to take up positions to support the attack. The initial bombardment was from the guns of the 12th Mountain Battery. Troops and tanks moved forward on a grand scale. The tanks and some of the Sikhs probed forward and found that the Japanese had gone.[32]

The road block site was derelict; the attack planned by the 63rd Brigade would not be necessary. The long columns of motor transport carrying Burma Army drove northwards to Tharrawaddy subject only to long range sniping.

What had become of the Japanese force that had so resolutely defended the road block? It transpired that General Iida had given the 33rd Division orders to push on southwards for Rangoon. In turn the enterprising General Sakurai had ordered the 215th Regiment to advance directly on the capital alongside the railway line. During the night of 7/8 March the regiment crossed to the west of the Rangoon-Prome road at a point on the northern side of the road block; the troops then began a gruelling slog towards Rangoon down the railway. The 33rd Division's other regiment, the 214th Regiment, had been blocking the road and an arc of countryside to the north of Taukkyan. But it was not intended to permanently block the road. The allotted task of Takanobe's battalion was only to block the road until the 215th Regiment had crossed to the western side to reach the railway. Once that had been completed there was no necessity to maintain the road block. Thus, during the early hours of 8 March, the force astride the road withdrew from their positions back to the village of Yetho, on the eastern side of the road. The III/214th Battalion had lost 100 casualties defending the block; Takanobe was amongst the wounded.[33]

On 8 March the 215th Regiment entered a deserted Rangoon after a long march down the railway. General Sakurai belatedly realised that the British garrison had escaped. That had been a stroke of luck for Burma Army, but in a fast moving campaign in a heavily forested tropical landscape mistakes were likely to be made by both sides from time to time. Brigadier Davies commented: 'Surely this was one of the most remarkable instances of a missed opportunity ever recorded.'[34] Japanese commanders had been expecting the British to mount a determined defence of Rangoon. Japanese expectations may have included a last ditch defence of the capital like the Russian defence of Port Arthur in 1904–05, or as the Filipino-American army was under-taking at Bataan. British forces had at least attempted to defend Singapore, though without much success. Still, the main Japanese goal was the capture of the port of Rangoon so that reinforcements and supplies could arrive directly by sea; that had been achieved triumphantly by a relatively small force.

As the rising sun flag was raised over the governor's residence in Rangoon, the long column of Burma Army's transport drove northwards. Twenty-eight miles was covered on 8 March, and thirty-five miles the following day, before Burma Army stopped to rest and regroup. Some of the troops withdrawing from Pegu had reached Taukkyan only just in time to join the main Rangoon column heading northwards. The force driving north towards Prome was not subjected to air attack, nor was it closely pursued on the ground.

Alexander signalled Wavell that he had held on at Rangoon for as long as possible: 'There was for some time grave danger of whole army being surrounded or of being broken up into such small columns as could fight their way out on foot after abandoning and destroying their mechanised equipment and transport.'[35] Wavell conceded in his campaign despatch that his decision to hang onto Rangoon for as long as possible 'eventually placed General Alexander in a difficult position and led to his forces being nearly cut off'. Wavell added, however, that, 'On balance I am satisfied that we gained by the delay.'

13

Retreat from Rangoon

The fall of Rangoon encouraged Imperial General Headquarters in Tokyo to issue orders for the conquest of Upper Burma. The capture of both Singapore and Rangoon made it possible for the Japanese to send reinforcements to southern Burma directly from Singapore by sea. Additional troops would be needed to expel both British and Chinese forces from Burma. If Singapore had not fallen so swiftly, reinforcements would not have been so readily available. The rapid success of Japanese landing operations in the Dutch East Indies was also vital to releasing shipping and opening the sea lanes into the Indian Ocean. Japanese troops were landed on the tip of northern Sumatra to help cover the route to Burma through the Bay of Bengal.

On 15 March XV Army issued operational orders for the next phase of the campaign to sweep Allied forces from Burma. Japanese troops were to advance north along the Irrawaddy and Sittang valleys. The jungle-covered hills of the Pegu Yomas divided the two valleys in southern Burma. These parallel corridors were the main routes northwards from Rangoon and stretched all the way to Meiktila. Henceforward the primary Japanese objectives in Burma would be the capture of Mandalay, and the defeat of Chinese forces entering the colony. The 55th Division was to move up the Sittang valley towards Mandalay; the 33rd Division, after it had reorganised at Rangoon, was to move northwards along the Irrawaddy to the oilfields at Yenangyaung. Japanese casualties up to the fall of Rangoon were not heavy, and replacements were already on hand to refill the ranks of the infantry.[1]

Prior to the fall of Rangoon, the Japanese had relied on the rough overland route to Thailand for stores and munitions, whereas the British had enjoyed the luxury of Rangoon as their main logistical base. The tables had been neatly turned. There were no reliable road communications through the mountains of northern Burma leading to Bengal and Assam. Burma Army would have to eke out survival using whatever supplies were available in the Mandalay region and other nearby depots.

To defend central Burma, Allied commanders had the battered 17th Indian and 1st Burma Divisions, the 7th Armoured Brigade and two Chinese armies. British forces in the Irrawaddy valley had concentrated at Prome after the loss of Rangoon. The 6th Chinese Army was in the Shan States watching the frontier with Indochina and Thailand. The leading troops of the 5th Chinese Army were in the Sittang valley at Toungoo, south of which the 1st Burma Division held positions at Nyaunglebin.

By this stage of the campaign military movements were constantly impeded by the steady trek northwards of Indian refugees from Rangoon and the towns and villages of southern Burma. Marauding Burmese gangs armed with *dahs* – long knives – preyed upon Indian refugees. Captain James Lunt of the 2nd Burma Brigade recalled how one morning he was standing beside a railway line, watching the columns of Indian coolies pouring through Nyaunglebin:

> my eye was caught by a beautiful Indian woman, striding along like a Rajput princess, her child clasped to her left hip. She was tall and well-built, her black hair fastened in a bun, her pleated dark red skirt swinging like a kilt at every stride. Bangles at her wrists and ankles tinkled as she passed, her kohl-rimmed eyes meeting mine for a brief moment.

Lunt saw her again a few days later, many miles to the north, and then a third time in very different circumstances. He was driving away from Toungoo late in the day, past the long stream of refugees heading northwards.

> Suddenly there was a break in the refugee traffic, for perhaps a mile or so, until rounding a bend, we came across some bodies lying in the road. A bright red skirt caught my eye and we stopped the jeep. She lay there, her long black hair streaming out into a pool of fast congealing blood, her throat cut from ear to ear. One arm was raised across her face, warding off the blows. Her bodice had been ripped off, the haft of a knife protruding between her breasts. The bright red skirt had been pulled up above her waist in a final obscene gesture. The child, a little way apart, lay with its brains spilling out onto the tarmac. The bodies were still warm, the attack obviously having taken place only minutes previously. A shot from my orderly distracted me. Some men were running across the paddy fields beyond, Burmese with their *lungyis* pulled up above their knees so as to run faster.[2]

The unrecorded death toll of the civilian population, whether from disease or acts of violence, would certainly exceed that of the combatant armies.

Scott's 1st Burma Division had been reorganised so that each brigade had a mixture of Indian and Burma Rifles battalions. Not long after the fall of Rangoon, Japanese troops were discovered at Pyuntaza, eight miles south of Nyaunglebin. On 11 March the 1st Burma Brigade attacked the town, though a Japanese counter-attack overran a company of the 2/7th Rajputs. The 2nd Burma Brigade had advanced in support of the attack on Pyuntaza. The 5/1st Punjabis crossed the Sittang river and captured Shwegyin from a detachment of the Burma Independence Army. Scott's force held their ground until Chinese troops were firmly established at Toungoo, after which the 1st Burma

Division was ordered to start the long journey needed to join the 17th Indian Division in the Irrawaddy valley.

General Hutton had requested the formation of a new corps headquarters in Burma earlier in the campaign, and Alexander was also keen for that arrangement to be put in place. On 19 March Lieutenant-General W.J. Slim took command of a hastily improvised 'Burcorps' headquarters. Slim's arrival introduced a remarkable personality to the war in Burma. Born in 1891 and the son of a Birmingham hardware merchant, Slim had joined the army at the outbreak of the First World War. He was badly wounded in both the Gallipoli and Mesopotamian campaigns serving with the Warwickshire Regiment

Slim transferred to the Indian Army after the First World War as it was possible to live comfortably on an officer's pay in India. He joined the 6th Gurkha Rifles. Frontier service in a Waziristan tribal war in 1920 was followed by a brilliant performance at the Quetta Staff College and a stint at army headquarters. Slim was the Indian Army's representative at the Camberley Staff College from 1934–36; he later attended the Imperial Defence College. In appearance Slim was a strong-jawed man of medium height and stocky build; he possessed great ambition, a fine intellect and sound professional judgement.

When war broke out in 1939 Slim was one of the army's rising stars; he was given command of a brigade, which sailed for the Middle East and took part in the Abyssinian campaign against Italian forces. Slim was promoted to command the 10th Indian Division in May 1941, and served with the division in Iraq and Syria. Further promotion soon followed; Slim's commander at Baghdad told him by telephone that he was to return to India to take up another appointment. Slim was advised: 'A good soldier goes where he's sent and does what he is told.'[3]

After a brief visit to Burma about the time of Rangoon's fall, Slim had returned to Calcutta to meet with General Wavell at Government House. Slim flew to Burma again the following day. On the return flight the Lysander light aircraft was piloted by a young Sikh of the Indian Air Force. The aircraft refuelled at Chittagong; it then landed at Magwe airfield after sunset, on the eastern side of the glistening Irrawaddy river. The following morning, Slim flew on to Prome, the location of his new headquarters.[4]

Slim set up headquarters at the Law Courts at Prome. Scott said of Slim's arrival: 'He immediately imposed his personality to the extent that we felt that someone behind had taken charge of us. Up to then we had been left to our own devices.'[5] Slim's task was made easier as he and his divisional commanders, Scott and Cowan, were all officers of the 6th Gurkha Rifles, and had known one another for many years. This did much to restore harmony in the upper reaches of Burma Army.

'Burcorps' needed a headquarters staff and acquired many personnel from an already over-stretched Burma Army headquarters. Brigadier Davies, a tall, 'bony' man, became Slim's chief of staff; Lieutenant-Colonel F.C. Simpson, formerly 17th Division's GSO 1, was put in charge of administration.[6] Additional staff officers had to be flown in from India, amongst whom was Major Brian Montgomery, the younger brother of the soon-to-be-famous Montgomery of Alamein. He had recently held an appointment at Waziristan district headquarters, and was a punctilious disciplinarian who had many of the attributes of his elder brother. Major Montgomery had transferred into the Indian Army in 1936 after stints with the Royal Warwicks and King's African Rifles. In April Captain Walter Walker, a recent graduate of a shortened Quetta course and a future NATO commander, also joined Slim's staff.[7]

Slim's new headquarters was only the size of a properly staffed brigade headquarters. Such a small headquarters, however, could be transported in a relatively short column of vehicles to reduce the risk of air attack. The signals detachment possessed four wireless sets with batteries that needed recharging by pedal. The maintenance of reliable communications would be difficult. A lack of aerial reconnaissance and captured documents made intelligence assessments haphazard. Few British officers had much knowledge of the Japanese language.

The heavy fighting in south-east Burma had led to wholesale promotions within Burcorps and the 17th Division in particular. After Brigadier Hugh-Jones was evacuated suffering from dysentery, Lieutenant-Colonel Cameron of the 2/5th Gurkhas was made commander of the 48th Brigade. The new commander of the 63rd Brigade was Brigadier A.E. Barlow, the former CO of the Garhwal Rifles battalion in Scott's division.

With the sea route severed only small numbers of personnel could be flown to Burma from India. Just about the last British reinforcement to reach Burma were the officers and men of the 1st Royal Inniskilling Fusiliers, who were flown to Magwe airfield in central Burma from 8–13 March by United States B-17 heavy bombers.[8] The under-strength battalion of 474 had been hastily mobilised at Meerut. There were now six British infantry battalions in Burma.

On 10 March Burma Army headquarters had been reopened at Maymyo, Burma's summer capital near Mandalay and a pre-war military station. Maymyo was 3500 feet above sea level on a jungle-covered plateau, and was blessed with breezes by day and a cool night; the sky was a brilliant blue and flowering bushes lit up the greens of the jungle. Slim wrote of Maymyo: 'It was a delightful spot, with English houses in the best Surrey stockbroker style, each in its own spacious garden.'[9] Governor Dorman-Smith, Prime

Minister Sir Paw Tun and the civil administration also took up residence at Maymyo. The town became the home of many expatriates. Paul Frillman of the AVG passed through Maymyo and recalled: 'I even saw two proper blondes in long-skirted evening dresses, one blue, one pink, walking sedately with two young British officers. Off to a dance I supposed. They looked strange as Martians to me.'[10]

Prior to the fall of Rangoon, Hutton had ordered the transfer of three-quarters of all reserve supplies to the Mandalay area. Large quantities of stores were successfully transported from the capital. Motor fuel was obtained from the oilfield at Yenangyaung. Nonetheless, anxious staff officers at Maymyo had roughly calculated that sufficient stores and munitions were on hand to keep Allied forces in the field only until the monsoons broke in May; after that date a new and reliable line of communication would be required back over the mountains to north-east India.

The 17th Indian Division was relatively unmolested in the period immediately after the retreat from Rangoon to Prome. The Allied air forces were not so fortunate. Prior to the evacuation of Rangoon, Air Vice-Marshal Stevenson was ordered to take his headquarters to Calcutta. In addition to Stevenson and his staff, another 3000 airmen were evacuated to India by sea or air. The only radar station in Burma was relocated at Magwe, which became the main RAF base in the colony. No. 67 Squadron had been relieved and the last of the Buffaloes were flown to Dum Dum airfield at Calcutta. No. 113 Squadron's remaining Blenheim bombers also left for India.

The RAF in Burma was reorganised as two mixed wings of all aircraft types. On 11 March Burwing was formed at Magwe. This wing comprised the sixteen Hurricanes of No. 17 Squadron, nine Blenheim Mk IVs of No. 45 Squadron and six Tomahawks of the American Volunteer Group. The second wing was formed at Akyab, on the Arakan coast of western Burma, and included ten Hurricanes of No. 136 Squadron. In the meantime the Japanese 5th Air Division was re-deploying to southern Burma. Airfields at Mingaladon, Moulmein and Pegu were taken over by Japanese aviators, in addition to the airfields of Thailand and Indochina already available. RAF intelligence estimated Japanese air strength at 400 machines; the real figure was 260, but that was still a formidable force.[11]

Japanese reconnaissance aircraft had discovered Magwe airfield, but RAF reconnaissance had also discovered the recent build-up of Japanese aircraft near Rangoon. On 20 March at least fifty Japanese aircraft were spotted at Mingaladon. Group Captain H.S. Broughall, the commander of the Magwe wing, decided to launch a pre-emptive strike. At dawn on 21 March nine Blenheims and ten Hurricanes set out to raid Mingaladon. Squadron Leader

C.A.C. 'Bunny' Stone's Hurricanes started proceedings with a strafing attack as the Blenheims had lagged behind on the outward flight. The Blenheims had clashed with Japanese fighters, but managed to fly onwards to bomb the airfield as planned. A lot of damage was inflicted; Japanese records state that two aircraft were consumed by flames on the ground and another eleven aircraft badly damaged.[12]

Broughall was delighted with the results of the raid and another operation was prepared for later that day. In the interim, however, the Japanese launched their own offensive against Magwe airfield. At 1.30 p.m. twenty-five Japanese bombers and forty fighters attacked Magwe. The Japanese raid arrived as Allied pilots were being briefed and their aircraft re-armed and refuelled for another sortie. Four Japanese bombers were knocked down by the dozen Hurricanes and Tomahawks hastily scrambled to intercept, but heavy damage was inflicted to the base and aircraft on the ground. More raids followed later in the afternoon involving over 100 Japanese aircraft.

At Magwe the following morning – 22 March – a large formation of approaching Japanese aircraft was detected by radar at 8.04 a.m. Eighty-five aircraft pounded Magwe and few airworthy defending fighters were available to take to the skies. An afternoon raid by another ninety-four aircraft ruined Magwe as a viable base. The runways became unserviceable and a dozen Blenheims and fighters were damaged beyond repair on the ground. The surviving flyable AVG machines left for northern Burma, and the RAF's remaining flyable Blenheims and Hurricanes departed for Akyab. Heavy raids on Akyab on 23–24 and 27 March caused further RAF evacuations to India.

The panicky evacuation of Magwe by RAF ground staff was not good for the morale of army personnel, who did not have the luxury of pulling out of harm's way quite so rapidly. Major Montgomery wrote of the RAF's defeat at Magwe: 'I so well remember Slim's dismay and Taffy Davies' rage, when the news reached us at Prome that our air cover had vanished overnight. We sensed it had gone for good, and so it had.'[13] Akyab was retained by the RAF as an advanced landing ground, but the Japanese air force had achieved complete control of the skies of southern and central Burma.

The entry of Chinese forces into Burma complicated Allied command arrangements, but without Chinese intervention British forces faced a swift annihilation. To the surprise of British officials, an American general – Lieutenant-General Joseph Stilwell – had been appointed commander of the Chinese expeditionary force. Stilwell was Chiang Kai-shek's chief of staff in the Generalissimo's capacity as Allied Supreme Commander in the China theatre. Stilwell was also the senior American military officer in the

American-designated China-Burma-India region, and controller of Lend Lease supplies to China. The heavily burdened Stilwell was responsible to Washington; he was not formally part of the British command structure.

Born in 1883 and a West Point graduate, Stilwell had served in France in 1918. During the 1920s and 1930s he had acquired considerable experience of China in treaty port garrisons and diplomatic postings. Most recently Stilwell was United States military attaché in China from 1935–39; he was well familiar with the Byzantine workings of the Nationalist regime and the quagmire of the Sino-Japanese war.

As war clouds gathered for America in 1941, Stilwell was given command of the 7th Division and then III Corps. He was one of the most senior officers in the United States Army. When he was posted to China this cost him the opportunity to compete for senior commands in other theatres of war. Stilwell was a tough, brave and disputatious man, prone to expressing his views strongly, both audibly and in his diary. A journalist said of Stilwell: 'He did not look like a General, but like a tramp or a character actor on the films or a dissenting parson or even somebody out of Alice in Wonderland.'[14] Stilwell, with his steel-rimmed glasses and craggy appearance, would do his best to live up to his nickname of 'Vinegar Joe'.

Stilwell had first arrived at Chungking on 4 March after a long journey from the United States. He quickly gained the correct impression that Chiang held the British in low esteem and was suspicious of their motives. For the Burma campaign Stilwell's 5th and 6th Armies were commanded by Generals Tu Li-ming and Kan Li-chu respectively. The Chinese General Staff was represented in Burma by General Lin Wei.[15] Stilwell agreed to serve under Alexander in Burma so that Allied forces might have a locally unified command structure.

Stilwell flew from Chungking to Maymyo and Burma Army headquarters. A red brick Baptist mission house with a garden of flowering bushes was taken over by his staff. Stilwell paid a visit to Governor Dorman-Smith at Flagstaff House on 12 March to inform him that he was the commander of the Chinese armies in Burma. General Tu Li-ming, commander of the 5th Army, later presented himself to the Governor in a similar capacity. When Dorman-Smith expressed surprise at this ambiguous arrangement the Chinese general said:

> Ah, Your Excellency, the American General only thinks that he is commanding. In fact he is doing no such thing. You see, we Chinese think that the only way to keep the Americans in the war is to give them a few commands on paper. They will not do much harm as long as we do the work.[16]

Chiang Kai-shek retained a system of liaison officers in Burma whereby orders issued by Stilwell to subordinate Chinese generals also needed the agreement of Chiang and the Chinese General Staff. Chinese divisional and regimental commanders were very reluctant to take offensive action without the certain knowledge they had the support of their political superiors.

Stilwell soon had his first meeting with Alexander. He wrote in his diary for 13 March:

> Alexander arrived. Very cautious. Long sharp nose. Rather brusque and stand-offish. Let me stand around ... Astonished to find ME – mere me, a goddam American – in command of Chinese troops. 'Extrawdinary!' Looked me over as if I had just crawled out from under a rock.[17]

Despite the outbursts in his diary, and to his American staff, Stilwell and senior British commanders managed to get along on a day-to-day basis. Stilwell's opinion of Alexander would improve with time.

The British were not entirely sure what to make of such a high ranking American general sent to Burma by his government without any troops. Stilwell was an emperor with no clothes, though something similar might have been said of Alexander. It was far easier for Allied political leaders to fly individual generals to Burma than to send substantial reinforcements. By this stage of the war, however, British commanders were in no position to question too carefully anything Washington might do or not do; they were grateful for any help they could get. At this time a new American air force command was also being established in India. Major-General Lewis Brereton, who had previously held a post in Java, was appointed commander of the 10th Air Force. This new air command had great future potential for Allied forces in the China-Burma-India theatre.

Stilwell's 5th and 6th Chinese Armies were a valuable addition to the Allied cause in Burma, but they had obvious military limitations. Chinese infantry units lacked transport, artillery, medical services and signalling units; soldiers wore rope sandals and porters carried supplies in bundles suspended from bamboo poles by grass rope. Civilian trucks used on the Burma Road were pressed into service to support the Chinese armies in the field. Discipline in Chinese units was often lax but arbitrarily cruel when imposed.

The Chinese 5th Army comprised the 200th, 22nd and 96th Divisions. The army had motored down the Burma Road to Lashio. General Tai An-lan's 200th Division was sent southwards to Toungoo in the Sittang valley, but the rest of the army remained well to the north beyond supporting distance. The 8500-man 200th Division was China's only mechanised formation; it was equipped with Lend Lease vehicles and artillery.[18] The commander of the 5th Army had declined to reinforce the division at Toungoo, despite the instructions of Stilwell, as Chiang Kai-shek had ordered the rest of the army to concentrate near Mandalay. Under pressure from Stilwell, Chiang agreed that the 22nd Division might assist the 200th Division in an emergency; but the 22nd Division moved southwards only to Pyinmana, which was still sixty miles to the north of Toungoo. Chiang was reluctant to concentrate his forces as he feared the political consequences of a decisive defeat.

The Chinese 6th Army had taken up positions in the Shan States to watch the border with northern Thailand. At this point in time there were no Japanese troops in northern Thailand, but Allied commanders could not be sure of that. The 66th Army had also been promised by Chungking for service in Burma if needed.

Governor Dorman-Smith and his wife embarked on a five-day tour of the Shan States on 21 March to show the flag. At Loilem the Governor met General Ch'en, the commander of a division in the 6th Army. Ch'en sympathised with Dorman-Smith's dilemma. 'We are sorry for you. You have been defeated so often. But don't lose heart. Look at us. We now know all about war, as we've been fighting the Japanese for the last ten years. You too will learn if you stick to it.'[19] This discussion was only one of many things to test Dorman-Smith's patience and humour as the crisis in Burma deepened. By late March over 100,000 Indian refugees from Rangoon and southern Burma had assembled in camps around Mandalay. Outbreaks of cholera were starting to sweep the camps; Burma's crumbling civil administration was poorly placed to render assistance.

The Japanese invasion of Burma was about to enter a new phase. General Iida's XV Army had rested and reorganised after the capture of Rangoon and was ready for the next battle. On the night of 20/21 March Japanese troops of the 55th Division advancing northwards along the Sittang valley encountered Chinese forces to the south of Toungoo. The Japanese 112th Regiment attacked astride the main road, whilst the 143rd Regiment bypassed Toungoo to the west and cut off the northern exit to the town. On 26 March the Japanese attacked Toungoo directly: the 112th Regiment from the south-west, and the 143rd Regiment from the north-west. The Japanese attack was held up by the Chinese defenders.

Strong Japanese reinforcements were due to land at Rangoon. The 56th Division arrived by sea on 25 March. The division had been recruited from a district of north-west Kyushu; it had been held in reserve for the battle at Singapore, for which it was not required. The 56th Division was ordered to reinforce the 55th Division at Toungoo. The 56th Division's motorised reconnaissance regiment was the first unit to set out northwards from Rangoon; it crossed to the east bank of the Sittang near Toungoo. The main town and the bulk of the Chinese 200th Division was on the west bank. The small Chinese flank guard on the east bank was surprised by reconnaissance troops on 28

March, and overrun by midday of the following day. The vital bridge across the Sittang at Toungoo fell into the hands of the Japanese intact. At 7 a.m. on 30 March Chinese forces in Toungoo were again subjected to a strong attack. Resistance finally crumbled and the 200th Division retreated northwards. Japanese accounts speak highly of the protracted Chinese effort to defend the town.

A furious Stilwell flew to Chungking to complain that the 200th Division had been left to fight alone at Toungoo; he threatened to resign. Chiang pacified the American with various tepid assurances.[20] Stilwell's troubles, however, were just beginning. The Japanese were planning to send motorised forces in a north-east direction from Toungoo to roll up the Chinese 6th Army on the Shan plateau.

So long as the Chinese held Toungoo, General Alexander had intended to maintain a front stretching from Toungoo in the Sittang valley to Prome on the eastern bank of the Irrawaddy. Toungoo and Prome were eighty miles apart and separated by jungle-clad mountains. Once the battle for Toungoo got underway, Stilwell had asked the British to undertake offensive action in the Irrawaddy valley to support the Chinese. When Alexander met Chiang Kai-shek at Chungking on 28 March the Generalissimo had repeated the request. In consequence, Slim was ordered to attack southwards from Prome, rather than fight a defensive battle for the town.[21] At this time the 17th Indian Division and 7th Armoured Brigade were in the Prome area. The 1st Burma Division was assembling to the north of Prome after recently transferring from the Sittang valley.[22]

The Japanese 33rd Division was ordered by General Iida to push north-wards from Rangoon along the Irrawaddy valley. Japanese patrols made contact with Slim's troops in the closing days of March. To the south of Prome was the town of Paungde; between those two places a rocky ridge divided the main road from the railway. After receiving orders from Alexander to attack, Slim planned to push a motorised column south from Prome along the main road to seize Paungde. Once that town had been taken a further thrust southwards was contemplated for the following day. Brigadier Anstice was to lead the attack with a force that included the 7th Hussars and several infantry battalions. Early on 29 March the force passed through the village of Shwedaung, which lay on the east bank of the Irrawaddy eight miles south of Prome. The Gurkhas of the 48th Brigade covered the more easterly railway corridor.

By this time the bulk of the Japanese 33rd Division had concentrated to attack Prome. The 214th Regiment was astride the main road, whilst the 215th Regiment was moving along the west bank of the Irrawaddy. The leading troops of the 213th Regiment had recently arrived at Rangoon by sea

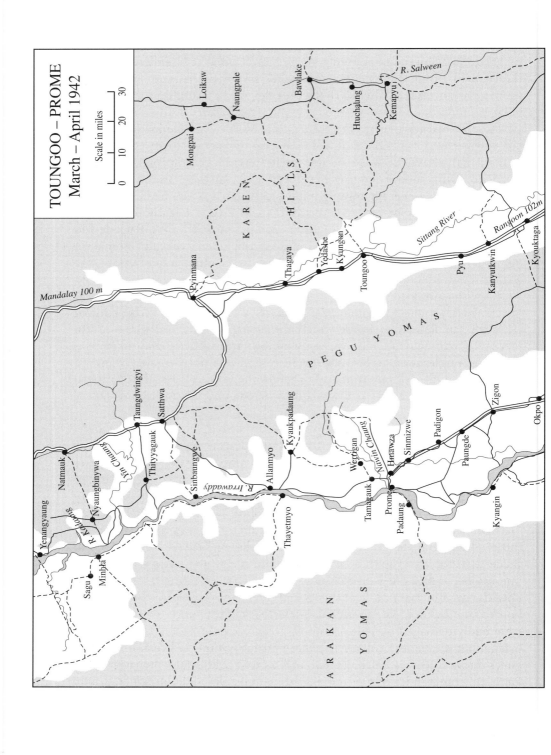

TOUNGOO – PROME
March – April 1942

Scale in miles

0   10   20   30

Mandalay 100 m

R. Salween

Loikaw

Naungpale

Bawlake

Huchalng

Kemapyu

Mongpai

KAREN   HILLS

Pyinmana

Thagaya

Yedashe

Kyungon

Toungoo

Sittang River

Rangoon 102m

Pyu

Kanyutkwin

Kyouktaga

PEGU YOMAS

Taungdwingyi

Satthwa

Kyaukpadaung

Zigon

Okpo

Natmauk

Thityyagauk

Pin Chaung

Sinbaungwe

Allanmyo

Werfgan

Nawin Chaung

Hmawza

Sinmizwe

Padigon

Paungde

Nyaungbinywa

R. Irrawaddy

Tamagauk

Prome

Kyangin

Yenangyaung

R. Kyaukpadaung

Thayetmyo

Padaung

Sagu

Minhla

ARAKAN   YOMAS

and would soon join the division. On the evening of 28 March the II/215th Battalion crossed the Irrawaddy to the east bank and marched through the night to reach Shwedaung by dawn on 29 March with the intention of cutting the road to Prome. By that time Anstice's motorised column had passed southwards towards Paungde. The bed of the Kala Chaung ran through the village of Shwedaung from east to west; the river was dry at this time of year. Japanese troops took up positions to block the road as it ran through the village.

During the daylight hours of 29 March Anstice's column pressed southwards to Paungde and fighting developed with Japanese troops near that town. But when General Cowan got news that the Japanese had blocked the road at Shwedaung, he ordered Anstice back to Prome. Clearly things were not developing as Burcorps headquarters had planned. The 48th Brigade and 2nd Royal Tanks were sent southwards along the railway corridor to make a demonstration in support of the withdrawal of Anstice's column along the road through Shwedaung.

The 16th and 63rd Indian Brigades were at Prome. Each brigade was instructed to dispatch a battalion to attack Shwedaung from the north and clear the Japanese road block. On the afternoon of 29 March the 4/12th Frontier Force encountered a large Burma Independence Army force in a village one mile north of Shwedaung. The BIA were overrun and dispersed with heavy losses. The Frontier Force then pressed on to the northern outskirts of Shwedaung, but was held up by a well-organised Japanese defence.

Whilst the Frontier Force were attacking Shwedaung from the north, British forces under Anstice's command had arrived at the outskirts of the village from the south. The village was composed of two-storey houses of wood and bamboo with corrugated iron or thatch roofs. After dark an attempt to break through the village by the Glosters in bright moonlight failed in the face of machine gun and mortar fire.

Two troops of the 7th Hussars were subsequently ordered to burst through the road block at the southern end of Shwedaung. The first Hussar troop succeeded in driving up the road through the village and onwards to Prome. The second troop, however, was halted by a bullock cart that had been pushed onto the road in the middle of the village. The leading tank was hit by petrol bombs and the crew baled out. The troop attacked again but two more tanks were badly damaged by petrol bombs. The troop's fourth tank reached the bridge, but a Japanese soldier used an anti-tank mine to break one of the tank's tracks. The crew baled out, two of whom were killed. Lieutenant Kildair Patteson, commander of the troop's leading tank, was taken prisoner, beaten and tied to the cart; he later managed to work free of his bonds and escape as

British shell fire fell uncomfortably close. A further attack by British infantry at 2 a.m. on 30 March was also halted. During the night Colonel Harada ordered reinforcements to cross the river to join the Japanese battalion in the village.[23]

At dawn on 30 March a column of British vehicles stretched for a mile south of Shwedaung. Open paddy on either side of the road offered protection from ambush. The next attack on the southern face of the village began at 7.30 a.m.; the 414th Battery fired a bombardment and B Squadron of the 7th Hussars advanced up the road with supporting infantry on both flanks, the Glosters and West Yorks to the left and the Cameronians and Dukes to the right. The tanks broke into the village and the infantry and column of vehicles followed. A scout car raced for the bridge that marked the northern end of the Japanese position, but hit an anti-tank mine half-way across. Two tanks following behind toppled down the embankment on either side of the bridge.[24] According to L.E. Tutt of the 414th Battery:

> We were almost out of ammunition as were the tanks. The battery formed up behind the tanks of the Hussars and the rest of the convoy of trucks followed behind. The tanks led off, blasting in every direction with everything that they had. We followed and immediately most of the enemy fire was directed at the soft-skinned vehicles. We copped everything, bullets, mortar bombs and grenades. For the first time we saw the Japanese using their version of Molotov cocktails to set any tanks which stopped on fire. One of our twenty-five pounders received a direct hit and was literally blown off the road. The headlong rush slowed and stopped. We were under very heavy machine-gun fire from a house at the very edge of the road. Lieutenant Simcox took over one of the subsections and they unhooked the gun. He fired over open sights and with about our last ammunition blew the house and the machine gunners to smithereens.[25]

Despite the effort that had been made, the column was again brought to a halt. In desperation British commanders ordered those who remained trapped in the village to break up into small groups and head northwards any way possible. On the northern side of Shwedaung, British and Indian troops had again attacked that day but without making much progress. At 4 p.m. this force was ordered to return to Prome; the 4/12th Frontier Force had lost eighteen killed and forty-five wounded in the engagement.[26]

Opposite Shwedaung, on the western side of the Irrawaddy, a Royal Marine detachment had occupied the village of Padaung as a flank guard. During the previous night the village had been stormed by Japanese troops of the III/215th Battalion. The marines fought their way out of the trap but seventeen men were taken prisoner, lined up in the village square after daylight and bayoneted to death – with one exception. A sergeant later turned up with three bayonet wounds; he had managed to escape from the massacre.[27]

The foray south of Prome on 29-30 March cost Burcorps 400 casualties and 200 vehicles. The 7th Hussars lost ten tanks, the artillery two field guns, the Dukes 122 and Cameronians 69 casualties. The Japanese lost seventy-five dead at Shwedaung and Paungde and took 113 prisoners.[28] The war diary of the 7th Hussars recorded: 'The next morning [31 March] we moved to where we had been before this useless venture had begun. The Regiment only had thirty-eight tanks now and had lost a number of B vehicles. We had been forced to fritter ourselves away in country entirely unsuitable to tanks.'[29] Hutton, Alexander's chief of staff, wrote that it was 'clear after the Prome operations that the morale of the troops, including the British battalions, was very low'.[30]

Needless to say, the Japanese 33rd Division's next objective was Prome, a large town on the east bank of the Irrawaddy river serviced by a railway branch line from Rangoon. Dense scrub jungle encroached upon the outskirts of Prome, and jungle-covered hills dominated the southern approaches to the town, which had been heavily bombed. The 63rd Brigade was in occupation of Prome, with the 16th Brigade nearby to the east; the 48th Brigade was further away to the south-east at Hmawza, astride the railway. The battered units that had taken part in the Shwedaung action were sent to the rear to regroup.

Slim's corps headquarters had withdrawn northwards to Allanmyo. On the afternoon of 1 April he was visited by Wavell and Alexander. As the Chinese were pulling out from Toungoo, the generals decided there was no longer any point fighting a major action for Prome. But before a further retreat could be arranged, on the evening of 1 April the Japanese attacked Prome along the road from Shwedaung. A company of the 5/17th Dogras was overrun in the initial push. During the night troops of the 215th Regiment penetrated Prome's defences on the river flank. From there the situation speedily unravelled for the 63rd Brigade, and the decision was made to abandon the town. Meanwhile a Japanese turning movement along the railway was successfully held-up by the Gurkhas of the 48th Brigade.

To the north of Prome the delta region began to merge with the dry zone of central Burma. On 2 April the 17th Indian Division marched northwards towards Allanmyo across a landscape with little water in searing heat. The presence of bullock carts slowed the pace of the march and beat up a fine dust. Late in the day the columns were subjected to heavy air attack; the Japanese air force now enjoyed complete aerial supremacy; the mere sound of an aircraft caused troops to look for cover and morale plummeted. After a brief halt during the night the trek continued the following day. A limited number of motor vehicles were on hand and used in relays to carry exhausted men to their final destinations. Further air attacks pushed casualties for the two-day march to over 200.[31]

At the start of the campaign Burma had been a prosperous and friendly land for British forces. As Burcorps tramped northwards, with the Japanese snapping at their heels, the local population seemed to grow hostile and demoralised soldiers became bitter and sullen. The entire Allied position in Burma was in danger of complete collapse.

14

The Imperial Japanese Navy and the Indian Ocean

The fall of Rangoon had implications for the war in the Indian Ocean far beyond the plight of Allied forces in central Burma. The capture of Burma's capital city and the Andaman and Nicobar Islands gave Tokyo command of the eastern half of the Bay of Bengal. Japanese troop convoys could sail to Rangoon from Singapore, but, in addition to that, a whole new theatre of war was opened up to the Imperial Japanese Navy. From newly conquered bases in South-east Asia, the IJN could threaten the exposed coast of eastern India and Ceylon, which lay at the southern tip of the sub-continent.

The Royal Navy's Eastern Fleet had been re-established at Ceylon after the Singapore Naval Base became untenable. Ceylon was the hub of the shipping lanes that criss-crossed the Indian Ocean. The ocean had been a British lake since the wars of Napoleon, but that state of affairs was under grave threat. The loss of Burma would endanger Britain's position in north-eastern India; but the combined loss of Burma and Ceylon was a threat to the entire Indian coastline all the way from Bombay to Madras and Calcutta. Ceylon was also a necessary stepping stone in any prospective Axis plan for Japanese forces to join hands with the Germans and Italians in the Middle East. In the early months of 1942 the world lay at the feet of the Axis powers; they seemed to be masters of contemporary warfare.

The crisis that threatened the Allies in the Indian Ocean urgently required a fresh round of high-level decision-making in London. The First Sea Lord, Admiral Sir Dudley Pound, wrote to Prime Minister Churchill on 8 March:

> There can be little doubt that there is a very good chance of the Japanese sending an expeditionary force against Ceylon. Equally, there can be no doubt that its loss would undermine our whole strategical position not only in the Far East but also in the Middle East. The Japanese battle fleet installed in Ceylon would be able seriously to interfere will all our Middle East convoys, our whole trade in the Indian Ocean and indeed the security of India itself.[1]

The Royal Navy's ability to reinforce Ceylon was compromised by recent losses at sea. Apart from the sinking of *Prince of Wales* and *Repulse* off Malaya, the heavy cruiser *Exeter* had been scuttled in the East Indies. In the

Mediterranean the aircraft carrier *Ark Royal* and battleship *Barham* had been lost at sea, and the battleships *Queen Elizabeth* and *Valiant* damaged by mines in Alexandria harbour.[2]

In London, Sir Earle Page, the Australian government's envoy, had been made aware of the weakness of Ceylon's army garrison, which comprised two brigades of the 34th Indian Division, a brigade of local volunteers and just one battery of field artillery. Page suggested to his government on 24 February that Australian troops might be used to temporarily reinforce Ceylon. An exasperated Prime Minister Curtin replied two days later that Page was not advocating the Australian viewpoint sufficiently. Canberra's stated policy was to secure the speedy return of Australian forces to their homeland.[3] The Australian government, however, relented; landing troops at Ceylon would help to 'create an atmosphere of goodwill', and repair some of the damage done to Anglo-Australian relations by the recent refusal to land the 7th Australian Division at Rangoon.

The 6th Division was sailing from the Middle East behind the 7th Division. Curtin cabled Churchill on 2 March to offer two brigades of the 6th Division for Ceylon; the division's headquarters and the third brigade would sail onwards to Australia. A state of high alarm had reigned in Canberra in the immediate aftermath of the fall of Singapore, but promised American troop commitments to the south-west Pacific and Australia had eased the Australian government's anxieties since that time.

Curtin's government, however, only permitted the main body of the 6th Division to land at Ceylon on the understanding that they would be relieved by troops of the 70th British Division after a few weeks. The 70th Division was also sailing to India from the Middle East. Churchill's intention, though, was to keep the Australians at Ceylon for a much longer period, and to send the main body of the 70th Division to eastern India.[4]

The effort to build up the defences of Ceylon was likely to come into conflict with the demands of the desperate campaign underway in Burma. On 13 March the War Office signalled India Command some grim news:

> We agree with your conception of forming a bastion in North-East India but the problem is to decide what portion of our slender resources it is right to allot to this area vis-à-vis Ceylon of the importance of which you are fully aware. In our view the security of our Indian Empire depends in the last resort on our ability to control sea communications in the Indian Ocean. For this we must have secure naval bases, and the only ones in sight for some time to come are in Ceylon … For these reasons we consider that defence requirements of Ceylon must be given priority although we agree that north-east India is very important and also appreciate potential internal security problems with which you may be faced in Bengal and Eastern India.[5]

From Delhi Wavell replied to the Chiefs of Staff on 15 March: 'Present policy seems to be to crowd unduly large proportion of slender resources, land and air, into Ceylon where their purpose is purely defensive ... we cannot afford to over insure.'[6] Wavell feared that if the Japanese landed troops at Ceylon, the defending garrison would be unable to repel the invaders, no matter how strongly the island was reinforced.

The Western presence at Ceylon – a 'tear-drop' in the Indian Ocean – was already several centuries old by the time of the Second World War. Ceylon had been a stepping stone for early navigators pressing eastwards across the Indian Ocean from the Cape of Good Hope; mariners were greeted by a fertile land inhabited by friendly people. The Portuguese had first arrived at the start of the sixteenth century, though they were later supplanted by the Dutch. In turn, the British took control of Ceylon at the close of the eighteenth century, and had remained the resident colonial power since that time.

The capital city of Ceylon was Colombo. Ships sailed by Moors had used the site of Colombo as long ago as the twelfth century. The Portuguese had developed a fort at that place on the mid-western coast for strategic reasons. The fort was named in honour of Christopher Columbus, the navigator who had discovered the Americas for western Europeans. By the twentieth century the old Portuguese fort was long gone; the modern Fort district featured Queen's House – the British governor's residence – government offices, solid commercial buildings and the general post office. The clock tower of the post office could be seen twenty miles out to sea and was a de facto lighthouse for the port.[7]

A large artificial harbour had been completed in 1885; the first stone of the 4000-foot breakwater was laid by the Prince of Wales, the future Edward VII. The mile-square port had become crowded by the 1930s. Colombo received a greater annual tonnage of shipping than all the harbours of India and Burma combined. A forest of steamer funnels, masts and sails from all nations greeted an observer on the quayside. There were no deep water landings; small craft and a large work force were needed for loading and unloading shipping.

Colombo was built on a flat plain that stretched for miles in all directions. In 1942 a population of 350,000 lived in a clean environment as a tropical city had no need of residential fires for heating. The city was swept by drenching tropical showers during the rainy season. In the evening at Colombo, the sun sank into the western sea; the light faded from picturesque gardens of orchids and flowering shrubs. The English language and European dress were widespread. Prior to Japan's entry to the war, British prestige remained high at Ceylon.

The bulk of Ceylon's population lived in the south-west corner of the island as rainfall was plentiful in that region. The central part of the island was mountainous. Tea, rubber, rice and coconuts were amongst Ceylon's principal agricultural industries. The colony's cosmopolitan population was over six million: four million of whom were indigenous Sinhalese, one and a half million Tamils and the balance Moors, Malays, Eurasians and Europeans. The rains of the south-west monsoon lasted from late April to July. Thunder and lightening signified the coming of the wet season.

The commander of the Royal Navy's Eastern Fleet, Vice-Admiral Sir Geoffrey Layton, was made Commander-in-Chief of Ceylon in early March with authority over the governor, Sir Andrew Caldecot, and the civil administration. Lieutenant-General Sir Henry Pownall was appointed commander of the army garrison on the island. Port facilities at Ceylon for the Royal Navy were not lavish; for instance the naval base at Colombo did not have a dock large enough for a battleship. Trincomalee, on the north-east coast, was an anchorage rather than a fully developed base.

Ceylon was, in theory at least, an unsinkable aircraft carrier. Air Vice-Marshal J.H. D'Albiac's No. 222 Group was the RAF command responsible for the island's air defences. The group's air strength at the end of March comprised fifty Hurricanes, fourteen Blenheims, six Catalinas and a collection of obsolete Fulmars. Two Hurricane squadrons – Nos 30 and 258 – were based at Ratmalana near Colombo; a third Hurricane squadron – No. 261 – was stationed at China Bay airfield outside Trincomalee. Some of the Hurricanes had been disembarked from the fleet carrier *Indomitable*, after it had become clear they would not arrive in time at Singapore. No. 258 Squadron had flown Buffaloes in the Malayan campaign. The surviving pilots of the squadron were pleased to graduate to a more up to date fighter-type. A squadron of Blenheim bombers, and some Fleet Air Arm Swordfish torpedo-bombers, were the only aircraft at Ceylon able to attack enemy warships off-shore.

Admiral Sir James Somerville was sent from Gibraltar to take command of the Eastern Fleet in place of Layton, who now had duties ashore as CIC. Born in 1882, Somerville was the son of an English landowner and his Tasmanian-born wife. Somerville had joined the Royal Navy prior to the First World War; his interwar appointments included a stint in command of the East Indies station. On the eve of the war against Nazi Germany he was diagnosed with pulmonary tuberculosis and placed on the retired list. When war broke out Somerville was recalled for service at the Admiralty, and helped to improvise the Dunkirk evacuation.[8]

On 27 June 1940 Somerville was appointed to command Force H at Gibraltar. He demonstrated he was a determined fleet commander when Force H bombarded the French fleet in port at Mers-el-Kebir in Algeria. Subsequently, Force H was involved in convoy operations to Malta, and the long campaign in the north Atlantic, including the successful hunt for the German battleship *Bismarck* in May 1941.

As a personality Somerville was a straightforward and popular commander; he was also something of a wit and raconteur, with little fear of higher authority. Somerville had been knighted twice, receiving the KB in 1939 and KBE in 1941. When he heard the news, Admiral Cunningham of the Mediterranean Fleet congratulated Somerville by signalling: 'What, twice a knight at your age?'[9] On a more sober note, Somerville had been subject to a Board of Enquiry after Force H's action with the Italian fleet off Cape Spartivento in November 1940. (Cape Spartivento is the southern-most point of Sardinia). Force H had clashed with an Italian force whilst escorting a convoy to Malta. Somerville had broken off the engagement as he felt that the safety of the convoy was his foremost priority. The Admiralty ordered a board to assemble at Gibraltar to investigate whether Somerville had broken off action prematurely. According to Vice-Admiral A.U. Willis: 'The Court of Enquiry upheld Somerville's actions to the hilt, but the Admiralty's suspicions obviously rankled and I think he must have been very averse to laying himself open to an accusation of this sort again.'[10]

Somerville sailed for the Indian Ocean aboard the fleet aircraft carrier *Formidable* on 17 February. The long voyage gave the admiral plenty of time to reflect upon the decline of Britain's fortunes in the Far East. Somerville observed in a letter to Admiral Pound at the Admiralty that the Royal Navy could not stop a major Japanese invasion of Ceylon, but the prospects of opposing a smaller hit-and-run attack were more promising. If that happened Somerville felt that the 'best counter is to keep an Eastern Fleet in being, and to avoid losses by attrition'. This might be achieved by keeping the fleet at sea as much as possible and by making 'feints to the east of Ceylon from time to time'. Enemy calculations could be influenced merely by the fact that a significant opponent was at large in the Indian Ocean. If the Japanese successfully invaded Ceylon, 'it will be extremely difficult, but not necessarily impossible to maintain our communications to the Middle East. But if the Japanese capture Ceylon and destroy the greater part of the Eastern Fleet, then I admit the situation becomes really desperate.'[11]

At Colombo Vice-Admiral Layton agreed with Somerville's line of thinking. He wrote to the Admiralty on 14 March: 'It would be folly to … risk our fleet in action with superior enemy forces in the defence of Ceylon, or other purposes until they have had some time for training together.'[12] On 18 March the Admiralty signalled agreement that the Eastern Fleet was not to be sacrificed to save Ceylon. Wavell was informed by the Chiefs of Staff that steps were underway to build up the Eastern Fleet, though it would be unable to intervene on the coast of Burma. Somerville arrived at Colombo by aircraft on 24 March and took command of the Eastern Fleet from Layton two days later. The two admirals were both strong personalities but old friends; they would cooperate effectively in the days ahead.

About the time of Somerville's arrival at Ceylon, the main body of the 6th Australian Division was also disembarking at Colombo. This division's war services included the campaigns in Libya, Greece and Crete. The 16th Brigade arrived in the liner *Orontes*; the 17th Brigade in the liner *Otranto*; the Dutch transport *Westerland* carried another 2800 men. A number of smaller vessels carried vehicles and supplies. Earlier in March Ceylon's original garrison of the 34th Indian Division had been joined by a brigade of the 70th British Division and the 21st East African Brigade. The arrival of the Australians built up General Pownall's command to the equivalent of two divisions.

Indian, Australian, British and African troops landed at Ceylon found themselves in a tropical landscape of semi-jungle, wild flowers and greenery. The humid climate was healthy and the population contented. Water buffalo, elephants and sugar monkeys had replaced the flies and sand the Australians had known only too well in the Nile delta. Many of the newly arrived troops were entrained to the south-west coast; the old Portuguese fort at Galle was made a headquarters. At this time the threat of invasion was high and a major Japanese incursion into the Indian Ocean widely predicted.

The fall of Singapore had opened up a range of new possibilities for the Japanese in the Indian Ocean, quite apart from the transport of reinforcements to southern Burma. There was the prospect of an invasion of Ceylon or landings at any number of places along the east coast of India between Madras and Calcutta. Japan's leadership was in general agreement that the best war strategy was to plan for a fresh round of offensive operations. It was important to maintain momentum and retain the initiative.

Admiral Isoroku Yamamoto and the Combined Fleet staff played a dominant role in naval strategy during the early months of 1942. Yamamoto's principal strategic desire was to renew the offensive in the central Pacific against the United States Pacific Fleet, but he was willing to support a brief foray into the Indian Ocean to cripple the Royal Navy's Eastern Fleet. There was backing for an Indian Ocean operation across the upper reaches of the Imperial Japanese Navy, though only as a hit-and-run raid. The Naval General Staff in Tokyo had their eyes on an offensive in the south-west Pacific to isolate Australia from the United States. The Imperial Japanese Army was already over-stretched by its conquests in eastern Asia and the western Pacific, and had no interest in an amphibious operation against Ceylon or eastern India. The army's commitment to Burma was a significant drain on finite reserves.[13]

From the time of the fall of Singapore Yamamoto's headquarters began drawing up contingency plans for a raid on Ceylon. War games for the operation were held aboard the Combined Fleet's flagship *Yamato*. Ideally, the British fleet was to be lured into battle somewhere between Ceylon and Sumatra.[14] On 9 March Yamamoto appointed Vice-Admiral Kondo to command the operation against Ceylon. Kondo was to have two subordinate task forces: Vice-Admiral Nagumo's aircraft carrier task force, and Vice-Admiral Ozawa's detachment of cruisers and destroyers.

Kondo's Southern Force had issued orders for an Indian Ocean operation by mid-March. Nagumo's Mobile Striking Force of five fleet aircraft carriers left Starling Bay, Celebes in the East Indies on 26 March (the sixth fleet carrier *Kaga* had returned to Japan for repairs). The fleet sailed westwards through the strait to the north of Timor bound for the Indian Ocean. Admiral Nagumo was a stern and aggressive man; he was by background a torpedo specialist, though by the early months of 1942 he had become an experienced commander of carriers.

Japanese naval aircrew were highly experienced and their aircraft had a performance equivalent to contemporary land-based aircraft. Nagumo's carriers – *Akagi, Zuikaku, Shokaku, Soryu* and *Hiryu* – were supported by four fast battleships, two heavy cruisers, one light cruiser and eleven destroyers; half a dozen submarines were already on reconnaissance patrols in the Bay of Bengal. On 1 April the task force refuelled south of Java and was ready for a prolonged foray into the Indian Ocean. An air strike on Ceylon was timed for 5 April.

Whilst Nagumo was raiding Ceylon, Ozawa's cruisers and destroyers would sweep deep into the Bay of Bengal to disrupt Allied shipping movements along the eastern coast of India. Ozawa's five heavy cruisers, one light cruiser and eleven destroyers were accompanied by the light aircraft carrier *Ryujo*. The force had already put to sea from Mergui on the Tenasserim coast of Burma, and was marking time to the south of the Andaman Islands waiting for the carrier operation to commence.

The RAF was expected to put up serious opposition in the skies of Ceylon. A Japanese aviator recalled: 'This time we had to expect greater losses [than in recent operations] but our Zekes [Zeros] had shown themselves far superior to all other enemy fighters and we had no doubt that we would win in the air and destroy the fleet and this great British base.'[15] At the start of March Japanese intelligence had estimated Allied naval forces in the Indian Ocean as three battleships, two aircraft carriers, four heavy and eleven light cruisers and several hundred carrier and land-based aircraft.[16] Further reinforcements were expected to join the British fleet at Ceylon. This substantial force needed neutralisation and seemed strong enough on paper to warrant the attention of Imperial Japan's fleet carriers. Japanese intelligence gathering efforts were often impressive, but the Royal Navy's auxiliary base in the southern Maldives at Addu Atoll, to the south-west of Ceylon, had not been discovered.

The Admiralty had done its best to build up the Eastern Fleet despite heavy commitments and losses in the war against the European Axis. By late March Somerville's fleet at Ceylon comprised the modernised battleship *Warspite*, four elderly *Royal Sovereign*-class battleships, the new fleet aircraft carriers *Indomitable* and *Formidable*, the old aircraft carrier *Hermes*, two heavy cruisers, five light cruisers, sixteen destroyers and seven submarines. *Warspite*, a veteran of the battle of Jutland in 1916, had only recently returned to service after repairs in North America for damage incurred off Crete in the Mediterranean Sea.

The battleships *Revenge*, *Royal Sovereign*, *Ramillies* and *Resolution* formed the Royal Navy's 3rd Battle Squadron (*Royal Oak*, the other R-class battleship, had been torpedoed at Scapa Flow in 1939). The R-class had been constructed from 1913–17. The battleships had eight fifteen-inch guns, but could only manage a top speed of nineteen knots for brief periods; they had been built primarily for service in the North Sea and cruises of short duration. The old guns needed relining and had poor elevation. Inadequate water distillation plants meant that the battleships would run short of water before running out of fuel. Somerville observed: 'My old battle-boats are in various states of disrepair and there's not a ship at present that approaches what I should call a proper standard of fighting efficiency.'[17] The Eastern Fleet's second-in-command, and commander of the 3rd Battle Squadron, was Vice-Admiral Willis. He wrote candidly in his memoirs: 'Being no seeker of glory I viewed the prospect of facing the Japanese Navy with the old out-of-date R-class battleships quite unsuited for service in the tropics, with gloom to put it mildly.'[18] Churchill simply called them 'coffin-ships'. The R-class had spent the war up to this time escorting convoys in the Atlantic.

Somerville's fleet aircraft carriers – *Indomitable* and *Formidable* – were newly constructed ships with armoured flight decks and engines capable of a maximum speed of thirty knots. *Formidable* had spent a long period in the United States undergoing extensive repairs for damage suffered in the Mediterranean at the hands of the Luftwaffe. On the voyage from European waters to Cape Town, Somerville had not been impressed by standards of training on *Formidable* after the crew's long lay-off in port.

The Royal Navy's new class of fleet carriers were well-built ships, but they embarked only half the aircraft of a similar-tonnage Japanese or American fleet carrier. United States carriers parked aircraft on a crowded deck to maximise the numbers that could be embarked, whereas the Royal Navy's new carriers housed a smaller number of aircraft in hangers below the armoured deck. Rear-Admiral Denis Boyd's *Indomitable* and *Formidable* carried only eighty-three aircraft in total, and half of these were obsolete Albacore torpedo-bombers. Some Albacores, however, carried radar sets to make night operations a realistic possibility.[19] Obsolete Fulmars and modern Sea Hurricanes and Martlet fighters made up the rest of the carriers' complement of aircraft (the Martlet was the Fleet Air Arm's version of the American Wildcat fighter). The Eastern Fleet's third carrier, *Hermes*, dated from 1919 and was the world's first carrier to be built from the keel up. *Hermes* had been stationed in the Indian Ocean for raider hunting and could only embark a dozen aircraft.

The Eastern Fleet at the end of March 1942 was in far better shape than the force that had been at Admiral Phillips' disposal at Singapore the previous December. From the Admiralty in London, Pound warned Layton to be on his guard against the Japanese 'Pearl Harbouring' Ceylon.[20] Part of Somerville's fleet had been detached and sent to Addu Atoll, 650 miles southwest of Colombo. Admiral Willis and *Resolution* arrived on 26 March to find the rest of the R-class battleships, *Indomitable* and *Hermes* present.

Addu Atoll – otherwise known as Port T for purposes of secrecy – was the most southern of the Maldive Islands, a deep-water lagoon was surrounded by a ring of barren coral islands. Enervating tropical heat did not make the atoll a natural place for human habitation; four deep channels ran through the reef; the lagoon was as large as Scapa Flow, the Royal Navy's fleet base in northern Scotland. A Royal Marines detachment had built the base in secret as an emergency anchorage before the war. A small airfield, tankers and auxiliary shipping were available to support a fleet. The anchorage, however, lacked adequate anti-submarine defences; a submarine could potentially sit outside the reef and fire torpedoes through the gaps. Anti-aircraft defences were also poor, but Addu Atoll was less exposed to surprise attack than Ceylon. In fact, the Japanese did not know of the base's existence, though British commanders could not be sure of that.

British intelligence had received general information that a Japanese thrust across the Indian Ocean towards Ceylon was imminent. It had been difficult for the Japanese to hide the extent to which shipping for the offensive was concentrated in the East Indies. It also made intuitive sense that the Japanese would make a major foray into the Indian Ocean at some stage.

Across March the codebreakers of the Far East Combined Bureau at Colombo had monitored the rising level of interest in the Indian Ocean in Japanese signals. Radio signals can be listened into with the necessary equipment tuned to the correct frequency. The Japanese were known to use sets of letters in their codes for geographic place-names. The repetition of those sets of letters in signals quickly drew the attention of codebreakers. Across mid-March there were repeated references to an impending operation in area 'D', and an air raid planned for 2 April on 'DG'. Those places remained a mystery until on 28 March, when a Japanese radio operator spelled out the target name phonetically as KO-RO-N-BO. The mystery was solved.[21]

The information was passed to Admiral Somerville, who commented:

> We did not know in what strength the Japanese would stage this attack. We anticipated a cut and run operation by a force consisting of two or three battle-ships and a couple of carriers escorted by some cruisers and destroyers. We rather expected the Japanese aircraft would attack at dawn, and that the Japanese would then make an immediate get-away to the eastward, in order to avoid attack by the British land-based aircraft in Ceylon.[22]

On the afternoon of 30 March the various divisions of the Eastern Fleet put to sea from Colombo, Trincomalee and Addu Atoll. The warships were to rendezvous on 31 March eighty miles south of Ceylon's Dondra Head.

Somerville and his staff were aboard *Warship*; the battleship left Colombo with *Formidable* and a force of cruisers and destroyers. At the rendezvous Somerville signalled Willis: 'So this is the Eastern Fleet. Never mind. There's many a good tune played on an old fiddle.' Somerville's chief of staff, Commodore Ralph Edwards noted in his diary: 'It is difficult to believe that any British force has been less drilled and well equipped to meet an enemy.'[23] The historically-minded might have made a comparison of Somerville's warships with the ramshackle Tsarist Russian fleet of Admiral Rozhestvensky, which had steamed half-way around the world to its destruction by the guns of the Japanese navy at the Tsushima Straits in 1905.

The Eastern Fleet, however, was the largest Royal Navy battle fleet to gather at sea since the war began. Twenty-nine warships were assembled in total: five battleships, three aircraft carriers, seven cruisers and fourteen destroyers. The crews of these vessels amounted to over 15,000 officers and ratings. The South African journalist, Ken Dimbleby, was a member of *Cornwall*'s crew:

> The meeting of the forces comprising the Eastern Fleet was a memorable occasion, especially for those of us who had never sailed in a fleet. The tropical sea was calm and a rich blue, creased white by the bow waves and wakes of the warships. On the horizon appeared small black dots. They became bigger; more black dots; gradually they all took shape; battleships, aircraft-carriers, cruisers and destroyers. Signals were flashed from the flagship. The forces merged and manoeuvred into position. Cruisers wheeled while destroyers, the terriers of the seas, sped to take up their stations. The battleships formed up in line ahead with the flagship, *Warspite*, a stately leader of the fleet.[24]

The Eastern Fleet spent 31 March at sea to the south of Ceylon. Somerville wanted to evade a Japanese air attack by daylight, but, after the Japanese had dashed themselves against Ceylon's air defences, he hoped to slip within range for a moonlight strike by the Fleet Air Arm's torpedo-bombers.

The fleet was divided by necessity into a fast and a slow division. An aircraft carrier needs to steam rapidly into the wind to launch aircraft, and the slower ships could not keep pace with a new fleet carrier. The R-class battleships, *Hermes* and other slower warships formed the slow division – Force B. This force included the cruisers *Caledon*, *Dragon* and the Dutch *Heemskerk* and eight destroyers. Force A, the fast division, comprised *Warspite*, *Formidable*, *Indomitable*, four cruisers – *Cornwall*, *Dorsetshire*, *Enterprise* and *Emerald* – and six destroyers.

On 1 and 2 April Somerville sailed his fleet eastwards – towards the likely Japanese approach route – by night, and then reversed course to the west by daylight. The weather was calm and training exercises occupied the fleet under a burning sun. Somerville commented: 'The trouble is that the Fleet I now have is much bigger than anything anyone has had to handle before during this war. Everyone is naturally very rusty about doing their Fleet stuff – most ships have hardly been in company with another ship during the war.'[25] Reconnaissance aircraft failed to sight any enemy shipping. Somerville wrote to his wife on 2 April: 'Still no news of the enemy. I fear they have taken fright which is a pity because if I could have given them a good crack now it would have been very timely. Unfortunately I cannot stand about indefinitely waiting for them.'[26] Fresh water was running short on the R-class battleships. Willis warned Somerville that they would have to use salt water in the boilers if the fleet did not return to harbour within the next few days.

There was still no report of the Japanese fleet during the night of 2/3 April. The Japanese seemed to have cancelled any operation against Ceylon. Both divisions of the Eastern Fleet headed for Addu Atoll on 3 April to replenish supplies and refuel. The heavy cruisers *Dorsetshire* and *Cornwall* were detached to sail to Colombo, the former to continue a refit, the later to meet a convoy due in a week's time. The aircraft carrier *Hermes* and a destroyer were also sent to Trincomalee for maintenance and to load stores.[27] Allied shipping movements in the Indian Ocean began to return to normal. All parts of the Eastern Fleet had reached Addu Atoll by mid-afternoon of 4 April. Somerville commented that it was a 'bloody awful looking place, which beats the band for an abomination of heat and desolation'.[28] Oil tankers and water-boats set about resupplying the warships in blistering heat, beneath a blue tropical sky.

Whilst the Eastern Fleet had been on station to the south of Ceylon, land-based Catalina flying-boats of No. 205 Squadron were patrolling deep across the ocean to the east and south-east of the island. Late in the afternoon of 4 April a report was received at Colombo that a large Japanese fleet was in sight. At 4 p.m. the wireless operator of Squadron Leader L.J. Birchall's Catalina reported a hostile fleet 360 miles south-east of Ceylon and steering for the island. Birchall, a Canadian pilot, recalled: 'As we got close enough to identify the lead ships, we knew at once what we were into, but the closer we got the more ships appeared, and so it was necessary to keep going until we could count and identify them all. By the time we did this there was very little chance left.'[29] The Catalina was shot down by Zeros before many details of the fleet's composition could be dispatched by radio. Japanese naval signallers detected the Catalina's radio transmissions and assumed that the fleet's presence had been reported to Ceylon. The survivors from the ditched flying boat were rescued by a Japanese destroyer.

The report was passed to Eastern Fleet's flagship at Addu Atoll. Somerville wrote of these developments forcefully:

> Damn and blast it looks as if I've been had because a Catalina has just reported a large enemy force 350 miles south-east of Ceylon – evidently the party I've been waiting for and here I am miles away and unable to strike. However I couldn't have stayed any longer as my miserable old battleboats were running out of water and short of fuel. But it's maddening to think they've slipped me this time.[30]

Somerville predicted that the Japanese would raid Ceylon 'and then shin out of it as fast as they could to the East'. He gave orders for the fleet to head back to sea in order to attempt a night air strike as the Japanese were retiring eastwards from Ceylon. British naval torpedo-bombers were dangerously obsolete for daylight operations, but the Fleet Air Arm was trained for night flying. The successful raid against the Italian fleet at Taranto in 1940 was a night operation.

The Eastern Fleet had been refuelling when the sighting report was received and that delayed sailing. Force A put to sea at 2.15 a.m. on 5 April; Force B followed after daylight. At Ceylon shipping in port was ordered to disperse out to sea in expectation of a raid at dawn on 5 April. Forty-eight ships in Colombo harbour hastily departed, though twenty-one merchant ships and eight fleet auxiliaries were still present the following morning.[31] The heavy cruisers *Cornwall* and *Dorsetshire* sailed southwards from Colombo at 10 p.m. on 4 April with the intention of rejoining the Eastern Fleet. Crew ashore on leave had been hastily recalled from their festivities.

15

Admiral Nagumo's Raid on Ceylon

At dawn on 5 April, Easter Sunday, Nagumo's carriers were 300 miles south of Ceylon. A strike force stood ready on deck for launch. The Japanese were hoping to surprise the Eastern Fleet in port at Colombo. Japanese commanders may have deliberately timed the foray into the Indian Ocean for a raid on Easter Sunday. Sunday morning had also been the time of the Pearl Harbor strike.[1]

The Japanese carriers steamed into the wind as dawn was breaking. The decks were crowded with aircraft, engines warming up, goggled aircrew waiting to take-off with their canopies open and silk scarves fluttering in the wind. Fifty-three level-bombers (Nakajima Type 97), thirty-eight dive-bombers (Aichi Type 99) and thirty-six fighters (Mitsubishi Type 00) set out for Colombo. The 127 aircraft were led by Commander Mitsuo Fuchida, who had achieved great fame for his leadership of the raid on Pearl Harbor. The dive-bombers were to attack first, covered by the fighters; level-bombers were then to drop their bomb loads to add to the chaos. The aircraft crossed the Ceylonese coast in thundery weather, amid dense but broken cloud. A radar station was planned for Colombo, but it was not yet completed.

As Fuchida's force was nearing its target a formation of six Swordfish torpedo-bombers was sighted at a lower altitude. The Swordfish of No. 788 Squadron were making an ill-timed flight from Trincomalee to an airfield near Colombo. British aircrew assumed that the approaching monoplanes were Hurricanes; Zeros, however, pounced to polish off the biplanes in no time.[2]

Just before 8 a.m. the Japanese strike force arrived over Colombo. By now thunder clouds, strong gusts of wind, showers and mist had reduced visibility.[3] The dive-bombers flew over the harbour; at the signal of their leader the aircraft turned down into a steep sixty-five degree dive, some aimed at shipping, others directed at the installations along the shore. The fixed undercarriage of the dive-bombers made them look like birds of prey with talons out-stretched.

The peaceful Easter Sunday morning was shattered by the sounds of screaming aero-engines and weaponry; anti-aircraft guns threw exploding shells and tracer skywards; one dive-bomber exploded in a flash a thousand feet above the harbour. An excited spectator recorded the scene. 'You've never seen anything like it. An absolute shambles – planes on fire, ships on fire, buildings on fire, the guns crashing away at some high bombers which had broken out of cloud in perfect formation, just like a Hendon Air Show.'[4] Tall columns of water rose into the air from bombs that missed their targets; low-flying aircraft strafed whatever flashed before them.

The destroyer *Tenedos* and armed merchant cruiser *Hector* fell victim to the raiders. A blazing *Hector* settled on the harbour's bottom. An eyewitness reported:

> When the raid occurred we were completing the refit of the Destroyer HMS *Tenedos* which was lying at the end of our jetty. A stick of bombs fell, some on the jetty and the remainder on the stern of the destroyer setting off the after magazine and torpedo warheads. The resulting explosion was of considerable force and forty feet of our very solid reinforced concrete jetty disappeared entirely and the destroyer was sunk. Parts of the destroyer actually fell in our works machine shop area some 150 yards from the jetty.[5]

The submarine depot ship *Lucia*, a venerable vessel launched in 1907, and another merchant ship were also damaged. *Lucia* had been preparing to load torpedoes onto a submarine moored alongside at the time of the attack. A bomb dropped right through the ship and out the bottom without exploding.

Near the city's cathedral was an asylum with a large chimney; Japanese aviators possibly mistook the asylum for a power station. The institution was heavily bombed and about fifty people were killed.[6] The severity of the raid caused an exodus of Colombo's population, many of whom left their homes for the villages and countryside of the hinterland. Most of the dock workforce vanished as well. Eighty-five civilians died in the bombing; almost as many were badly injured. The raid lasted an hour and twenty minutes.

The main RAF airfield near Colombo was at Ratmalana. There was an auxiliary landing strip at Colombo racecourse. Forty-two defending fighters took to the skies to greet the raiders: thirty-six Hurricanes and six Fulmars. The last Hurricanes were getting airborne as the first Japanese aircraft arrived. Hurricane fighters were not quite the match of a Zero in terms of speed or manoeuvrability, but they were strongly built and well armed. The Fulmar, however, was an out-of-date two-seater fighter-bomber. In the aerial battle that followed, fifteen Hurricanes and four Fulmars were shot down. Japanese carrier pilots were highly experienced aviators. RAF and Fleet Air Arm pilots claimed nineteen enemy aircraft destroyed and several 'probables', but the Japanese listed their losses as seven aircraft in total – six dive-bombers and a Zero.[7] The Japanese pilot Lieutenant Ibusuki Masanobu shot down a Hurricane, which ditched in the ocean. The Hurricane's pilot climbed out of his cockpit whilst Masanobu circled overhead. The two men waved to each other and both lived to fight another day.[8] Some Blenheim bombers at Ratmalana took off to bomb the Japanese fleet, but could not find them and returned with bomb loads still on the racks.

As the raid on Colombo was taking place, Somerville's fleet steamed towards Ceylon from Addu Atoll. Force B was 100 miles astern of the faster Force A. Late in the morning Somerville received a report of Japanese warships 250 miles from his fast division. The Japanese were within torpedo-bomber range, but Somerville did not want to risk a daylight strike with his ancient carrier aircraft. Meanwhile the heavy cruisers *Dorsetshire* and *Cornwall* were sailing south from Colombo to a rendezvous with Somerville.

The heavy cruisers were commanded by Captain A.W.S. Agar VC on *Dorsetshire* and Captain P.C.W. Manwaring on *Cornwall*. Agar was the senior of the two captains; he had been born in Ceylon, the youngest of thirteen children of an Irish tea planter.[9] Agar won his Victoria Cross when his coastal motorboat sank a Bolshevik Russian cruiser in Krondstadt harbour in the Baltic on 17 June 1919. He was also awarded the DSO for his part in another motorboat raid on Krondstadt on the night of 17/18 August 1919 in which a Bolshevik armoured cruiser and dreadnought battleship were sunk.

The heavy cruisers *Dorsetshire* and *Cornwall* had a main armament of eight-inch guns. In theory their maximum speed was over thirty knots. The heavy cruisers were thinly armoured as they had been built to conform with the 10,000 ton limit allowed by the Washington Naval Treaty. The treaty, however, had not limited the length of a cruiser; *Cornwall* was 630 feet in length and thus longer than *Warspite* or any of the R-class battle-ships. This was compensated for by a narrowness of beam, sixty-eight and a half feet as against 104 feet for *Warspite*.[10] The ships' anti-aircraft armament included eight four-inch guns and two multiple-barrel pom-poms. Each of the warships carried over 100 South Africans amongst their British crew. *Dorsetshire* and *Cornwall* were two of fifteen heavy cruisers to be launched by British shipyards from 1926–29.

Since the outbreak of war, the cruisers had both spent long and dangerous periods at sea. On 8 May 1941 *Cornwall* sank the German auxiliary cruiser *Pinguin*; the raider was no match for a heavy cruiser. The engagement caused only a single fatality aboard *Cornwall*. An engineer lieutenant died of heat exhaustion after ventilation fans broke down. Aboard *Pinguin* a huge explosion sank the ship and killed 554 men, including 213 Allied prisoners of war held below deck. There were only eighty-four survivors of all nation-alities.[11] *Dorsetshire*'s role in the war also had moments of drama. She gave the German battleship *Bismarck* her *coup de grâce* with torpedoes in the North

Atlantic. More recently, *Dorsetshire* had forced the German supply ship *Python* to scuttle on 1 December 1941.

Captain Agar's pair of cruisers had sailed from Colombo in a south-west direction. As *Dorsetshire* was leaving Colombo harbour, the Executive Officer, Commander C.W. Byas, had remarked to another officer, 'I think we are for it this time'.[12] During the night of 4/5 April Somerville signalled Agar to take the cruisers to a rendezvous at Longitude 77.35 East.[13] This rendezvous compelled the cruisers to steam a southerly course that was closer than desirable to the Japanese fleet known to be rapidly approaching Ceylon from the east. Agar later wrote that he was unaware of the full extent his ships were in danger as he did not know Japanese naval aircraft had such a long range. He assumed they had much the same limited range as Fleet Air Arm aircraft.

At 8 a.m. on 5 April *Dorsetshire* received a delayed report that placed Japanese warships only 150 miles to the east. Agar increased speed to twenty-seven and a half knots; that was *Cornwall*'s maximum speed. The warships closed up at action stations; tension and suspense began to mount amid the heat below deck. Under these circumstances *Cornwall*'s usual Sunday morning church service on the quarter deck could not be held. The chaplain, the Reverend J.M. Bird, broadcast over the loudspeaker instead: 'We pray not for our personal safety, but for courage to do our duty'.[14] *Cornwall*'s Meteorological Officer, Lieutenant B.M. Holden, was no stranger to Japanese air attack; he had survived the sinking of the *Repulse* the previous December, before subsequently joining *Cornwall*'s company.

To the south of Ceylon the weather was calm; there was a slight haze with wisps of cloud, but visibility was perfect across the sea. At 11 a.m. the two British heavy cruisers were discovered by a Japanese scout from Nagumo's fleet. Lookouts briefly saw a dot in the sky, twenty miles astern. This was a reconnaissance seaplane catapulted from a Japanese warship. The dot disappeared but at midday another aircraft was sighted astern. Agar broke radio silence to report that he was being shadowed; the message was relayed from Colombo to Somerville and the Eastern Fleet. Agar recalled that he then had an even harder decision to make:

> whether to turn the two ships immediately to the westward so as to get them farther out of range of the enemy striking force, or whether to press on as arranged towards the rendezvous, which was now only ninety miles away. I decided to press on, because if I turned to the west it might expose the Fleet to the 'shadower', who was now on my tail ten miles away and obviously determined to stay there.[15]

After a while the shadower made off and an uneasy lull followed.

At 1.40 p.m. the heavy cruisers were 300 miles south–south-west of Ceylon. *Cornwall* had no radar; *Dorsetshire* had only an early type of apparatus, which had shown 'confused streaks' on its screen earlier in the day. All of a sudden lookouts on *Dorsetshire* sighted three aircraft in the sky high above the warships; anti-aircraft guns quickly opened fire. *Cornwall* was a mile astern of *Dorsetshire*. A rating aboard *Dorsetshire* remarked that the aircraft were 'bringing us a nice packet of Easter eggs'.[16]

The sky soon filled with large formations of Japanese dive-bombers, each of which carried a 250-kilogram bomb. Fifty-three dive-bombers proceeded to conduct a very efficient attack from out of the sun, ahead of their victims. The aircraft fell upon the warships in waves of three, one after another at short intervals. Bombs were released at a height of a thousand feet. Anti-aircraft weaponry was fired at full pace, the crews dressed in anti-flash gear and tin helmets. An eight-barrel pom-pom could fire 720 graze-fused shells a minute. Flames shot from the muzzles of the four-inch guns.

On *Dorsetshire* Captain Agar watched as dive-bombers fell downwards to attack his ship:

> We could see the bombs falling, black and shiny, blunt-nosed ... I ordered immediately the helm to be put over twenty-five degrees to keep the ship turning as soon as the planes were sighted, but in spite of this the first one scored a hit near the catapult and started a fire. The next one fell close to the bridge, the blast throwing us to the deck ... There followed afterwards, in quick succession, a series of thuds and heavy thumps as further bombs exploded in the engine and boiler rooms ... The ship kept on turning to starboard with the steering gear jammed, and I could see little from the bridge through the inferno of smoke and fire. The few guns we had left were firing intermittently but most were out of action after the first two bomb hits. There followed a frightful explosion as a bomb reached one of our magazines.[17]

Dorsetshire's steering gear was disabled by the first set of hits. The ship's wireless office was wrecked and most of the port side anti-aircraft guns put out of action. *Dorsetshire* was turning hard to starboard when the steering jammed and this caused the ship to keep turning in a circle. At least six more hits followed; the stricken cruiser was soon ablaze from bridge to stern; boiler damage caused a loss of speed. The order to abandon ship was passed by shout and gesture. The crew scrambled down the sides of the cruiser under sporadic machine gun fire from low-flying aircraft. Steam escaping from broken boilers and the scream of the ship's damaged siren added to the cacophony. *Dorsetshire*, listing heavily to port, capsized and sank eight minutes after the first attack.

Cornwall soon shared the fate of *Dorsetshire*. The first three dive-bombers scored a hit and two near misses. The explosions in the water alongside heaved *Cornwall* out of the sea. Towers of water were sent high into the air and drenched men on deck. Captain Manwaring later reported: 'The effect of these [the near misses] was very great, lifting the ship bodily by their force, causing her to whip heavily from end to end and carrying away all the wireless aerials and nearly shaking the mast down.'[18] At the port pom-pom, Able Seaman Wally Muller recalled:

> A high-pitched whine intruded suddenly upon the senses, growing in the space of a second or two to an ear-shattering roar, then passed overhead and away. Almost immediately the ship shuddered violently with the sound of the muffled explosion of a near miss, but even before stunned realisation took hold, the scream of a second dive-bomber rent the air and there was the fearsome concussion as a bomb exploded in the ship.[19]

An aircraft pulling out of its dive crashed astern after hits from a pom-pom.

Underwater damage to *Cornwall* flooded the engine and boiler rooms; the electric power system was damaged and only emergency lamps remained lit; the sick bay was destroyed by a bomb hit and the chaplain killed. After suffering at least seven bomb hits, *Cornwall* was brought to a halt. To those below deck it was unclear at first if she had been hit by a torpedo or bombs. The ship's company had to escape upwards through narrow hatches in semi-darkness. Fireballs rolled through the confined spaces of the lower deck; badly burnt men reached the upper deck in a state of collapse. Ken Dimbleby reached the upper deck and recalled the following:

> I glanced instinctively across the ocean to see how *Dorsetshire* was faring on our starboard side. She was slightly astern of us and listing acutely to port ... Smoke and steam were billowing from the big cruiser as she heeled over farther on to her side and sank stern first, her bows almost vertical as she slid down to her ocean grave.[20]

Aboard *Cornwall*, at 1.55 p.m. the order was given to abandon ship. Many boats had been smashed by the bombing; men in the water would need their lifebelts.

Cornwall sank by the bows with a seventy-degree list. As the ship sank, the stern lifted out of the water, one propeller turning, the colours still flying. Those men trapped below deck went with the wreck to the ocean's floor. The attack was over in fifteen minutes, leaving survivors clinging to wreckage in the calm seas, and whatever boats and rafts could be released in time. An oil slick lay upon the surface of the sea.

The radar on Somerville's flagship had detected the swarm of aircraft that pounded *Cornwall* and *Dorsetshire*. Later in the afternoon a reconnaissance aircraft from the main fleet saw wreckage and survivors in the water near where Agar's ships should have been. It was fortunate for the Royal Navy that Japanese scouts did not find the Eastern Fleet's fast division to the south of where the cruisers sank. For the rest of that day, and the following night,

Somerville's fleet steered away from the danger zone. The admiral grimly noted: 'We were no longer the hunters, we were the hunted.'

Only on the morning of 6 April did Somerville's fast division head back east again to look for the cruisers' survivors. This was a course of action fraught with danger. Somerville no longer had any wish to encounter his enemy and hoped that the Japanese had departed the scene. That proved to be the case; Nagumo had steered south-east after recovering his aircraft on the afternoon of 5 April, and was pulling away from the Eastern Fleet.

The survivors of the sunken cruisers, many covered in oil, were discovered in two groups, two miles apart, in calm seas. The sunburnt, hungry and thirsty men had spent thirty hours in the water by the time the cruiser *Enterprise* and two destroyers picked them up on the afternoon of 6 April. It took an hour to collect the survivors; 1122 of 1546 crew were rescued from shark-infested tropical waters. Sharks had not molested the living as they could feast upon the corpses of the dead. Nineteen officers and 214 men died on *Dorsetshire*; ten officers and 181 men died on *Cornwall*. Both captains survived the sinking. Agar remarked: 'I can only say that the attack was well timed, well delivered, and most courageously executed by our enemies.' On *Akagi*, Commander Fuchida commented, 'rather than exultation over the proficiency of the bombardiers, [I] could only feel pity for those surface ships assailed from the air at odds of forty to one'.[21] The dive-bombers had achieved very high levels of accuracy in the clear, windless conditions.

When Admiral Layton, ashore at Ceylon, heard news of the loss of the cruisers, he felt compelled to signal the Admiralty that the Eastern Fleet was in danger from a superior Japanese force and faced 'immediate annihilation'. At sea Somerville's signallers intercepted the message. Layton had no authority over Somerville but he could express his views.

During 6 April the Eastern Fleet received reliable information that the Japanese task force in the Indian Ocean probably comprised four battleships and five aircraft carriers.[22] This made it crystal clear that a major offensive was underway. Alarmingly, aerial reconnaissance reported sighting two hostile submarines to the south-west of Somerville's fleet astride the line of retreat to Addu Atoll. Suspicions grew amongst British commanders that Nagumo's carriers might have hooked southwards to intercept a retirement to that anchorage. Layton sent a signal from Ceylon mentioning the possibility. Somerville sailed north-westwards and then south-westwards to approach Addu Atoll cautiously from the west, preceded by a screen of reconnaissance aircraft.

Eastern Fleet returned to Addu Atoll at 11.30 a.m. on 8 April. Rear-Admirals Boyd and Willis came aboard *Warspite* for discussions with the Eastern Fleet's commander and staff. Willis told Somerville that, 'I thought he had

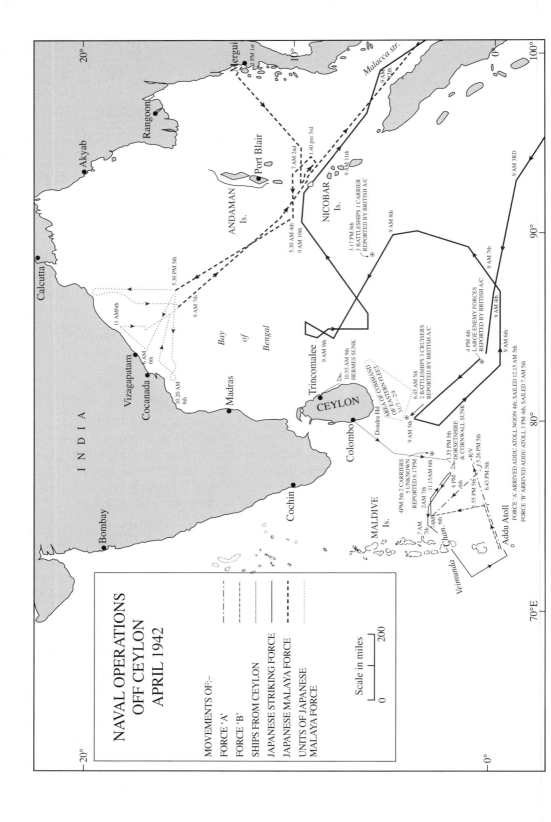

NAVAL OPERATIONS
OFF CEYLON
APRIL 1942

MOVEMENTS OF:–

FORCE 'A'

FORCE 'B'

SHIPS FROM CEYLON

JAPANESE STRIKING FORCE

JAPANESE MALAYA FORCE

UNITS OF JAPANESE
MALAYA FORCE

Scale in miles

0   200

INDIA

Bombay

Calcutta

Cochin

Madras

Cocanada
Vizagapatam

Akyab

Rangoon

Mergui
PM 1st

Port Blair
ANDAMAN
Is.
7 AM 2nd
1.40 pm 3rd

NICOBAR
Is.
9 AM 11th

3.17 PM 8th
3 BATTLESHIPS 1 CARRIER
REPORTED BY BRITISH A/C
9 AM 8th

9 AM 7th

9 AM 3RD

9 AM 4th

9 AM 6th

4 PM 4th
LARGE ENEMY FORCES
REPORTED BY BRITISH A/C

6.45 AM 5th
2 BATTLESHIPS 3 CRUISERS
REPORTED BY BRITISH A/C

Bay
of
Bengal

5.30 AM 4th
9 AM 10th

5.30 PM 5th

9 AM 7th

11 AM 6th

7 AM
6th
10.20 AM
6th

CEYLON
Trincomalee
Dondra Hd
Colombo

10.55 AM 9th
HERMES SUNK

9 AM 9th

9 AM 5th

AREA OF COMMAND
OF EASTERN FLEET
31/3 – 2/4

4PM 5th 2 CARRIERS
5 UNKNOWN
REPORTED 6.17PM

2AM 7th
11.15AM 6th

7.55 PM 5th
DORSETSHIRE
& CORNWALL SUNK

5.26 PM 5th

6.43 PM 5th

6 PM
6th

7 AM
7th

7 AM
7th

7.55 PM 5th

R/V

Veimunda

MALDIVE
Is.

Chan.

Addu Atoll

FORCE 'A' ARRIVED ADDU ATOLL NOON 4th; SAILED 12.15 AM 5th
FORCE 'B' ARRIVED ADDU ATOLL 3 PM 4th: SAILED 7 AM 5th

Malacca str.
9.12th

20°

10°

0°

20°

70°E

80°

90°

100°

0°

taken grave risks with the fleet, the preservation of which ought to be the main object.'[23] In London the Admiralty had reached the same conclusion. The Eastern Fleet was advised to send the R-class battleships to the safety of Aden or Zanzibar. Somerville ordered Force B to sail for Kilindini on the coast of Kenya, after refuelling was completed.

Nagumo, however, was not finished with Ceylon. His carriers had sailed eastwards on 6 April to a point 500 miles from Ceylon, and then began to circle northwards in an arc. Profiting from criticism of his timidity off Hawaii, Nagumo and his fleet prepared to return for a second raid on Ceylon. The Japanese warships refuelled at sea; the port of Trincomalee was the next target.

The coast of Ceylon has relatively few bays and inlets, but Trincomalee is one of the world's most beautiful natural harbours. Located on the north-east coast, Trincomalee overlooks the Bay of Bengal. The town was isolated from the main merchant shipping routes that radiated from Colombo, but Trincomalee's seclusion made it an ideal site for a naval base. The harbour entrance is guarded by two formidable headlands that shelter a vast inner harbour. To the north of the inner harbour is the picturesque Dutch Bay, and a rocky peninsula where 400 foot-high cliffs rise from the blue water of the bay.

The Portuguese had built a settlement at Trincomalee, which was rebuilt by the Dutch. In 1775 a young Horatio Nelson had visited the harbour; he pronounced it the finest in the world. Colonel Arthur Wellesley, the future Duke of Wellington, also visited in 1800 for the assembly of an expeditionary force. In 1852 Trincomalee became the presumed resting place of Rear-Admiral Sir Charles Austen, the younger brother of the novelist Jane Austen. The spacious, tree-shaded town featured Buddhist and Hindu temples and the neo-baroque fronted St Mary's Cathedral. A jungle hinterland cut off Trincomalee from the rest of Ceylon, but a railway had been built from Colombo to open up the region.[24] The port's naval facilities included fifty oil tanks in the nearby jungle.

On the afternoon of 8 April a Catalina flying-boat reported sighting three battleships and an aircraft carrier 470 miles south-east of Trincomalee.[25] All shipping was ordered to clear the harbour. The land bridge between Ceylon and India is covered by shallow water; large ships leaving Trincomalee cannot hook north-westwards to safety around the northern point of Ceylon. Therefore the aircraft carrier *Hermes* and destroyer *Vampire* were ordered to head southwards down the east coast of the island. The tanker *British Sergeant*, fleet auxiliary *Athelstane* and corvette *Hollyhock* did likewise. The old 7200 ton monitor *Erebus* and a merchant ship remained in harbour. The *Erebus* dated from 1916 and mounted two fifteen-inch guns.

The strike force destined to raid Trincomalee on 9 April comprised ninety-one bombers (Kates) and forty-one fighters (Zeros). Fuchida was in command and the strike force was drawn from all five carriers. Val dive-bombers were to remain on deck ready to attack any enemy warships sighted. The Japanese force was launched before dawn and reached Trincomalee at 7.25 a.m. The raiders' bombs did heavy damage to the dockyard and other shore installations; fuel tanks and an ammunition depot were destroyed. The Japanese official account recorded that the bombing caused a 'spectacular display of fireworks'. *Erebus* was damaged; the merchant ship *Sagaing* was set on fire and beached. *Sagaing* was rumoured to be carrying a large supply of whisky in its cargo hold. Heavy anti-aircraft fire was reported over the base by returning Japanese aircrew.

The radar station at Trincomalee had detected the incoming raiders in good time. From China Bay airfield seventeen Hurricanes of No. 261 Squadron and six naval Fulmars, put ashore from *Hermes*, took to the skies in fine weather. In the aerial combats that followed eight Hurricanes and three Fulmars were shot down. Several Japanese aircraft were destroyed as well, though not nearly as many as were claimed by Allied pilots and anti-aircraft gunners on the ground. China Bay airfield was bombed and strafed by the raiders. One particular anti-aircraft gun was destroyed, and the crew killed, when a damaged Japanese aircraft crash-dived onto the emplacement.[26]

Meanwhile nine Blenheim bombers of No. 11 Squadron were dispatched from the Racecourse airstrip near Colombo to bomb the Japanese carriers. At 10.25 a.m. the Blenheims found the carriers far out at sea. The Japanese fleet, unused to air attack, was caught unawares and the Blenheims made their bombing run after an approach flight partly covered by cloud. Bombs fell near *Akagi*, but no hits were made. The bomb misses caused white columns of water to rise high into the air close to the carrier. Zeros soon pounced and managed to shoot down five of the Blenheims on their return flight. All of the surviving bombers were damaged – No. 11 Squadron was ruined.

At the time of the raid the aircraft carrier *Hermes* and the Australian destroyer *Vampire* were at sea sixty-five miles south of Trincomalee. *Hermes* was not carrying any aircraft. A float-plane from a Japanese battleship spotted the carrier, and at 9.45 a.m. a dive-bomber force of eighty-five aircraft, and a small escort of fighters, took-off into blue skies from Nagumo's fleet. The float-plane's signal was intercepted and read at Colombo. The RAF at Trincomalee was instructed to provide air cover for *Hermes*; the carrier was ordered to reverse course and head back to port.[27]

Dive-bombers attacked *Hermes* with ruthless efficiency shortly after 10.30 a.m. An officer on the carrier noted that 'the attack was carried out perfectly, relentless and quite fearlessly, and was exactly like a highly organised deck display. The aircraft peeled off in threes diving straight down on the ship out of the sun.'[28] The carrier took evasive action; anti-aircraft guns opened fire. It was all to no avail, and the deck was soon torn to ribbons by the blasts of 250-kilogram bombs. The carrier became a flaming wreck. Some of the dive-bombers plunged so low they risked damage from their own bomb blasts. As many as thirty-seven hits were scored on *Hermes* in ten minutes. The crippled carrier listed to port so severely that the flightdeck was lapped by the sea. *Hermes* sank at 10.55 a.m. in shallow water. A hit on the bridge had killed Captain R.F.J. Onslow. The leader of the dive-bombers, Lieutenant-Commander Takashige Egusa, would claim that sinking *Hermes* had been easier than hitting a target ship in peacetime.

The destroyer *Vampire* was nearby and soon followed the carrier to a watery grave. Dive-bombers delivered two near misses before a hit on the boiler room brought the ship to a halt. Further hits knocked the bow off, and the crew abandoned ship. At 11.02 a.m. *Vampire* was blown apart by an explosion in the after-magazine.[29]

Nineteen officers and 283 men died on *Hermes*; one officer and seven men died on *Vampire*. Six hundred survivors were fished out of the warm water by the hospital ship *Vita*, which happened to be sailing in a southerly direction nearby. *Vita* was unmolested in her task and lowered lifeboats and a motorboat to rescue the survivors. The hospital ship reached Colombo that evening. As many as ten men from *Hermes* are believed to have successfully swum the five miles from the sinking ship to the shore.

There were enough dive-bombers with undelivered bombs to sink other Allied shipping fleeing from Trincomalee. The tanker *British Sergeant* was attacked by six dive-bombers. The crew left the sinking tanker in boats and headed for shore. The corvette *Hollyhock* and fleet auxiliary *Athelstane* were also sunk. *Athelstane*'s crew survived but the corvette suffered many casualties, including fifty-three dead.[30]

At first the Japanese dive-bombers that sank *Hermes* were unopposed as the damaged China Bay base had no aircraft ready to take to the skies. Eventually eight Fulmars of No. 806 Squadron arrived on the scene from Ratmalana airfield. The Fulmars had left their observers and rear gunners behind as, on this occasion, they were said to be 'excess baggage'. In the dogfights that followed the pilots of the Fulmars claimed to have shot down several dive-bombers for the loss of two of their own aircraft.[31]

After the raid on Trincomalee, Admiral Nagumo decided to end the operation in the Indian Ocean. The Japanese fleet headed back towards the Malacca Strait and the East Indies on the night of 9/10 April. The Japanese were disappointed that the main Allied fleet in the Indian Ocean had not been destroyed. Nagumo had remained unaware that the Royal Navy was using a secret base at Addu Atoll; he would doubtless have made different decisions if he had known.

On 11 April the English-language *Japan Times and Advertiser* published details of the Imperial Japanese Navy's latest victory over the Western powers. 'The might of the British Empire once depended upon its strong navy which once dominated the seven seas of the world … These serious setbacks suffered by the British Navy and Air Force in the Indian Ocean are nothing but an elegy for the downfall of that once mighty Empire.'[32] Forty-eight British aircraft (RAF and Fleet Air Arm) were lost in the brief aerial campaign, and other aircraft were damaged on the ground. According to Japanese figures the Ceylon operation cost eighteen aircraft destroyed and thirty-three damaged.[33] Losses of Japanese carrier aircraft around Ceylon may have had a marginal impact on future events in the Pacific theatre, though that is unclear.

The dive-bombing performance of Japan's naval aviators had been phenomenal, but not every operational aspect of the fleet's performance was above criticism. The anti-aircraft defences of Nagumo's carriers had made no impression on the Blenheim bombers' raid. Likewise, Japanese aerial reconnaissance did not find the Eastern Fleet.[34] Later in the war the Japanese would pay a heavy price for defects of that kind.

Whilst Nagumo's carriers had raided Ceylon, Admiral Ozawa's task force swept across the Bay of Bengal towards the eastern coast of India. On 6 April *Ryujo*'s aircraft bombed Vizagapatam and Cocanada. Panic and alarm was spread along India's eastern seaboard. An air raid warning at Madras caused a general exodus. The 19th Indian Division was concentrated to defend the coastline near the city. Major-General G.N. Molesworth recalled that there were so few anti-aircraft guns in India that, 'near Madras and Vizagapatam, palm trees were cut down and the trunks stuck up at an angle of forty-five degrees in the hope that Japanese planes would mistake them for defences'.[35] Churchill and the Chiefs of Staff in London had been anxious that the Japanese might invade Ceylon, but they did not think there was much risk to the Madras region as long as Ceylon remained in Britain's possession.

At sea Ozawa's force sank twenty-three merchant ships totalling 112,000 tons from 4–9 April.[36] There were further shipping losses at this time to Japanese submarines operating on the west coast of India. The port of Calcutta became crowded with merchantmen unable to sail.

Nagumo's carriers reached Singapore on 11 April and returned to Japan a week later. The British and Japanese forces recently opposed in the Indian Ocean were now thousands of miles apart. Once it was clear that the Japanese carrier force had withdrawn to the East Indies, the Eastern Fleet sailed for

Bombay, though the port was not large enough to be a permanent fleet base. Somerville had considered taking his warships to Colombo for a short stay, but, after the sinking of *Hermes*, he was ordered by the Admiralty not to proceed to Ceylon. Somerville wrote to his wife on 10 April: 'I can do nothing now to help Ceylon. They have practically no air force left so it looks to me as if the Japs can walk in any time they like.'[37]

In Royal Navy circles Somerville was criticised for detaching *Dorsetshire*, *Cornwall* and *Hermes* from the rest of Eastern Fleet at a time of crisis. Somerville explained to the Admiralty: 'Since no news of enemy [was] received by a.m. 3rd [April] it appeared enemy's intentions quite possibly misjudged or operation postponed'.[38] Prior to the devastating dive-bombing of the heavy cruisers, Somerville had not understood how heavy a punch the Japanese fleet carriers could deliver. He reported:

> The novel aspect of the attack, viz, using fighter dive-bombers, was not appreciated until p.m. 6th on return of *Enterprise* with survivors. I then realised that, with very limited number of high-performance fighters I had available and vulnerability of 'R' class to this form of attack, it would be necessary to avoid an encounter until we were better equipped.[39]

Churchill was not impressed by the extent of the Eastern Fleet's losses, in return for which the Japanese cause had received little damage. Yet he was obliged to defend Somerville's actions to the House of Commons in a secret session.

Somerville's fleet arrived at Bombay on 13 April. The admiral met with General Wavell and Air Marshal Sir Richard Peirse that evening, and gave them the grim news that the Royal Navy would not be able to prevent landings at Ceylon or southern India. With the situation rapidly crumbling in Burma, this was a further blow for Wavell, who was surprised to find that command of the seas was forfeited given the long list of warships belonging to the Eastern Fleet. Wavell and Somerville found common cause against the news that 'hundreds of bombers' were regularly attacking targets in Germany. Somerville wrote to the Admiralty: 'In this connection I must confess that the majority of senior officers of the Eastern Fleet are sceptical of the results achieved by these attacks on Germany, who can presumably "take it" as well as the United Kingdom.'[40] Wavell later wrote in his despatch that this period was India's most dangerous hour:

> Our Eastern Fleet was powerless to protect Ceylon or Eastern India; our air strength was negligible; and it was becoming increasingly obvious that our small tired force in Burma was unlikely to be able to hold the enemy, while the absence of communications between Assam and Upper Burma made it impossible to reinforce it.

The threat to eastern India had caused many merchant ships to be directed to Bombay and Karachi for unloading, rather than Calcutta. Goods then had to be sent on long rail journeys across India to strain further a rail system already at breaking point.

The modern units of the Eastern Fleet at Bombay did not remain long in that port, and soon departed for eastern Africa to join the R-class battleships. At Kilindini, a large deep-water inlet, the fleet was at least able to directly cover the shipping route from South Africa to the Nile delta. Hostile Vichy French forces at Madagascar were the principal threat in that part of the Indian Ocean.

Given the speed with which the Vichy French had turned over Indochina to the Japanese, there was concern in London that the Japanese might launch a *coup de main* across the Indian Ocean to seize Madagascar. A fleet of Japanese submarines based at Diego Suarez could feast upon Allied shipping heading for the Middle East. To prevent that eventuality, a British expeditionary force made a surprise landing on Madagascar on 5 May. Two days later the French at Diego Suarez surrendered to bring that phase of the operation to a successful conclusion; sporadic fighting in other parts of the island would linger on for months.

In the aftermath of Nagumo's raid, the possibility of an invasion of Ceylon remained high, but giant turtles swimming ashore at night were the only invaders to appear out of the gloom to startle beach posts manned by Australian infantry. The Imperial Japanese Navy was no longer greatly interested in the Indian Ocean; instead the fleet was getting ready for another round of offensive operations, but this time in the south-west Pacific against the United States Navy.

16

The Oilfields of Yenangyaung

April is the hottest month of the year in Burma. In the morning there is already a closeness in the air; long hours of stifling heat lie ahead. A fierce light blazes from a sun high in the ultramarine sky; humidity, dust and thirst plagues man and beast alike. In April of 1942 British, Indian, Gurkha, Burmese and Chinese troops retreating northwards into Upper Burma knew little of what was happening in the skies and seas around Ceylon. The commanders of those troops, however, were only too well aware that the Royal Navy had lost all control of the seas off southern Burma.

The Japanese army was about to disembark additional reinforcements at Rangoon. The 18th Division was due on 7 April to give General Iida's XV Army four divisions. Two tank regiments were also expected at Rangoon in a major convoy; the regiments each had thirty-six tanks. Further artillery, engineering, railway and transport reinforcements were accompanying the larger formations.

A high priority for the Japanese air force was the bombing of the principal urban target in Upper Burma – the city of Mandalay. The former seat of the Kingdom of Ava had thus far escaped the attentions of the Japanese air force, but that period of grace had ended. On 3 April fifty Japanese bombers flew from bases in Thailand to pound the defenceless city.[1] The streets and bazaars were crowded when the bombers struck just after 11 a.m. The American journalist Jack Beldon observed the raid. 'The pilots leisurely fixed the town under their sights, as a scientist fixes a bug beneath a microscope, pinned it to earth, and stabbed it with hundreds of explosive plummets.' A west wind from the Irrawaddy blew sparks over those districts that were down wind to spread the conflagration. Before long half of Mandalay seemed to be on fire; the mains water supply failed; firemen were reduced to pumping water out of the moat around the palace. According to Beldon:

> Toward this palace Darrell Berrigan of the United Press and I drove slowly in a jeep. Smoke from the rest of the city poured over the palace grounds, hiding them in a haze. An ox stood by the side of the moat with a mortal wound in his neck, slowly nodding with a glazed look in his eyes as the blood oozed down across his white front and dripped onto the ground. A man in a bicycle carriage sat with his feet up in the air, killed in the very act of getting out. A tall fellow with

a cigar raised to his lips … leaned against a tree, frozen dead like a figure buried in Pompeii. Another man sat on the ground with an umbrella over his shoulder in one hand, his other hand gesticulating and his mouth open, killed in the act of saying something.[2]

The railway station and nearby freight cars were set on fire; the hospital lost power; the danger of looters and dacoits loomed large as night fell; the authorities lost control of the city.

Governor and Lady Dorman-Smith toured the city three days after the raid. Lady Dorman-Smith wrote in her diary:

> The scenes beggar description. Acre after acre of streets are burnt completely flat. The streets are littered with burnt trees, telephone wires down everywhere, burnt out gharries, one with the remains of the pony – just too appalling for words … The smell was awful. It looks absolutely hopeless to begin to clear the mess. There was no warning. The first thing the bombs. The wind helped a lot as it kept shifting and fanning the flames. Rangoon was nothing to this destruction.[3]

Most of Mandalay's population fled and the life of the city ceased.

General Slim's Burcorps, at this time, was far to the south of Mandalay marching northwards into central Burma's 'dry zone', an arid, flat landscape broken by scrub, nullahs and bare hills. A Japanese attempt to encircle British forces at Allanmyo, a town on the east bank of the Irrawaddy north of Prome, found them already gone. On 8 April Burcorps halted its northward retreat and took up new positions with the right flank astride the Irrawaddy. A forty-mile front was established from the river to Taungdwingyi, a town at the terminus of a railway branch line. This extended front was vulnerable to infiltration. Alexander instructed Slim to hold Taungdwingyi firmly so as to maintain contact with Chinese forces further to the east on the main route running northwards from Toungoo to Mandalay. Attempts to arrange for Chinese troops to relieve part of the 17th Division at Taungdwingyi amounted to nothing, even though Alexander made the request of Generalissimo Chiang in person.

General Scott's 1st Burma Division was deployed with the 2nd Burma Brigade at Minhla on the west bank of the Irrawaddy. The 1st Burma Brigade was on the east bank of the river at Migyaungye, and the 13th Indian Brigade extended the line eastwards. The battalions of the Burma Rifles had continued to waste away from desertion as the families and homes of most of the soldiers were left farther and farther to the rear. British infantry units, however, were in no better shape numerically as a consequence of high rates of wastage from sickness and few, if any, replacements. The 1st Cameronians were reduced to 215 all ranks; over 200 men had been evacuated sick, apart from battle losses. The 1st Glosters were down to seven officers and 170 men; Lieutenant-Colonel Bagot was amongst those evacuated to hospital.

The main body of the 17th Division was positioned at Taungdwingyi, and the division's 48th Brigade was ten miles to the west at Kokkogwa astride the lateral road leading to Scott's division. Taungdwingyi was surrounded by open paddy, which at least provided adequate fields of fire. Generals Alexander and Slim paid the garrison a visit. Slim told a group of officers: 'General Cowan and I were at the Staff College together – but I'm bound to say that some of the things that we learnt there don't seem to work too well out here!'[4]

Burcorps headquarters had been established at Magwe, from where a road led southwards to the lateral road that ran from the Irrawaddy to Taungdwingyi. Japanese aircraft patrolled the road at regular intervals hunting for Allied vehicles. Slim recalled:

> Once when I was visiting his area, Curtis, who commanded 13 Brigade, went ahead in a closed car with the Colonel of the Inniskillings [R.G.S. Cox] beside him. A Japanese fighter swooped and riddled the back of their car. The Colonel was killed instantly, and when we came up we found Curtis bleeding from three wounds, all luckily superficial. Bandaged but completely unshaken, he took me round his positions without any further reference to the incident. I have rarely seen a better instance of steady nerves.[5]

The driver of the car had also been killed. The rear of the vehicle was cut open by machine gun fire.

General Iida's XV Army had four divisions available for the next phase of the campaign. On the eastern flank the 56th Division was to advance on Lashio; in the centre of the front the 18th and 55th Divisions were to advance along the rail and road routes leading from Toungoo to Mandalay; on the western flank the 33rd Division was to push northwards up the eastern bank of the Irrawaddy.

The 33rd Division would have to tackle both divisions of Burcorps unaided by other Japanese formations in Burma. General Sakurai's division paused for three days at Allanmyo to resupply and rest. The division had been reinforced by the 213th Regiment and the 26th Independent Engineer Regiment. The engineers were equipped with landing craft and steel motor-boats; the Japanese intended to take full advantage of the watery highway of the Irrawaddy, which was the traditional route from lower to upper Burma, and the fabled road to Mandalay. Sakurai's plan was for the 215th Regiment to pin the 17th Division at the eastern end of the front, whilst the 213th and 214th Regiments attacked the 1st Burma Division and pushed up the east bank of the Irrawaddy towards Magwe.

The Japanese advance from Allanmyo began at sunset on 9 April. The first of Slim's brigades to come into contact with the Japanese was the 48th Brigade at Kokkogwa. The brigade was fortunate as it had absorbed five Gurkha battalions and 500 replacements. These men had been reorganised to form three reasonably strong battalions – the 1/4th, 2/5th and 1/7th Gurkhas. The battalions had taken up positions in an arid countryside littered with thorn bush scrub. The Gurkhas were supported by eight twenty-five-pound field guns of the 1st Indian Field Regiment and the 2nd Royal Tanks (less one squadron which was with Scott's division). There was no barbed wire available and in places the thorn bushes were woven into an old-fashioned zariba entanglement of the type used in the Sudan in the 1890s. There were telephone lines running between battalion and brigade headquarters, but otherwise signalling depended on the equally old-fashioned method of runners.

Gurkha patrols made contact with Japanese troops to the south of Kokkogwa on 10 April. On the night of 11/12 April the fast-advancing I/215th Battalion probed the 48th Brigade's perimeter from the south-east, whilst the II/215th Battalion attacked from the west. At one point a violent thunderstorm broke and flashes of lightening lit up the landscape. The engagement lasted into the afternoon of 12 April before the Japanese withdrew.[6] The following night of 12/13 April, the Gurkhas were again probed, but an attack was not pressed home. Brigadier Cameron later said that 'Kokkogwa was the best effort made by the 48th Brigade in Burma'.[7] Recorded Japanese casualties for the battle included forty-two dead. The 215th Regiment's attack was repelled, but General Sakarai had only intended it to be a diversion.[8]

Whilst the 215th Regiment was keeping the 17th Indian Division occupied at Kokkogwa, the main offensive was getting underway near the Irrawaddy. The 213th Regiment was to advance up the east bank of the river towards Magwe; further east the 214th Regiment was to push northwards directly on Yenangyaung and the oilfields. The 214th Regiment was known as the 'White Tigers' as a soldier's cap badge featured the head of that creature. The regiment successfully crossed the lateral road running between the 13th and 48th Brigades undetected on the night Kokkogwa was first attacked.[9]

At this time the 2nd Burma Brigade was on the west bank of the Irrawaddy; the 1st Burma Brigade was on the east bank. Advancing Japanese troops of the 213th Regiment encountered troops of the 1st Burma Brigade south of the Yin Chaung. The 1st Burma Rifles was scattered outside Migyaungye on 13 April. The 2nd KOYLI was now part of the 13th Brigade, and was heavily engaged in an isolated position on 14–15 April. The Yorkshiremen gave as good as they got as they fell back northwards. The front was clearly crumbling and Slim ordered the 1st Burma Division to retreat to the Yin Chaung, which was a river ten miles south of Magwe. The 48th Brigade at Kokkogwa withdrew westwards to Taungdwingyi to rejoin the rest of the 17th Division.

Meanwhile the 214th Regiment was resting in hiding fifteen miles to the east of Magwe. On 15 April the regiment resumed its northward march and reached a new position only twelve miles south-east of Yenangyaung, still undetected. Burcorps intelligence was almost blind by this stage of the campaign; the local population could see that the British were loosing the war and had little incentive to be of assistance. Aerial reconnaissance had vanished with the RAF's departure, and signals interception was not practical in the absence of officers with knowledge of the Japanese language.

Yenangyaung was less than forty miles north of Magwe. Slim visited Yenangyaung at 1 p.m. on 15 April. Shortly afterwards he gave the order to destroy the oilfields. Teams of engineers set fire to millions of gallons of oil held in storage. The oilfields comprised 5000 wells that could produce over 250 million gallons of oil a year. A forest of oil derricks, a pumping station, workshops and a residential town lay close to the eastern bank of the Irrawaddy. The town of Yenangyaung had been evacuated; troops of the Glosters found bungalows with wardrobes full of clothes, children's toys and books. Dining rooms with crockery from the last meal still lay on tables. An officer commented: 'One could have had a morning coat or a tennis-racquet, but necessities like combs or razors to replace kit lost in action were not there.'[10]

To the south of Magwe the 1st Burma Brigade was in the front line. On the Irrawaddy's east bank, the brigade was deployed behind the Yin Chaung with the 5th Burma Rifles on the right and 2/7th Rajputs on the left; the battered 1st Burma Rifles and B Squadron 2nd Royal Tanks was in reserve; the 23rd Mountain Battery provided artillery support. At 1 a.m. on 16 April Japanese troops of the 213th Regiment advanced with bayonets fixed across the white sand of the river bed and the shallow stream. Defensive machine gun and artillery fire did not retard the progress of the Japanese infantry for long. The right-hand company of the 5th Burma Rifles collapsed and the battalion was bundled back in disorder. The Rajputs' sector was also penetrated and the battalion's headquarters overrun. The situation remained alarmingly fluid until the tank squadron intervened to hold up the advance of the Japanese at dawn.

There was no alternative but for Scott's division to set out on another retreat, of which there had been so many for British forces in this campaign. There was no natural water source available at this time of year in the stretch between the Yin Chaung and Yenangyaung, where by the afternoon of 16 April the demolitions at the oilfields had been completed. The horizon was blanketed by an apocalyptic pall of black smoke; flames rose over 500 feet into the air; storage tanks, the power station and mechanical equipment had been wrecked. The Japanese air force had not bombed the oilfield as Japanese commanders wanted to capture them undamaged.

The 1st Burma Division marched northwards towards Yenangyaung in the heat of forty-three degrees Celsius. By nightfall of 16 April Magwe had been left behind to the south. Columns of vehicles, guns, ambulances, men, mules and horses trudged across sandy, arid hills. Jack Beldon, the *Daily Mail*'s correspondent, watched the scene on the night of 16/17 April:

> The beards of the men were heavy and filthy, their faces caked with dust, and their uniforms were grimed and stained and torn. Sweat, which had poured out of their bodies on the long day's march in the sun, had dried in streaks of white salt across their shirt fronts, and waterbags clacked dry against soldiers' hips as they advanced with slow steps and their bodies slumped forward.[11]

During the night Beldon came upon General Scott alongside the road with a staff officer and a cocker spaniel. A lantern lit the group. In the distance the flames of the oilfields shone against the night sky; the acrid smell of burning and the sounds of random explosions added to a scene of despair. The weary Scott was in a reflective mood, and said that the elusive Japanese 'vanishes into thin air like a jinni'. According to Beldon:

> After a while his [Scott's] musings ceased and he came out of his reverie. From his notebook he tore a piece of paper. 'Will you take a note to my wife in Maymyo?' he asked. When he had finished scribbling and given the folded soiled paper to me, he said: 'Tell her about us, tell her all about it; don't leave anything out. She's a soldier's wife and she'll understand.' I still have that note, for I was destined never to deliver it. Now it is wrinkled and dirty, and the writing is scarcely legible, but the mood is still there. 'Darling, We are OK. Tired, hell of a day but still fighting – keep smiling – I doubt if you'd recognise me, beard and filthy – the reporter will tell you all about me. I adore you. B.'[12]

Scott went on to say: 'If my troops could get only one complete night of rest, a day without marching in the sun, with plenty of water to drink, they would soon be back in fighting trim.'[13] There was little prospect of that in the immediate future.

On 17 April the march northwards continued; ahead of the troops, flames and dense black clouds of smoke rose high in the sky from the oilfields. The ground was bare of cover; the heat was intense; water ran short and men had only their personal bottles to rely upon. To the south of Scott's division, the Japanese 213th Regiment had entered Magwe. They were probed from the east by the 7th Hussars, which was operating from the 17th Indian Division's sector. A Japanese battalion was diverted to fend off the tanks, but the main body of the 213th Regiment marched northwards in the wake of the 1st Burma Division.

During the day the depressing news reached Scott that the Japanese had cut off his division's retreat through Yenangyaung. Colonel Sakuma's 214th Regimental group had broken cover the previous night and quickly seized the vital town. To the north of Yenangyaung was the Pin Chaung, an unbridged river with a good ford and low water levels in the dry season. Japanese troops placed blocks on the road both north and south of the ford in the Pin Chaung. The village of Twingon to the south of the river was given a strong garrison.[14]

By nightfall on 17 April Scott's division had arrived just south of Yenangyaung after an exhausting day's march. As the situation was clearly drifting out of hand, Slim had requested reinforcements from his superiors. Alexander and Stilwell agreed to make a division of the Chinese 66th Army available. The army had entered Burma earlier in the month. The Chinese soldiers carried an assortment of weapons and were supported by a train of porters and animals carrying supplies. A British liaison officer referred to them as 'Genghiz Khan's horde', as they seemed to have materialised from a bygone century.

The 38th Division's commander, General Sun Li-jen, had attended the Virginia Military Academy and spoke excellent English with an American accent. The American missionary surgeon Gordon Seagrave described Sun as a 'tall, handsome figure, looking much younger than his years, going round his wounded in the hospital wards, listening patiently, treating the enlisted men much more courteously than their sergeants or lieutenants would have done'.[15] Slim put a squadron of British tanks and a troop of field artillery under General Sun's command to encourage Allied solidarity.

Burcorps' plan for 18 April was for the Chinese force to clear the Japanese road block north of the ford in the Pin Chaung, whilst Scott's troops cleared the road block at Twingon to the south of the ford. As the road to Twingon ran through Japanese-occupied Yenangyaung, the 1st Burma Division would advance along a bypass road that skirted the eastern side of the town. To help cover this manoeuvre, a detachment that included the Cameronians and 5th Mountain Battery was to capture the village of Nyaunghla, to the immediate south of Yenangyaung. The 1st Burma Brigade was to remain in reserve and keep an eye on the division's southern front, where pursuing Japanese troops were bound to appear at some stage. The 2nd Burma Brigade remained on the western side of the Irrawaddy, and was under the direct command of Burcorps headquarters.

Scott's advance got underway at 6.30 a.m. on 18 April. Nyaunghla was occupied though stiff opposition was encountered north of the village. The bypass road to the east of Yenangyaung ran up onto a bare and desolate ridge. There was no shade for men and animals on a day when the temperature reached in excess of forty degrees Celsius. The broken country was a sterile and stony waste; the watercourses had dry beds of sand and pebbles. A forest of skeletal oil derricks added to the surreal environment, as did the smell of burning oil. The 13th Indian Brigade advanced with the 5/1st Punjabis on the left, and the 1/18th Garhwalis Rifles on the right. The 1st Royal Inniskilling Fusiliers was the brigade's reserve battalion. As the Punjabis moved onto the portion of the ridge overlooking Twingon, artillery, mortar and medium machine gun fire began to cause casualties. The village was defended by elements of two battalions of the 214th Regiment. The Punjabis were held up and lost ground to a counter-attack, but the Garhwalis and Inniskilling Fusiliers retook the high ground and fought their way into the eastern part of Twingon.

Needless to say, Japanese resistance in Twingon was ferocious. An Inniskilling major told an American journalist: 'Our men were worn out but they had guts. They crouched low with bayonets fixed and charged forward like the Guards on a parade ground – or, at least, they thought they did. The plain fact is they were so worn out that they stumbled forward like drunken men hardly able to hold their rifles.'[16] The attack on Twingon broke down and British troops were driven out of the ruined village.

One detachment of Inniskillings, about ninety strong, skirted Twingon to reach the river a mile to the north. Foreign troops were seen on the north bank and assumed to be Chinese as they appeared to give the pre-arranged recognition signal. Parties of exhausted men desperate for water met and fraternised on the sandy expanse of the Pin Chaung. But the Chinese proved to be Japanese troops and the Inniskillings were taken prisoner.[17]

To the north of the Pin Chaung Chinese troops had advanced to reach the river in places, but the Japanese successfully defended a small bridgehead covering the vital ford crossing. At 4.30 p.m. Scott spoke to Slim from the radio van of the 2nd Royal Tanks. The two generals were able to carry out radio conversations in the clear with the help of Gurkhali and personal references. Scott said his men were exhausted and suggested a breakout across the river somewhere to the east of the Twingon ford. This had not hitherto been considered as a crossing at any place other than the ford might cause the loss of all motorised transport. Slim refused the request; he said that a strong Chinese force would attack again the following morning. Scott told his commander and old friend: 'All right, we'll hang on and we'll do our best in the morning; but, for God's sake Bill, make those Chinese attack!' Slim stepped out of the radio van to a waiting half-circle of subordinates:

> 'Well, gentlemen,' I said, putting on what I hoped was a confident, cheerful expression, 'it might be worse!' One of the group, in a sepulchral voice, replied with a single word: 'How?' I could cheerfully have murdered him, but instead I

had to keep my temper. 'Oh,' I said, grinning, 'it might be raining!' Two hours later, it was – hard.[18]

That evening Slim was ordered by Alexander to attend a conference at Pyawbwe, far to the rear, on the following day.

For the night of 18/19 April the 13th Indian Brigade took up positions on the ridge south of Twingon. The 1st Burma Brigade and divisional headquarters closed up from the south to form a night perimeter nearby. British forces had at least been spared from air attack during the day given the clouds of oil smoke and the close quarters nature of the fighting. The American journalist Darrell Berrigan recorded the scene:

> An Inniskilling Major, with two other officers and myself, walked forward to inspect the outposts. We passed groups of men resting beside the road, dark shadows from which a voice quietly said, 'A Company, sir', 'B Company, sir'. There were other lumps of black shadow which were silent, Irish, Indian and Japanese dead, lying in heaps off the road ... The Inniskilling Major had me worried when he continued to walk more than a hundred yards past the last listening post, but he was not satisfied that his men were holding a wide enough perimeter. Returning, we stopped beside a derrick where the Major struck a match; for a fleeting moment it flickered over the bodies of two Inniskilling officers. The tired voice of the Major came from the darkness; 'These officers must be buried, according to regimental custom, tonight.'[19]

Scott's exhausted division passed a relatively quiet night on the ridge after the extreme heat of the day; howling heard outside the perimeter was assumed to be a ruse by Japanese patrols. During that night of 18/19 April Japanese troops at Twingon were reinforced by the I/214th Battalion, which had been in divisional reserve before arriving at Yenangyaung by boat on the Irrawaddy. All three battalions of the 214th Regiment were now in occupation of the village.[20]

At 6.30 a.m. on 19 April the 13th Brigade made another attempt to advance on Twingon from the ridge. The Inniskillings and a company of Garhwal Rifles reached the fringe of the village, but were halted by heavy firing. The Inniskillings' commanding officer, Major S. B. McConnell, was killed by a sniper. The heat of the day was again extreme and thirst was a terrible problem for the combatants, some of whom stole away to drink from the shallow waters of the Pin Chaung.

As the morning wore on there was little sign of Chinese intervention from the north and General Scott's patience gave out. Slim was absent from his headquarters that day to attend a conference with Alexander and Stilwell; in consequence, on this occasion Scott felt able to act on his own initiative. Troops had reported a rough track leading down to the Pin Chaung upstream

from the ford, and at 2 p.m. Scott ordered a breakout. By this time men
and animals alike were desperate to quench their thirst. The mules of the
mountain artillery galloped for the river when they smelt the water; once
they had drunk what they needed, the animals rallied to their handlers to
carry their loads to safety. The main column of vehicles was shelled and
mortared as it headed for the river. The sandy banks of the chaung were
too soft for vehicles, most of which had to be abandoned, along with heavy
equipment. The tracked tanks were able to keep going and crossed the river
at a relatively shallow point. Some of the wounded were carried across on the
tanks, but others were left behind to the tender mercies of the Japanese. A
gunner officer re-crossed the river after nightfall and found the wounded left
behind had been bayoneted to death or had their throats cut.

Meantime the Chinese attack across the Pin Chaung, supported by a
squadron of British tanks, had finally got moving at 3 p.m. that afternoon.
Chinese troops crossed the river and captured a hamlet west of Twingon,
though Twingon was not attacked. The captured detachment of Inniskillings
were recovered and released by advancing Chinese troops.

By dark Scott's division had retreated several miles to the north of the
Pin Chaung. The Japanese official history commented: 'The enemy's fighting
spirit suddenly collapsed. He abandoned his vehicles and retreated northwards. Soon he went to pieces. It was a rout.'[21] Lieutenant Carmichael of the
mountain artillery saw a bullock cart go by as his weary mules were drinking
at a stream. A pair of legs hung limply from the back of the cart. An officer
walking alongside told Carmichael that it was General Scott, in a state of
collapse from exhaustion.[22] Scott, who had recently turned fifty, and Brigadier
Roughton, the sub-area commander at Yenangyaung, were taken to the rear
in a Bren carrier. Scott soon recovered his strength, but Roughton died from
heat exhaustion.[23]

The following day – 20 April – Chinese troops south of the Pin Chaung
clashed again with the Japanese. General Slim had returned from his
conference with Alexander, and he ordered the Chinese 38th Division to pull
back to the north of the river. The Chinese intervention had played a part in
helping the 1st Burma Division to break clear. A grateful Slim was impressed
with the performance of General Sun Li-jen: 'He was alert, energetic and
direct. Later I found him a good tactician, cool in action, very aggressively
minded, and, in my dealings with him, completely straight-forward.'[24] Over
the next few days Chinese troops and the 7th Armoured Brigade covered the
retreat northwards of the shattered 1st Burma Division.

The battle of Yenangyaung cost Scott's division almost 1000 killed,
wounded and missing. Three hundred Allied prisoners were taken by the
Japanese, roped in batches and marched off southwards. The injured and

exhausted were shot or bayoneted if they held up the column's progress. After a grim journey the survivors were interned at Rangoon. Equipment losses included four tanks, ten guns of various types, many invaluable mortars and 200 vehicles. The casualties of the Japanese 214th Regimental group were forty dead and 100 wounded; these were modest losses given the scale of the victory.[25]

The battle of Yenangyaung was certainly a low point in Slim's military career. General Sakurai's 33rd Division won a resounding victory at the expense of both divisions of Burcorps. Sakurai's plan worked brilliantly; his forces made a convincing diversionary attack on the 17th Indian Division, and then neatly side-stepped westwards to roll up the vulnerable 1st Burma Division. In his memoirs Slim blamed Alexander's headquarters for insisting that Taungdwingyi be strongly held by the 17th Division; he conceded, however, that he might have done more to strengthen the 1st Burma Division and the Yenangyaung flank of Burcorps' extended front.[26]

A new crisis was about to envelop Allied forces in Burma, hard on the heels of the Yenangyaung debacle. On this occasion the well planned and executed Japanese blow fell on the Chinese armies, rather than Burcorps. At Toungoo the Japanese 55th Division had been reinforced by Lieutenant-General Renya Mutaguchi's 18th Division and the 1st Tank Regiment, both of which had recently arrived at Rangoon. The 18th Division had taken part in the triumphant capture of Singapore; Mutaguchi was keen to add to his laurels.

At this time the Chinese 5th Army was positioned astride the road leading northwards from Toungoo to Mandalay; the 6th Army was in the Shan States of north-eastern Burma; the 66th Army was in general reserve. British military and Burma Road motor transport had been pressed into service to distribute rice and other basic supplies to Chinese troops in the field. The official strengths of the Chinese 5th, 6th and 66th Armies were 60,000, 40,000 and 30,000 respectively. British liaison staff, however, felt that a combined figure of 70,000 for all three Chinese armies was a more accurate tally.[27]

The Japanese advance on Mandalay was resumed from Pyinmana, a town to the north of Toungoo. In fierce fighting near Pyinmana on 20–21 April the 18th Division lost seventy killed. After the Chinese defence had collapsed, Japanese troops made rapid progress northwards; on 25 April a squadron of the 1st Tank Regiment occupied Pyawbwe, to the south of Meiktila. Meiktila was an important communications junction south of Mandalay; Burcorps' line of communication to Mandalay ran through Meiktila.[28]

In conjunction with the push northwards from Toungoo, the Japanese 56th Division advanced swiftly into the Shan States, which lay to the north-east

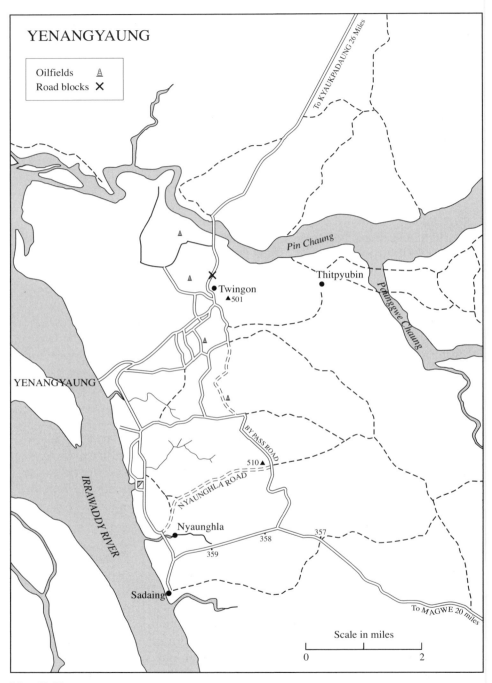

Map K Yenangyaung

of Toungoo. Lieutenant-General Masao Watanabe's 56th Division was newly raised, but its ranks included many recalled reservists who had seen service in the Sino-Japanese war. The division was allocated 250 lorries and the 14th Tank Regiment. Watanabe's motorised troops rushed into the Shan States along good roads to the east and north-east of Toungoo; captured fuel helped Japanese formations stay on the road. The first Chinese division encountered was swiftly routed and Loikaw fell on 20 April. Stilwell ordered the 6th Army's remaining two divisions to concentrate at Loilem on the road running eastwards from Meiktila to the Salween river. It was all to no avail. Japanese pressure soon compelled the rest of the Chinese 6th Army to retreat eastwards towards the Salween and the Thai frontier.

The Japanese 56th Division continued northwards from Loilem towards the Mandalay-Lashio road. On 29 April Lashio was captured in the face of only light resistance. Lashio was located north-east of Mandalay, and was the western railhead of the Burma Road. The Japanese advance on the ground had been so swift that a parachute operation planned to seize Lashio had to be cancelled as the town was already in Japanese hands. Stilwell sent the 5th Army's 200th Division eastwards from Meiktila to protect the flank of the rest of that army and Burcorps. The 200th Division pushed aside the Japanese forces they encountered and retook Loilem; from there, however, to Stilwell's consternation, the division drove onwards to cross the Salween river and depart the campaign.[29]

The Allied position in Burma had collapsed. This raised the question as to whether British forces should retreat into China or India, or possibly a combination of the two alternatives. At first General Wavell was inclined – for political reasons – to favour a retreat by at least part of Burma Army to China. Alexander was given orders by Wavell on 18 April to cover the route leading back to India, and maintain contact with Chinese forces. But the onward rush of events made it steadily clear that a retreat to north-east India was the only alternative.

On 21 April Alexander met Chiang's chief liaison officer, General Lin Wei, to arrange the final evacuation of Burma. Alexander gave instructions on 23 April that the bulk of Chinese forces should withdraw north-east towards their homeland, whilst Burcorps and the Chinese 38th Division made plans to head for India via the Chindwin valley. Mandalay was on the exposed eastern bank of the Irrawaddy; the city would not be defended.[30]

On 25 April Alexander, Stilwell and Slim held a conference at Kyaukse, to the north of Meiktila. All commanders agreed that an immediate retreat to India and China had become necessary. It was clear that Allied forces could no longer hope to maintain a front anywhere in Burma during the fast-approaching monsoon season. The next location of Alexander's headquarters was Shwebo, to the north-west of Mandalay; but Governor Dorman-Smith decided to re-establish the civilian administration at Myitkyina, which was on the upper waters of the Irrawaddy in the far north of Burma. When Dorman-Smith left Maymyo for the last time he travelled to Myitkyina via Mandalay. Near that city he recalled that he saw 'numbers of Buddhist monks in their yellow robes lying dead on the roadside. Chinese soldiers had shot them out of hand'.[31] The Governor reached his new headquarters by rail on 28 April.

General Hutton had asked to be relieved as Alexander's chief of staff several weeks before; he had found his relegation unbearable and had not always agreed with Alexander's decisions. Hutton borrowed a quotation from a life of the Duke of Wellington to describe his dilemma: 'Of all the awkward situations in the world that which is most so is to serve in a subordinate capacity in an Army which one has commanded'.[32] Major-General T.J.W. Winterton arrived from India to become Burma Army's new chief of staff. For an interim period Hutton remained at Alexander's headquarters in an advisory capacity; he finally left for India on 26 April. By this time the end of the campaign was well in sight.

Whilst calamity and despair was overwhelming British and Chinese forces alike, General Iida calmly prepared for the final stage of XV Army's triumphant conquest of Burma. Iida was hoping to catch and destroy his opponents to the south of Mandalay and the broad Irrawaddy river; he ordered his subordinates 'to strike wide and deep in rear of the Allied forces, so as to cut their lines of retreat and thus destroy them in one blow'.[33]

Allied commanders, however, were well aware of the danger they faced. Burcorps remained in Meiktila only long enough to cover the Chinese 5th Army's retreat to Mandalay; Meiktila was evacuated on the evening of 25/26 April. On 27 April the 2nd Royal Tanks fought a rearguard action to the north of Meiktila, whilst the 48th Brigade prepared a position at Kyaukse, thirty miles south of Mandalay, to cover the approaches to the Ava bridge over the Irrawaddy. The regimental historian of the 7th Gurkhas described Kyaukse as

> a small township at the toe of a low rocky ridge ... Like all Burmese villages it is well treed and gives the appearance of a thickly wooded island in the plain. A brisk stream runs through the town from which numerous irrigation channels take off and flow along the roadsides to the open fields. The banks of all these waterways are thickly covered with gardens and banana groves.[34]

The town had been damaged by bombing. Brigadier Cameron was ordered to hold Kyaukse until 6 p.m. on 29 April. The 48th Brigade had an infantry strength of 1700; the brigade was supported by the 7th Hussars, one troop of the 414th Field Battery and twelve guns of the 1st Indian Field Regiment. The railway and road heading northwards to Mandalay joined close together at Kyaukse. The shallow River Zawgyi ran through the town, and was a good tank obstacle. A high ridge looked over the town from the north-east. There were good fields of fire to the south-west of Kyaukse, but to the south and south-east of the town banana plantations, patches of jungle and thick scrub retarded observation.[35]

On 27 April the last troops of the 5th Chinese Army passed through Kyaukse in big American Lend Lease lorries. That evening the rest of Burma Army leap-frogged back through the town as well. On the evening of 28 April patrols of the 48th Brigade sent south from Kyaukse made contact with advancing Japanese tanks and motorised infantry.

The 48th Brigade's forward defensive line was just south of Kyaukse. On the western flank the 1/4th Gurkhas looked out across open fields that had been partly inundated by opening a water sluice. On the eastern flank the 2/5th Gurkhas had posts on the ridge that overlooked the town. The 1/7th Gurkhas, in the centre of the brigade's front, were astride the road and railway that approached Kyaukse from the south. The 1/3rd Gurkha Rifles remained in reserve.

In the evening of 28 April Japanese foot patrols made contact with the 1/7th Gurkhas dug-in either side of the road. D Company was to the east of the road in thick vegetation with its left flank against a bend in the Zawgyi river. At 10 p.m. D Company was attacked by a two-company Japanese force that emerged from the jungle under the bright moonlight. The Gurkhas opened fire at 100 yards and the Japanese ran back after a lot of confused screams and shouting. Another attack after midnight was also repelled by small arms and mortar fire. Before dawn, after the moon had set, a further attack on D Company was driven off. On the high ground to the east, the 2/5th Gurkhas skirmished with Japanese patrols during the night; the 1/4th Gurkhas on the western flank were undisturbed. The artillery had fired enthusiastically during the hours of darkness; the war diary of the 1/7th Gurkhas commended Captain Ranbir Bakshi, the forward observation officer, for 'exceptionally fine work'.[36] A night battle was confusing for troops and commanders alike.

After dawn tanks swept the 48th Brigade's front. Japanese troops were found in a small hamlet just south of the front line. Brigadier Cameron ordered a counter-attack and at 8 a.m. Captain O.R. Gribble's B Company of the 1/7th Gurkhas left the brigade's perimeter. The Gurkhas' morale was high and the hamlet and a nearby banana grove were swiftly overrun; many Japanese dead were counted, included thirty-eight beneath a large culvert under the main road. According to Japanese sources an advanced dressing station was located under the culvert and an army doctor, Lieutenant Katayama, amongst those killed.[37]

The attack on Kyaukse during the night of 28/29 April had been mounted principally by the 18th Division. The 114th Regiment had sent a battalion onto the ridge to the east of Kyaukse, whilst the 55th Regiment made the frontal attack on the town. On the 55th Regiment's left flank, to the west of the railway, a battalion of the 55th Division had also advanced, but was held up when it suffered losses from artillery and mortar fire.[38] A tank regiment was sent on a turning movement to the west of Kyaukse, but rough ground had retarded its progress.

During the daylight hours of 29 April Japanese 150 millimetre guns shelled the 48th Brigade's positions accurately, though without causing many casualties. Strong Japanese patrols seemed to be searching for the brigade's flanks. The planned withdrawal of the 48th Brigade went ahead at 6 p.m.; the Gurkhas marched to motor transport north of Kyaukse and a clean break was made. The brigade had lost only three killed and seven wounded; Japanese dead were estimated at over 200, though a figure of sixty was closer to the actual tally.[39] Slim described the Kyaukse action as 'a really brilliant example of rearguard work. It not only enabled the last of the Chinese to cross the Ava Bridge without molestation and gave us all a breathing space, but it inflicted heavy casualties on the enemy at extremely small cost to ourselves.' The 18th Division's attack at Kyaukse was a clumsy frontal push rather than a swift flanking movement of the sort that often proved successful during Japan's campaigns in South-east Asia. General Sakurai of the 33rd Division might have approached the battle more creatively.

The 48th Brigade retreated through the 63rd Brigade at the Myitnge river and continued on to the Ava bridge. The 63rd Brigade was the last Allied formation to cross the only bridge over the Irrawaddy. The Ava bridge was almost three-quarters of a mile long and featured eleven main girder spans; the bridge carried a double rail track and a road on either side of the railway. Major Darley of the 24th Field Company was in charge of the demolitions.

About midday on 30 April a tight formation of twenty-seven Japanese bombers flew towards the bridge at 8000 feet. The formation leader rocked his wings and all the bombers dropped their loads together. The bombs fell to earth with an almighty crash, but the target was the village of Sagaing at the northern end of the bridge. It was hardly in the interests of the advancing Japanese to damage the structure.

General Cowan gave the order to blow the Ava bridge at 11.20 p.m. on the night of 30 April. The demolitions caused one span to fall down and another subsequently collapsed. The bridge would not be repaired for thirteen years. The colonial regime was destroying some of its principal accomplishments in Burma. There was at least no repeat of the fiasco at the Sittang river. Slim wrote of the destruction of the bridge that it was 'a sad sight and a signal that we had lost Burma'.

On a lighter note, General Wavell had conceived the plan of sending Peter Fleming, an officer in the Grenadier Guards and elder brother of the novelist Ian Fleming, to implement a ruse that was reminiscent of a similar ruse carried out prior to the third battle of Gaza in 1917, a campaign in which Wavell had taken part. A car was deliberately crashed over a thirty-foot drop near the Ava bridge soon after it was wrecked; a letter case was left in the car for the Japanese to discover; a scribbled document headed 'Notes for Alexander' listed inflated figures for British reinforcements said to be on the way to India. The ruse, however, did not have any obvious or immediate impact on events.[40]

The bulk of Burcorps crossed the Irrawaddy at the Ava bridge, but the 1st Burma Division crossed by ferry to the west at Sameikkon. The boats were crewed by sappers and Royal Marines; 500 oxen and 250 bullock carts crossed with the soldiers.

The Japanese did not interfere with Burcorps' transfer across the Irrawaddy. General Iida had been under the impression that British forces would cross the river in the vicinity of Myingyan, which was to the south of Sameikkon. On 29 April he had ordered the 55th Division to head westwards from near Kyaukse to Myingyan, whilst the 33rd Division marched on that town from the south. When Japanese troops reached Myingyan they found it empty of British troops.

The fall of Mandalay soon followed the destruction of the Ava bridge. The bomb-damaged city was on the east bank of the Irrawaddy to the north-east of the bridge. Late on the afternoon of 1 May Japanese troops of the 18th Division entered the city unopposed.

General Iida's plan for the final conquest of Burma was for the 33rd Division to press onwards to Monywa on the Chindwin river; from there further advances to the north might cut off Burcorps' retreat to India. The 55th Division was to advance northwards to Myitkyina, whilst the 56th Division pressed up the Burma Road to the bridge over the Salween river on the Chinese side of the frontier. The 18th Division was to clear any Chinese forces still in the Shan States. Captured Lend Lease stocks of fuel and vehicles were gratefully pressed into service by Japanese troops always operating at the end of tenuous lines of communication.

Surprisingly, Japanese troops managed to secure undamaged the Gokteik viaduct on the railway running between Mandalay and Lashio. This was a great coup as the viaduct ran 825 feet above a river far below. The viaduct was not blown down as British commanders had been hesitant to order the demolition for fear that might damage relations with the Chinese leadership.[41]

17

The Retreat to India

At the close of April 1942 Burma Army was poised to commence the final stage of its long retreat into the mountains of north-east India. On 30 April General Wavell signalled the War Office: 'War Cabinet must really make up their minds whether or not they propose to defend India and Ceylon seriously. At present we are getting continual messages stressing vital importance of Ceylon and at the same time our means of defending it are being removed.'[1] The colony of Burma was clearly lost and north-eastern India might be next on Japan's list.

The advance guard of an army of civilian refugees had already arrived in India from Burma, well ahead of General Alexander's Burma Army. Seventy thousand people had sailed from Rangoon prior to the city's capture by the Japanese; another 100–200,000 people had reached Akyab, on the western coast of Burma, and from there marched to Chittagong. A growing torrent of humanity was taking the route from the Chindwin river to Imphal in Manipur state; 30,000 people in March and a greater number in April. More refugees were gathering in northern Burma to commence the hard trek through the mountains to Imphal.[2] This was also the route Burcorps was planning to use for its retreat to the hoped-for sanctuary of north-east India.

At the end of April, in the wake of the destruction of the Ava bridge, both the 1st Burma and 17th Indian Divisions were on the north bank of the Irrawaddy to the west of Mandalay. Burcorps' ration strength was 6500 British, 22,000 Indian and Gurkha and 4000 Burmese troops. Another 1600 animals also required feeding.[3]

The Chindwin valley was the intended route of retreat to India for almost all of Burma Army. The exception was the 2nd Burma Brigade, which was to return to India via the Myittha valley. The Myittha valley lay to the west of the Chindwin. There was concern that the Japanese might use this route if it was left unguarded. On 28 April the 2nd Burma Brigade left Pakokku on the Irrawaddy's west bank to march for the Myittha valley. From that time there was no longer any sizeable Allied force on the Irrawaddy's western bank.

Burcorps' retreat to India was gathering pace, but the enterprising General Sakurai and his 33rd Division, briefly rested after their triumph at Yenangyaung, was poised to strike again where Slim's army least expected. The

Japanese 215th Regiment advanced up the west bank of the Irrawaddy to reach Pakokku on 29 April. The town was unoccupied as the 2nd Burma Brigade had departed the previous day. Lorries then carried the 215th Regiment from Pakokku, over a rough but passable track, to a point on the west bank of the Chindwin across the river from the town of Monywa. Monywa was fifty miles north of the confluence of the Chindwin and Irrawaddy rivers. The 1st Burma Division was planning to retire northwards through Monywa, which was full of refugees and rear echelon military personnel.

By the evening of 30 April Japanese patrols had discovered that the town across the river was not strongly held. Colonel Harada displayed the high level of initiative common to Japanese commanders in Burma, and sent the I/215th Battalion and two guns across the Chindwin during the night. The troops crossed the 600-yard-wide river just south of Monywa.

At this time Slim's headquarters was at Songon, sixteen miles north of Monywa, and seemingly far from the assumed location of the front line. The headquarters was in a grove of trees next to a Buddhist monastery. After dinner news was received by Slim that Monywa was under attack; explosions could be heard in the distance. Japanese artillery was shelling the town from across the river to distract attention from the crossing underway nearby. Slim ordered Scott to deal with the intruders, and Burcorps headquarters hastily packed up for re-location to Ye-U. Scott received Slim's order but at 5 a.m. his own headquarters, which was south-east of Monywa at Ma-U, was suddenly overrun by Japanese soldiers rushing out of the darkness. Scott and his chief staff officer beat a rapid retreat. The headquarters ciphers and other secret documents were carried to safety with them.

Only a small combatant garrison was in Monywa; they had little chance of withstanding a determined assault. The southern part of the town was entered by Japanese troops after daylight on 1 May. The whole town was soon in Japanese hands.[4] During the morning Colonel Harada ordered the II/215th Battalion to cross the river in launches and reinforce the troops in Monywa. That afternoon the regiment's headquarters and a mountain artillery battalion also crossed the river to build up a strong Japanese force in the town.

After daylight on 1 May, Scott wasted no time getting a counter-attack underway to re-take Monywa. The 63rd Brigade had arrived by train from the 17th Division. The brigade advanced along the road leading towards Monywa from the south: the 2/13th Frontier Force Rifles was to the left of the road, and the 1/10th Gurkhas to the right. The 1/11th Sikhs and tanks of the 7th Hussars moved close behind in support. The troops passed Ma-U and the scene of the recent scuppering of divisional headquarters. The brigade pushed onwards and the Frontier Force came under artillery and mortar fire from across the river. There was heavy firing from in front; two tanks were knocked out; the

advance ground to a halt. Brigadier Barlow put the Sikhs into an outpost line
to the south of Monywa; the other two battalions were withdrawn to Ma-U
to regroup.

That evening Scott ordered the 63rd Brigade to attack again the following
day, whilst the 13th Brigade marched across country to Zalok on the Monywa-
Shwebo road. From there the 13th Brigade was to attack Monywa from the
east. Scott held the 1st Burma Brigade in reserve. This brigade no longer had
any Burma Rifles units and comprised the 2nd KOYLI – only 150 strong – the
depleted 2/7th Rajputs, reorganised into a two-company unit, and the 1/4th
Gurkhas. The Gurkhas had been borrowed from the 48th Brigade.

On 2 May the 63rd Brigade attacked Monywa again. The advance from
Ma-U commenced at 8.40 a.m., the 1/11th Sikhs on the left and the 1/10th
Gurkhas on the right. The Sikhs fought their way into the southern part of
the town, but the Gurkhas were mortared in marshland and veered away
from the objective. Meanwhile the 13th Brigade had advanced westwards
from Zalok at dawn to reach the small village of Shaukka. From there the
advance continued across open paddy fields towards trees and scrub to
the immediate east of Monywa. The 1/18th Garhwalis were to the left of the
road leading from Zalok to Monywa and the 5/1st Punjabis to the right. The
Garhwalis reached within fifty yards of the railway line that ran along the
eastern face of Monywa, before they were pinned down by machine gun and
mortar fire. The advance of the Punjabis was also halted by Japanese fire; one
company managed to capture the town's railway station, but were driven out
by a counter-attack early in the afternoon.

As the attack had stalled, at 3 p.m. General Scott committed his reserve
brigade to the battle. The 1st Burma Brigade was to attack Monywa from the
south by leap-frogging through the 63rd Brigade. It was another very hot day
and drinking water was a luxury, but the 1/4th Gurkhas advanced briskly
on a narrow frontage between the road and railway line. The 2/7th Rajputs
moved to the right of the Gurkhas, but were held up in the marshland that
had stopped an earlier attack. The Gurkhas were finally halted by Japanese
posted in a pagoda near the railway station.

The pagoda was heavily mortared and preparations were underway for a
further assault when orders were received to wait. Earlier in the afternoon
Scott received an instruction, probably from Alexander, to bypass Monywa
to the east. Slim knew nothing of this order and later questioned if it was a
Japanese ruse, but in all likelihood there had been a breakdown in communications between army and corps headquarters. The Gurkhas withdrew from
their hard-won position in Monywa after dark.[5]

During the night of 2/3 May Scott's division marched across country and
rejoined the road to the north of Monywa. By the evening of 4 May the troops

had reached Ye-U with the help of motor transport. The sudden Japanese capture of Monywa had caused a crisis, but it had been weathered. According to Japanese sources, the attack on Monywa by Allied troops was pressed home in the face of heavy fire. The 215th Regiment's historical record stated:

> From the morning of 2nd May, the enemy started a full strength attack from all directions. The enemy infantry advanced under artillery cover, shells bursting all over the town. They were supported by tanks and tried to break through our 1st battalion several times, but were repelled … The enemy – Indian and Gurkha soldiers – attacked very bravely, many falling under our fire, but they kept coming on over their dead.[6]

The Japanese claimed to have taken 400 prisoners, many of whom were administration troops rounded up when Monywa was originally seized. A Japanese scout force sent along the road from Monywa towards Ye-U was led by six captured British tanks, most of which had been recovered from the Shwedaung battlefield. This caused predictable confusion amongst British forces when the vehicles were encountered.[7]

Burma Army's final task was to rapidly retreat from Ye-U to Kalewa on the west bank of the Chindwin river, after which the troops would be required to toil northwards into the hills of the Indian state of Manipur to reach the Imphal plateau. On 3 May the 16th Brigade, the 48th Brigade and the headquarters of the 17th Division arrived at Ye-U from Shwebo.[8] Slim sent the 16th Brigade to secure the crossing of the Chindwin river from Shwegyin to Kalewa. Lines of communication troops began crossing the river; 2300 wounded and sick required evacuation by land and the retreating army was accompanied by many refugees. Supplies were running low; on 4 May the army was put on half-rations.[9] The monsoon was due mid-May and would swiftly turn streams into torrents, and tracks to impassable quagmire. Men scanned the sky daily for black storm clouds rather than for the Japanese air force. The small garrison at Akyab, on the western coast of Burma, was withdrawn to Chittagong.

Transport aircraft evacuated civilians and military casualties from the airfields at Myitkyina and Shwebo for as long as that was possible. (Captain Lunt had been admitted to hospital and was flown out of Myitkyina on 27 April.) Fourteen thousand people were flown out of northern Burma, of whom less than 5000 were Indian: Europeans, Anglo-Indians and Anglo-Burmese comprised the bulk of the passengers. Governor Dorman-Smith also left Myitkyina for India; civilian administration in Burma had collapsed completely and there was nothing more that he could do. On 6 May airborne evacuation was suspended after two transports were destroyed by the strafing of Japanese fighters as they were loading refugees on the airfield.

It was not long before Japanese troops reached Myitkyina. A fast-moving Japanese force entered the town on 8 May. Ten thousand refugees fled north-westwards through the jungle of the Hukawng valley in the hope of reaching Assam. Many Chinese troops of the 5th Army and Sun Li-jen's 38th Division were cut off from China when the Japanese occupied Myitkyina. These troops either skirted around the town and headed north-east for China along tracks, or joined the columns heading north-westwards for India.

After the rout of the Chinese armies there was no further place for General Stilwell in Burma. He had already sent most of his headquarters staff to India by air from Shwebo. Stilwell and his personal staff left Shwebo in jeeps with the intention of heading for Myitkyina, but the route proved too dangerous. Stilwell and a party of 100 Americans, Chinese and other Allied personnel left Indaw and travelled westwards through thick country to the Chindwin river. The detachment had to abandon their vehicles when the track became no more than a footpath. Stilwell's party pressed onwards over the hills to reach Imphal on 20 May. Stilwell turned sixty years of age during the exodus. Upon arrival at Imphal he famously said of the campaign:

> In the first place, no military commander in history made a voluntary retreat. And there's no such thing as a glorious retreat. All retreats are as ignominious as hell. I claim we got a hell of a licking. We got run out of Burma, and it's humiliating as hell. I think we ought to find out what caused it, go back, and retake Burma.

Some people questioned why Stilwell had not simply flown out of Burma like other senior officers. An American observer summed up Stilwell as the 'best damned four-star battalion commander in the army'. There was no doubting, however, Stilwell's steely determination and resolute spirit.

To reach India Burcorps would have to traverse the dirt track through the jungle from Ye-U to Shwegyin on the east bank of the Chindwin. The track was 107 miles in length, unmetalled and broken by frequent dry watercourses. The final stage of the retreat began on 4 May. Alexander wrote in his despatch: 'Anyone seeing this track for the first time would find it difficult to imagine how a fully mechanised force could possibly move over it.' The track, which ran in places along the dry bed of a stream, would be impassable for motor vehicles once the rains came; the sandy beds were already too difficult for many civilian cars. The Governor's black Rolls-Royce was amongst the many vehicles that had to be abandoned en route. The 1st Burma Brigade left the track at Pyingaing and marched northwards to cross the Chindwin at Pantha.

The 48th Brigade spent four days at Pyingaing as Burcorps' rearguard. Transport, troops and other jetsam and flotsam streamed through. The history of the 5th Royal Gurkha Rifles recorded:

It was during this journey that the Battalion first had evidence of the magnitude and horror of the refugee problem. Numbers of refugees had been seen from time to time earlier in the campaign, but now the withdrawal had caught up with the main stream which had become canalised on to the one and only narrow and indifferent road … the weary stream of men, women and children, carrying the remnants of their poor belongings, shuffled listlessly on through the dust, a pitiful and heart-rending sight.[10]

On the night of 8/9 May the 48th Brigade left Pyingaing and marched twenty-five miles to meet motor transport that deposited them two miles from Shwegyin about 3 a.m. on 10 May.

The village of Shwegyin was on the east bank of the Chindwin, six miles downstream from Kalewa on the west bank. Shwegyin was just north of the mouth of the Shwedaung Chaung; patches of palm and banana trees grew nearby. An adjoining stretch of level paddy 300 yards wide and 600 yards long was called the 'Basin'. The Basin was dotted with lumps of bushes and surrounded by steep, tree-covered hills and ridges.

There was a ferry service along the short stretch of river from Shwegyin to Kalewa. Six sternwheeler steamers were available, but almost all vehicles would have to be abandoned for lack of space. Brigadier Ekin was in administrative control of the embarkation. The Chittagonian steamer crews preferred to work by night for fear of air attack, though there were only occasional sightings of Japanese aircraft across this fraught period. The river level was visibly rising from day to day; the monsoon was not far off.

A boom of sampans was roped together on the Chindwin a mile and half south of Shwegyin. A detachment of troops was posted on the west bank to cover the boom. Further south a flank guard under the command of Major Eric Holdaway and Major Mike Calvert of the Bush Warfare School was put in position to keep the Chindwin under observation. Holdaway's force comprised two companies of Gurkhas and a miscellaneous party of British soldiers.

General Cowan and the 17th Division's headquarters arrived at Shwegyin on the evening of 8 May. By this time all army and corps supply and transport troops had crossed the river to Kalewa, along with a large part of the 7th Armoured Brigade and several other combatant units. On 9 May most of the remaining tanks were destroyed near the river bank; the 63rd Brigade left for Kalewa that evening.

General Iida had given Sakurai's 33rd Division the order: 'Not one Allied soldier is to get back to India.' In response Sakurai had dispatched a regimental-sized force up the Chindwin valley to intercept Burcorps. The detachment left Monywa on the evening of 4 May and included an engineer regiment equipped with forty motorboats and barges. One part of the force advanced by land along the Chindwin's bank; other troops were sent directly up river by boat. On the night of 8/9 May the water-borne advance guard passed up the river unobserved by Major Holdaway's flank guard. Holdaway had received orders to withdraw northwards the following day, and had already left the river to establish a night perimeter inland.[11] The Japanese advance guard disembarked nine miles to the south of Shwegyin; the troops set out for that village during the night of 9/10 May.

On the morning of 10 May the British force remaining on the east side of the river at Shwegyin included the 48th Brigade, 1/9th Jats, 1st Indian Field Battery, 12th Mountain Battery and a troop of the 3rd Light AA Battery.[12] The Jats were responsible for defending the southern flank of the basin, but they had only two rifle companies available as their third company was on the west bank opposite Shwegyin; the fourth rifle company had been evacuated by sea from Rangoon. Troops of the 1/7th Gurkhas had bivouacked over night in rice fields behind the Jats.

Slim's headquarters was in the jungle outside Kalewa, on the western side of the Chindwin. Slim was anxious to see how the final stage of the evacuation was coming along. Accompanied by an aide, he reached the jetty at Shwegyin about 5.30 a.m. on 10 May. It was getting light and as the two men stepped ashore machine gun and mortar fire broke out on the south side of the Basin. A stream of red tracer bullets passed overhead. Slim crossed an open space and came upon soldiers of the 1/7th Gurkhas crouched behind bushes, mounds and any other cover they could find. Slim had commanded a battalion of the 7th Gurkhas before the war, and an old comrade – Sudedar-Major Saharman Rai – appeared smiling from behind a bush. 'I asked him coldly what he was laughing at and he replied that it was very funny to see the General Sahib wandering along there by himself not knowing what to do!'[13] Slim wanted to dive for cover, but had felt compelled to set an example.

At first light the Japanese had attacked the Jats holding the south and south-eastern flank of the Basin. The Jats, with the help of the 1/7th Gurkhas, held off the initial assault by troops of the II/213th Battalion. The 48th Brigade's headquarters was made responsible for the developing battle, and the 1/3rd and 1/4th Gurkhas came up to occupy positions covering the eastern flank of the Basin. This was completed only just in time to forestall the advance of the II/214th Battalion.[14] To support this attack the Japanese used a horse team to drag up a mountain gun. The gun opened fire on the Basin about midday, but was promptly destroyed by the direct fire of the Bofors anti-aircraft battery; Gurkha infantrymen loudly cheered the success.

Slim had remained at Shwegyin as the battle on the southern and eastern flanks of the Basin got underway. He saw what would prove to be the last steamer draw alongside the jetty. The twenty-five pounders of the armoured brigade were embarked, and other troops awaited their turn to board. One hundred Indian refugees huddled miserably in the shelter of the nearby bank. Slim recalled:

> One poor woman near the tank from which I was speaking [on the tank's radio], lay propped against the side of the track dying in the last stages of small pox. Her little son, a tiny boy of four, was trying pathetically to feed her with milk from a tin a British soldier had given him. One of our doctors, attending the wounded at the jetty, found time to vaccinate the little chap, but nothing could be done for his mother. She died and we bribed an Indian family with a blanket and a passage on the steamer to take the boy with them.[15]

As the loaded ferry was casting off the remaining refugees were permitted to board the vessel. Smith Dun, a Karen officer, found a young woman nearby giving birth in the back of a stranded lorry. Ferries were no longer able to use the jetty, but three more craft came inshore under a cliff to the north of the jetty to make the last evacuations from the river. Slim returned to his headquarters by launch and authorized the abandonment of Shwegyin that night.

Late in the afternoon the 48th Brigade was ordered by General Cowan to retreat northwards after nightfall along the river bank to a point directly opposite Kalewa. The troops could be ferried across the river from there. At 7.55 p.m. a barrage was fired by all guns on Japanese-held positions around the Basin to cover the retreat. One unit's war diary recorded:

> The chief contribution came from the Bofors whose tracer shells lit up the descending darkness. It was a cheering sound the like of which we had not heard during our time in Burma. At 8.15 the guns ceased fire, and five minutes later we received the order to go. As we left the Basin enormous fires were getting a good hold on the dumps of stores and ammunition, tanks and lorries. It was an eerie night in the gathering gloom and distressing to think so much material had to be left behind. From the Japanese there wasn't a sound. They had apparently had enough.[16]

The British force marched along tracks that were in places no more than a narrow jungle footpath; there were long delays as men and mules stumbled forward in the darkness.

The Japanese did not immediately follow up Slim's retreating force; they set to work gathering together the prisoners and equipment left in the Basin, which had become the final graveyard of Burma Army. The Basin and surrounding area was strewn with hundreds of vehicles; fires burned amongst the abandoned stores. Burcorps casualties in the Shwegyin action were 150 killed and wounded; Japanese losses were eighty killed and 160 wounded. British shelling, which had involved firing off just about all remaining ammunition, caused many casualties.[17]

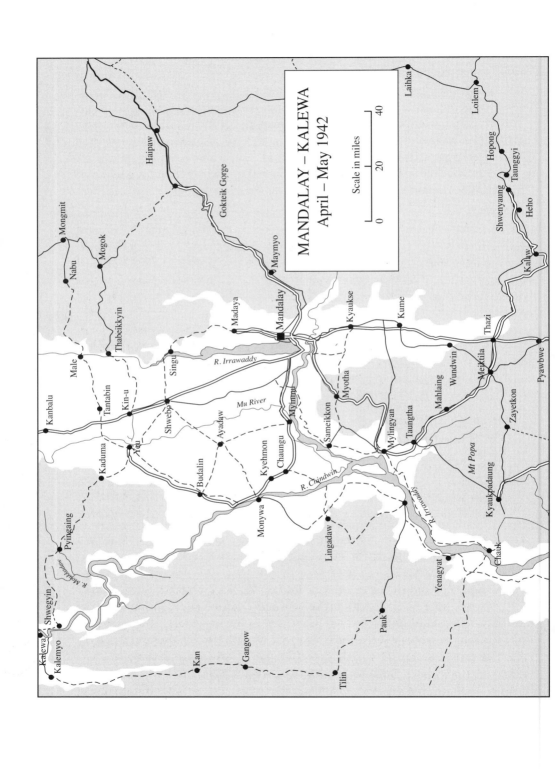

MANDALAY – KALEWA
April – May 1942

Scale in miles

0   20   40

On 11 May Cowan's troops crossed the Chindwin from the river bank opposite Kalewa. Burma Army's rearguard left Kalewa on the morning of 12 May; some troops marched onwards by land, whilst others caught steamers upriver to Sittaung. At Sittaung the boats were scuttled and the troops marched along a path to Tamu; five elephants helped to carry the baggage. The Japanese occupied Kalewa in the evening of 12 May. After a pause Sakurai's men pushed on up the Chindwin by boat, though without making further contact with Burcorps.[18]

The first heavy monsoon rains fell as the rearguard left Kalewa, though the weather remained fine for the following week. Brigadier Davies recalled: 'Everyone realised from the humblest private, that within the first few days of the initial heavy main downpour the road to Assam, the lifeline of the Army, would disintegrate into an impassable morass. There was a dreadful tension in the air. Would the weather hold?'[19] Once the rains set in the highest mountain peaks would be lost in the clouds.

Kalewa was 200 miles from railhead at Dimapur. The road from Kalewa to Tamu was fit for vehicles in the dry season; a mule track led from Tamu to Palel at the southern end of the Imphal plain; a dry season road ran from Palel to Imphal. Finally, from Imphal an all-weather section of road ran to Dimapur to complete the route.

The village of Tamu was just inside the Indian frontier; it was at a height of 500 feet, but the 5000-foot Shenam pass had to be crossed to reach Palel. A three-day march was needed to climb the pass, which was held by the 1st Brigade of the 23rd Indian Division. Wavell had decided that the Shenam pass would be the new front line. The 23rd Division's history described the pass and nearby hill features as standing out like 'a bastion of an ancient fortress, glowering defiance at the east'.[20] Once across the pass the route headed down hill to Palel. Motor transport at Palel was on hand to take the weary troops onwards to Imphal and camps in the surrounding area. The 48th Brigade reached Palel on 21 May; the 63rd Brigade marched in the following day. These men were the last organised units of Burma Army. The colony of Burma had been left far behind. Drenching rains of the monsoon broke on the evening of 18 May.

Imphal, the bomb-damaged capital of Manipur state, was set in a large valley 2500 feet above sea level. The Imphal plain was like an oasis in the hills, surrounded by forbidding tracts of wilderness. Local commanders in Manipur were unimpressed by the ragged state of Burma Army. The best of the fighting units retained their organizational core to the finish; but rear echelon units, stragglers from combatant units and refugees formed mobs that gave the unmistakable impression of a complete rout.

On 20 May Lieutenant-General N.M.S. Irwin's IV Corps headquarters assumed command of all troops in the frontier region; Burma Army headquarters and General Alexander had no further role to play. The newly mobilised 23rd Indian Division, commanded by Major-General Reginald Savory, was given the responsibility of watching the routes leading to Imphal. The division, however, was arriving 'piecemeal in Assam at a pace more befitting a funeral procession'.[21] At Imphal malaria was rife as the rains caused mosquitoes to flourish; the monsoon quickly turned the landscape into a swamp.

Civilian refugees staggered back to India alongside or trailing after the army. The Kabaw valley became known as the 'valley of death'. On one occasion Brigadier Ekin watched an elderly Indian man completing the last stage of the long journey:

> He staggered along on spindly legs, and over his meagre shoulders was a long wooden pole with a small bucket-like receptacle at each end – the classic Indian peasant method of carrying water. In each bucket was a baby boy, one aged one year and the other two; these two mites eyed the outside world in silent and thumb-sucking bewilderment. The old man ... [said] that these were his grandsons, all that were left alive of his family which had started from Rangoon eight-strong – the grandmother, father, mother, uncle and aunt had died on the way.[22]

The stream of refugees heading for Imphal became a torrent. On a single day – 24 May – 5000 refugees staggered over the Shenam pass. The army could do little to alleviate their distress. An observer recorded:

> They came through our lines, emaciated with hunger, clad in rags, without covering for their feet, their bodies a mass of sores, riddled with all the common diseases of the East. Weakened by the ravages of cholera, dysentery, smallpox and malaria, their strength overtaxed, they were the wrecks of human beings.[23]

Over 400,000 refugees made the trek by land from Burma to India. One hundred and ninety thousand people reached Imphal via Tamu after crossing the Chindwin river. Thousands more trekked through northern Burma to Ledo and Assam. These poor wretches suffered the full force of the monsoon in the Hukawng valley.[24]

During June the flow of refugees into Shenam slowed, though their emaciated condition was even worse than before. At the end of June the arrivals ceased; the soldiers in the front line remained in possession of a drenched wilderness. Patrols found tracks littered with decaying corpses. Seaforth Highlanders would need to wear their gas masks to clear the dead from the road between Tamu and Palel. Estimates of the total number of civilians who died making an enforced journey from Burma to India range from 10,000–50,000 men, women and children.[25]

Approximately 30,000 troops of Burma Army returned to India. The 1st Burma and 17th Indian Divisions ended the campaign with a combined strength of 12,000–13,000; corps and army troops made up the balance of the 30,000. Twenty-eight field, mountain and anti-tank guns were brought out with the troops, but virtually all other equipment was lost except for weaponry and gear that could be carried.

The strength of some units was very low by the time they reached Imphal; many men had been evacuated sick alongside the wounded. Stragglers separated from their units joined up with other parts of the retreating army to make the final leg of the journey to India. For example, on 11 June the Royal Inniskilling Fusiliers had only 114 officers and other ranks present. The 2nd KOYLI reached Imphal with nine officers and seventy men. A number of other battalions were crippled by losses to a similar extent.[26]

About 800 men of the Burma Rifles reached India. The 2nd Battalion, many of whom were Karens, was the only unit still in good shape. The 4th Burma Rifles was a composite unit comprising men from a range of units. About half of Burmese personnel stayed in the army after the loss of Burma; the other half headed back for their homes when given the option of discharge.[27]

Some Indian and Gurkha units had low sick rates and received reinforcements to retain a useful fighting strength to the end of the campaign. The 4/12th Frontier Force Regiment and 2/5th Gurkhas reached Imphal with 300–400 men each.[28] The 1/4th and 1/7th Gurkhas also had enough men to field battalions of a reasonable strength. The 1/9th Jats, which had begun the campaign in awkward circumstances at Kawkareik, recovered well and had three rifle companies present at Shwegyin.

The casualties of British forces in Burma are as follows:[29]

	Killed	Wounded	Missing	Total
Officers	133	126	115	374
British other ranks	348	605	647	1600
Viceroy's commissioned officers	63	60	83	206
Indian/Gurkha other ranks	706	1678	5472	7856
Burmese units	249	126	3052	3427
Total	1499	2595	9369	13,463

The Japanese claimed to have taken 4918 prisoners in Burma, and that is believed to be an accurate figure. The bulk of prisoners were Indians and Gurkhas; 350 were European and only fifty Chinese. Of Burma Army's missing, almost 4500 remain unaccounted. Many of these would have been Burmese who had left for their homes; the remainder were unrecovered dead.[30] With the inclusion of those 'missing presumed dead', the complete toll of Burma Army killed was roughly 3000. Additional wounded would be amongst the prisoners of war.

It is difficult to reconstruct a detailed casualty list for many units of Burma Army, though some information is available. The two original British garrison battalions in Burma suffered heavily in the five-month campaign. The 2nd KOYLI started the campaign with only 550 officers and men; approximately 160 were killed and another eighty made prisoner. The 1st Glosters suffered the deaths of eight officers and 156 other ranks; eleven officers were amongst the many wounded.[31] The five Gurkha battalions in Burma lost 800 dead at the Sittang battle alone. For the campaign as a whole, the 1/4th Gurkhas got off relatively lightly with one British officer, three Gurkha officers and 103 Gurkha other ranks killed, died of wounds and missing presumed dead. The 2/5th Gurkhas returned a post-war casualty list of thirty-nine killed, seventy-five wounded, 149 POWs and 280 missing.[32] The 1/3rd Gurkhas and 7/10th Baluch also suffered crippling losses in southern Burma of a similar magnitude.

Japanese casualty figures for the campaign amounted to 2431 deaths from combat and illness.[33] The divisional tallies were as follows: 18th Division 123, 33rd Division 730, 55th Division 702, 56th Division 286, army units 590. No precise figure for wounded is given by Japanese sources. In the Malayan campaign, however, a Japanese army lost almost two wounded for each soldier killed. It is likely that XV Army's casualty experience was similar, which would yield a round figure of 4500 wounded.

The Allied air forces lost 116 aircraft in Burma, of which sixty-five were incurred in aerial combat. Japanese records reveal a very similar tally as 117 aircraft were destroyed, sixty of those in aerial combat.[34] Air force casualties were small compared to the army's losses, but often constituted a large proportion of a particular unit's aircrew. The American Volunteer Group lost twenty-three pilots killed in combat and accidents, which was almost a quarter of the total. Churchill wrote of the AVG: 'The victories of these Americans over the rice paddies of Burma are comparable in character if not in scope with those won by the RAF over the hop fields of Kent in the Battle of Britain.'[35] The fighter pilots of the RAF and AVG held their own in the air against the Japanese, often in the face of considerable odds. But on the ground the RAF in Burma was roundly defeated, and driven out of the colony by Japanese air attacks well in advance of Allied ground forces. The Japanese army and navy air forces won a handsome victory in South-east Asia across the early months of 1942.

Little is known of the losses of the Chinese armies in Burma. The Japanese took virtually no Chinese soldiers prisoner as a matter of routine. The

Chinese had only rudimentary medical services; it is unlikely that sufficient transport was available to evacuate wounded and sick with a retreating and routed army. British liaison officers had estimated Chinese forces in Burma at 70,000; given the speed of the final Japanese advance northwards from Toungoo, it seems plausible that thousands of Chinese soldiers must have fallen into Japanese hands. These men were presumably killed on the spot with the ruthlessness typical of the Imperial Japanese Army. The Chinese death toll for the campaign remains unrecorded and unknowable.

18

The Consequences of Defeat

The loss of Burma was a terrible Allied defeat; routed British and Chinese forces were forced to flee the colony and seek sanctuary in the mountains of north-east India and south-west China respectively. Captain Lunt recalled: 'Our liveliest memories of the retreat are of confusion, disorder and near-escapes from disaster, all of which were brought about by the relentless pressure of the enemy.'[1] When General Slim reflected on the 1942 campaign he wrote that the Japanese had been 'bold to the point of foolhardiness, and so aggressive that never for one day did they lose the initiative'. The thousand-mile, three and a half-month retreat destroyed both the armed forces and civil government of British Burma. 'It made me feel sick at heart,' wrote Lunt, 'to see the little country towns turned into flaming ruins, the columns of Indian peasants on their long trek back to India dying by the way-side from cholera, or cut down in their tracks by murderous Burmese gangs who hated the Indians above all others.'[2] The overthrow and humiliation of the regime was a revolution for the people of Burma; their world was turned upside down. The two main self-justifications for British rule had been the creation of a stable internal government and protection from foreign invasion. On both those counts failure was complete.

Burman discontent with British rule was made abundantly clear by the sudden appearance of the Japanese-sponsored Burma Independence Army. Lieutenant Pat Carmichael of the Indian Mountain Artillery conceded: 'I think we loathed the Burmans almost as much as we did the Japanese, for their persistent treachery and murderous attacks on refugees.'[3] Burmese villagers were often suspected of giving away the positions of British troops to the invaders. In mid-April Lieutenant Gerald Fitzpatrick of the 2nd KOYLI had a group of twenty-seven Burmans shot as they were believed to be bandits and spies.[4]

Burma Army was defeated but, despite that, General Iida's 'oriental blitzkrieg' came to a halt at the Chindwin river. The huge jungle-covered mountain range that straddled the Indian-Burmese frontier was an immense barrier. At this time a large part of the Indian Army, including its best-trained formations, was in the Middle East or POW camps at Singapore. A new army would have to be raised to defend north-east India. India was fortunate to have huge manpower reserves to draw upon for that task.

General Wavell reorganised the army in India so that Eastern Command was primarily responsible for the Indian-Burmese frontier. The Eastern Army controlled two corps headquarters: IV Corps in Manipur and Assam with the 17th and 23rd Indian Divisions, and XV Corps in Bengal with the 14th and 26th Indian Divisions. The 70th British Division was in reserve at Ranchi in Bihar province.

British forces at Imphal regrouped behind the shield provided by the mountains. Calcutta became the main base for the army in Manipur and Assam. The single line metre-gauge rail to Dimipur would struggle, however, to support a full-scale campaign. The Assam-Bengal railway had been built to serve the tea plantations of the region; a ferry was needed to cross the unbridged Brahmaputra river; trains might sit stationary in sidings for several days on either bank of the river.

The remnants of Burma Army were re-absorbed into the Indian Army. Scott's 1st Burma Division was broken up; the 17th Indian Division was in need of a long period of rest and rebuilding. The 23rd Indian Division was deployed to hold the front line at Imphal for the duration of the 1942 monsoon season. Of the division's three infantry brigades, at the end of June the 1st and 49th Brigades were located to the south of Imphal at Shenam and Palel, whilst the 37th Brigade watched the tracks leading to the Imphal plain from the east.

The monsoon rains at Imphal are amongst the heaviest in the world. Scottish soldiers of the 1st Seaforth Highlanders, who had arrived in India the previous year after stints at Shanghai and Singapore, felt that the weather at Imphal was even gloomier than their homeland. Once the monsoon was fully underway the tops of mountains became shrouded in a perpetual mist. For the first thirteen days of July rain fell at Imphal without cease. Malaria was rampant and the sickness rate reached 40 per cent. Troops were bored and drenched, and reduced to living in leaky bamboo huts; forward patrols and outposts battled with the elements and nature; mules were vital for carrying supplies along tracks that were impassable to motor transport. The 23rd Division was put on half rations for over two months. From September the weather began to slowly improve, but there was still no sign of the Japanese to the west of the Chindwin river.[5]

Distant events in the Asia-Pacific region would have a decisive impact on Japanese plans for Burma and India. In the Philippines, the Japanese overran Bataan early in April. On 6 May the last bastion of resistance in the Philippines, the island fortress of Corregidor, also fell. With the final conquest of northern Burma and Corregidor, the Japanese invasion of South-east Asia was largely complete. A further round of operations soon got underway to take the Solomon Islands and Papua New Guinea. This was intended to drive a wedge between Australia and North America. An amphibious operation against Port Moresby, on the south coast of Papua New Guinea, was set in motion. In the subsequent battle of the Coral Sea from 4–8 May the Japanese and Americans each lost an aircraft carrier sunk; a second Japanese carrier was badly damaged.

Admiral Yamamoto's long planned general offensive in the central Pacific went ahead within a few weeks of the Coral Sea battle. Yamamoto's attack on Midway Island, to the north-west of Hawaii, was designed to draw the United States Pacific Fleet into a decisive battle. But United States code breakers had discovered the outline of the Japanese plan. On 4 June four Japanese aircraft carriers were sunk in the famous battle of Midway. From this point the Imperial Japanese Navy was forced to adopt a defensive posture and the whole complexion of the war in the Pacific changed.

As a seaborne operation against Port Moresby was no longer practical, in late July 1942 Japanese forces began to advance towards that town by land along the Kokoda trail. Only a small Australian garrison was in Port Moresby at that time. The 7th Australian Division had reached Australia several months before and, after long delays, was dispatched to Papua New Guinea. The headquarters of the division was established at Port Moresby on 18 August. Meanwhile the brigades of the 6th Australian Division at Ceylon had finally sailed from Colombo and arrived at Melbourne in early August.

On 7 August 1942 the Americans took an early advantage of their victory at Midway by landing marines at Guadalcanal, at the southern end of the south-west Pacific's Solomon Islands. Fighting on land, at sea and in the air around Guadalcanal soon developed into a ferocious and epic war of attrition. The main fleet of the Imperial Japanese Navy, and readily available army reserves, were drawn into a prolonged campaign in the Solomons. The new commitments in the Solomons and New Guinea meant that Tokyo's military planners were in no position to contemplate major offensives anywhere else.

In the later half of 1942 Japanese intentions in the Indian Ocean remained unclear, though the likelihood of an invasion of Ceylon or eastern India had receded given the scale of losses at Midway and the Coral Sea. There was speculation amongst Allied commanders that the Japanese might attempt a land invasion of north-east India. This view was not without foundation. In July Imperial General Headquarters in Tokyo ordered XV Army to draw up plans for an invasion of Manipur and Assam. An advance to the Brahmaputra river might cut the air route to China and further isolate Chiang's regime. On 22 August Tokyo ordered that active preparations commence. But that order was later reversed, and on 23 December 1942 Imperial GHQ directed Southern Army to suspend offensive planning given the scale of the crisis unfolding in the Solomon Islands.[6] The Japanese were content to blockade south-west China from ground they had gained in Upper Burma, and had no further territorial ambitions in that quarter.

Once the Japanese offensive had run out of steam, Wavell decided to take the first steps needed to regain the initiative. In Delhi he looked at a map of Burma and said: 'Think how stretched they must be! This is the moment to hit the Japs if only we could! If I had one division in India fit to fight I'd go for them now!'[7] Wavell told London that in the up-coming dry season he was keen to carry out any possible offensive action. Wavell wrote to the Chiefs of Staff on 17 September: 'We may find Japanese opposition very much lower than we expect in Burma if we can only act with boldness and determination ... The Jap has never fought defensively and may not be much good at it.'[8] For the dry season of 1942–43, Wavell decided to launch a limited counter-offensive to capture the port of Akyab in the isolated Arakan region of western Burma. He did not have the forces available to attempt more than that.

Plans were also laid for a brigade-strength guerrilla-style operation behind Japanese lines on the eastern side of the Chindwin. This force was to be led by Colonel Orde Wingate, and would be reliant on animal and air transport. The Clinthe, a mythological beast often seen on Burmese pagodas, was chosen as the new formation's badge; the Clinthe was half-lion, half-eagle.

From the end of October 1942 the Japanese air force carried out occasional raids on RAF airfields in Assam, Manipur and south-eastern Bengal. The first night raid on Calcutta took place at the end of December; only a few bombers were involved but great panic was caused in the crowded port city. The following month a RAF nightfighter managed to shoot down several bombers and the raids promptly ended.[9]

The United States military presence in the China-Burma-India theatre continued after the Japanese conquest of Burma, and the severance of the land route to south-west China. The American Volunteer Group was absorbed into the USAAF on 4 July 1942 and re-named the China Air Task Force. Some of the AVG's pilots remained in China but most left for home and other roles in the war effort. Chennault, the senior American aviator in China, rejoined the American military as a brigadier-general. He would later say of his time in China: 'I always found the Chinese friendly and cooperative. The Japanese gave me a little trouble at times, but not very much. The British in Burma were quite difficult sometimes. But Washington gave trouble night and day throughout the whole war!'[10] Chennault felt that Washington's limited commitment to Nationalist China was the deciding factor in the region. Chennault also believed that General Stilwell did little to progress the cause of the Western allies in China as the later was such an abrasive personality.[11] Stilwell, however, was an American general without an American army and that crippled his mission at every turn. After the loss of Burma, Stilwell remained the senior American military commander in the CBI theatre; his dealings with Chiang Kai-shek and the Chungking regime were far from finished.

Despite a multitude of commitments, Washington did its best to gradually build up an air transport service from India to China. The 10th United States Air Force was based in India, and an India-China Ferry Command was set up to oversee the airlift. Transport aircraft began flying the treacherous 500-mile journey from airfields in the Brahmaputra valley to Kunming, across snow-capped peaks over 15,000 feet high. The so-called 'Hump' route was difficult to navigate and losses were caused by the weather rather than enemy fighters. In mid-1942 only a trickle of supplies was flown to Kunming. The tonnage figure for December 1942 was still only 1227 and it would not rise greatly the following year.[12] In December 1942 American personnel in the CBI theatre numbered 17,000.

During 1942 the Government of India faced considerable challenges on the home front. Nationalist agitation for political reform had the potential to disrupt and deflect the government's direction of India's war effort. An attempt to defuse the situation was made by the London government when Sir Stafford Cripps, a former ambassador to the Soviet Union and socialist politician, arrived in India in March 1942 to spend three weeks in the country for constitutional discussions that lasted into April.

Cripps' offer to the leaders of the Hindu-dominated Congress Party from the British Cabinet was that, after the war, a constituent assembly should draft a new constitution for India. In the meantime, Congress, which was the strongest nationalist grouping, was invited to join the central government. The Muslim League's growing demand for Pakistan – a homeland for Muslims – was given a good hearing as the British in India had come to rely on Muslim support.

Not surprisingly, the negotiations failed. The Congress leadership desired a dominant role in the central government, and wanted the defence ministry handed over to Indian politicians.[13] Churchill, however, had no intention of abandoning British control of India during a great conflict. The British-led regime still had the support of the princes – who reigned over 40 per cent of India – and the traditional coalition of business interests and military communities that was the buttress of the imperial regime.

In April Mahatma Gandhi began using the slogan 'Quit India' in his reported speeches. From May to July Gandhi regularly spoke of the need for a new civil disobedience campaign to paralyse the government. On 14 July the Congress Party's Working Committee published a resolution calling for the end of British rule in India. The Congress leadership was due to meet in Bombay on 8 August, and British officialdom expected that to bring the crisis to a head. In the early hours of 9 August Gandhi and other Congress Party leaders were arrested; the arrested men were interned at Ahmednagar in Deccan; the elderly Gandhi was held at the Aga Khan's palace.

A wave of rioting, strikes and sabotage broke out in many parts of India in response to the arrest of the Congress leaders. Disturbances began in Bombay and Delhi, and spread to other cities of eastern and southern India, before moving into the countryside. Government services such as the railways, telegraph, police and post office were directly attacked. The railways leading to Calcutta were damaged in many places. Communications were disrupted in Bengal, Bihar and the United Province. The police proved ineffective in the crisis and a large military force was deployed to support the civilian author-ities. Fifty-seven infantry battalions were involved in the operation. Troops were posted to guard rail bridges and junctions; Eastern Army used aircraft to strafe mobs damaging railway tracks near Patna.[14] The Muslim League took no part in events and Muslim regions of the country remained calm.

It took six weeks to restore order, but by late September the worst of the crisis had passed and the country came back under government control without the need for a declaration of martial law. The insurrection had been localised and piecemeal. The government believed that the arrest of the Congress leadership had disorganised the planning of the insur-rection; Congress spokesmen said that the government's actions had caused a 'non-violent' movement to slide into violence. Thousands of Congressmen and political dissidents were jailed, often for lengthy periods. There was no evidence of collusion between the Japanese and the Congress Party, though many British officials felt that the government was opportunistically attacked at a time of international calamity.

The North-West Frontier Province, despite a garrison adding up to several divisions, had also flared up during the summer months to add to India Command's anxieties. The mountains of Waziristan was the scene of a long-running tribal insurgency led by the Faqir of Ipi. The Waziristan agencies had a strong permanent military presence, but a tribal army managed to lay siege to a government post in the upper Tochi valley in May. Two extra brigades had to be sent to North Waziristan so that a divisional-strength relief column could be assembled. The column set about restoring order from the end of July.[15]

By the end of 1942 the war with Japan had severed all economic links between South-east Asia and the rest of the world. Large regions of India were dependent on the import of rice, much of which came from Burma. Burma was the world's largest rice exporter; millions of foreign people relied on the colony's agriculture. With the whole of South-east Asia in Japanese hands there was no alternative place from which India could import rice. In the event of a rice famine in India, the import of additional supplies from Burma was the traditional safeguard.

During 1943 Bengal, with an estimated population of sixty-one million, fell into the grip of the worst famine seen in India since the first decade of the twentieth century. This was a shock as it was half-believed that British India had solved the problem of famine. The shortage of rice in Bengal was not great but in a desperately poor subsistence economy any shortage was a potential catastrophe; there was little margin for error. Bengal consumed roughly a third of India's rice supply, and Bengali diets gained 80 to 90 per cent of calories from rice; other less dependent rice-consuming states and provinces of India were able to reorganise their local food markets to avoid a famine.[16]

Famine conditions in Bengal would set in by May 1943 and reached a peak towards the end of the year. Once rural Bengal began to experience severe food shortages, people fled from the countryside to larger towns and the great city of Calcutta. The crop of December 1943 relieved famine conditions, but epidemics of malaria, cholera and smallpox swept through the province. The central government's Famine Commission report would point out that the famine badly effected perhaps a tenth of the population, but the consequent epidemics afflicted almost the whole population. There were a million deaths in Bengal in 1943 above the average expected level of mortality. The Famine Commission stated that for 1943–44, 'we must conclude that about one and a half million deaths occurred as a direct result of the famine, and the epidemics which followed in its train'.[17] If the famine period is extended to 1946, the toll rises to as high as three million deaths above average expected levels of mortality. After all, trade and administrative conditions did not return to normal until after the war.

On the eve of the Second World War South-east Asia had accounted for 70 per cent of the world's rice exports; Burma's share was 37 per cent, the majority of which went to India and Ceylon. The sudden ripping of so much of a particular commodity out of the world trading system was bound to cause a crisis somewhere. To make matters worse, the impact of the loss of Burmese rice on the Indian market was out of all proportion to the amounts of rice lost. Rampant wartime inflation had already put the Indian rice market under stress. By one measure the price of rice in September 1941 was 69 per cent above the level of August 1939; then from November 1942 to May 1943 the wholesale price of rice went up a further 300 per cent. Once rice became too expensive for the peasantry to purchase, the distribution network in the countryside vanished and famine was unavoidable.[18] Ultimately, price inflation probably did more to cause famine than anything else, but it was the loss of Burma and South-east Asia that directly caused the Indian rice market to collapse.

The Famine Commission observed in its report that the Bengal government had been slow to halt the export of rice out of the province following the loss of Burma.[19] The arrival of refugees from Burma added to the food demand on Bengal.

The Quit India movement also had a crippling impact on the railways and local government across a vital period of months that stretched well beyond the main period of crisis. Wartime shipping shortages and the Imperial Japanese Navy's control of the Bay of Bengal compounded an already bad situation.

The Government of India in Delhi came in for its share of criticism. It was several decades since the last major famine, and the civil service was out of practice at responding to that circumstance. There was no widespread crop failure in Bengal during 1942 from drought, which was the traditional warning sign to officialdom that famine was in the offing. News of the famine was devastating to the morale of officials who had sincerely dedicated their life's work to the prevention of just such a calamity.

The Japanese did not invade Bengal in 1942 or 1943, which masks their impact on the province. Famine in Bengal, however, was as much a consequence of the loss of Burma as the bombing of British cities by the Luftwaffe was a consequence of the fall of France to Nazi Germany. In the early 1940s Bengal was British territory, and what happened there is also part of the story of Britain's war. Bengal is generally brushed under the carpet and forgotten. That more people died in Bengal during the Second World War than the rest of the British empire combined is a matter for reflection.

What had gone wrong for Allied forces in Burma in 1942? Part of the explanation can be traced back to the previous century. The British had originally annexed Burma to be the Indian empire's outer eastern bastion. But India's main military priority was the North-west Frontier facing central Asia. Russia was Britain's most feared potential enemy in Asia; the rise of Japan as a threat was unforeseen. No strategic roads or railways were built from north-east India into Burma; the peacetime garrison of Burma was modest once the territory was pacified. These policies persisted until 1937, when Burma was re-separated from India.

The eruption of full-scale war between China and Japan in 1937 set the eastern part of Asia ablaze long before war broke out in Europe. The so-called Burma Road from Upper Burma into south-west China was a way to ship

Western aid to Nationalist China, after the Chinese seaboard was subject to Japanese occupation. Yet the Japanese still seemed remote from the affairs of Burma, a colonial society that looked out upon the broad expanses of the Bay of Bengal. The danger that Japan posed to the British empire did not become fully apparent until the later half of 1940, when the Japanese entered northern French Indochina and joined the Axis.

By this time France had fallen to Germany, and Italy had entered the war. Prime Minister Churchill was later to write: 'Our priorities during 1941 stood: first, the defence of the Island [Britain], including the threat of invasion and the U-boat war; secondly the struggle in the Middle East and Mediterranean; thirdly, after June, supplies to Soviet Russia; and, last of all, resistance to a Japanese assault.'[20] Churchill drew comfort from the likelihood that if the Japanese embarked on war with the European powers in Asia that would drag America into the war. The Middle East was the most active theatre during 1941 and drew in a steady stream of reinforcements from Britain and other parts of the empire; even within South-east Asia, Malaya had first call on reinforcements entering the region right down until late January 1942.

The garrison in Malaya was the primary shield of Burma, which remained towards the bottom of London's priorities – somewhere between Hong Kong and Jamaica. The Japanese would be hard pressed to attack Burma in strength whilst the Allied position in Malaya remained strong. Not a lot changed in Burmese military life from 1939 to late 1941 as there was no infusion of reinforcement to make it clear that the colony was in peril.

The outbreak of war in the Pacific did not greatly impact Burma at first. The Japanese invasion of Malaya and advance towards Singapore dominated the attention of commanders in the region. Chiang Kai-shek's regime offered troops to help defend the Burma Road, though General Wavell was slow to whole-heartedly welcome the arrival of a large Chinese army in the colony. Thailand was highly vulnerable to Japanese aggression; the Thai government had little choice but to cooperate with Tokyo. This exposed Burma to the possibility of invasion by land. The bombing of Rangoon on 23 and 25 December 1941 was a warning of what was to come. British commanders at Rangoon had hoped for strong resistance in Malaya to delay a major Japanese invasion of Burma. Yet British forces were soon in full retreat towards Singapore.

By mid-January 1942 General Iida's XV Army in southern Thailand was ready to invade Burmese Tenasserim. The opening engagements of the campaign that followed were not an auspicious start for British forces. As in Malaya, inexperienced and dispersed colonial formations struggled to perform effectively against well-trained, determined and experienced Japanese troops. The 17th Indian Division's rearguard action at Moulmein did not gain much time given the risk that was run by fighting a battle in front of a broad estuary. The 1st Burma Division remained in the Shan States in case the Japanese invaded Upper Burma from northern Thailand; Mandalay and the Burma Road were too important to leave undefended.

At his Java headquarters, General Wavell was gambling on being able to reinforce Burma by sea faster than Japanese troops could enter the colony by land. At this time Wavell could not be sure what reinforcements London might make available for Burma; the port of Rangoon had to be kept open whilst that was arranged.

After the loss of Moulmein the line of the Salween river was the next defensible geographic barrier; but the two most likely crossing places for Japanese troops – Martaban and Kuzeik – were each defended by only a single battalion. General Smyth, the 17th Division's commander, might have put stronger forces into those places. The Japanese were not long delayed at the Salween river, which in turn made it necessary to fight a battle at the Bilin river for as long as practical. General Hutton was expecting the 7th Armoured Brigade and other reinforcements at Rangoon; he wanted to hold the Japanese as far to the east of the port city as possible.

The 17th Division offered battle at the Bilin river from 16–20 February, and fought an effective rearguard action under difficult circumstances. Contact was only broken, and the retreat resumed, once it became clear that the highly mobile Japanese were edging past both flanks of the British force.

The routing of Smyth's division as it marched from Bilin to the Sittang river hastened the loss of Rangoon. Slim later told Smyth: 'Jackie, you dropped your Field-Marshal's baton into the Sittang river.'[21] The retreat from the Bilin river was too unhurried for an army caught up in a desperate campaign against a capable opponent. The Japanese were able to push troops through the jungle, past the northern flank of British forces lingering at Kyaikto, to seize hills near the eastern end of the Sittang bridge on the morning of 22 February. Smyth and his staff had insufficiently appreciated the vital importance of that ground.

The Sittang bridge was blown by engineers before dawn on 23 February to leave the bulk of the 17th Division cut off on the eastern side of the river. The debacle was a military tragedy for British forces. Generals Wavell and Hutton felt that Smyth had been given enough time to get his division behind the Sittang river. The full severity of the disaster was avoidable.

Smyth returned to India after his dismissal by Wavell. In India he was taken to task for proceeding on active service without being passed fit; that was against military regulations, which were in place for good reason. In the post-war years Smyth recovered much of his old dynamism and ambition. He became a member of parliament, government minister, writer, journalist and lived to the age of eighty-nine. Over the years Smyth would write a succession of books and articles that included discussions of the campaign in southern Burma. This indicates that Smyth was greatly troubled by the battle of the Sittang bridge. The officer on the spot who ordered the bridge to be wrecked, Brigadier Hugh-Jones, was also deeply affected by what happened. After the war, in 1952, he would walk into the sea and drown himself.[22]

General Slim commented that the Sittang fiasco was:

> the decisive battle of the first [Burma] campaign. After it, however gallantly our troops fought, there was little hope of holding Rangoon. And when Rangoon went … the whole army in Burma was cut off from the outside world almost as effectively as had been the two brigades on the east bank of the Sittang.[23]

The premature collapse of the 17th Division at the Sittang river undermined attempts to mount a prolonged defence of Rangoon, despite the eleventh-hour arrival of the 7th Armoured Brigade. The crisis became even more acute when the Australian government refused to allow the 7th Australian Division to be landed at Rangoon. Canberra foresaw a battle for northern Australia and wanted Australian formations returning from the Middle East for that campaign. The British official historian of the war against Japan, Major-General S. Woodburn Kirby, concluded in 1958 that at best only a single brigade of the 7th Division could have reached Rangoon in time, such was the speed of events in southern Burma.[24] But that was a polite fiction to deflect controversy. Given Wavell's determination to land the 63rd Indian Brigade at Rangoon in early March, there can be little doubt that all three brigades of the 7th Division could have been landed if permitted to do so. The whole question of the destination of Australia's seaborne troops draws attention to the failure of Indian Army formations in the Middle East to return to India at a time of great danger.

The escape of General Alexander's Burma Army from Rangoon along the road leading to Prome was certainly a lucky break for British forces, but the Japanese cordon closing around the capital in early March was weak in numbers and full of holes. Rangoon was entered by Japanese forces on 8 March; this was another triumph for XV Army hard on the heels of the Sittang victory.

After the loss of Rangoon, the aim of the campaign from the British viewpoint was to fight a delaying action, though without an effective overland line of communication to India there was only a slender chance of the campaign lasting beyond the onset of the monsoon. When Chinese forces began to enter Burma it soon became apparent that the Chungking regime was unwilling to send troops deep into southern Burma. The Chinese leadership was worried that the Japanese would thrust through the Shan

States from northern Thailand to directly cut the Burma Road.[25] The Chinese 200th Division fought well at Toungoo, but the town was lost by the end of March. Burcorps was also forced to retreat northwards after a confused battle south of Prome in the Irrawaddy valley.

General Stilwell's task as commander of Chinese forces in Burma was badly undermined by political interference; his thankless role in China would have confounded the most skilful of diplomats. Alexander later wrote: 'We hoped that the Chinese would be able to do more than they did – and perhaps we should have known how logistically weak they were, and what a rotten system of command they had from Chiang Kai-shek downwards.'[26] It is unlikely, however, that Chinese opinions of British forces were any rosier at this stage of the war.

Alexander's appointment to Burma was largely a political gesture in the absence of something more substantial. The relief of Hutton probably made no difference to the course of events. The die was already well and truly cast. Hutton, though, might have won more sympathy by sticking out the campaign to the end. On 2 July 1942 Wavell wrote to Hutton: 'I admit quite frankly that I misjudged the situation ... [I] never expected the Japanese to get along as fast as he did, or in such strength'.[27] Hutton received no further posting in the army. He wrote bitterly after the war:

> Wavell could no doubt have found me military employment in India ... He could have pressed my case more strongly with the authorities at home, but I realised that my seniority and the P.M.'s prejudice against anyone who he felt had failed him was an obstacle, but the real obstacle was no doubt Wavell himself.[28]

Hutton's next posting was in the upper reaches of the civilian government of India; he became secretary to the War Resources and Reconstruction Committee.

The period encompassing the early months of 1942 was the ideal time for the Japanese to run riot in the Indian Ocean. The fall of Singapore and the Dutch East Indies opened up the Indian Ocean for the Imperial Japanese Navy. Admiral Nagumo's carrier raid against Ceylon in April 1942 involved the principal warships of the IJN, and compelled the Royal Navy to withdraw from the eastern Indian Ocean. This was the only occasion in the war when the Royal Navy put a fleet to sea to contest the passage of the strongest surface fleet at the disposal of the Axis powers. This was in stark contrast to the First World War, when the Royal Navy's primary task had been to bottle up Germany's battle fleet in the North Sea to maintain maritime supremacy for the Allies. Admiral Somerville's Eastern Fleet was as strong a force as the Admiralty could assemble in 1942; the navy had been neglected for a generation, and the damage done to the institution was beyond repair. The sailing of Japanese troops to Rangoon without interference was a stark illustration of the collapse of British seapower on the internal sea lanes of the British empire. The arrival of Japanese reinforcements at Rangoon sealed the fate of Burma, despite the entry to the colony of Chinese forces that were of greater numerical strength than Alexander's depleted army.

The war in the air in Burma did not go well for the RAF. There were plenty of airfields but not enough aircraft. Air Vice-Marshal Stevenson would report that thirty-two crashed enemy aircraft were found on the ground up until the fall of Rangoon. This was far fewer than claimed shot down by Allied aircrew. Stevenson added: 'Technical examination of these – although many were burnt or otherwise destroyed beyond recognition – established the quality of equipment about which little was previously known.'[29] Without the spirited presence of the American Volunteer Group, the RAF's defeat in Burma might have been more rapid. The heavy and successful Japanese raids on Magwe airfield on 21–22 March left the Allied armies without air cover for the rest of the campaign.

In the absence of major British reinforcement, military planning in Upper Burma could only erect a house of cards that fluttered away in the first gust of hostile wind. In the intense heat of April, the 1st Burma Division was routed near the oilfield of Yenangyaung. Whilst that was taking place, the rest of General Iida's XV Army broke the Chinese front to the north of Toungoo and in the Shan States. An Allied retreat out of northern Burma could not be long delayed. Mandalay was abandoned; the Ava bridge was wrecked; the western end of the Burma Road fell into Japanese hands.

During the final stage of the retreat to India a horde of refugees and Dorman-Smith's civil administration accompanied British forces, which were marching only just ahead of the fast-approaching monsoon. Given the extent of the rout of May 1942, it was just as well for the Indian Army that the mountains of north-east India were sufficiently impenetrable to bring the progress of the Japanese to a halt. The war in the Far East was going to be a prolonged affair.

From his Delhi headquarters, General Wavell continued to command the British war effort in India after the loss of Burma. Some of Wavell's subordinates found his outlook unrealistic, but to military and political leaders in distant London his determination and well-reasoned reports were reassuring. Wavell's reputation for possessing a clear mind and balanced temperament was sufficiently robust to withstand a string of setbacks that would have terminated the career of a lesser man. He would be promoted field-marshal in January 1943.

General Slim observed that Allied troops in Burma had been fearful of the jungle. 'To us it appeared only as an obstacle to movement and vision; to the

Japanese it was a welcome means of concealed manoeuvre and surprise.'[30] In the later part of 1942 two training divisions were established in India with jungle operations in mind. As a leader Slim had impressed many people in Burma with his composure and robust personality. He was marked out for greater things and took command of XV Corps in Bengal not long after the final retreat to Imphal. General Cowan remained in command of the 17th Indian Division, a post he had held since Smyth's relief. Cowan had the division's sign changed from a streak of lightening to a black cat; this was possibly because Tokyo Rose, an English-language radio broadcaster, announced that 'the division whose sign is a yellow streak' had been thrown out of Burma.[31] Brigadier Cameron also stayed at his post with the Gurkhas of the 48th Brigade.

Some senior officers, however, did not return to the main front after the loss of Burma. General Scott was awarded the DSO for his services as commander of the 1st Burma Division. After the division was broken up he took command of a training formation. He went on to be the Indian Army's Inspector of Infantry until June 1943. James Lunt wrote of Scott: 'Always alert and cool, he was at the same time friendly and relaxed. Had Bruce Scott's fate taken him to the Middle East rather than to Burma he might well have risen to the highest rank. He had the temperament to take the rough with the smooth.'[32] Scott finished his career as GOC of the Peshawar divisional district from 1943–46. Peshawar was a large garrison town close to the Khyber pass. Brigadiers Curtis, Bourke, Hugh-Jones, Jones and Ekin were all given commands of military districts or training units in India. In particular, Jones was commandant of the Indian Military Academy from 1942–44; Hugh-Jones had a posting as Deputy Director-General of Recruiting.

As for the junior officers and rank and file of the British, Indian, Gurkha and Burmese units that had fought in Burma; for some the 1942 campaign was just the beginning of their military experience of the Japanese and Burma; for others transfer, ill-health and injury meant they would play no further part in the conflict.

The performance of General Iida's XV Army had been brilliant; though the sheer quality of the Japanese campaign to conquer Burma was somewhat overshadowed by the triumphs achieved elsewhere in South-east Asia and the Pacific during this phase of the war. Japanese troops were highly motivated and had already gained experience of mobile warfare in China. The capture of Rangoon was Iida's main objective in the opening phase of the campaign. Tokyo needed to capture Rangoon to deny the port to Allied forces, and to seal off the land route to Nationalist China.[33]

After Rangoon had been taken it was a straightforward task to ship Japanese reinforcements directly to southern Burma. Japanese engineers repaired long stretches of railway to support the advance of XV Army on Mandalay. Japanese officers were impressed by the Chinese defence of Toungoo and Pyinmana. Colonel Miyawaki, commander of the 213th Regiment, wrote that 'the British were weaker than the Chinese'.[34] The Burma Independence Army proved useful to the Japanese for reconnaissance tasks and gathering information, though not for fighting. The Burmese nationalists, however, were very important to winning over the support, or at least neutrality, of the civilian population from the outset. This was in stark contrast to what Japanese forces usually experienced in China.[35] By April 1942 the Japanese were supreme in Burma by land and in the air, as well as at sea off-shore; the sheer speed of their victory owed much to this triple layering of success.

Everything seemed to work well for General Iida in Burma; he relentlessly pushed forward his army rather as General Yamashita had in Malaya. Iida returned to Tokyo from Burma in March 1943; two years later, after a lengthy period at army GHQ, he was sent to command XXX Army in Manchuria. Iida was made a POW after the Soviet intervention in the Far East and spent five years in captivity in Siberia; he died in Japan in 1980 at the age of ninety-two.

The 55th Division's General Takeuchi was retired from the army in 1943, but General Sakurai of the 33rd Division was to be a thorn in the side of Allied forces in Burma for the rest of the war. In January 1944 he took command of XXVIII Army in the Arakan region of western Burma. After the war he was a POW at Rangoon until 1947; Sakurai died in 1985 at the age of ninety-five.[36]

There were many capable leaders amongst XV Army's subordinate commanders. Decorations and awards were handed out very sparingly in the forces of Imperial Japan. The highest standards of courage and sacrifice were the expected minimum. Still, exceptions were sometimes made; after the campaign letters of citation were awarded to the 33rd Division, 214th and 215th Regiments, 56th Division and 56th Reconnaissance Regiment.[37]

After the conquest of Burma the Japanese set up a military administration in June 1942. General Iida headed the new administration and was assisted by a body of officials sent from Japan. XV Army's four divisions all remained in Burma after the monsoon season of 1942. The 55th and 56th Divisions took up positions in north-east Burma facing China; the 33rd Division watched the Indian frontier from the Chindwin river; the 18th Division formed a reserve in southern Burma. The Japanese later set about building a railway from Thailand to Burmese Tenasserim with the assistance of forced labour. Tenasserim was under the control of the Japanese headquarters at Singapore and many prisoners of war held there were used as labourers on the railway. POWs at Rangoon gaol were not employed on the Thai-Burma railway as they were held prisoner by a different Japanese command.[38]

The Japanese disbanded the Burma Independence Army; it had outlived its usefulness from the Japanese viewpoint. Aung San, however, continued to work for the Japanese as the commander of a newly formed local defence force. On 1 August 1942 the Japanese installed U Ba Maw, the former prime minister, as the head of a puppet government. Until recently Ba Maw had been a political prisoner of the British. The Thakins were not given a controlling role in the administration, but took part in a junior capacity.[39]

Ba Maw was on friendly terms with General Iida whilst the later remained in Burma. Iida was dismayed when civil servants and businessmen arrived at Rangoon from Japan with the intention of treating the territory as an occupied enemy country – rather like Manchuria or China.[40] But Tokyo had no intention of fully sharing power with Burmese nationalists, especially in a territory adjacent to an active front line. Burmese collaboration with the occupation authorities was led on by promises of qualified autonomy within the framework of the Greater East Asia Co-prosperity Sphere.

Nevertheless, the balance of power between Europe and Asia was undergoing a profound transformation. There is no question that the Japanese conquest of Burma made the colony immediately independent of Britain. By the last months of 1942 the only British in Burma – more or less – were incarcerated in Rangoon gaol. British influence and control of Burmese political and social life had been abruptly ended. Burma would never be the same again in the aftermath of the British expulsion.

The future of the British empire in Asia was uncertain in July 1942. Wavell pointed out to the authorities in London:

> The loss of Burma has been from a strategical point of view our most serious reverse of the Japanese war. It has deprived our Chinese allies of a flow of munitions to continue their long resistance; it has made the establishment of air bases within effective range of Japan a matter of extreme difficulty; it has exposed India to a serious threat of invasion; and it has had a disastrous effect on British prestige in the East.[41]

London decided to retain Sir Reginald Dorman-Smith's Government of Burma in exile at Simla, the traditional summer capital of India. The well-intentioned Dorman-Smith would be needed were the Union Jack ever to be raised again over Rangoon.

What was to become of Nationalist China and the regime of Generalissimo Chiang? The Allied defeat in Burma had caused Anglo-American forces to loose direct contact with the Nationalist armies of China, the force engaging so much of the Imperial Japanese Army. In 1942 Anglo-American fortunes in the war were at their lowest ebb. Nationalist China and Chiang Kai-shek therefore had a much greater importance in Allied calculations than would later seem to be the case. But, if Nationalist China intended to be a great power, like the Soviet Union, it had to substantially stand on its own feet; limited Allied assistance could be sent to Chungking by air transport, but Chiang's regime had to survive and flourish on its own merits within Chinese society. The Allied defeat in Burma played its part in the eventual post-war destruction of the Nationalist regime on the Chinese mainland. The 1942 campaign in Burma was the only time in the war when large Chinese and Western armies fought the Japanese side-by-side.

In the meantime, Burma under Japanese rule steadily slid back towards the kind of subsistence society that had existed before the arrival of the British had forced the modern world upon the region. Life in Japanese-occupied Burma was bleak. The agricultural economy was ruined; the populace learnt to fear the Japanese military police – the sinister *Kempeitai*. The port city of Rangoon began what would prove to be a long period of decay and stagnation.

Late in 1942 a military campaign to regain Burma by land from north-east India seemed a formidable undertaking. Churchill would reflect that, 'Going into swampy jungles to fight the Japanese is like going into the water to fight a shark.' The prospect of Allied victory in Burma was distant; a great deal of hard work and sacrifice would be needed to make the eventual achievement of that goal a reality. A Japanese invasion of north-east India in early 1944 had to be repelled before an advance into northern Burma became possible. The re-conquest of Burma by General Slim and the Indian Army in 1945 was a triumphant reversal of the local military situation. Many – if not most – of the individual Japanese soldiers who took part in General Iida's campaign of 1942 did not survive the war.

British forces retook Rangoon on 2 May 1945, just before the onset of the monsoon season. On 16 October Dorman-Smith returned to Rangoon as governor armed with promises of further political reform. Self-government would be granted at an early opportunity. British institutions, however, had been discredited by the Japanese occupation. Aung San had broken with the Japanese; his Burma National Army was a force to be reckoned with. The war had deeply scarred the body politic of Burma; the country's future constitutional development would not favour those of moderate views.

British administrators played a caretaker role in Burma from 1945–48, but they merely floated upon the surface of public life. Dorman-Smith left Burma in June 1946; another governor completed a transfer of power that failed to protect the status of minority communities. The future of Burma had received scant attention in London; Burma was badly over-shadowed by the constitutional crisis underway in neighbouring British India.

The stagnation of Rangoon continued after Burma's independence in

1948. The unrestricted export of Burma's raw materials and crops by private companies did not find favour with Burma's new rulers. A corrupt and foolish state-run economic system was imposed instead. A complex civil war between Burma's majority and minority groups soon erupted and burned and simmered for decades. Even in the early years of the twenty-first century Rangoon's relatively undeveloped downtown district still boasted plenty of colonial architecture dating from the British period. The Japanese conquest of Burma in 1942 completely knocked the country off the prosperous trajectory it seemed to be rapidly and inevitably steering in the decades leading up to the Second World War.

Notes

Notes to Preface

1. H.L. Thompson, *New Zealanders with the Royal Air Force*, iii (Wellington, 1959), p. 269.
2. D. Ford, *Flying Tiger: Claire Chennault and His American Volunteers, 1941–1942* (Washington, 2007), p. 122.

Notes to Chapter 1: British Burma and Imperial Japan

1. J.W. Fortescue, *A History of the British Army*, xi (London, 1923), p. 349.
2. N. Tarling (ed.), *The Cambridge History of Southeast Asia*, iii (Cambridge, 1992), p. 35.
3. Cheng Siok–Hwa, *The Rice Industry of Burma, 1852–1940* (Kuala Lumpur, 1968), p. 1.
4. Ibid., pp. 201, 206, 217.
5. Ibid., pp. 198, 221, 241–43.
6. M. Collis, *The Burmese Scene* (London, 1943), p. 36.
7. Tarling, *The Cambridge History of Southeast Asia*, iii, p. 240.
8. J. Lunt, *The Retreat from Burma, 1941–1942* (London, 1986), p. 35.
9. B. Prasad, *Defence of India: Policy and Plans* (New Delhi, 1963), p. 138.
10. R. Callahan, *Burma, 1942–1945* (London, 1978), p. 14.
11. C.M. Bell, *The Royal Navy, Seapower and Strategy Between the Wars* (Stanford, California, 2000), p. 3.
12. E.L. Dreyer, *China at War, 1901–1949* (London, 1995), pp. 181–82; His-Sheng Ch'I, *Nationalist China at War* (Ann Arbor, Michigan, 1982), pp. 12, 37, 48.
13. Bell, *The Royal Navy*, pp. 44, 187.
14. Callahan, *Burma, 1942–1945*, p. 16.
15. F. Wakeman, *Policing Shanghai, 1927–1937* (Berkeley, 1995), p. 277.
16. Edgar Snow, *Scorched Earth* (London, 1941), p. 45.
17. F. Wood, *No Dogs and Not Many Chinese* (London, 1998), p. 278.
18. H. Knatchbull-Hugessen, *Diplomat in Peace and War* (London, 1949), p. 126.
19. His-Sheng Ch'I, *Nationalist China at War*, p. 55.
20. S.E. Morison, *History of United States Naval Operations in World War II*, iii (Boston, 1948), p. 15; W. Murray and A.R. Millett, *A War to be Won* (Cambridge, Massachusetts, 2000), p. 151.

21. Callahan, *Burma, 1942–1945*, pp. 25–26.

22. M. Byrd, *Chennault: Giving Wings to the Tiger* (Tuscaloosa, Alabama, 1987), p. 93.

23. W. Cornelius and T. Short, *Ding Hao: America's Air War in China, 1937–1945* (Gretna, Louisiana, 1980), p. 9.

Notes to Chapter 2: Preparations for War

1. J. Lunt, *The Retreat from Burma, 1941–1942* (London, 1986), pp. 39–41.

2. B. Prasad (ed.), *The Retreat from Burma, 1941–42* (Calcutta, 1959), p. 31.

3. D. Ford, *Flying Tiger: Claire Chennault and His American Volunteers, 1941–1942* (Washington, 2007), p. 109.

4. M. Collis, *Last and First in Burma* (London, 1956), p. 26.

5. C. Bayly and T. Harper, *Forgotten Armies: The Fall of British Asia, 1941–1945* (London, 2004), pp. 8–13.

6. Kaushik Roy, 'Military Loyalty in the Colonial Context: A Case Study of the Indian Army During World War II', *Journal of Military History* (April, 2009), p. 504; Rafiuddin Ahmed, *History of the Baloch Regiment, 1939–1956* (Uckfield, East Sussex, 2005), p. 1.

7. Ahmed, *Baloch Regiment*, p. 9.

8. J. Thompson, *The War in Burma, 1942–45* (London, 2002), p. 405; Kaushik Roy, 'The Construction of Regiments in the Indian Army: 1859–1913', *War in History*, 2001, 8 (2), p. 128.

9. T. Gould, *Imperial Warriors* (London, 2000), pp. 2–3.

10. Ibid., pp. 8, 13.

11. Roy, 'The Construction of Regiments', pp. 132–34.

12. Ahmed, *Baloch Regiment*, p. xi.

13. Prasad, *The Retreat from Burma*, p. 48.

14. C.F. Romanus and R. Sunderland, *Stilwell's Mission to China* (Washington, 1953), pp. 10, 33–35.

15. W.F. Craven and J.L. Cate, *The Army Air Forces in World War II*, i (Chicago, 1948), p. 724.

16. A. Draper, *Dawns Like Thunder* (London, 1987), pp. 48–50; E.L. Dreyer, *China at War, 1901–1949* (London, 1995), p. 267.

17. Ford, *Flying Tiger*, pp. 27–29; M. Byrd, *Chennault: Giving Wings to the Tiger* (Tuscaloosa, Alabama, 1987), p. 105.

18. Craven and Cate, *The Army Air Forces*, i, pp. 485–89.

19. Maochun Yu, *The Dragon's War: Allied Operations and the Fate of China, 1937–1947* (Annapolis, Maryland, 2006), p. 35; Ford, *Flying Tiger*, p. 45.

20. Maochun Yu, *The Dragon's War*, p. 32; J. Klinkowitz, *With the Tigers Over China, 1941–1942* (Lexington, Kentucky, 1999), p. 25.

21. R. Callahan, *Burma, 1942–1945* (London, 1978), p. 29.

22. H.L. Thompson, *New Zealanders with the Royal Air Force*, iii (Wellington, 1959), p. 270.

23. Collis, *Last and First in Burma*, p 42.

24. Ibid., pp. 43–44.
25. Ibid., pp. 41–42; Prasad, *The Retreat from Burma*, p. 33.

Notes to Chapter 3: The Outbreak of War in South-east Asia

1. S. Woodburn Kirby, *The War Against Japan*, ii (London, 1958), p. 443; B. Prasad (ed.), *The Retreat from Burma, 1941–42* (Calcutta, 1959), p. 61.
2. I.L. Grant and Kazuo Tamayama, *Burma 1942: The Japanese Invasion* (Chichester, 1999), p. 47.
3. Ibid., pp. 332–33.
4. Ibid., pp. 371, 374.
5. Ibid., pp. 374, 376–77.
6. Ibid., p. 49.
7. Prasad, *The Retreat from Burma*, pp. 66–67.
8. Kirby, *The War Against Japan*, ii, p. 18.
9. M. Collis, *Last and First in Burma* (London, 1956), p. 46.
10. Grant, *Burma*, p. 45.
11. D.S. Daniell, *Cap of Honour: The Story of the Gloucestershire Regiment (The 28th/61st Foot), 1694–1950* (London, 1956), pp. 236, 266, 268.
12. Prasad, *The Retreat from Burma*, p. 55.
13. Ibid., p. 73; R. Lewin, *The Chief: Field-Marshal Lord Wavell* (London, 1980), p. 156.
14. Prasad, *The Retreat from Burma*, pp. 440–43.
15. S. Woodburn Kirby, *The War Against Japan*, ii (London, 1958), pp. 13–14.
16. Prasad, *The Retreat from Burma*, p. 454; Grant, *Burma*, p. 41.
17. J. Latimer, *Burma: The Forgotten War* (London, 2004), p. 43.
18. R. Callahan, *Burma, 1942–1945* (London, 1978), p. 39; Collis, *Last and First in Burma*, p. 50.
19. M. Byrd, *Giving Wings to the Tiger* (Tuscaloosa, Alabama, 1987), p. 143; D. Ford, *Flying Tiger: Claire Chennault and His American Volunteers, 1941–1942* (Washington, 2007), pp. 95–96.
20. Ford, *Flying Tiger*, pp. 98–105.
21. C. Shores, B. Cull and Yasuho Izawa, *Bloody Shambles*, i (London, 1992), p. 241.
22. Ibid., p. 242; H.L. Thompson, *New Zealanders with the Royal Air Force*, iii (Wellington, 1959), p. 272.
23. J. Klinkowitz, *With the Tigers Over China, 1941–1942* (Lexington, Kentucky, 1999), p. 71.
24. Ford, *Flying Tiger*, p. 116.
25. Shores, *Bloody Shambles*, i, pp. 245–46.
26. Ford, *Flying Tiger*, pp. 117–18.
27. Ibid., pp. 119–20.
28. Ibid., p. 121.
29. Collis, *Last and First in Burma*, p. 56.
30. Shores, *Bloody Shambles*, i, p. 243.

31. Ibid., p. 245; Ford, *Flying Tiger*, p. 126.

32. Ford, *Flying Tiger*, p. 127.

33. Shores, *Bloody Shambles*, i, p. 249.

34. Ibid., p. 250; Thompson, *New Zealanders with the Royal Air Force*, iii, pp. 272–73.

35. Shores, *Bloody Shambles*, i, p. 251.

36. Lewin, *Lord Wavell*, p. 159; Latimer, *Burma: The Forgotten War*, p. 43.

37. Ford, *Flying Tiger*, pp. 129, 135.

38. Maochun Yu, *The Dragon's War: Allied Operations and the Fate of China, 1937–1947* (Annapolis, Maryland, 2006), p. 39.

39. Ford, *Flying Tiger*, p. 134.

40. J. Lunt, *The Retreat from Burma, 1941–1942* (London, 1986), p. 82.

41. Collis, *Last and First in Burma*, p. 59.

42. Kirby, *The War Against Japan*, ii, p. 24.

Notes to Chapter 4: The Invasion of Burma

1. M. Collis, *Last and First in Burma* (London, 1956), p. 60.

2. R. Lewin, *The Chief: Field-Marshal Lord Wavell* (London, 1980), p. 161; A. Draper, *Dawns Like Thunder* (London, 1987), p. 29.

3. I.L. Grant and Kazuo Tamayama, *Burma 1942: The Japanese Invasion* (Chichester, 1999), p. 42.

4. G.N. Molesworth, *Curfew on Olympus* (Bombay, 1965), pp. 209–11.

5. B. Prasad (ed.), *The Retreat from Burma, 1941–42* (Calcutta, 1959), p. 456.

6. C. Shores, B. Cull and Yasuho Izawa, *Bloody Shambles*, i (London, 1992), p. 254.

7. J. Smyth, *Milestones* (London, 1979), p. 50; G. Corrigan, *Sepoys in the Trenches* (Staplehurst, Kent, 1999), p. 211.

8. Smyth, *Milestones*, p. 65.

9. Ibid., p. 149.

10. K.P. MacKenzie, *Operation Rangoon Jail* (London, 1954), p. 16.

11. J. Lunt, *The Retreat from Burma, 1941–1942* (London, 1986), p. 87.

12. Ibid., p. 97.

13. J. Smyth, *The Only Enemy* (London, 1959), pp. 169–70.

14. J.N. Mackay, *History of the 7th Duke of Edinburgh's Own Gurkha Rifles* (London, 1962), p. 168.

15. P. Carmichael, *Mountain Battery* (Bournemouth, 1983), p. 3.

16. Grant, *Burma*, p. 372.

17. Ibid., pp. 49, 372.

18. Draper, *Dawns Like Thunder*, p. 38.

19. Grant, *Burma*, pp. 51–52.

20. Collis, *Last and First in Burma*, p. 65.

21. Mackay, *7th Gurkha Rifles*, p. 161.

22. Grant, *Burma*, pp. 62–63.

23. Ibid., p. 64; Prasad, *The Retreat from Burma*, p. 96.

24. T. Carew, *The Longest Retreat* (London, 1969), p. 63; Grant, *Burma*, p. 64.

25. Grant, *Burma*, p. 65.

26. Carew, *The Longest Retreat*, p. 63; Draper, *Dawns Like Thunder*, p. 35; Mackay, *7th Gurkha Rifles*, p. 164; Grant, *Burma*, p. 66; S. Woodburn Kirby, *The War Against Japan*, ii (London, 1958), p. 29.

27. Mackay, *7th Gurkha Rifles*, p. 165.

28. Carew, *The Longest Retreat*, p. 71; Draper, *Dawns Like Thunder*, p. 36; Mackay, *7th Gurkha Rifles*, p. 166.

29. Grant, *Burma*, p. 64.

30. Prasad, *The Retreat from Burma*, p. 105.

Notes to Chapter 5: Battle of Moulmein

1. R. Lewin, *The Chief: Field-Marshal Lord Wavell* (London, 1980), p. 173.

2. B. Prasad (ed.), *The Retreat from Burma, 1941–42* (Calcutta, 1959), p. 253.

3. H. Probert, *The Forgotten Air Force: The RAF in the War Against Japan, 1941–1945* (London, 1995), p. 85.

4. C. Shores, B. Cull and Yasuho Izawa, *Bloody Shambles*, i (London, 1992), p. 264.

5. C.R. Bond and T. Anderson, *A Flying Tiger's Diary* (College Station, Texas, 1984), p. 88.

6. I.L. Grant and Kazuo Tamayama, *Burma 1942: The Japanese Invasion* (Chichester, 1999), p. 70.

7. Ibid., p. 72.

8. J. Lunt, *Imperial Sunset* (London, 1981), p. 364.

9. S. Woodburn Kirby, *The War Against Japan*, ii (London, 1958), p. 30; A. Draper, *Dawns Like Thunder* (London, 1987), p. 36; J. Smyth, *Milestones* (London, 1979), p. 173.

10. J. Lunt, *The Retreat from Burma, 1941–1942* (London, 1986), p. 108.

11. Ibid., p. 102.

12. C. Mackenzie, *Eastern Epic* (London, 1951), p. 422.

13. Lunt, *The Retreat from Burma*, p. 112.

14. Ibid., p. 113.

15. Kirby, *The War Against Japan*, ii, p. 32; W.E.H. Condon, *The Frontier Force Regiment* (Aldershot, 1962), p. 397; Prasad, *The Retreat from Burma*, p. 115.

16. Grant, *Burma*, p. 77.

17. Condon, *The Frontier Force Regiment*, p. 397.

18. M. Farndale, *History of the Royal Regiment of Artillery*, vi (London, 2000), p. 83.

19. Lunt, *Imperial Sunset*, p. 364.

20. Lunt, *The Retreat from Burma*, p. 116.

21. Ibid.

22. T. Carew, *The Longest Retreat* (London, 1969), p. 77; Grant, *Burma*, p. 78.

23. C. Chenevix Trench, *The Indian Army and the King's Enemies, 1900–1947* (London, 1988), p. 199; R.P. Pakenham-Walsh, *History of the Corps of Royal Engineers* (Chatham, 1958), p. 161.

24. Grant, *Burma*, p. 78.

Notes to Chapter 6: The Defence of the Salween River

1. Regimental Committee, *History of the 5th Royal Gurkha Rifles (Frontier Force)*, ii, 1929–1947 (Aldershot, 1956), pp. 150–52.

2. Ibid., p. 157; J.N. Mackay, *A History of the 4th Prince of Wales's Own Gurkha Rifles*, iii, 1938–1948 (London, 1952), pp. 71–73; C.N. Barclay, *The Regimental History of the 3rd Queen Alexandra's Own Gurkha Rifles*, ii, 1927–1947 (London, 1953), pp. 17–22.

3. C. Shores, B. Cull and Yasuho Izawa, *Bloody Shambles*, ii (London, 1992), p. 256.

4. I.L. Grant and Kazuo Tamayama, *Burma 1942: The Japanese Invasion* (Chichester, 1999), pp. 80–81.

5. M. Collis, *Last and First in Burma* (London, 1956), p. 84; G.N. Molesworth, *Curfew on Olympus* (Bombay, 1965), pp. 212–14.

6. B. Prasad (ed.), *The Retreat from Burma, 1941–42* (Calcutta, 1959), pp. 469, 471.

7. R. Callahan, *Burma, 1942–1945* (London, 1978), p. 34.

8. Prasad, *The Retreat from Burma*, p. 122.

9. J.M.A. Gwyer and J.R.M. Butler, *Grand Strategy*, iii (London, 1964), p. 466.

10. S. Woodburn Kirby, *The War Against Japan*, ii (London, 1958), p. 37; J. Lunt, *The Retreat from Burma, 1941–1942* (London, 1986), p. 98.

11. Collis, *Last and First in Burma*, p. 88.

12. Lunt, *The Retreat from Burma*, p. 128.

13. J. Smyth, *Milestones* (London, 1979), p. 199.

14. Grant, *Burma*, p. 82.

15. Ibid., p. 85.

16. Ibid., p. 86.

17. J.N. Mackay, *History of the 7th Duke of Edinburgh's Own Gurkha Rifles* (London, 1962), p. 170.

18. T. Carew, *The Longest Retreat* (London, 1969), p. 87.

19. J. Thompson, *The War in Burma, 1942–45* (London, 2002), p. 11; Grant, *Burma*, p. 88.

20. Grant, *Burma*, pp. 92–93.

21. Ibid., p. 89; Kazuo Tamayama and J. Nunneley (eds), *Tales by Japanese Soldiers of the Burma Campaign, 1942–1945* (London, 2001), p. 33.

22. Thompson, *The War in Burma*, p. 12.

23. Carew, *The Longest Retreat*, p. 90.

24. J. Latimer, *Burma: The Forgotten War* (London, 2004), p. 54.

25. C. Mackenzie, *Eastern Epic* (London, 1951), p. 430; Grant, *Burma*, p. 90.

26. A. Draper, *Dawns Like Thunder* (London, 1987), p. 66; Grant, *Burma*, p. 91.

27. Thompson, *The War in Burma*, p. 12; Rafiuddin Ahmed, *History of the Baloch Regiment, 1939–1956* (Uckfield, East Sussex, 2005), pp. 60–61, 251.

28. Tamayama and Nunneley, *Tales by Japanese Soldiers*, p. 247; Ahmed, *Baloch Regiment*, p. 61.

Notes to Chapter 7: The Battle of Bilin River

1. J. Latimer, *Burma: The Forgotten War* (London, 2004), p. 54.
2. I.L. Grant and Kazuo Tamayama, *Burma 1942: The Japanese Invasion* (Chichester, 1999), p. 94.
3. M. Farndale, *History of the Royal Regiment of Artillery*, vi (London, 2000), p. 85.
4. J. Smyth, *Milestones* (London, 1979), p. 177.
5. Grant, *Burma*, p. 96.
6. V. Schofield, *Wavell: Soldier and Statesman* (London, 2006), p. 249; T. Pocock, *Fighting General: The Public and Private Campaigns of General Sir Walter Walker* (London, 1973), p. 55.
7. Grant, *Burma*, p. 97.
8. C. Mackenzie, *Eastern Epic* (London, 1951), p. 432; A. Draper, *Dawns Like Thunder* (London, 1987), pp. 81–82.
9. J.N. Mackay, *History of the 7th Duke of Edinburgh's Own Gurkha Rifles* (London, 1962), p. 174; B. Prasad (ed.), *The Retreat from Burma, 1941–42* (Calcutta, 1959), p. 144.
10. Prasad, *The Retreat from Burma*, p. 144.
11. Grant, *Burma*, p. 99.
12. Prasad, *The Retreat from Burma*, p. 145.
13. Ibid.
14. Mackenzie, *Eastern Epic*, p. 433; Grant, *Burma*, p. 97.
15. Grant, *Burma*, pp. 97, 102.
16. Prasad, *The Retreat from Burma*, p. 147; Grant, *Burma*, p. 102.
17. S. Woodburn Kirby, *The War Against Japan*, ii (London, 1958), p. 61.
18. J.N. Mackay, *A History of the 4th Prince of Wales's Own Gurkha Rifles*, iii, 1938–1948 (London, 1952), p. 83.
19. Grant, *Burma*, p. 103; Prasad, *The Retreat from Burma*, p. 148.
20. Grant, *Burma*, p. 194.
21. Prasad, *The Retreat from Burma*, p. 154.
22. Grant, *Burma*, p. 98; Regimental Committee, *History of the 5th Royal Gurkha Rifles (Frontier Force)*, ii, 1929–1947 (Aldershot, 1956), p. 160.
23. Grant, *Burma*, p. 104.
24. Prasad, *The Retreat from Burma*, p. 457.
25. Grant, *Burma*, p. 100.
26. Kirby, *The War Against Japan*, ii, p. 64.
27. Ibid.
28. Prasad, *The Retreat from Burma*, p. 155; Mackenzie, *Eastern Epic*, p. 434; Grant, *Burma*, p. 106.
29. Kirby, *The War Against Japan*, ii, p. 64.
30. Grant, *Burma*, p. 106.
31. Cabinet Office, *Principal War Telegrams and Memoranda, 1940–1943, Far East* (London, 1976), p. 75.
32. Grant, *Burma*, p. 107.

33. Prasad, *The Retreat from Burma*, p. 156; Grant, *Burma*, p. 107; Kirby, *The War Against Japan*, ii, p. 65.
34. Kirby, *The War Against Japan*, ii, pp. 79–80.

Notes to Chapter 8: Confusion at Kyaikto

1. C.N. Barclay, *The History of the Duke of Wellington's Regiment, 1919–1952* (London, 1953), pp. 11–14.
2. G. Astor, *The Jungle War* (Hoboken, New Jersey, 2004), p. 60.
3. I.L. Grant and Kazuo Tamayama, *Burma 1942: The Japanese Invasion* (Chichester, 1999), p. 114.
4. J. Lunt, *The Retreat from Burma, 1941–1942* (London, 1986), p. 134.
5. B. Prasad (ed.), *The Retreat from Burma, 1941–42* (Calcutta, 1959), p. 161.
6. Grant, *Burma*, pp. 112–13, 120.
7. Ibid., p. 111.
8. C.N. Barclay, *The Regimental History of the 3rd Queen Alexandra's Own Gurkha Rifles*, ii, 1927–1947 (London, 1953), p. 26.
9. Grant, *Burma*, pp. 114–15.
10. A. Draper, *Dawns Like Thunder* (London, 1987), p. 92.
11. C. Mackenzie, *Eastern Epic* (London, 1951), p. 437; Grant, *Burma*, p. 116.
12. J.N. Mackay, *A History of the 4th Prince of Wales's Own Gurkha Rifles*, iii, 1938–1948 (London, 1952), p. 87; Prasad, *The Retreat from Burma*, p. 163; Grant, *Burma*, p. 116.
13. Prasad, *The Retreat from Burma*, p. 164; Mackenzie, *Eastern Epic*, p. 438.
14. Regimental Committee, *History of the 5th Royal Gurkha Rifles (Frontier Force)*, ii, 1929–1947 (Aldershot, 1956), p. 163.
15. Barclay, *3rd Gurkha Rifles*, ii, p. 26.
16. Draper, *Dawns Like Thunder*, p. 93.
17. J.N. Mackay, *History of the 7th Duke of Edinburgh's Own Gurkha Rifles* (London, 1962), p. 176.
18. J. Latimer, *Burma: The Forgotten War* (London, 2004), p. 59.
19. G. Astor, *The Jungle War* (Hoboken, New Jersey, 2004), p. 61; K.P. MacKenzie, *Operation Rangoon Jail* (London, 1954), p. 26.
20. Grant, *Burma*, p. 117.
21. C. Shores, B. Cull and Yasuho Izawa, *Bloody Shambles*, ii (London, 1993), p. 272.
22. Prasad, *The Retreat from Burma*, pp. 164–65.
23. W.E.H. Condon, *The Frontier Force Regiment* (Aldershot, 1962), p. 339; Grant, *Burma*, p. 119.
24. Grant, *Burma*, pp. 113, 120.
25. S. Woodburn Kirby, *The War Against Japan*, ii (London, 1958), p. 81.
26. Cabinet Office, *Principal War Telegrams and Memoranda, 1940–1943, Far East* (London, 1976), pp. 75, 81; Prasad, *The Retreat from Burma*, p. 461.
27. Kirby, *The War Against Japan*, ii, p. 81.
28. Ibid., p. 82.

29. Lunt, *The Retreat from Burma*, p. 152; L. Allen, *The Longest Retreat, 1941–1945* (London, 1984), p. 51.

30. R. Callahan, *Burma, 1942–1945* (London, 1978), p. 34.

31. Prasad, *The Retreat from Burma*, p. 162; Grant, *Burma*, p. 120.

Notes to Chapter 9: The Sittang Bridge

1. J. Smyth, *Leadership in War, 1939–1945* (London, 1974), p. 169.

2. I.L. Grant and Kazuo Tamayama, *Burma 1942: The Japanese Invasion* (Chichester, 1999), p. 113.

3. Regimental Committee, *History of the 5th Royal Gurkha Rifles (Frontier Force)*, ii, 1929–1947 (Aldershot, 1956), p. 163; C. Mackenzie, *Eastern Epic* (London, 1951), p. 439.

4. Grant, *Burma*, pp. 120–21; B. Prasad (ed.), *The Retreat from Burma, 1941–42* (Calcutta, 1959), p. 165; S. Woodburn Kirby, *The War Against Japan*, ii (London, 1958), p. 68.

5. J. Thompson, *The War in Burma, 1942–45* (London, 2002), p. 18.

6. Mackenzie, *Eastern Epic*, p. 439.

7. Prasad, *The Retreat from Burma*, p. 166.

8. Smyth, *Leadership in War*, p. 170.

9. Prasad, *The Retreat from Burma*, p. 169.

10. Grant, *Burma*, p. 122.

11. Kirby, *The War Against Japan*, ii, p. 68.

12. K.P. MacKenzie, *Operation Rangoon Jail* (London, 1954), p. 30; Grant, *Burma*, p. 123.

13. A. Draper, *Dawns Like Thunder* (London, 1987), pp. 97, 100.

14. W.E.H. Condon, *The Frontier Force Regiment* (Aldershot, 1962), p. 399; Grant, *Burma*, p. 123.

15. R.P. Pakenham-Walsh, *History of the Corps of Royal Engineers* (Chatham, 1958), p. 162; Prasad, *The Retreat from Burma*, p. 167; Grant, *Burma*, p. 125; C.H.T. MacFetridge and J.P. Warren (eds), *Tales of the Mountain Gunners* (Edinburgh, 1973), pp. 133–34.

16. Grant, *Burma*, p. 128.

17. Regimental Committee, *5th Royal Gurkha Rifles*, ii, p. 164; C.N. Barclay, *The Regimental History of the 3rd Queen Alexandra's Own Gurkha Rifles*, ii, 1927–1947 (London, 1953), pp. 28–29.

18. MacKenzie, *Operation Rangoon Jail*, p. 32.

19. Thompson, *The War in Burma*, p. 18.

20. Grant, *Burma*, p. 130; Barclay, *3rd Gurkha Rifles*, ii, pp. 29–30.

21. Grant, *Burma*, p. 141.

22. Prasad, *The Retreat from Burma*, p. 170; Grant, *Burma*, p. 124.

23. Draper, *Dawns Like Thunder*, p. 103.

24. Barclay, *3rd Gurkha Rifles*, ii, p. 30.

25. J.N. Mackay, *History of 7th Duke of Edinburgh's Own Gurkha Rifles* (London, 1962), p. 178; Grant, *Burma*, pp. 127, 141.

26. G. Astor, *The Jungle War* (Hoboken, New Jersey, 2004), p. 61.
27. C. Shores, B. Cull and Yasuho Izawa, *Bloody Shambles*, ii (London, 1993), p. 272.
28. Grant, *Burma*, p. 128.
29. Mackenzie, *Eastern Epic*, p. 441.
30. Prasad, *The Retreat from Burma*, p. 174; Grant, *Burma*, p. 131.
31. Prasad, *The Retreat from Burma*, p. 462.
32. Draper, *Dawns Like Thunder*, p. 107.

Notes to Chapter 10: The Demolition of the Sittang Bridge

1. I.L. Grant and Kazuo Tamayama, *Burma 1942: The Japanese Invasion* (Chichester, 1999), p. 132.
2. W.E.H. Condon, *The Frontier Force Regiment* (Aldershot, 1962), p. 400.
3. M. Farndale, *History of the Royal Regiment of Artillery*, vi (London, 2000), p. 88.
4. L. Allen, *Burma: The Longest War, 1941–1945* (London, 1984), pp. 40–41.
5. Grant, *Burma*, p. 133; S. Woodburn Kirby, *The War Against Japan*, ii (London, 1958), p. 71.
6. J. Smyth, *Leadership in War, 1939–1945* (London, 1974), p. 172; C. Mackenzie, *Eastern Epic* (London, 1951), p. 446.
7. C.N. Barclay, *The History of the Duke of Wellington's Regiment, 1919–1952* (London, 1953), p. 120; Grant, *Burma*, p. 133.
8. Mackenzie, *Eastern Epic*, p. 446.
9. A. Draper, *Dawns Like Thunder* (London, 1987), p. 111; Grant, *Burma*, p. 133.
10. Draper, *Dawns Like Thunder*, pp. 111, 114; Grant, *Burma*, p. 133.
11. Grant, *Burma*, p. 134; B. Prasad (ed.), *The Retreat from Burma, 1941–1942* (Calcutta, 1959), p. 175.
12. Draper, *Dawns Like Thunder*, p. 112.
13. C. Chenevix Trench, *The Indian Army and the King's Enemies, 1900–1947* (London, 1988), p. 206.
14. Grant, *Burma*, pp. 129, 135.
15. C.N. Barclay, *The Regimental History of the 3rd Queen Alexandra's Own Gurkha Rifles*, ii, 1927–1947 (London, 1953), p. 33.
16. Ibid., p. 34; Grant, *Burma*, p. 136; Kirby, *The War Against Japan*, ii, p. 72.
17. Regimental Committee, *History of the 5th Royal Gurkha Rifles (Frontier Force)*, ii, 1929–1947 (Aldershot, 1956), p. 169.
18. Ibid., p. 170.
19. Kirby, *The War Against Japan*, ii, p. 72.
20. Grant, *Burma*, p. 137.
21. G. Astor, *The Jungle War* (Hoboken, New Jersey, 2004), p. 61.
22. Barclay, *Duke of Wellington's Regiment*, pp. 116–19; Kirby, *The War Against Japan*, ii, p. 73; T. Carew, *The Longest Retreat* (London, 1969), p. 139.
23. J. Smyth, *The Only Enemy* (London, 1959), p. 204.

24. J. Lunt, *The Retreat from Burma, 1941–1942* (London, 1986), p. 155.
25. Barclay, *3rd Gurkha Rifles*, ii, p. 36.
26. Kirby, *The War Against Japan*, ii, pp. 73, 445; Prasad, *The Retreat from Burma*, p. 406.
27. Carew, *The Longest Retreat*, p. 145; Regimental Committee, *5th Royal Gurkha Rifles*, ii, pp. 172, 177.
28. Lunt, *The Retreat from Burma*, p. 163.
29. J.N. Mackay, *A History of the 4th Prince of Wales's Own Gurkha Rifles*, iii, 1938–1948 (London, 1952), p. 123; J.N. Mackay, *History of the 7th Duke of Edinburgh's Own Gurkha Rifles* (London, 1962), p. 180; Grant, *Burma*, p. 139.
30. Grant, *Burma*, p. 139.
31. K.P. MacKenzie, *Operation Rangoon Jail* (London, 1954), pp. 39–40.
32. Cabinet Office, *Principal War Telegrams and Memoranda, 1940–1943, Far East* (London, 1976), p. 99.
33. Grant, *Burma*, p. 142.
34. Lunt, *The Retreat from Burma*, p. 136.
35. Allen, *Burma: The Longest War*, p. 650; Grant, *Burma*, p. 141.
36. J. Thompson, *The War in Burma, 1942–45* (London, 2002), p. 22.
37. J. Latimer, *Burma: The Forgotten War* (London, 2004), p. 63.
38. Thompson, *The War in Burma*, p. 22.
39. R. Lewin, *The Chief: Field-Marshal Lord Wavell* (London, 1980), p. 177.
40. Draper, *Dawns Like Thunder*, p. 126.
41. Ibid.
42. Ibid., p. 74.
43. Grant, *Burma*, p. 147.

Notes to Chapter 11: Rangoon in the Front Line

1. A. Warren, *Singapore, 1942: Britain's Greatest Defeat* (London, 2002), pp. 180–81.
2. D. Horner, *High Command* (Sydney, 1982), p. 157.
3. Ibid.
4. G. Hermon Gill, *Royal Australian Navy, 1939–1942* (Canberra, 1968), p. 594.
5. W.S. Churchill, *The Second World War*, iv (London, 1951), pp. 138–39.
6. L. Wigmore, *The Japanese Thrust* (Canberra, 1957), p. 464.
7. Churchill, *The Second World War*, iv, p. 142.
8. Gill, *Royal Australian Navy, 1939–1942*, p. 601.
9. Horner, *High Command*, p. 158; Churchill, *The Second World War*, iv, p. 145; Gill, *Royal Australian Navy, 1939–1942*, p. 601.
10. Churchill, *The Second World War*, iv, p. 137.
11. A.J. Marder, M. Jacobsen, J. Horsfield, *Old Friends, New Enemies: The Royal Navy and the Imperial Japanese Navy*, ii (Oxford, 1990), p. 52.
12. Gill, *Royal Australian Navy, 1939–1942*, p. 622.
13. Marder, *Old Friends, New Enemies*, ii, p. 78.
14. A. Draper, *Dawns Like Thunder* (London, 1987), p. 132.

15. B. Perrett, *Tank Tracks to Rangoon* (London, 1978), p. 29.
16. G. Astor, *The Jungle War* (Hoboken, New Jersey, 2004), pp. 63–64.
17. M. Collis, *Last and First in Burma* (London, 1956), p. 92.
18. Perrett, *Tank Tracks to Rangoon*, p. 24.
19. J. Klinkowitz, *With the Tigers Over China, 1941–1942* (Lexington, Kentucky, 1999), p. 81.
20. Collis, *Last and First in Burma*, p. 93.
21. Perrett, *Tank Tracks to Rangoon*, p. 30.
22. Collis, *Last and First in Burma*, p. 98.
23. S. Woodburn Kirby, *The War Against Japan*, ii (London, 1958), p. 84.
24. Collis, *Last and First in Burma*, p. 99.
25. B. Prasad (ed.), *The Retreat from Burma, 1941–42* (Calcutta, 1959), p. 204.
26. I.L. Grant and Kazuo Tamayama, *Burma 1942: The Japanese Invasion* (Chichester, 1999), p. 149.
27. Ibid.
28. Collis, *Last and First in Burma*, p. 102.
29. R. Callahan, *Burma, 1942–1945* (London, 1978), p. 35; Grant, *Burma*, p. 149.
30. Collis, *Last and First in Burma*, p. 105.

Notes to Chapter 12: Wavell Takes Charge

1. B. Prasad (ed.), *The Retreat from Burma, 1941–42* (Calcutta, 1959), p. 461.
2. S. Woodburn Kirby, *The War Against Japan*, ii (London, 1958), p. 86.
3. J. Lunt, *The Retreat from Burma, 1941–1942* (London, 1986), p. 155.
4. A. Draper, *Dawns Like Thunder* (London, 1987), p. 128; I.L. Grant and Kazuo Tamayama, *Burma 1942: The Japanese Invasion* (Chichester, 1999), p. 150.
5. Draper, *Dawns Like Thunder*, p. 128.
6. J. Smyth, *The Only Enemy* (London, 1959), p. 171.
7. Draper, *Dawns Like Thunder*, p. 130.
8. Grant, *Burma*, p. 145.
9. J. North (ed.), *The Alexander Memoirs, 1940–1945* (New York, 1962), p. 91.
10. R. Callahan, *Burma, 1942–1945* (London, 1978), p. 36.
11. Grant, *Burma*, p. 152.
12. Kirby, *The War Against Japan*, ii, p. 88; Grant, *Burma*, p. 155.
13. Grant, *Burma*, p. 160; C.N. Barclay, *The History of the Cameronians (Scottish Rifles)*, iii, 1933–1946 (London, 1947), p. 69.
14. Grant, *Burma*, pp. 158–59.
15. J. Latimer, *Burma: The Forgotten War* (London, 2004), p. 68; Grant, *Burma*, pp. 159–60.
16. Regimental Committee, *History of the 5th Royal Gurkha Rifles (Frontier Force)*, ii, 1929–1947 (Aldershot, 1956), p. 176; Grant, *Burma*, pp. 162–64.
17. B. Perrett, *Tank Tracks to Rangoon* (London, 1978), pp. 39–40.
18. Lunt, *The Retreat from Burma*, p. 170.
19. Draper, *Dawns Like Thunder*, p. 160.

20. J. N. Mackay, *A History of the 4th Prince of Wales's Own Gurkha Rifles*, iii, 1938–1948 (London, 1952), p. 123; Grant, *Burma*, p. 165.
21. L. Allen, *Burma: The Longest War, 1941–1945* (London, 1984), p. 45.
22. B.N. Majumdar, *Administration in the Burma Campaign* (Delhi, 1952), p. 14.
23. M. Collis, *Last and First in Burma* (London, 1956), p. 116.
24. S.W. Roskill, *The War at Sea, 1939–1945*, ii (London, 1956), p. 20.
25. T. Carew, *The Longest Retreat* (London, 1969), pp. 156–57.
26. Grant, *Burma*, pp. 177–78.
27. Ibid., p. 176.
28. Carew, *The Longest Retreat*, pp. 159–60; C.N. Barclay, *The History of the Duke of Wellington's Regiment, 1919–1952* (London, 1953), p. 123; D.S. Daniell, *Cap of Honour: The Story of the Gloucestershire Regiment (The 28th/61st Foot), 1694–1950* (London, 1951), pp. 271–73.
29. Daniell, *Cap of Honour*, pp. 272–74; Kirby, *The War Against Japan*, ii, p. 97.
30. Grant, *Burma*, p. 181.
31. Ibid.
32. G. Astor, *The Jungle War* (Hoboken, New Jersey, 2004), p. 69.
33. Grant, *Burma*, pp. 181–82.
34. Lunt, *The Retreat from Burma*, p. 167.
35. Cabinet Office, *Principal War Telegrams and Memoranda, 1940–1943, India* (London, 1976), p. 32.

Notes to Chapter 13: Retreat from Rangoon

1. I.L. Grant and Kazuo Tamayama, *Burma 1942: The Japanese Invasion* (Chichester, 1999), p. 372; B. Prasad (ed.), *The Retreat from Burma, 1941–1942* (Calcutta, 1959), p. 58.
2. J. Lunt, *The Retreat from Burma, 1941–1942* (London, 1986), p. 173.
3. R. Lewin, *Slim: The Standardbearer* (London, 1977), p. 82.
4. W. Slim, *Defeat into Victory* (London, 1956), pp. 31–34.
5. G. Evans, *Slim as Military Commander* (London, 1969), p. 67.
6. Slim, *Defeat into Victory*, pp. 35–36.
7. T. Pocock, *Fighting General: The Public and Private Campaigns of General Sir Walter Walker* (London, 1973), p. 57.
8. S. Woodburn Kirby, *The War Against Japan*, ii (London, 1958), p. 213.
9. Slim, *Defeat into Victory*, p. 23.
10. J. Klinkowitz, *With the Tigers Over China, 1941–1942* (Lexington, Kentucky, 1999), p. 107.
11. C. Shores, B. Cull, Yasuho Izawa, *Bloody Shambles*, ii (London, 1993), pp. 347–49.
12. Ibid., pp. 350–52.
13. R. Lewin, *The Chief: Field-Marshal Lord Wavell* (London, 1980), p. 85.
14. M. Collis, *Last and First in Burma* (London, 1956), p. 118.
15. B.W. Tuchman, *Stilwell and the American Experience in China, 1911–45* (New York, 1970), p. 267.

16. Ibid., p. 270.

17. C. Mackenzie, *Eastern Epic* (London, 1951), p. 461.

18. E.L. Dreyer, *China at War, 1901–1949* (London, 1995), p. 269; L. Allen, *Burma: The Longest War, 1941–1945* (London, 1984), pp. 59–60.

19. Collis, *Last and First in Burma*, p. 133.

20. Grant, *Burma*, pp. 191–92; Collis, *Last and First in Burma*, pp. 142–43.

21. C.F. Romanus and R. Sutherland, *Stilwell's Mission to China* (Washington, 1953), p. 97; Grant, *Burma*, pp. 203–04.

22. J.N. Mackay, *History of the 7th Duke of Edinburgh's Own Gurkha Rifles* (London, 1962), p. 185; Regimental Committee, *History of the 5th Royal Gurkha Rifles (Frontier Force)*, ii, 1929–1947 (Aldershot, 1956), pp. 176–77.

23. J. Thompson, *The War in Burma, 1942–45* (London, 2002), p. 29; Grant, *Burma*, pp. 205–6, 210.

24. Grant, *Burma*, p. 214.

25. G. Astor, *The Jungle War* (Hoboken, New Jersey, 2004), pp. 77–78.

26. Grant, *Burma*, p. 214; W.E.H. Condon, *The Frontier Force Regiment* (Aldershot, 1962), p. 403.

27. Grant, *Burma*, p. 218; J. Thompson, *Royal Marines* (London, 2000), p. 288.

28. Lunt, *The Retreat from Burma*, p. 193; Prasad, *The Retreat from Burma*, p. 250; Grant, *Burma*, p. 216.

29. B. Perrett, *Tank Tracks to Rangoon* (London, 1978), p. 51.

30. Grant, *Burma*, p. 229; Lunt, *The Retreat from Burma*, p. 194.

31. Grant, *Burma*, pp. 226–27.

Notes to Chapter 14: The Imperial Japanese Navy and the Indian Ocean

1. A.J. Marder, M. Jacobsen and J. Horsfield, *Old Friends, New Enemies: The Royal Navy and the Imperial Japanese Navy*, ii (Oxford, 1990), p. 96.

2. A. Jackson, *The British Empire and the Second World War* (London, 2006), p. 274.

3. L. Wigmore, *The Japanese Thrust* (Canberra, 1957), pp. 459–60; D. Horner, *High Command* (Sydney, 1982), p. 158.

4. D. McCarthy, *South-West Pacific Area – First Year* (Canberra, 1959), p. 118.

5. B. Prasad, *Defence of India: Policy and Plans* (New Delhi, 1963), p. 153; B. Prasad (ed.), *The Retreat from Burma, 1941–1942* (Calcutta, 1959), p. 464.

6. Prasad, *The Retreat from Burma*, p. 464.

7. H. Williams, *Ceylon: Pearl of the East* (London, 1950), p. 319.

8. D. Macintyre, *Fighting Admiral: The Life of Admiral of the Fleet Sir James Somerville* (London, 1961), pp. 16, 20, 44–45, 52.

9. K. Dimbleby, *Turns of Fate: The Drama of HMS Cornwall* (London, 1984), p. 146.

10. Marder, *Old Friends, New Enemies*, ii, pp. 102, 125.

11. S.W. Roskill, *The War at Sea, 1939–1945*, ii (London, 1956), pp. 22–23; Marder, *Old Friends, New Enemies*, ii, p. 109.

12. Marder, *Old Friends, New Enemies*, ii, p. 110.

13. Ibid., p. 90.

14. Ibid., p. 87.

15. R. Hough, *The Longest Battle: The War at Sea, 1939–45* (London, 1987), p. 150.

16. Marder, *Old Friends, New Enemies*, ii, p. 94.

17. P.C. Smith, *The Great Ships Pass* (London, 1977), p. 308.

18. Marder, *Old Friends, New Enemies*, ii, p. 103.

19. Ibid., p. 113; C. Shores, B. Cull, Yasuho Izawa, *Bloody Shambles*, ii (London, 1993), p. 386.

20. Marder, *Old Friends, New Enemies*, ii, p. 105.

21. M. Smith, *The Emperor's Code: The Breaking of Japan's Secret Ciphers* (New York, 2000), pp. 128–29.

22. Marder, *Old Friends, New Enemies*, ii, p. 117.

23. Ibid., p. 119.

24. Dimbleby, *Turns of Fate*, p. 150.

25. Macintyre, *Fighting Admiral*, p. 186.

26. Marder, *Old Friends, New Enemies*, ii, p. 122.

27. Jackson, *The British Empire and the Second World War*, p. 295.

28. Marder, *Old Friends, New Enemies*, ii, p. 123.

29. Shores, *Bloody Shambles*, ii, p. 394.

30. M. Simpson (ed.), *The Somerville Papers* (Aldershot, 1995), p. 399.

31. Jackson, *The British Empire and the Second World War*, p. 296.

Notes to Chapter 15: Admiral Nagumo's Raid on Ceylon

1. D. Macintyre, *Fighting Admiral: The Life of Admiral of the Fleet Sir James Somerville* (London, 1961), p. 189.

2. C. Shores, B. Cull, Yasuho Izawa, *Bloody Shambles*, ii (London, 1993), p. 396.

3. M. Smith, *The Emperor's Code: The Breaking of Japan's Secret Ciphers* (New York, 2000), p. 130; A. Jackson, *The British Empire and the Second World War* (London, 2006), p. 296.

4. R. Hough, *The Longest Battle: The War at Sea, 1939–45* (London, 1987), p. 152.

5. Jackson, *The British Empire and the Second World War*, p. 299.

6. C. Jeffries, 'O.E.G.': A Biography of Sir Oliver Ernest Gonetilleke* (London, 1969), p. 54.

7. S. Woodburn Kirby, *The War Against Japan*, ii (London, 1958), p. 119; S.W. Roskill, *The War at Sea, 1939–1945*, ii (London, 1956), p. 26; Shores, *Bloody Shambles*, ii, p. 404.

8. A.J. Marder, M. Jacobsen, J. Horsfield, *Old Friends, New Enemies: The Royal Navy and the Imperial Japanese Navy*, ii (Oxford, 1990), p. 127.

9. A. Agar, *Footprints in the Sea* (London, 1959), p. 17.

10. K. Dimbleby, *Turns of Fate: The Drama of HMS Cornwall* (London, 1984), p. 20.

11. Ibid., pp. 27, 79–81.

12. Marder, *Old Friends, New Enemies*, ii, p. 128.

13. Ibid., p. 129.

14. Dimbleby, *Turns of Fate*, p. 161.
15. Marder, *Old Friends, New Enemies*, ii, p. 129.
16. Ibid., p. 130.
17. Agar, *Footprints in the Sea*, p. 307.
18. Dimbleby, *Turns of Fate*, p. 165.
19. Ibid.
20. Ibid.
21. Marder, *Old Friends, New Enemies*, ii, p. 131.
22. Ibid., p. 132.
23. Ibid., p. 133.
24. H. Williams, *Ceylon: Pearl of the East* (London, 1950), pp. 338–41.
25. Marder, *Old Friends, New Enemies*, ii, p. 134.
26. Shores, *Bloody Shambles*, ii, pp. 420–22; Marder, *Old Friends, New Enemies*, ii, p. 134.
27. G. Hermon Gill, *Royal Australian Navy, 1942–1945* (Canberra, 1968), p. 20.
28. Kirby, *The War Against Japan*, ii, p. 124; Shores, *Bloody Shambles*, ii, pp. 424–25.
29. Gill, *Royal Australian Navy, 1942–1945*, p. 21.
30. Ibid., p. 21.
31. Shores, *Bloody Shambles*, ii, pp. 427–28.
32. Marder, *Old Friends, New Enemies*, ii, p. 143.
33. Shores, *Bloody Shambles*, ii, p. 429.
34. Marder, *Old Friends, New Enemies*, ii, p. 145.
35. G.N. Molesworth, *Curfew on Olympus* (Bombay, 1965), p. 217.
36. Roskill, *The War at Sea*, ii, p. 28.
37. Marder, *Old Friends, New Enemies*, ii, p. 138.
38. M. Simpson (ed.), *The Somerville Papers* (Aldershot, 1995), p. 407.
39. Ibid., p. 408.
40. Macintyre, *Fighting Admiral*, p. 198.

Notes to Chapter 16: The Oilfields of Yenangyaung

1. C. Shores, B. Cull, Yasuho Izawa, *Bloody Shambles*, ii (London, 1993), p. 361.
2. J. Beldon, *Retreat with Stilwell* (New York, 1943), pp. 64–65.
3. M. Collis, *Last and First in Burma* (London, 1956), p. 143.
4. I.L. Grant and Kazuo Tamayama, *Burma 1942: The Japanese Invasion* (Chichester, 1999), p. 232.
5. W. Slim, *Defeat into Victory* (London, 1956), p. 61.
6. Regimental Committee, *History of the 5th Royal Gurkha Rifles (Frontier Force)*, ii, 1929–1947 (Aldershot, 1956), p. 181; Grant, *Burma*, pp. 235–37.
7. J.N. Mackay, *History of the 7th Duke of Edinburgh's Own Gurkha Rifles* (London, 1962), p. 188.
8. Grant, *Burma*, p. 239.
9. Ibid., pp. 243–44.

10. D.S. Daniell, *Cap of Honour: The Story of the Gloucestershire Regiment (The 28th/61st Foot), 1694–1950* (London, 1951), p. 281.

11. Beldon, *Retreat with Stilwell*, p. 97.

12. Ibid., p. 104.

13. Ibid., p. 105.

14. Grant, *Burma*, p. 252.

15. L. Allen, *Burma: The Longest War, 1941–1945* (London, 1984), p. 66.

16. Ibid., p. 67.

17. Grant, *Burma*, p. 225.

18. Slim, *Defeat into Victory*, p. 75.

19. F. Fox, *The Royal Inniskilling Fusiliers in the Second World War* (Aldershot, 1951), pp. 41–42.

20. Grant, *Burma*, p. 256.

21. Allen, *Burma: The Longest War*, p. 69.

22. J. Lunt, *The Retreat from Burma, 1941–1942* (London, 1986), p. 216.

23. Grant, *Burma*, p. 259; R.E.S. and D.A. Tanner, *Burma 1942: Memories of a Retreat* (Stroud, Gloucestershire, 2009), p. 75.

24. Lunt, *The Retreat from Burma*, p. 214; Grant, *Burma*, p. 250.

25. Grant, *Burma*, pp. 259–60.

26. Slim, *Defeat into Victory*, p. 62.

27. S. Woodburn Kirby, *The War Against Japan*, ii (London, 1958), p. 475.

28. Grant, *Burma*, p. 262.

29. Ibid., p. 265.

30. Allen, *Burma: The Longest War*, p. 70; R. Callahan, *Burma, 1942–1945* (London, 1978), p. 37.

31. Collis, *Last and First in Burma*, p. 156.

32. Allen, *Burma: The Longest War*, p. 52.

33. R. Lyman, *Slim: Master of War* (London, 2004), p. 51.

34. Mackay, *7th Gurkha Rifles*, p. 190.

35. Regimental Committee, *5th Royal Gurkha Rifles*, ii, p. 186.

36. Mackay, *7th Gurkha Rifles*, p. 191; Grant, *Burma*, p. 274.

37. Mackay, *7th Gurkha Rifles*, p. 192; Grant, *Burma*, p. 275; Regimental Committee, *5th Royal Gurkha Rifles*, ii, p. 188.

38. Grant, *Burma*, p. 275.

39. Ibid., p. 278.

40. Allen, *Burma: The Longest War*, p. 70; V. Schofield, *Wavell: Soldier and Statesman* (London, 2006), pp. 262–63.

41. Grant, *Burma*, pp. 284–85.

Notes to Chapter 17: The Retreat to India

1. Cabinet Office, *Principal War Telegrams and Memoranda, 1940–1943, India* (London, 1976), p. 165.

2. H. Tinker, 'A Forgotten Long March: The Indian Exodus from Burma, 1942',

Journal of Southeast Asian Studies, VI, 1975, pp. 1–15; S. Woodburn Kirby, *The War Against Japan*, ii (London, 1958), p. 192.

3. Kirby, *The War Against Japan*, ii, p. 473.
4. I.L. Grant and Kazuo Tamayama, *Burma 1942: The Japanese Invasion* (Chichester, 1999), p. 289.
5. Ibid., pp. 291–92.
6. J. Lunt, *The Retreat from Burma, 1941–1942* (London, 1986), pp. 246–47.
7. Grant, *Burma*, p. 293.
8. Ibid., p. 294.
9. Kirby, *The War Against Japan*, ii, p. 473.
10. Regimental Committee, *History of the 5th Royal Gurkha Rifles (Frontier Force)*, ii, 1929–1947 (Aldershot, 1956), p. 193.
11. Grant, *Burma*, pp. 299, 302–3.
12. Ibid., p. 302.
13. W. Slim, *Defeat into Victory* (London, 1956), p. 107.
14. Grant, *Burma*, p. 307.
15. Slim, *Defeat into Victory*, p. 110.
16. C. Mackenzie, *Eastern Epic* (London, 1951), p. 498.
17. Grant, *Burma*, p. 313.
18. Ibid., p. 315; Regimental Committee, *5th Royal Gurkha Rifles*, ii, p. 198.
19. R. Lewin, *The Chief: Field-Marshal Lord Wavell* (London, 1980), p. 104.
20. A.J.F. Doulton, *The Fighting Cock: History of the 23rd Indian Division, 1942–1947* (Aldershot, 1951), p. 12; Grant, *Burma*, pp. 319–20.
21. Doulton, *The Fighting Cock*, p. 10.
22. T. Carew, *The Longest Retreat* (London, 1969), p. 263.
23. Doulton, *The Fighting Cock*, p. 20.
24. Tinker, 'A Forgotten Long March', p. 2; Kirby, *The War Against Japan*, ii, p. 192.
25. Lunt, *The Retreat from Burma*, p. 271; Tinker, 'A Forgotten Long March', p. 2.
26. F. Fox, *The Royal Inniskilling Fusiliers in the Second World War* (Aldershot, 1951), p. 42; J. Latimer, *Burma: The Forgotten War* (London, 2004), p. 111.
27. Grant, *Burma*, p. 344.
28. W.E.H. Condon, *The Frontier Force Regiment* (Aldershot, 1962), p. 406; Regimental Committee, *5th Royal Gurkha Rifles*, ii, p. 185.
29. Grant, *Burma*, pp. 278–79; B. Prasad (ed.), *The Retreat from Burma, 1941–42* (Calcutta, 1959), pp. 394–95.
30. Grant, *Burma*, p. 379.
31. R.E.S. and D.A. Tanner, *Burma 1942: Memories of a Retreat* (Stroud, Gloucestershire, 2009), p. 73; D.S. Daniell, *Cap of Honour: The Story of the Gloucestershire Regiment (The 28th/61st Foot), 1694–1950* (London, 1951), p. 286.
32. J.N. Mackay, *A History of the 4th Prince of Wales's Own Gurkha Rifles*, iii, 1938–1948 (London, 1952), p. 123; Regimental Committee, *5th Royal Gurkha Rifles*, ii, p. 201.
33. Grant, *Burma*, p. 380.
34. Kirby, *The War Against Japan*, ii, p. 210.

35. Maochun Yu, *The Dragon's War: Allied Operations and the Fate of China, 1937–1947* (Annapolis, Maryland, 2006), p. 45.

Notes to Chapter 18: The Consequences of Defeat

1. J. Lunt, *The Retreat from Burma, 1941–1942* (London, 1986), p. xviii.
2. Ibid., p. xix.
3. R.E.S. and D.A. Tanner, *Burma 1942: Memories of a Retreat* (Stroud, Gloucestershire, 2009), p. 77.
4. Ibid., p. 103; J. Latimer, *Burma: The Forgotten War* (London, 2004), p. 100; Lunt, *The Retreat from Burma*, p. 174.
5. A.J.F. Doulton, *The Fighting Cock: History of the 23rd Indian Division, 1942–1947* (Aldershot, 1951), pp. 28, 36–37; R. Callahan, *Burma, 1942–1945* (London, 1978), p. 48.
6. I.L. Grant and Kazuo Tamayama, *Burma 1942: The Japanese Invasion* (Chichester, 1999), p. 325; S. Woodburn Kirby, *The War Against Japan*, ii (London, 1958), p. 308.
7. P. Mason, *A Matter of Honour* (London, 1974), p. 494.
8. Callahan, *Burma, 1942–1945*, p. 49.
9. H.L. Thompson, *New Zealanders with the Royal Air Force*, iii (Wellington, 1959), p. 289.
10. Maochun Yu, *The Dragon's War: Allied Operations and the Fate of China, 1937–1947* (Annapolis, Maryland, 2006), p. 45.
11. Ibid., p. 41.
12. W.F. Craven and J.L. Cate, *The Army Air Forces in World War II*, vii (Chicago, 1958), pp. 115, 117, 123.
13. G.N. Molesworth, *Curfew on Olympus* (Bombay, 1965), p. 222.
14. Ibid., p. 234; Kirby, *The War Against Japan*, ii, pp. 245–47.
15. A. Warren, *Waziristan, The Faqir of Ipi and the Indian Army: The North-West Frontier Revolt of 1936–37* (Karachi, 2000), p. 254.
16. A. Jackson, *The British Empire and the Second World War* (London, 2006), p. 323.
17. Government of India, *Famine Inquiry Commission: Report on Bengal* (New Delhi, 1945), pp. 1–2.
18. Sugata Bose, 'Starvation Amidst Plenty: The Making of Famine in Bengal, Honan and Tonkin, 1942–45', *Modern Asian Studies*, 1990, p. 716; Cheng Siok-Hwa, *The Rice Industry of Burma, 1852–1940* (Kuala Lumpur, 1968), pp. 201, 206, 217.
19. Government of India, *Famine Inquiry Commission: Report on Bengal*, pp. 13, 28.
20. Grant, *Burma*, p. 354.
21. J. Smyth, *Milestones* (London, 1979), p. 13.
22. Ibid., p. 191.
23. W. Slim, *Defeat into Victory* (London, 1956), p. 26.
24. Kirby, *The War Against Japan*, ii, p. 102.
25. Grant, *Burma*, p. 347.

26. R. Lewin, *The Chief: Field-Marshal Lord Wavell* (London, 1980), p. 96.

27. Latimer, *Burma: The Forgotten War*, p. 66.

28. A. Draper, *Dawns Like Thunder* (London, 1987), p. 173; C.N. Barclay, *On Their Shoulders* (London, 1964), p. 144.

29. D. Ford, *Flying Tiger: Claire Chennault and His American Volunteers, 1941–1942* (Washington, 2007), p. 218.

30. Slim, *Defeat into Victory*, p. 123.

31. Grant, *Burma*, p. 323.

32. Lunt, *The Retreat from Burma*, p. 69.

33. Grant, *Burma*, p. 329.

34. Lunt, *The Retreat from Burma*, p. 283.

35. Grant, *Burma*, pp. 327, 329, 331.

36. Ibid., pp. 332–33.

37. Ibid., p. 328.

38. Ibid., p. 337.

39. M. Collis, *Last and First in Burma* (London, 1956), p. 185; Latimer, *Burma: The Forgotten War*, p. 123.

40. L. Allen, *Burma: The Longest War, 1941–1945* (London, 1984), pp. 560–62.

41. Grant, *Burma*, p. xiv.

Bibliography

Ahmed, Rafiuddin, *History of the Baloch Regiment, 1939–1956* (Uckfield, East Sussex, 2005).

Allen, L., *Burma: The Longest War, 1941–1945* (London, 1984).

Astor, G., *The Jungle War* (Hoboken, New Jersey, 2004).

Barclay, C.N., *On Their Shoulders* (London, 1964).

Barclay, C.N., *The History of the Cameronians (Scottish Rifles)*, iii, 1933–1946 (London, 1947).

Barclay, C.N., *The History of the Duke of Wellington's Regiment, 1919–1952* (London, 1953).

Barclay, C.N., *The Regimental History of the 3rd Queen Alexandra's Own Gurkha Rifles*, ii, 1927–1947 (London, 1953).

Bayly, C. and Harper, T., *Forgotten Armies: The Fall of British Asia, 1941–1945* (London, 2004).

Beldon, J., *Retreat with Stilwell* (New York, 1943).

Bell, C.M., *The Royal Navy, Seapower and Strategy Between the Wars* (Stanford, California, 2000).

Bond, B. and Tachikawa, Kyoichi, *British and Japanese Military Leadership in the Far Eastern War, 1941–1945* (London, 2004).

Bond, C.R. and Anderson, T., *A Flying Tiger's Diary* (College Station, Texas, 1984).

Bose, Sugata, 'Starvation Amidst Plenty: The Making of Famine in Bengal, Honan and Tonkin, 1942–45', *Modern Asian Studies*, 1990, pp. 699–727.

Brown, I., *Economic Change in South-East Asia, c. 1830–1980* (Kuala Lumpur, 1997).

Byrd, M., *Chennault: Giving Wings to the Tiger* (Tuscaloosa, Alabama, 1987).

Cabinet Office, *Principal War Telegrams and Memoranda, 1940–1943* (London, 1976).

Callahan, R., *Burma, 1942–1945* (London, 1978).

Carew, T., *The Longest Retreat* (London, 1969).

Carmichael, P., *Mountain Battery* (Bournemouth, 1983).

Chenevix Trench, C., *The Indian Army and the King's Enemies, 1900–1947* (London, 1988).

Cheng Siok-Hwa, *The Rice Industry of Burma, 1852–1940* (Kuala Lumpur, 1968).

Churchill, W.S., *The Second World War*, iv (London, 1951).

Collis, M., *Last and First in Burma* (London, 1956).

Condon, W.E.H., *The Frontier Force Regiment* (Aldershot, 1962).

Cornelius, W. and Short, T., *Ding Hao: America's Air War in China, 1937–1945* (Gretna, Louisiana, 1980).

Corrigan, G., *Sepoys in the Trenches* (Staplehurst, Kent, 1999).

Craven, W.F. and Cate J.L., *The Army Air Forces in World War II*, i–vii (Chicago, 1948–58).

Daniell, D.S., *Cap of Honour: The Story of The Gloucestershire Regiment (The 28th/61st Foot), 1694–1950* (London, 1951).

Dimbleby, K., *Turns of Fate: The Drama of HMS Cornwall* (London, 1984).

Donnison, F.S.V., *British Military Administration in the Far East, 1943–46* (London, 1956).

Doulton, A.J.F., *The Fighting Cock: History of the 23rd Indian Division, 1942–1947* (Aldershot, 1951).

Draper, A., *Dawns Like Thunder* (London, 1987).

Dreyer, E.L., *China at War, 1901–1949* (London, 1995).

Farndale, M., *History of the Royal Regiment of Artillery*, vi (London, 2000).

Ford, D., *Flying Tiger: Claire Chennault and His American Volunteers, 1941–1942* (Washington, 2007).

Fortescue, J.W., *A History of the British Army*, xi (London, 1923).

Fox, F., *The Royal Inniskilling Fusiliers in the Second World War* (Aldershot, 1951).

Fuchida, Mitsuo and Okumiya, Masatake, *Midway* (Annapolis, 1992).

Gill, G. Hermon, *Royal Australian Navy, 1942–1945* (Canberra, 1968).

Gillison, D., *Royal Australian Air Force, 1939–1942* (Canberra, 1962).

Gould, T., *Imperial Warriors* (London, 1999).

Grant, I.L. and Tamayama, Kazuo, *Burma 1942: The Japanese Invasion* (Chichester, 1999).

Greenough, P.R., *Prosperity and Misery in Modern Bengal: The Famine of 1943–44* (New York, 1982).

Heathcote, T.A., *The Military in British India* (Manchester, 1995).

Horner, D., *High Command* (Sydney, 1982).

Hough, R., *The Longest Battle: The War at Sea, 1939–45* (London, 1987).

India, Government of, *Famine Inquiry Commission: Report on Bengal* (New Delhi, 1945).

Jackson, A., *The British Empire and the Second World War* (London, 2006).

Jeffries, C., *'O.E.G.': A Biography of Sir Oliver Ernest Goonetilleke* (London, 1969).

Kirby, S. Woodburn, *The War Against Japan*, ii (London, 1958).

Klinkowitz, J., *With the Tigers Over China, 1941–1942* (Lexington, Kentucky, 1999).

Latimer, J., *Burma: The Forgotten War* (London, 2004).

Lewin, R., *Slim: The Standardbearer* (London, 1977).

Lewin, R., *The Chief: Field-Marshal Lord Wavell* (London, 1980).

Lunt, J., *Imperial Sunset* (London, 1981).

Lunt, J., *The Retreat from Burma, 1941–1942* (London, 1986).

Lyman, R., *Slim: Master of War* (London, 2004).

McCarthy, D., *South-West Pacific Area – First Year* (Canberra, 1959).

MacFetridge, C.H.T. and Warren, J.P. (eds), *Tales of the Mountain Gunners* (Edinburgh, 1973).

Macintyre, D., *Fighting Admiral: The Life of Admiral of the Fleet Sir James Somerville* (London, 1961).

Mackay, J.N., *A History of the 4th Prince of Wales's Own Gurkha Rifles*, iii, 1938–1948 (London, 1952).

Mackay, J.N., *History of the 7th Duke of Edinburgh's Own Gurkha Rifles* (London, 1962).

Mackenzie, C., *Eastern Epic* (London, 1951).

MacKenzie, K.P., *Operation Rangoon Jail* (London, 1954).

Majumdar, B.N., *Administration in the Burma Campaign* (Delhi, 1952).

Maochun Yu, *The Dragon's War: Allied Operations and the Fate of China, 1937–1947* (Annapolis, Maryland, 2006).

Marder, A.J., Jacobsen, M., Horsfield, J., *Old Friends, New Enemies: The Royal Navy and the Imperial Japanese Navy*, ii (Oxford, 1990).

Mason, P., *A Matter of Honour* (London, 1974).

Molesworth, G.N., *Curfew on Olympus* (Bombay, 1965).

Moon, P. (ed.), *Wavell: The Viceroy's Journal* (London, 1973).

Moreman, T.R., *The Jungle, the Japanese and the British Commonwealth Armies at War, 1941–45* (London, 2005).

Nand, Brahma (ed.), *Famines in Colonial India* (New Delhi, 2007).

North, J. (ed.), *The Alexander Memoirs, 1940–1945* (New York, 1962).

Okumiya, Masatake and Horikoshi, Jiro, *Zero: The Story of the Japanese Navy Air Force, 1937–1945* (London, 1957).

Pakenham-Walsh, R.P., *History of the Corps of Royal Engineers* (Chatham, 1958).

Perrett, B., *Tank Tracks to Rangoon* (London, 1978).

Pocock, T., *Fighting General: The Public and Private Campaigns of General Sir Walter Walker* (London, 1973).

Prasad, B., *Defence of India: Policy and Plans* (New Delhi, 1963).

Prasad, B. (ed.), *The Retreat from Burma, 1941–42* (Calcutta, 1959).

Probert, H., *The Forgotten Air Force: The Royal Air Force in the War Against Japan, 1941–1945* (London, 1995).

Regimental Committee, *History of the 5th Royal Gurkha Rifles (Frontier Force)*, ii, 1929–1947 (Aldershot, 1956).

Richards, D. and Saunders, H.St.G., *Royal Air Force, 1939–1945*, ii (London, 1954).

Romanus, C.F. and Sunderland, R., *Stilwell's Mission to China* (Washington, 1953).

Roskill, S.W., *The War at Sea, 1939–1945*, ii (London, 1956).

Roy, Kaushik, 'Military Loyalty in the Colonial Context: A Case Study of the Indian Army during World War II', *The Journal of Military History*, April 2009, pp. 497–529.

Roy, Kaushik, 'The Construction of Regiments in the Indian Army: 1859–1913', *War in History*, 2001, 8 (2), pp. 127–48.

Schofield, V., *Wavell: Soldier and Statesman* (London, 2006).

Shores, C., Cull, B., Yasuho Izawa, *Bloody Shambles*, i–ii (London, 1992–93).

Simpson, M. (ed.), *The Somerville Papers* (Aldershot, 1995).

Singer, N.F., *Old Rangoon: City of the Shwedagon* (Stirling, Scotland, 1995).

Slim, W., *Defeat into Victory* (London, 1956).

Smith, M., *The Emperor's Codes: The Breaking of Japan's Secret Ciphers* (New York, 2000).

Smith, P.C., *The Great Ships Pass* (London, 1977).

Smyth, J., *Leadership in War, 1939–1945* (London, 1974).

Smyth, J., *Milestones* (London, 1979).

Smyth, J., *The Only Enemy* (London, 1959).

Stewart, A., *The Underrated Enemy* (London, 1987).

Stewart, A.T.Q., *The Pagoda War* (London, 1972).

Tanner, R.E.S. and D.A., *Burma 1942: Memories of a Retreat* (Stroud, Gloucestershire, 2009).

Tarling, N. (ed.), *The Cambridge History of Southeast Asia*, iii (Cambridge, 1992).

Thompson, H.L., *New Zealanders with the Royal Air Force*, iii (Wellington, 1959).

Thompson, J., *The Royal Marines* (London, 2000).

Thompson, J., *The War in Burma, 1942–45* (London, 2002).

Tinker, H., 'A Forgotten Long March: The Indian Exodus from Burma, 1942', *Journal of Southeast Asian Studies*, VI, 1975, pp. 1–15.

Tuchman, B.W., *Stilwell and the American Experience in China, 1911–45* (New York, 1970).

Warren, A., *Singapore 1942: Britain's Greatest Defeat* (London, 2002).

Warren, A., *Waziristan, The Faqir of Ipi and the Indian Army: The North-West Frontier Revolt of 1936–37* (Karachi, 2000).

Warren, A., *World War II: A Military History* (Stroud, Gloucestershire, 2008).

Weinberg, G.L., *A World at Arms* (Cambridge, 1994).

Wigmore, L., *The Japanese Thrust* (Canberra, 1957).

Williams, H., *Ceylon: Pearl of the East* (London, 1950).

Wilson, D., *When Tigers Fight* (New York, 1982).

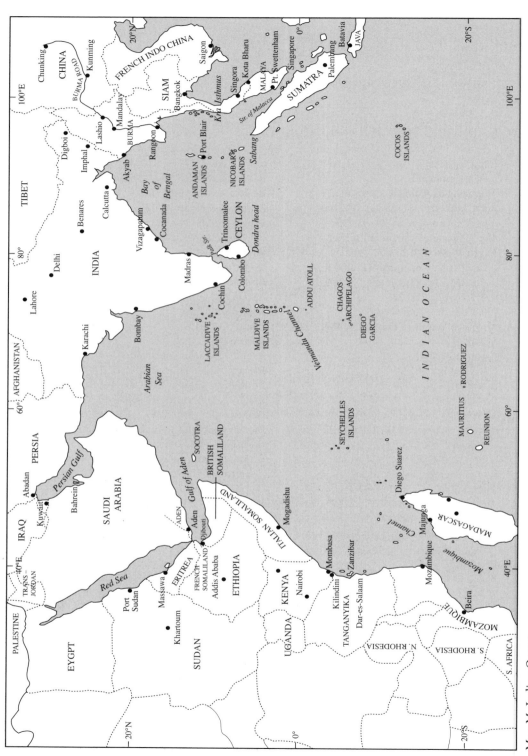

Map M Indian Ocean

Index